Marion Zimmer Bradley

MW00908176

McFarland Companions to Young Adult Literature

Gary Paulsen: A Companion to the Young Adult Literature
by Mary Ellen Snodgrass (2018)

Marion Zimmer Bradley: A Companion to the Young Adult Literature
by Mary Ellen Snodgrass (2020)

Marion Zimmer Bradley

A Companion to the Young Adult Literature

MARY ELLEN SNODGRASS

McFarland Companions to Young Adult Literature

McFarland & Company, Inc., Publishers
Jefferson, North Carolina

ALSO BY THE AUTHOR AND FROM MCFARLAND

Rachel Carson: A Literary Companion (2020); *Lee Smith: A Literary Companion* (2019); *Coins and Currency: An Historical Encyclopedia*, 2d ed. (2019); *Gary Paulsen: A Companion to the Young Adult Literature* (2018); *World Epidemics: A Cultural Chronology of Disease from Prehistory to the Era of Zika*, 2d ed. (2017); *Brian Friel: A Literary Companion* (2017); *Settlers of the American West: The Lives of 231 Notable Pioneers* (2015); *Who's Who in the Middle Ages* (2013; paperback 2001); *Isabel Allende: A Literary Companion* (2013); *World Epidemics: A Cultural Chronology of Disease from Prehistory to the Era of SARS* (2011; paperback 2003); *Encyclopedia of World Scriptures* (2011; paperback 2001); *Leslie Marmon Silko: A Literary Companion* (2011); *Peter Carey: A Literary Companion* (2010); *Jamaica Kincaid: A Literary Companion* (2008); *Kaye Gibbons: A Literary Companion* (2007); *Walter Dean Myers: A Literary Companion* (2006); *World Shores and Beaches: A Descriptive and Historical Guide to 50 Coastal Treasures* (2005); *Barbara Kingsolver: A Literary Companion* (2004); *August Wilson: A Literary Companion* (2004); *Amy Tan: A Literary Companion* (2004)

LIBRARY OF CONGRESS CATALOGUING-IN-PUBLICATION DATA

Names: Snodgrass, Mary Ellen, author.
Title: Marion Zimmer Bradley : a companion to the young adult literature / Mary Ellen Snodgrass.
Description: Jefferson, North Carolina : McFarland & Company, Inc., Publishers, 2020 | Series: McFarland companions to young adult literature | Includes bibliographical references and index.
Identifiers: LCCN 2020031338 | ISBN 9781476679525 (paperback) ∞
ISBN 9781476640433 (ebook)
Subjects: LCSH: Bradley, Marion Zimmer—Criticism and interpretation. | Young adult fiction, American—History and criticism.
Classification: LCC PS3552.R228 Z86 2020 | DDC 813/.54 [B]—dc23
LC record available at https://lccn.loc.gov/2020031338

BRITISH LIBRARY CATALOGUING DATA ARE AVAILABLE

ISBN (print) 978-1-4766-7952-5
ISBN (ebook) 978-1-4766-4043-3

On the cover: Front cover image © 2020 Shutterstock

Printed in the United States of America

McFarland & Company, Inc., Publishers
Box 611, Jefferson, North Carolina 28640
www.mcfarlandpub.com

For Martin Otts,
the Patrick Beaver Library's
Man Friday

Each soul comes back again and again
to complete its mission on earth.
—Marion Zimmer Bradley, *The Forest House*

Every life has a death and every light a shadow. Be content
to stand in the light and let the shadow fall where it will.
—Mary Stewart, *The Hollow Hills*

Table of Contents

Acknowledgments

Allegheny Campus Library, Pittsburgh, Pennsylvania

Belk Library, Appalachian State University, Boone, North Carolina

California State University Library, Long Beach

Chicago Public Library, Chicago, Illinois

Claremont College Library, Claremont, California

Dudley Library, California State University at Long Beach

Duke University Library, Durham, North Carolina

Fondren Library, Southern Methodist University, Dallas, Texas

Green Library, Florida International University, Miami, Florida

Greensboro Public Library, Greensboro, North Carolina

Harold B. Lee Library, Brigham Young University, Provo, Utah

H.C. Buley Library, Southern Connecticut State University, New Haven

Nogales-Santa Cruz Library, Nogales, Arizona

San Francisco Chronicle, California

San Francisco Public Library, California

Torreyson Library, University of Central Arkansas, Conway

University of Georgia Library, Athens

Ventura County Library, Ventura, California

Warren Wilson College Library, Asheville, North Carolina

Special thanks go to reference librarians Martin Otts and Beth Bradshaw of the Patrick Beaver Library in Hickory, North Carolina, and to my publicist and consultant Joan Lail. I am indebted to lending institutions that maintain sci-fi and fantasy collections from mimeographed newsletters and short-run fanzines. Stars in your crowns, all around.

Preface

For the sci-fi/fantasy admirer, teacher, literary historian, reviewer, and feminist reader, *Marion Zimmer Bradley: A Companion to the Young Adult Literature* introduces a multitalented writer from varied perspectives. The 86 topics cover her most appealing YA novels—*The Catch Trap, Survey Ship, The Fall of Atlantis, The Firebrand, The Forest House*, and *The Mists of Avalon*—along with the graphic slave narrative in *Warrior Woman*, the Lythande novella *The Gratitude of Kings*, and, from the Darkover series, *The Shattered Chain, The Sword of Aldones*, and *Traitor's Sun*. Separate entries on dominant themes—rape, divination, religion, violence, womanhood, adaptation, dreams—comb stories and longer works for the author's insights about the motivation of institutions that oppress marginal groups, especially females. Overviews compare specific subjects—heroines, knights of the Round Table, Christianity, and exotic beings. General entries group peripheral titles of Bradley's canon pertaining to costume, sex, ritual, storytelling, ambition, sisterhood, feuds, and details, the subjects that set her fiction apart from the ordinary. Genealogies elucidate complex clan septs of Atlanteans, Trojans and Akhaians, Greek Gods, the Pendragon dynasty, Darkover offspring, and the author's family tree.

Glossing defines and identifies the sources of 464 terms and phrases from stories, essays, poems, and novels to explain usage in context, as with these models:

costume winding sheet, breechclout, serge, basque, dalmatica, fustian, kirtle
culture lughnasad, talisman, sigil, *ceilidh*, croft, lexicon, midden, handfasting
fantasy chimera, roc, were-dragon, bane wolf, maenad, will-o'-the-wisp
food pastille, posset, barm, tile meats, tisane, bannock, comfit, mead
foreign language *ex officio, noblesse oblige, patron, soeur, salve, samurai*
geography barrow, fells, cairn, tor, firth, Giants' Dance, Hibernia, *locus*
government archon, Roman wall, citadel, lordling, vizier, aedile, keep
health moonblood, amnesiac, narcosynthesis, sphincter, simples, rheum
literature strophe, picara, collective unconscious, doppelgänger, hamartia
music clavier, sistrum, threnody, cadenza, liturgy, bodhran, chitarrone
occult clairaudience, poltergeist, scry, fetch, glamour, hearth-witch, rune
plants wicker-withes, nosegay, dark leaf, anis, bladder wrack, holt
religion Palladium, avatar, haruspex, agape, Vestal, chantry, chela
science nebula, vector, psychodynamics, azimuth, biofeedback, dymaxion
transportation VTOL, cariole, pillion, prop plane, scull, spinnaker, dray cart
weaponry elf bolt, spatha, nock, deadfall, skein, code duello, strappado

Lists include sources of terms by title and page numbers.

Appendix A: A Guide to Places encompasses modern geographical terms—Kent, Glastonbury Tor, Skye, Libya, Montmartre—as well as mythic locales—Hy-Brasil, Atlantis, Ys—and archaic names and their current designations, e.g., Mona/Anglesey, Lothian/Scotland, Judea/Palestine, New Hebrides/Vanuatu, and Hibernia/Ireland.

For discussion and composition subjects and research, Appendix B: A Guide to Writing, Art and Research Topics suggests 39 ideas for titles, computation, historical background, community projects, comparative literature, letter writing, contrasting scenes, and wisdom and character analysis. A separate bibliography of primary and secondary sources, both print and electronic, precedes the index, which points readers to fundamental titles, issues, and cultural and literary subjects, particularly names, Pax Arthuriana, original sin, Mariology, Gothic, Beltane, and allegory. The overall work encompasses major aspects of the canon of Marion Zimmer Bradley.

Introduction

An under-appreciated American genius, Marion Zimmer Bradley achieved mastery of short story, vignette, novella, myth, fantasy, essay and op-ed pieces, oratory, satire, narrative verse, allegory, and historical fiction. Over a six-decade career begun in childhood, she allowed intellectual curiosity to guide explorations of mature subjects, from religious fanaticism, plutocracy, trade wars, abortion, suicide, incest, and homosexuality to necrophilia, hallucinogenic drugs, inter-species breeding, and galactic empires. In early stories, she dabbled in classic lore in "Well Met by Moonlight" and took small steps into the paranormal, aiding Max to levitate amid flames in "Phoenix" and helping Andy to conceive a form of metempsychosis in "Measureless to Man" to rehouse dying Martians in chimpanzee bodies. For background, the autodidact researched a variety of subjects—astronomy, herbalism and alchemy, medieval warfare, weaponry, Greek mythology, midwifery, scripture, and astrophysics, a useful study for *Darkover Landfall* and *Survey Ship*, a plunge into extra-planetary pioneering by a teen crew. Sure-footed in untried territory, she created diction, kenning, and dilemmas to match the demands of fantasy, the occult, and science fiction, including a community mixer in "The Dance at the Gym" to reduce hostility between feuding space outposts.

Essential to Bradley's expert fiction, characterization, like the strength of the mythic Antaeus, remained earthbound. She nourished interaction with normal behaviors and responses, turning the Greek Akhilles in *The Firebrand* into a sulky, teen triggerman and the priestess Morgaine in *The Mists of Avalon* into the mother of a monster and the conflicted acolyte of a mystic goddess. Glimpses of parenting in Helen of Troy and Queen Imandra of Colchis retain the wonder of pregnancy, childbirth, and rearing a toddler, the topics of "The Wind People" and "Women Only." Subjects anchored in womanhood dominate plots with the ambivalence of first-time parents and fears for children fostered by strangers at distant firesides, the fate of Cynric, the fatherless boy and avenger in *The Forest House* and of the young Arthur Pendragon, future high king of Britannia in *The Mists of Avalon*. The role of the midwife/healer recurs in much of her storytelling, especially the communal delivery of Valentine in *The Shattered Chain* and Marisela's aid to Byrna in *Thendara House*. The details of women aiding women confers honor on a profession as old as clan survival, as necessary as fire and water.

The author's personal leanings toward humanism and justice defied categorization into other -isms—not feminism, Neopaganism, Protestantism, globalism, nor utopianism, as some critics assert. Her moral authority shone through plots set on historic earthly battlefields at Troy and Badon and on distant planets among humanoids and exotic animals as rare as banshees and flying salamanders, the comic relief in "The Gratitude of Kings." Her characters profited from open-hearted clemency and tolerance, boons to marooned breeder Dr. Judy Love in *Darkover Landfall*; Kevin Harper, a disabled singer advanced to the rank of the Merlin in *The Mists of Avalon*; South African surgeon David "Peake" Akami in *Survey Ship*; and Free Amazon Magdalen "Magda" Lorne in *City of Sorcery*. By setting action amid intertribal, international, and interplanetary conflict, she disclosed a conviction that wars, like the match-up of Romans with Celts and Celts with Saxons, may be inevitable, but are never merciful.

Bradley's altruism marked a series of editorial essays in *Sword and Sorceress* guiding her peers, imitators, and neophyte sci-fi authors Diana Lucile Paxson and Elisabeth Waters toward publication. While issuing playful poems and tales under the pseudonyms Astro, Miriam Gardner, and Astra of the Spheres, Bradley created a serious master saga—Darkover, the fictional laboratory for examining human reactions to separation from Earth. The unexplored setting fostered group adaptation of institutions, from food production, worship, and environmental protection to educating the young and governing the populace, the work of the planet's seven domains—Aillard, Aldaran, Alton, Ardais, Elhalyn, Hastur, and Ridenow. Much of her speculative fiction reprised the trial-and-error inventions and industry of the Middle Ages, when cultures instituted the divine right of kings and set restrictions on aristocrats, guilds, and standing armies, topics dramatized in *Exile's Song* and *The Heritage of Hastur*. By imagining clingfire, crystal matrix, and the psychic powers of *laran*, she equipped futuristic realms with visionary armaments requiring policing to protect the vulnerable, a motif of *Hunters of the Red Moon*. The introduction of occult forms of reproduction in *The Alton Gift* questioned the bigotry of the 1900s toward modifications of male-female monogamy. Interspersing thugs and subjugators in the rovings of Lythande and rescues of the Renunciates, Bradley's fiction echoed the worst of her own time, from the scourges of pollution, urban gangs, rape, and Cold War espionage, the subject of "The Stars Are Waiting," to late twentieth-century thralldom, skulduggery, and genocide, a topic of *The World Wreckers*.

The author's work grew in popularity as the interests of readership extended to classicists, medievalists, and linguists, especially fans of Gaelic idiom and Scandic kenning. No longer bound to appease popular tastes, she abandoned writing for cash with such modern bodice rippers as "Mama, Don't Let Him Have My Babies!" for *True Experience*. True to her gender, she ventured to the outer rim of imagination for *The Winds of Darkover*, the fount of women's science fiction. Honors and awards accrued to Bradley's works along with esteem from critics, fans, and fellow writers and editors of fanzines. Still writing and plotting new ideas as her body failed in fall 1999, she criticized global militarism in her last co-authored novel, *Traitor's Sun*. Her staff fleshed out *Ghostlight*, *Zandru's Forge*, and other incomplete projects; collected manuscripts for *A World Divided*, *To Save a World*, *The Age of Chaos*, and other anthologies; and promoted the film version of *The Mists of Avalon*, her most popular novel.

Chronology of Marion Zimmer Bradley's Life and Works

A breacher of boundaries for a half century, Marion Zimmer Bradley created a network of speculative fiction to accommodate her interest in medieval history, Arthurian lore, opera, women's rights, scholarship, and life-affirming futuristic science. Integral to her career, the nurturing of young writers resulted in *Darkover* and *Sword and Sorceress* collections as well as writing contests and her workshops on short fiction. For the anthologies, the author chose 26 from a slush pile of 700 manuscripts. For the winning fiction, action places a female in settings demanding magic or sword fights.

In the style of Mary Shelley and Ursula K. Le Guin, Bradley's work probed faults in folk bias about female strengths and proposed means of correction. By appending episodes and opening the fantasy and sci-fi genres to women throughout English readership, she promoted the fantasy and sci-fi classics of her era—*The Lord of the Rings* and *Star Trek*, which she admired for drawing girls into sci-fi fandom. By affirming women's roles in history, she achieved what theorist Gloria Orenstein calls "a kind of truth that our written records deny" (Orenstein, 1990, 156).

June 3, 1930

A child of the Great Depression, Marion Eleanor Zimmer Bradley was born on an Albany dairy farm in New York state. Of Norwegian-Dutch-Frisian-Flemish ancestry, she bore the name of a 23-year-old maternal aunt Marion Eleanor of Clifton Springs, New York. Her colonial ancestors, who settled in New York and New Jersey, connect directly to the Massachusetts Bay Colony and Anne Bradstreet, America's first poet.

Marion's alcoholic father, Leslie Raymond Zimmer, farmed and worked day labor. Her mother, Evelyn Parkhurst Conklin Zimmer, preferred boy babies to girls and brainwashed Marion with the importance of males and the insignificance of females. Evelyn had a romantic bent and liked to read aloud from Nathaniel Hawthorne's *Tanglewood Tales for Boys and Girls* (1853).

1934

In the afterword of *The Fall of Atlantis,* the author mused on building temples from wood blocks and questioned how she knew about ancient architecture before she could read. She surmised that *Tanglewood Tales* provided images from the myths of Jason and the Argonauts, Theseus and the Minotaur, and Proserpina and Pluto. In the six-chapter text, "temple" appears three times. Marion also credited the illustrations of painter Mayfield Parrish, Henry Rider Haggard's lost world novels and media stories, Sax Rohmer's Fu Manchu adventures, and Roger Lancelyn Green's classic *Tales of Ancient Egypt*. From these, according to biographer and critic Diana Lucile Paxson, the author developed an "interest in the Western Esoteric tradition" that shaped her career (Paxson, 1999, 110).

1937

Marion dictated original fables and myths to her mother and obtained a first space exploration novel from the school library. She admitted, "As an ex-tomboy, I can sympathize with a little girl's wish to play knight" (Bradley, 1991, ix). With brothers Paul Edwin and Leslie R. Zimmer, she spent childhood immersed in fantasy adventure fiction by screenwriter and planetary romance specialist Leigh Douglass Brackett, classic short story writer Edmond Moore Hamilton, Prussian American author Henry Kuttner, and Catherine Lucille Moore, a pioneer of female sci-fi and fantasy. A reluctant writer, Marion aspired to sing opera, which she heard on radio broadcasts of *Metropolitan Opera* while she ironed. Her love of Gilbert and Sullivan and dramatic arias influenced the style of *The Mists of Avalon* and the adaptation of two operas—Bellini's *Norma* into *The Forest House* and Mozart's *The Magic Flute* into *Night's Daughter*, an ordeal plot resulting in human-animal hybridization.

1938

Marion's middle brother David was born and died in 1938. According to the author, she began plotting a writing career at age eight and profited from free reading in a nonrestrictive attic stocked with pulp fiction magazines *Argosy*, *Blue Book*, and *Weird Tales*. She arose at 5 a.m. to type prose. Key to her pro-woman canon lay the realization that "women have been reared on myths/legends/hero tales in which the men do the important things and the women stand by and watch and admire but keep their hands off" (Bradley, 1986). To empower females, she created plots rich in women's agency and courage.

1940

From a used copy of Sidney Lanier's *Tales of King Arthur*, a gift from maternal grandfather John Roscoe Conklin, Marion began perusing and absorbing Arthuriana. By age ten, she had memorized most of the anthology and its characters. Added medievalism derived from Hal Foster's comic strip *Tales of Prince Valiant* from her weekly issues of *Wednesday Comics*.

1942

At age twelve, Marion proclaimed her dedication to the occult. In the introduction to *Renunciates of Darkover,* she described herself as uninterested in makeup or football- and car-crazy boys. For a time in her teens she lived with her aunt, composer Marion Eleanor Conklin Chapman, in New York, and wrote monomythic stories from the perspective of Lew Alton, her alter ego and favorite character from *The Alton Gift.*

1943

The birth of little brother Paul created a family relationship that Marion later applied in *The Mists of Avalon* to the birth of Arthur and his mother Igraine's dependence on preteen daughter Morgaine as a surrogate mom and nanny.

1945

Marion characterized herself in the introduction to *The Forbidden Tower* as a rebel and nonconformist: "My obsession with science fiction was not a mild eccentricity but a sinister weirdness" (Bradley, 1977, v). Adept at skipping classes to read at the Albany state library, a regional sector of the Library of Congress, she recreated the concept of ancient scroll archives in *The Fall of Atlantis.* She studied psychology and parapsychology and read Sir Thomas Malory's compilation *Le Morte d'Arthur* and Scots anthropologist and folklorist James George Frazer's *The Golden Bough,* a ten-volume comparison of world mythologies. Personal involvement in global lore paralleled her concerns for gender equity as an alternative to tyrannic patriarchy. Immersed in comparative religion, she sought baptism as an Episcopalian.

1946

Undiagnosed symptoms suggest that Marion had rheumatic fever, which kept her housebound in her mid-teens. Although frequently bedfast with joint pain and fatigue, she graduated from high school at age sixteen. She found summer employment in the Thousand Islands north of Watertown, New York, and traveled by train through Utica on home visits to Albany. In retrospect, the author equated the joy of reading a copy of *Startling Stories* with other life-changing encounters—her first LSD trip or initial views of the British Museum, the Delphic shrine, or a performance of Giacomo Puccini's *Turandot* at Lincoln Center. Self-education forged a lifelong joy in science fiction and the occult.

1946 August

The writer of template fiction, whom colleagues assumed was a man, attended her first sci-fi convention. Although she preferred novels, she wrote novellas and short works, including "Saga of Carcosa" for *Astra's Tower* and "World After Destruction" for *Gorgon.* She loved the camaraderie of people who admired women in the profession. Secure among literary colleagues, she rejoiced that "[i]t's all just a game. We're all having fun here" (Bradley, 1991, ii).

1946 September

Supported by what she called the "commercial writing of romances for schlock paperback houses … a literary prostitute," Marion enrolled at New York State College for Teachers (Bradley, 1993, 3). On scholarship, she majored in music and completed five terms before lack of financial support and disillusion with three education departments caused her to quit.

1947

In an era of female fantasists writing under pen names—Jane Howes (pseud. of Wilmar House Shiras) and Edmond Hamilton (pseud. of Leigh Douglas Brackett Hamilton)—Marion used her real name to create a sci-fi magazine, *Astra's Towers,* under the pen name Astra of the Spheres. In her definition of fantasy, she contrasted technological outer space with "inner space … the science fiction of the mind" (Friedman, 1981, E4). She preferred longer fiction, but made inroads into the industry through short pieces and essays. Of the camaraderie of her peers, she delighted that they "regard one another not as rivals but as highly valued friends and colleagues, not temperamental prima donnas but like members of one large orchestra, or choir, whose allegiance is given only to the music" (Bradley, 1994, 1). She valued sci-fi stories for their "sense of wonder" (*Ibid.*, 2). To capture the moment, she followed the stratagem of "Run fast, stand still," her term for "Write quickly, then pause for thought" (Epstein, 1987, C5).

1947 June

At age seventeen, the author sold heart-throb fiction to pulp magazines—*True Confessions, Caper, True Experience*—and began writing *The Forest House,* a romance novel set in the first century CE on the Welsh island of Ynys Mon or Mona, now called Anglesey. The plot developed love interest between Roman legionary officer Gaius Macellius and Druidic priestess Eilan, a resetting of Vincenzo Bellini's opera *Norma* (1831). The novel, published in 1994, followed the arc of *Ancestors of Avalon* and anticipated events in *Lady of Avalon* and *The Mists of Avalon,* Marion's masterwork. She also wrote letters to the editor of *Thrilling Wonder Stories* and other sci-fi clearinghouses.

1947 November–December

A breakthrough in publication identified Marion as the author of the essay "Astra-Logically Speaking," the poems "Ode on Imitations of an Immortal" and "Lovecraftian Sonnetry," and the narratives "The Place in the Marshes," "The Chimes in the Cathedral" and "The Priestess," all for *Astra's Tower* and "The Inevitable Secret" in *Altitudes* and "World After Destruction" in *Gorgon*.

1948

Marion began submitting critiques and publishing in the fanzines *Allerlei, Gorgon, Nekromantikon, Day*Star, Fantasy Ambler, Geminis, Jr., Gemini FAPA, On the Ragged Edge, Catch Trap, Anduril, MEZRAB, Ugly Bird*, and *Anything Box*. She later applauded fans for providing feedback and guidance to the masters of sci-fi and fantasy. Her published works earned three cents per word. She received a fanzine rejection for "Genuine Old Master," a tale of a portrait artist that she later issued in October 1977 in *Galileo*. She spawned more ideas from a reading of the poems of James Stephens and from William Butler Yeats's *Irish Fairy and Folk Tale*.

1948 December

With the emergence of a town on planet Deneb in "Outpost," issued in *Spacewarp* fanzine, the author crafted the rudiments of Terrans and the Darkover series, "the biography of a planet" (Breen, 1979, vi). Of her "surprising amount of integration," Marion observed, "I just wrote the novels, and made up the languages, and gee whiz, they make sense!" (*Ibid.*). In the estimation of critic Rosemarie Arbur for *Twentieth-Century Science-Fiction Writers*, "By postulating a Terran Empire the main features of which are advanced technology and bureaucracy, and a Darkover that seems technologically backward and is fiercely individualistic, Bradley sets up a conflict to which there is no 'correct' resolution" (Arbur, 1982). Irish critic Linda Leith put the guiding principle into more universal terms—"the clash between opposites" (Leith, 1980, 29).

October 26, 1949

After dating the author by letter for a year, 51-year-old Robert Alden "Brad" Bradley wed Marion and settled in Rochester, Texas, where he worked as a railroad agent and telegrapher for the Atchison, Topeka and Santa Fe Railroad. She described hasty wedlock as "the only way for a young woman to get away from a bad home situation" (Bradley, 1984, 1). Southern fundamentalism sapped her enthusiasm for organized Christianity; the Texas mania for football seemed even more irrelevant.

1949 December

The story "Outpost" got a second issuance and $50 from a writing contest sponsored by *Amazing Stories*.

1950

The author bore son David Robert Bradley, who received the names of his father and a maternal uncle who was born and died in 1938. Marion preferred staying at home to rear David rather than farming him out to a sitter. In her own magazine, *Startling Stories*, and *Nekromantikon*, she continued publishing with "Women … At War," "Oh-Oh, Another Po,'" "Spaceman's Song," "Child of Fire," "The Vigil," "The Haunted Street," "Speaking of Hacks," "Nova," and "Of Cabbages and Kings," a phrase from Lewis Carroll's "The Walrus and the Carpenter." When David became an adult, he contributed to her novels and groomed the manuscript for *The Mists of Avalon*. David died in 2008 at age 58.

1952–1953

While living in Rochester, Texas, Marion began supplying a column to *Vega* and wrote "Dio Ridenow of Serre," a character in *Exile's Song* and *The Sword of Aldones*. She made initial sales of short-short fiction to *Vortex Science Fiction,* which issued "Keyhole" and "Women Only." The two stories about interspecies parenthood derived from the author's arguments with Brad over her longing for more children.

1954 April

From reading medical books, Marion refined the novella "Centaurus Changeling," additional speculative fiction about the interbreeding of species, one of her many perusals of human reproduction and polygamy. Critic Anthony Boucher, editor of *The Magazine of Fantasy & Science Fiction*, named the work her first important contribution to sci-fi for its details and perceptive themes of feminism and utopianism.

1954 May

The author issued "Year of the Big Thaw" in *Fantastic Universe* and the novella *Falcons of Narabedla* in *Dimensions*.

1954 October

Following the success of "Jackie Sees a Star" in September, Marion expressed interest in robot surrogacy in the sardonic, witty "The Crime Therapist," which appeared in *Future Science Fiction*.

1954 November

*Day*Star* featured the poem "Symphonic Suite."

1955

Marion began writing *Star of Danger*, which she completed a decade later. A young adult preface to Darkover, the narrative examines the friendship of male teens of different species, focusing on Larry, the motherless son of Terran Wade Montray. Walter Henry Breen later lauded the sci-fi series as "a mythos as well developed, as consistently conceived, and as thoroughly elaborated as [Tolkien's] Middle Earth" (Breen, 1975, n.p.).

1955 February

Marion sold the story "A Dozen of Everything" and the poems "Tomboy" to *Day*Star* and, to *Fantasy and Science Fiction*, "The Climbing Wave," picturing a return flight to Earth from Darkover.

1955 March

Fantastic Universe issued Marion's "Exiles of Tomorrow," a sci-fi conundrum on the punishment of Cara and Ryn Kenner's crimes by banishment to another year in the past or future. In one of her early musings on the interaction between reproduction and metaphysics, she concluded, "It isn't lawful for children to be born before their parents" (Bradley, 1955, 122).

1955 May

"The Sterner Season" appeared in *Day*Star*.

1955 Summer

The author penned the essay "Alas All Maturity" for *Vagabond*, "Child-Mother" for *Day*Star*, and the book *Summer Butterflies*, containing the title story and "Song to Patrice."

1955 October

Marion supported the Daughters of Bilitis, founded by Del Martin and Phyllis Lyon and named for the courtesan Bilitis, a contemporary of Sappho of Lesbos and practitioner of Sapphic love.

1956 March

For "Death Between the Stars," issued in *Fantastic Universe*, Marion named a starship Vesta, the Roman goddess of hearth and home.

1956 July

A next submission to the magazine, "Peace in the Wilderness," required manufacture of fake enemy spacecraft.

1957 May

A melodramatic raptor fantasy, *Falcons of Narabedla*, which appeared in *Other Worlds*, anticipated exotic animals in the author's bestselling Darkover series. The title featured the reverse spelling of Aldebaran, a giant star in the Taurus constellation named in 1252 Cor Tauri (bull's heart) by Moorish astronomers in Toledo, Spain. In the same month, Marion issued in *Venture* the story "Bird of Prey," the nucleus of the space opera *The Door Through Space* (1961). The opening scenario anticipates the cantina scene in Star Wars that introduces pilot Han Solo and Leia to the Wookie Chewbacca amid a backdrop of pirates, smugglers, scapegraces, and criminals. The dialogue—"We don't serve his kind here"—illustrates Marion's issues of speciesism in the Darkover series.

1958

Anything Box published "Introvert" and featured Marion's essay, "The Femfan's Lament," one of a series of op-ed pieces commenting on women's roles as sci-fi readers, writers, and publishers.

1958 March

Marion turned Cold War espionage into the story "The Stars Are Waiting" for *Saturn*. She wrote for *The Ladder,* the first Lesbian publication in the U.S., and began a bibliography of lesbian literature under the title *Astra's Tower*. Subsequent editions in 1959, 1960, and 1961 extended her research in female erotica.

1958 June

Satellite issued the story "Collector's Item."

1958 November

In *Amazing Stories,* Marion formally introduced the Darkover series with the novella *The Planet Savers,* the first of a four-decade project co-authored by Paul Edwin Zimmer, Jacqueline Lichtenberg, Mercedes Lackey, and Adrienne Martine-Barnes. The classic sci-fi novel introduced the use of matrix mechanics in defeating pandemic disease. The protagonist, Jason/Jay Allison, suffers a dissociative disorder that alienates him from others until the opposing personalities unite to form an integrated third persona.

In the introduction to her second Darkover anthology, Marion described the pre-feminist era, when "Women are not and were not encouraged to create universes of their own; especially in the days when I entered fandom" (Bradley, 2010, i). As the doyenne of fan fiction, she welcomed additions to the canon. In an assessment of the best in writing, she stated the centrality of character and "the ability to make the reader *feel* as if he or she were sharing some facet of Darkovan life," particularly the plight of refugees from a polluted, overpopulated Earth (Bradley, 1987, 1). For her own pleasure, she composed "out-takes," such as "The Shadow," which enlarged on the main flow with a sub-plot.

Deborah Jean Ross, one of the editors trained by Marion, extended the series in 2001 with the first of nine sequels. The isolation of a spaceship crew on an isolated planet foregrounds a feudal atmosphere similar to Anne McCaffrey's Pern series. The ongoing clashes of dynasties, races, ethnicities, and species upend earthly normality with bizarre powers and obstacles amid pageantry, chivalric manners, and the ultimate collapse of ideals. Over two decades, some 1,000 fans subscribed to the *Darkover Newsletter*. For the prominent gynocentrism, critics lauded Marion as the fount of feminist science fiction.

ca. 1959

The Breens established an occult group, the Aquarian Order of the Restoration. Marion continued her steady output of the poems "Leaf," "Two Christmas Cards, Out of Season," and "The Long Hot Summer" and stories—"Breather," "Conquering Hero," "To Err Is Human," and "The Wind People," a narrative about the risk of bearing children in space.

1960

Marion composed *Songs from Rivendell* to accompany poems in the novels of J.R.R. Tolkien and wrote a song, "Lament for Boromir" about a warrior in Gondor. Her stories included "The House on the Borderland" and "Seven from the Stars," the beginning of a longer version. In addition to her poem "The Wild One," she wrote for *Amra* the essay "…And Strange-Sounding Names" and for *Ladder*, "Behind the Borderline."

1961 spring

The author wrote "Giant Step" for *Mattachine Review* and "Crime Story" for *Day*Star* and the poems "Year's Beginning" and "Three Moods." In the essay "Men, Halflings, and Hero Worship" for *Astra's Tower*, she honored J.R.R. Tolkien for varying standard fictional motifs in *The Hobbit* and for focusing on thirty primary male characters and no love story.

1961 August

The author paid homage to Tolkien with the crossover stories "The Jewel of Arwen," a study of magical healing issued in *I Palantir,* and "Orcs and Elfstones" for *Day*Star.* The latter blesses the father with his daughter's wishes, "May the stars never fail for you … may the lands I shall not behold be ever more blessed and fair for your abiding there" (Bradley, 1964, 9). Of her authorship of *The Door Through Space,* Marion credited 1960s science: "Now that Sputniks clutter up the sky with new and unfamiliar moons, … there is a place, a wish, a need and hunger for the wonder and color of the world way out. The world beyond the stars" (Bradley, 1961, 4).

1962

In addition to issuing "Fannish Executioner's Song" in *Yandro* and *I Am a Lesbian* and "Blood Money" for the February issue of *Uncensored Confessions,* Marion published other speculative titles under the pseudonyms Lee Chapman, John Dexter, Valerie Graves, Morgan Ives, Elfrieda Rivers, and Astra Zimmer. Under the name Miriam Gardner, she wrote *The Strange Women* for Monarch. She sold her first long fiction, *The Sword of Aldones* and *Seven from the Stars,* which she later called a "novelette-length [Catherine Moore] Kuttner pastiche" (Bradley, 1984, 1). For a heavenly creator, she initiated Aldones, a sun deity similar to the Egyptian Ra and the Greek and Roman Apollo and the first Darkover ancestor. Critics noted the influence of Isaac Asimov and Robert Anson Heinlein in her examination of threats to life on earth.

1962 summer–fall

She completed for *WEB Terror Stories* "Treason of the Blood," a story of vengeance against a vampire, and the verse "Fragilities" for *Allerlei* and the poems "Reflections on the Fugghead" and "Fannish Executioner's Song" for *Yandro.*

1962 November–December

With "A Meeting in the Hyades," published in *Anduril* and *Astra's Tower Special Leaflet,* Marion created interlocking sword-and-cloak fantasies by pairing Regis Hastur over a campfire with Strider, a warrior in *The Lord of the Rings.* The writer ended the year with the "Cover-Up Girl" for *True Romance* and, for *Amazing Stories,* the narrative "Black and White" and the long short story of the spaceship *Erdenluft* and of shared primate bodies in "Measureless to Man."

1963

Marion earned a Hugo nomination and, a year later, a Nebula award for *The Sword of Aldones*, a classic of suspense and speculative fiction and number two in the nineteen-title Darkover series. Because of its survey of the pros and cons of decisions and the unleashing of defiant protagonists Callina and Dio, the novel generated a cult following and, in the 1970s, a fan club. In the same mode as *Heritage of Hastur*, the narrative introduces matrix mechanic Lew Alton, a bi-cultural son of a Terran mother and Darkovan sire, evidence of the primary subject of divided loyalties. The controlling theme contrasts bureaucratic earthmen to resident Darkovans, who abjure technological abstracts in favor of integrity and responsibility. Editor Mike Ashley noted that the series, which began as sci-fi, gradually transformed into fantasy.

1963 summer

The writer produced "Another Rib" for *Fantasy and Science Fiction*. Six months after issuance of "Phoenix," a tale of the hero Max in *Amazing Stories*, *The Colors of Space* appeared in print as a juvenile sci-fi novel. She chose Miriam Gardner as a pen name for *My Sister, My Love* and Morgan Ives for *Spare Her Heaven*. Dell incorporated "The Wind People" into the anthology *A Century of Science Fiction*.

1964

The author's introduction to *The Dark Intruder* celebrated her first short fiction anthology, containing seven stories that she composed from 1952 to 1962. She submitted to Monarch *Twilight Lovers* under the name Miriam Gardner and to *I, Palantir* another Tolkien tribute, "The Parting of Arwen." She earned regard for *The Bloody Sun*, which revisited the issue of the orphaning of Dorilys and the disparate parentage and divided cultures that confuse and alienate Jefferson Andrew Kerwin, Junior, an "orphan of space" (Bradley, 2003). In an era of scientific advancement, she stated her faith in the future of sci-fi: "Every step into the unknown future opens up a thousand new unknown futures—and only by the free play of the imagination can we guess, perhaps, where our dreams may be leading us" (Bradley, 1964, i).

1964 May

The author studied Bible while completing a BA in English, Spanish, and psychology from Hardin-Simmons University in Abilene, Texas, which she financed with royalties from her works.

May 19, 1964

The Bradleys divorced two years before Brad's death at age 67 on September 5, 1966, in Taylor, Texas. Marion gladly left the state and moved to Berkeley, California.

June 3, 1964

Marion wed an affable, charismatic mathematician and sociologist Walter Henry Breen, Jr., editor of *International Journal of Greek Love* (1965) and author of *Walter*

Breen's Complete Encyclopedia of U.S. and Colonial Coins, 1722–1977 (1988) and *Greek Love* (1964), which Marion edited. The couple produced Moira Evelyn Dorothy Greyland Breen Stern and Patrick Mark Greyland Breen, who suffered from diabetes. Marion continued to use Bradley as her professional surname.

1965

Marion submitted "Feminine Equivalents of Greek Love in Modern Literature" to Breen's journal. The essay contrasted woman-to-girl love as less sensual, less overtly sexual, and more sublimated than man-boy liaisons. While living at Greyhaven, a communal dwelling in the Claremont section of Berkeley Hills, she began a master's degree at the University of California, Berkeley, while writing *Castle Terror*, a tale of haunting featuring a psychiatric nurse. For daily quiet, she "bribed [her family] shamelessly for letting me alone" in the company of "the best company in the world: the characters who come out of my brain and mind. I had to learn to be sociable" (Bradley, 1984, 1). From intense work, she completed the essay "Block That Title" and issued *Star of Danger,* the third in the Darkover series.

1966

The author's output included writing *Knives of Desire* and *No Adam for Eve* and editing *Sybil Leek's Astrology* magazine.

May 1, 1966

At Milpitas, California, the author, brother Paul Edwin Zimmer, and neopagan writer Diana Lucile Paxson, Marion's sister-in-law, established the Society for Creative Anachronism (SCA), a group promoting reenactments of Medieval and Renaissance life. From 600 to 1,600 members performed in costume. Participants extolled chivalric qualities—courtly manners, excellence in combat, and skill at chess and other royal amusements—and vied for peerages proving command of stitchery, brewing, cookery, and dance. At Twelfth Night, Beltane, and Purgatorio, some 14,000 revelers feasted and reveled in selection of a monarch. The concept spread to members in Australia, Canada, Finland, Germany, Greece, Italy, Japan, New Zealand, Romania, South Africa, Sweden, and the UK.

1967

The author earned an MA from the University of California at Berkeley the same year she completed *Souvenir of Monique,* a doppelgänger novel of disappearance and suicide.

1968

While completing the doppelgänger mystery *Bluebeard's Daughter,* featuring Sybil as protagonist, and publishing "Two Worlds of Fantasy" in *Haunted,* Marion founded the Kingdom of the East. At home in Staten Island, New York, the imaginative setting expanded on SCA with heraldry, illumination, feasting, costumes, archery and fencing, and medieval drama and music.

1969

In a wide-ranging study of protagonists, the author chose a teenage boy to feature in *The Brass Dragon,* one of her less appreciated YA fictions. She submitted the essay "The Chief Value of Science Fiction" to *The Double-Bill Symposium.*

1970

For *The Winds of Darkover,* Marion made a gender breakthrough with a premier female protagonist at a time when "women's liberation was not even a shadow on the horizon" (Leith, 1980, 30). She orchestrated the romantic rescue of a virgin Keeper by Terran Andrew Carr in a relationship that results in marriage in the sequel, *The Forbidden Tower.* In answer to critics calling her a "literary prostitute," she retorted, "I like to write the kind of books I enjoy reading…. Also, I had kids to feed, and literary prostitution is legal and less hard on the conscience and the physique than the ordinary kind" (Bradley, 1970, vii).

1971

Always challenging herself to examine extremes of human possibilities, the writer translated Spanish poet Lope de Vega's *El Villano in Su Rincon* (The Villain in His Corner), a vilification of Iberian Muslims, and perused male homosexual bonding in *The World Wreckers,* a long work dramatizing economic imperialism plotted by Andrea Closson, head of Planetary Investments Unlimited.

1972

Marion published *Dark Satanic,* the poems "Katwen" and "In Search of Arkham" for *Allerlei* and "Shangri La" for *Allerleib,* and, under the pseudonym Valerie Graves, *Witch Hill,* the first of a series of mysteries on demonic possession. She reprised the foundations of Darkover with the explanatory essays "The Voice of the Myth-Maker" and "The (Bastard) Children of Hastur" and with an outer-space classic, *Darkover Landfall,* originally named *Summer of the Ghost Wind.* Because public discourse favored discussion of psychedelic drugs, she invented an hallucinogenic pollen spread by wind.

1973

Returned to California, the Breen family moved into Greenwalls, a house north of Oakland in Berkeley. The author composed the story "In the Steps of the Master" for

Sixth Sense, the essay "Translations from the Editorial" for *The Alien Critic,* and *Men, Halflings, and Hero Worship* for T-K Graphics. She collaborated with her brother, neo-paganism writer and poet Paul Edwin Zimmer, on *Hunters of the Red Moon* and *The Survivors,* cautionary narratives of kidnap and survival, especially to girls and women, which she published five years later.

1974

To stimulate fantasy writing, Marion wrote the monograph *The Necessity for Beauty* and launched Friends of Darkover, a collaborative fan club. For the composition of *The Spell Sword,* a Darkover quest-and-portal fantasy, she posed protagonist Andrew Carr as an explorer of another realm. In the estimation of critic Farah Mendlesohn, author of *Rhetoric of Fantasy,* Andrew's initiatory plunge into fantasy continues until he is "knowledgeable enough to negotiate with the world via the personal manipulation of the fantastic realm," where he embraces the powers of telepathy (Mendlesohn, 2008, 2).

1974 winter

A two-part essay, "My Life on Darkover" for *Fantasiae,* acknowledged Marion's affection for her off-planet saga.

1975

The writer published *Can Ellen Be Saved?* and began issuing *The Darkover Newsletter,* which ran for seventy issues over eighteen years. Breaking out of defined genre, page lengths, and deadlines, *The Heritage of Hastur* contained Marion's poem "The Outlaw." The work earned a Nebula nomination for the depth of action and character in a society that achieves a compact banning long-range weapons. As a result, individuals settle conflicts at arm's length on a one-to-one basis rather than through war, a theme that recurs in *The Sword of Aldones.* Contracts with Don Wollheim of DAW Books allowed Marion to write adventure, emotion, psychology, spirituality, and topical issues without artificial limits on plot and style.

January 1, 1975

Walter Breen issued a monograph, *The Gemini Problem: A Study in Darkover,* a critique of Marion's style, themes, and motivations for sci-fi writing.

August 1, 1975

The author completed *Endless Voyage* and *Endless Universe.* At Lughnasad, she stressed in *GE* magazine the harvest festival in "The Feminist Creation Myth."

1975 winter

Late in the year, Marion authored the essay "About the Birthgrave, by Tanith Lee," a book review for *Fantasiae.*

1976

Marion continued her frenetic pace with the stories "Hero's Moon," a revenge plot in "The Waterfall," and a nature befogged Diana in "The Day of the Butterflies," the novel *Drums of Darkness,* the essay "Children's Fantasy," and the monograph "Experiment Perilous: The Art and Science of Anguish in Science Fiction." She enjoyed writing the classic feminist text *The Shattered Chain,* a glimpse of female actualization and what critic Edward Frederick James, a medievalist at University College in Dublin, called "some of the most fundamental aspects of human relationships" (James, 1996).

1977

Of the writer's chosen genres, Marion stated, "I'm not apologizing for writing Gothics. I like writing them, and I like reading them, too…. I resolved to live and let live, read and let read, and I suggest that we all try to show tolerance for the reading and preferences of others" (Bradley, 1977, iv). Her nonfiction sparkled in *Costume and Clothing As a Cultural Index on Darkover,* a monograph on the old belief that "[c]lothes make the man." To illustrate alien anthropology, she chose primitive and aristocratic outfits for men and women as well as the distinctive tunics and footwear of horsemen and villagers.

1977 October

After release of the essay "Clunkers" and the stories "Who Am I, Where I Am, and Where I Came From," "The Bardic Revel," "The Engine," "The Immovable Object," and "A Genuine Old Master," Marion began to summarize her impact on female authors in the essay "An Evolution of Consciousness: Twenty-Five Years of Writing about Women in Science Fiction." *The Forbidden Tower* received a Hugo nomination, a Locus citation, and the Invisible Little Man Award, followed the next year by a Sense of Wonder Award. She received accolades from Paul McGuire, a book critic for *Science Fiction Review.*

1978

The Darkmoon Circle, celebrants of paganism, chose the room above Marion's garage as a ceremonial lodge. In a productive period, she added to the Darkover series the stories "Green Thumb," "Everything But Freedom," "Amazon Excerpt," "The Keeper's Price," and "The Lesson of the Inn"; the verse "Amazon Fosterlings' Rhyme," *The Maenads,* "A Parting Gift," "Spinning Song," and "Chieri Lament"; and the essays

"What's My Name in Darkovan?," "My Trip Through Science Fiction," "Now, Marion," and "Darkovans Have Dirty Minds, Too!" Collaborating with Walter, she also initiated *Starstone,* a fanzine that ran annually for five issues. In June 1978, the magazine announced the first of three short fiction contests, judged by Marion and four others. Prizes ranged from $5 to $20.

Critic Edward James termed the popular novel *Stormqueen!* a pseudo-medieval "heroic fantasy" featuring female sex slaves to the lordly Hasturans (James, 1996). A pronounced isolation of women in *The Ruins of Isis* received a so-so review from Greg Costikyan, a sci-fi satirist, for weak character development of a female starship pilot. To gibes from feminists, Marion replied, "I must say sales figures are an ample vindication" (Lefanu, 1988, 94).

1979

When the Breens divorced, Walter continued to write for his ex-wife, but lived apart in Oakland, California. The two collaborated on character sketches in the *Darkover Concordance.* Before traveling to England, she released the finished version of *The Survivors* and *Legends of Hastur and Cassilda.* Marion introduced the Lythande character in "The Secret of the Blue Star," printed in *Thieves' World.* The story discloses a tedious guardianship of the magician's gender while covering her on-the-march mercenary deeds. The story "Children of Cats" features Raella, a juvenile wizard, and the Lord of Sathorn, who murders his unfaithful wife. Her essays included "Editorially Speaking."

In the family saga *The Catch Trap,* Marion developed a fully realized homosexual relationship between male trapeze artists in the Flying Santellis during the repressive post–World War II era. She based circus research on real flyers, Antoinette Concello and Alfred Codona, whom she saw perform in Texas. A quarter century later, scientists Catherine Salmon and Don Symons conducted research on readers accustomed to male-female romance novels and found that 78 percent enjoyed *The Catch Trap.*

1980

Marion began collaborating with fantasy writer and opera singer Elisabeth Waters of Providence, Rhode Island. Marion trained Elisabeth as an editor and maintained their relationship for the rest of her life and in her will. The author completed the short-short story "Cross Currents" for *Obsc'zine* and reset the arms race in Darkover in *Two to Conquer,* which opens on a Celtic betrothal and concludes a chaotic era with a ban on psychic weapons of mass destruction. She also compiled *Checklist: A Complete, Cumulative Checklist of Lesbian, Variant and Homosexual Fiction* and the story "Thendara House," a significant setting in her study of sisterhood.

July 12, 1980

Del Rey's publication of *The House Between the Worlds* hooked readers on Marion's engaging style and fast-paced plots featuring elements of parapsychology,

Gothicism, and out-of-body adventures. She also issued *Two to Conquer* and *Survey Ship*, a follow-up on six graduates of a space exploration academy, and the stories "Maidenhood" and "Elbow Room," a tale of confession and penance. She edited a collection of nineteen short works in *The Keeper's Price*, which contained her story by the same name as well as "The Hawk-Master's Son" and "Blood Will Tell."

In "A Word from the Creator of Darkover," the introduction to *The Keeper's Price*, Marion admitted to becoming "a little unpopular in feminist circles by my persistent refusal to be typed as a 'woman writer' or to collaborate in telling my grievances against the publishing world which is supposedly in male-dominated hands or to identify with the extremes of feminism" (Bradley, 1980, 3). She identified the typing of women professionals as a form of apartheid. Dan Davidson, a book reviewer for the *Whitehorse* (Yukon) *Daily Star*, admired the collection: "All clearly spring from the joy these people have found in their hobby, and that, if nothing else, makes the book enjoyable" (Davidson, 1982, 244).

At age fifty, Marion achieved some resolution of earlier perplexities. She and her husband sought ordination into the Eastern Orthodox priesthood. The object of serious critical praise in *Science Fiction Studies*, she received from Susan Gubar inclusion with "Ursula Le Guin, Doris Lessing, Marge Piercy, and Joanna Russ, all of whom are contributing to what promises to be an *Aurora*—a new dawning—in SF" (Gubar, 1980, 16).

1981

Marion's involvement in Darkmoon Circle preceded the incorporation of the Center for Non-Traditional Religion. In the next decade, she returned to Episcopalianism. Her cross-genre efforts included *Sharra's Exile* and *The White Knight Cookbook*.

1981 August

Marion's story "Elbow Room" appeared in *The 1981 Annual World's Best SF.*

1982

Hawkmistress! invigorated the feminist themes of the Darkover series by freeing a fifteen-year-old girl from an odious betrothal. For background, Marion researched ring dancing, falconry, and the care and feeding of captive raptors.

1982 April

The author incorporated "A Sword Called Chaos," the story of Mhari, a vengeful rape survivor, and "The Lesson of the Inn" into a nineteen-title omnibus, *Sword of Chaos and Other Stories*. A generous mentor to young writers, she stated in the introduction an intention to retire from celebrities and let beginners "live for other writers than myself" (Bradley, 1982, 1).

1983

The author initiated a busy year with publication of "The Incompetent Magician," one of her most appealing fictions for its villain, the inept wizard Rastafyre and the thieving Roygan the Proud, whom she marks with a nose ring. With *Thendara House,* winner of a 1984 Prometheus Award second place, Marion developed the concept of a college of priestesses, the motif of *The Mists of Avalon.* Reviewer Paul Craig, in an interview for the Santa Rosa, California, *Press Democrat,* noted that "[s]he made the changeover with no difficulty, proving to a wider audience what her followers already knew—that she is an enormously skilled storyteller" (Craig, 1989, B5).

The author immediately began a second view of the prototype in *City of Sorcery,* a study of the high price of female security. Her promotion of Goddess worship resulted in what scholar Kristina Hildebrand of Uppsala University described as "the emerging Neopagan religious tradition" (Hildebrand, 2001, 112). The renewal of faith in the old days honored "those few who can come and go between the worlds" (Bradley, 1983, 16). For Marion's command of quest lore, Alyssa Rosenberg, a journalist for the *Washington Post,* proclaimed the writer a "titan of genre fiction" (Rosenberg, 2014).

February 1, 1983

With the help of son David, the author published *Web of Light* and *Web of Darkness,* reissued in one volume as *The Fall of Atlantis.* The text incorporated the words of David's deceased father as apothegms for each chapter as well as the philosophy of the Darkmoon Circle, a women's consortium that trained postulants to minister to others. The ceremonial traditions influenced creation of the character Viviane in *The Mists of Avalon.* Analyst Janice C. Crosby validated the work for "[giving] fictional flesh to hypotheses about matriarchal and matrifocal cultures" (Crosby, 2000, 32).

Following the arc of Malory's *Morte D'arthur,* T.H. White's *Once and Future King,* Alfred Lord Tennyson's *Idylls of the King,* Mark Twain's *A Connecticut Yankee in King Arthur's Court,* and Mary Stewart's Merlin trilogy, Marion reset Arthurian lore in a matriarchal trajectory under the metaphoric title *The Mists of Avalon,* her signal success in mainstream fiction. Within the text, Lancelet performs Middle Welsh ballads of Queen Arianrhod ("Silver Wheel") and Blodeuwedd ("Flower-Faced"), the blossom woman, two mythic characters from the Mabinogion, a collection of oral Celtic stories composed after 1100 CE.

Marion, who intended the international bestseller as a celebration of women's centrality to alternative religions, succeeded at what *New York Times* reviewer Maureen Quilligan called "mythic coherence" (Quilligan, 1983). Although Morgaine may have been a goddess before entering the Arthuriad, Marion declared in "The Once and Future Merlin" that "only Arthur and Merlin are immortal in any sense other than the literary" (Bradley, 1998). Of the question of a reconciliation between the ancient goddess faith and Christianity, she declared, "I do feel very strongly, not only that it can, but that it must" (Bradley, 1986). Her sister-in-law and colleague, Diana Lucile Paxson, concurred that *The Mists of Avalon* relayed "in accessible fictional form things that people badly needed to hear" (Paxson, 1999, 110).

The publisher ruled out the original title—*Mistress of Magic*—because it echoed racier titles. Despite winning the Locus Poll Award for best fantasy novel in 1984, Marion still incurred "[dismissal] as a writer of historical romance, and/or a producer of 'best-sellers'" (Wynne-Davies, 2016, 176). *The Mists of Avalon* inspired Marion to recreate episodes from the Dark Ages, a revised focus on the past that critic Julius Evola calls "the starting point of a whole subgenera of fantasy novels" (Evola, 2018). The *New York Times* praised the huge undertaking and the drama of events in settings both real and magical. Isaac Asimov rated the retelling of Arthur's saga the best of its kind. Royalties from the book paid for Marion's kitchen makeover and a new car.

1983 May

At the onset of cardiac disease and diabetes, Marion began editing and writing introductions to the annual *Sword and Sorceress* series with "The Heroic Image of Women: Woman as Wizard and Warrior" and continued from volumes I to XVII. In the introduction, she stated that fiction "about both men and women, is, I hope, a sign of the times" (Bradley, 1984, I, 13). The fantasy collections stress self-determined female protagonists in plots based on warfare, adventure, and magic.

1984 October

In addition to completing the story "Oathbreakers" and the novel *The Inheritor,* Marion published in *The Magazine of Fantasy & Science Fiction* one of her most successful short works, "Somebody Else's Magic," a story set in the fictional crime nest Thieves Quarter. Replete with the old-fashioned language of country folk, the plot depicts the remains of the priestess Laritha attacked by necrophiliacs.

1985

Of changes in printing costs and quality, the author's 1985 essay "Fandom: Its Value to the Professional" followed the arc of the times:

> I published my first fanzine on a pan hectograph which cost me five dollars, paying a dollar for a ream of paper, thirty cents for a special hectograph ribbon and about a dollar for thirty three-cent stamps to mail it out with…. Just to keep perspective, a stamp is now twenty cents; paper is about ten dollars a ream, and my latest novel is advertised to sell at $3.50 [Bradley, 1985].

She added to her canon *Night's Daughter* and *Warrior Woman,* the essay "On Night's Daughter and Mozart's *The Magic Flute,*" and her popular stories "House Rules"; "Sea Wrack," the tale of a dangerous mermaid; and "Bonds of Sisterhood," a glimpse of women sharing a torture chamber.

The author collected major works—*The Planet Savers, The Colors of Space, The Door Through Space, Year of the Big Thaw*—in *The Best of Marion Zimmer Bradley.* For the anthology *Free Amazons of Darkover,* she chose the embedded woman-to-woman union in "The Legend of Lady Bruna" and "Knives," a cautionary tale of the domineering stepfather who prefers an illiterate woman for wife and a winsome stepdaughter as bedmate. In the mode of *The Shattered Chain*, Marion composed "To Keep the Oath," a short story about the meeting of Camilla n'ha Kyria and Kindra n'ha Mhari, leader of the Free Amazons. Of the author's pace, in the essay "Fandom: Its Value to the Professional," Marion claimed to do the best writing at the output of fifteen–twenty pages a day. In the prologue to *Warrior Woman,* she stated a philosophy of human inequalities:

> Beyond our work lie a million billion suns lighting a million billion other worlds, and uncountable men and women struggling to live and thrive. And on some of them men build cities, and dwell in them served by giant brains and robots, and on others men struggle to survive in desert or virgin forest, with sword throwing-stick and whatever powers their unknown gods have given to their bodies and their minds.
> So it is.
> So will it be ever, worlds without end [Bradley, 1985, 3].

1986 August

In *The Magazine of Fantasy & Science Fiction,* Marion issued the novella "The Wandering Lute," a segment of *The Complete Lythande,* a collection of twenty tales that disclose the mistreatment of women by Tashgen and other womanizers. Of the protagonist's nature, *Publishers Weekly* described the armed pilgrim as "discreet and nebulous to the point of anonymity" ("Review," 1986, 82). Her musical instruments— lute and harp—and the blue star on her forehead draw questions from the typically narrow-minded rubes of small villages. Essential among her replies to the intrusive lie the commercial deals that fund her decades of meandering. Her essays "Thoughts on Avalon" and "The Evolution of Women's Fantasy" increased stress on female accomplishments in the genre.

1987

For the fourth Darkover anthology, *The Other Side of the Mirror,* Marion contributed an introduction and the tales "Everything But Freedom," "Oathbreaker," and "Bride Price," a feminist theme found in her short and long fiction of women's loss in marrying older men. For the Lythande series, she composed "The Walker Behind," a tale of pig charmers at the Hag and Swine saloon, and "Bitch," a plot that turns women into ravenous dogs. Marion also offered the *San Francisco Chronicle* the story "The Dance at the Gym," a vignette expressing the mental and emotional hesitance of a satellite outpost member caught up in a feud.

October 1, 1987

Drawing on Walter's knowledge of Greek classics, Marion paralleled her venture into Arthurian motifs with *The Firebrand,* a matriarchal alternative to Homer's epic of the eastern Mediterranean discontent preceding the destruction of Troy. An intriguing study of catastrophe, female silencing, and regret, a new story of the Princess Cassandra/Kassandra details the clearing of her ears by snakes to attune her senses to prophecy. According to South African classicist Elke Steinmeyer, Marion extends "Cassandra's snake affinities by taking her off to Colchis, there to follow in the serpent-tending Medea's footsteps" (Evans, 2017).

In addition to the telepathic visions of Troy's fall, the text includes current interpretations of the mythic Jason and the Golden Fleece based on a method of straining freshets to isolate flakes of gold. Another history-based theory concludes that the Trojan War erupted against Priam for enforcing tolls on merchant ships passing through the Dardanelles into the Sea of Marmora. For unraveling the international conflicts of the past, the historical novel earned a 1988 Locus Award and translation into twelve languages.

1987 November

Marion's *Red Sun of Darkover* anthology contained an introductory essay plus the stories "The Shadow" and "The Ballad of Hastur and Cassilda," a song-story performed by Lady Rohana Ardais. The verse narrative became the last of the author's four-decade career in poetry, which began in 1947. The foretelling of modern bafflement earned the author a fervid audience for prophecy. As explained by Zambian analyst Carla Namwali Serpell, "Maybe science fiction future is actually just a lens on the present" (Serpell, 2019, 11).

1988

A quarterly, *Marion Zimmer Bradley's Fantasy Magazine*, first appeared in print and flourished for fifty issues until 2000. Walter's arrest for sexual abuse of children precipitated Marion's first stroke and, six months later, a heart attack, which required two years of rehabilitation. During this period, she limited appearances and concentrated on editing rather than writing. She snarled, "Brain scans show a lot of my brain is turned to granola—but I can still read and write and walk and talk. And edit" (Bradley, 1991).

For the collection *Four Moons of Darkover*, the author incorporated "Man of Impulse" and "House Rules." She composed the short-short story "The Final Bet" and a tribute to the wise crone in "The Malice of the Demon," plus insightful essays for the beginning writer—"A New Magazine," "Dear Editor: Stop Right There," "Programming the Centipede," "The Devil Made Me Do It," "Trialogue," "A Subject I Wish Had Never Come Up," and "The Evolution of Women's Fantasy."

1989

Marion detailed the creation and keeping of a Wiccan holy space with earth, air, wind, and fire in her essay "The Household Altar." The details substantiated beliefs that

Marion was a Wiccan priestess. The validation of the occult in the story "The Haunted Street" grew in part from celebration of the inclusion of women, whom patriarchal faiths excluded, alienated, and subordinated as unworthy of God's praise. She contributed to author tutorials with the essays "Rejection, Continued," "Rejection, Rejection…. Acceptance!," "A View from the Other Side of the Desk," and "The Nine Basic Science Fiction Plots." A settling of inter-dynastic feuding in *The Heirs of Hammerfell* brought to the Darkover series a lasting peace.

1990

With *Black Trillium,* Marion took up the medieval quest novel with a flurry of period details—citadels, labyrinths, merchant guilds, incantations, and caravans traveling secret routes—and such archaisms as *anon, equerry, citadel,* and *oddlings,* a swamp race she added to her list of exotic beings.

1990 spring

Marion's essays "The Major Question," "More Rejection," and "Introduction: And Contrariwise" continued coaxing beginners to write. The narrative "Firetrap," co-written by Elisabeth Waters, appeared in the seventeen-story collection *Domains of Darkover.* In the introduction, she commented on the ongoing series, which had reached twenty books, and revealed plans for additions: "If I want anything—and I probably do—it's to make some special new point with each new book" (Bradley, 1990, 2).

May 9, 1990

The Breen marriage ended in divorce after Walter revealed an ongoing molestation of a thirteen-year-old boy.

1990 July

Marion submitted the essays "God Hears Short Prayers Just as Well as Long Ones" and "The Attraction of Fantasy" and a one-page piece, "Hello Daddy, This Is Margaret." She followed in October by "The Fine Art of Collecting Rejection Slips" and an interview with Diana Paxson.

1991

After treatment in a rehabilitation hospital for stroke, Marion composed the tutorial "When I Ignore My Own Guidelines" and the short-short piece "Footsteps." The story "The Footsteps of Retribution" reached into human perfidy for the kidnap of Mary from her grandmother. The author reported to fans, "I am a pretty lucky individual; brain scans show a lot of my brain is turned to granola—but I can still read and write and walk and talk. (And edit.)" (Bradley, 1991, 22). In the introduction to the *Encyclopedia of the Strange, Mystical & Unexplained,* the author commented an era of social approbation: "In these troubled times, we need information, and we need it badly" (Bradley, 1991, ix).

1991 October

Marion added a light-hearted Lythande story to the series by depicting her as an exterminator of vermin in "The Wuzzles." To focus the medieval occult on a barn, she sketched a pentagram, an emblem of Wiccan faith. In advice to the beginner, she published "The Perfect Cover Letter" in *Marion Zimmer Bradley's Fantasy Magazine,* a periodical issued four times a year.

October 3, 1991

Police arrested 61-year-old Walter Breen at Superior Galleries in Beverly Hills on eight felony counts of child abuse. In reference to his crimes and accusations against Marion, critic Nicole Evelina assured readers, "Regardless of what Bradley may or may not have done, the work stands on its own" (Tichelaar).

November 5, 1991

Marion added *Leroni of Darkover* to her series, containing an introduction and 22 stories. Her opening words ridiculed feminist orthodoxy and accusations that she had "sold out years ago to the male establishment" (Bradley, 1991, 2).

1991 winter

A resurgent spirit inspired the essays "Fantasy vs. Disney" and "Announcement: Off with the Old and On with the New" and introductions for *Harper's Encyclopedia of Mystical and Paranormal Experience.*

1992

To *Grails: Quests, Visitations and Other Occurrences,* the author contributed the exemplum "Chalice of Tears," which introduced the gentle female character Manuela and the ancient divination via tarot cards. She returned to tutorials with the essay "What I Reject and Why."

1992 March

Marion's husband began a sentence of thirteen years at Chino's California Institute for Men for child molestation. Grief contributed to her failing health from congestive heart failure and diabetes. Because author Jean Lamb accused the author of plagiarizing a fan's story, Marion disbanded the Friends of Darkover, an outlet for beginning fantasy writers.

1992 late spring–fall

The author's wit and enthusiasm resurged in the essays "Twice the Work and Half the Money," "Discovery," "Holes in My Yard," "Tools of the Trade," and "The Art of Speaking Forsoothly." In late fall, she submitted "Excellence or Elitism?" to the winter issue of *Marion Zimmer Bradley's Fantasy Magazine*.

1993

Recorded Books issued a 51-hour audio version of *The Mists of Avalon* read by Davina Porter, the award-winning narrator of *Madame Bovary, Anna Karenina, Moll Flanders, Josephine, Canterbury Tales, The Red and the Black, Far from the Madding Crowd, Tess of the d'Urbervilles,* and the *Outlander* series.

April 27, 1993

Walter Breen died at the Chino prison of cancer before he could be transferred to San Quentin State Prison.

1993 October

At a difficult time in her career, Marion achieved heightened critical attention in *Journal of Popular Culture, Extrapolation,* and *Mythlore,* and mocked protagonist Gareth Lindir in the story "Ten Minutes or So" with the name of a young, inexperienced Knight of King Arthur's Round Table. She produced more essays on composition: "Happy Endings," "I'm Not in This Business for My Health," "Convenient Earthquake," "Do You Know the Way to Miskatonic!," "The Sense of Wonder," "Suspension of Disbelief," and "At Science Fiction Conventions, Fans Can Sometimes Be a Second Family." While writing *The Forest House* and *Rediscovery,* a perusal of child sex slaves, she anthologized fourteen stories for the sci-fi collections *Marion Zimmer Bradley's Darkover, Towers of Darkover,* and *Jamie and Other Stories*.

1994

The author composed the essays "Dialogue," "My Very Own Slush Pile," "The One Reason for Rejection," and "Grabbing the Reader" and reissued the story "Chalice of Tears," featuring the humble pilgrim leader Manuela. "To Kill the Undead" reflected on Catholic refusal to bury Haymil, a suicide, in hallowed ground. Book reviews burgeoned in *Kirkus, Extrapolation, Entertainment Weekly,* and *Publishers Weekly* and in critical volumes.

1994 April

With Diana Paxson, Marion began the six-volume Avalon series, which Diana continued after Marion's death. For the 23-story anthology *Snows of Darkover,* Marion wrote "The Word of a Hastur," a tale lauding probity as a virtue. The introduction stated the author's pride in advancing the careers of Paxson, Mercedes Lackey, Deborah Wheeler, and Elisabeth Waters.

1995

Marion wrote the essay "The Writer's Tool Box" and polished *Lady of the Trillium* and *Tiger Burning Bright,* a psychological thriller depicting the army of Emperor Balthasar. With the fictional "The Pledged Word," she introduced Nimue's acceptance into the Avalon sisterhood. The short-short Lythande story "Fool's Fire" and "Here There Be Dragons" picture the mercenary's efforts to drive off menace with a crucifix. Time-Warner hired actor Natasha Richardson to narrate the audio version of *The Mists of Avalon.*

1995 June

In anticipation of her 65th birthday, Marion wrote in the prologue to "The Word of a Hastur": "Big deal; but it means I get a discount pass on the Berkeley buses" (Bradley, 1994, 193).

1996

In the anthology *Space Opera,* the author published another Lythande episode, "To Drive the Cold Winter Away," a dirge for discordant townsfolk who endure the outlawing of music, the cause of unending winter. The essay "What Is a Short Story" extended the author's tutorials for authors with parameters and incisive definitions.

May 17, 1996

Marion starred as featured writer at the sixth yearly sci-fi and fantasy convention, held in Salt Lake City, Utah.

1996 June

At the Audie Awards, Natasha Richardson achieved a second place for Best Solo Performance for recording *The Mists of Avalon* for Time Warner. Marion issued *Exile's*

Song, a continuation of the Darkover series with the adulthood of Margaret, daughter of Lew Alton.

August 29, 1996

The author attended the 54th annual World Science Fiction Convention in Anaheim, California, to discuss the realm of sci-fi authorship with a panel of experts. For feminists, according to scholar Rhoda K. Unger, imaginative stories provided "role models for independence and intellectual inquiry" (Unger, 2009, 117).

September 1, 1996

Marion published the gothic novel *Glenraven* with Bastei, a German company in Cologne. She set the story in a minuscule country between France and Italy still wrapped in medieval magic. She followed with the quirky mini-story "Toe Heaven."

1997

Marion began the year with the essay "Why Did My Story Get Rejected?" After completing *Gravelight* and *The Shadow Matrix,* her plotting of the urban romance *Witchlight,* a sequel to *Ghostlight,* earned strong support from Sybil S. Steinberg, a reviewer for *Publishers Weekly.* Steinberg noted a lack of energy in the narrative, but applauded the author's ability to "spin a wicked web of tangled relationships and motivations" (Steinberg, 1996, 56).

1997 June

The issuance of *Lady of Avalon,* a prequel to *The Mists of Avalon* and sequel of *The Forest House,* traced the bloodlines of Viviane and Igraine with historic detail and promotion of female strengths. An episode accounts for the conjuring of a misty veil separating the women's training center at Avalon from Inis Within.

Marion continued the Lythande series with "North to Northwander," a brief revival of the mercenary's delight in womanhood. For *Ghor, Kin-Slayer,* she added "Doom of the Thrice-Cursed" to the story catalog. She turned to the time-honored story of the woman disguised as a man in the fantasy novella *The Gratitude of Kings,* a Christmas gift book from ROC featuring Lythande as a female wizard who must thwart a misalliance at a wedding. The novella found fans in Italy, France, Portugal, and Germany. More critiques appeared in *Publishers Weekly* and *Mosaic.*

October 18, 1997

Paul Edwin Zimmer, Marion's younger brother and collaborator, died of a heart attack in Schenectady, New York at age 54.

1998

Marion continued advising writers with the essay "What's Your Story About, Anyway?" With *The Forests of Avalon* and *Heartlight,* the third in Marion's Light series, themes moved from extreme paranormal to posit a world view of wars between light and shade, good and evil, symbolized by a veteran returning from combatting Nazism and his crusade between 1960 and 1998. As elements of struggle, the author references wars in Korea and Vietnam, a missile crisis in Cuba and the Kennedy assassination, Watergate, Irangate, and Desert Storm. Reviewer Sybil S. Steinberg of *Publishers Weekly* noted that the author "barely fictionalized versions of real-life esoteric sites and practitioners" in New York and San Francisco (Steinberg, 1998, 53).

January 5, 1998

From *Publishers Weekly,* Marion's *Lady of Avalon* won a Listen Up award for sci-fi/fantasy. For *TV Guide,* she wrote "The Once and Future Merlin."

April, 1998

Co-authorship of *In the Rift* with Holly Lisle yielded Kate Beacham, a tough, fearless woman warrior who combats a malevolent sorcerer during an anti–Wicca war in Fort Lauderdale.

1998 July

For *Niekas,* Marion satisfied period tastes for ghoulish fiction with "A Clutch of Vampires."

1998 October

The tutorial series continued with "Grammar I learned in Fifth Grade" and "Death, Taxes, and the Writer." Echoing Clarissa Pinkola Estes's *Women Who Run with the Wolves,* Marion's foreword to *In Search of the Woman Warrior* acknowledged the mythic forerunners of modern pacesetters and added, "These days, we need her" (Bradley, 1998, ix). She mused on a paradox: "Why Arthurian legends had so many women who did absolutely nothing" (*Ibid.,* viii). Another fact puzzled her, why the *Sword & Sorceress* anthology thrived in Europe and the U.S. She concluded, "A lot of people want to read about strong women," a fact inspiring the Shakespearean whimsy "Well Met by Moonlight," a story of Titania and Oberon, mates from the fairy world retrieved from the 1595 comic romance *A Midsummer Night's Dream* (*Ibid.*).

1999

In her final publications, Marion still cherished fun in the essay "Sex and Bad Language" and Lythande's ballad in "Goblin Market," a title taken from the feminist rescue narrative by Christina Rossetti.

1999 January

In *Traitor's Sun,* the author charged warmongers with complicating normal life: "Very little was spent on the day-to-day existence of ordinary people, whose lives became even more difficult" (Bradley, 1999, 3). She made no effort to conceal criticisms of American politics and the waste of tax money on the Pentagon and mounting firepower. As an outlet for satire, she depicted a traveling puppet show that disgusts its audience with ribald dialogue.

September 25, 1999

Marion entered Alta Bates Medical Center in Berkeley, California, on September 21 and died four days later of heart failure. Mourners spread her ashes over Glastonbury Tor, a sandstone hill in Somerset, England, terraced during the late 600s CE near Cadbury Castle, a hill fort identified as King Arthur's Camelot. Her papers, fanzines, and manuscripts survive at Boston University.

2000

A posthumous World Fantasy Award for Lifetime Achievement acknowledged the author's career. Accolades appeared in newspapers and in *Foundation, Sagewoman,* and *Extrapolation.*

April 19, 2000

A tribute at the Surroundings Gallery in Worcester, Massachusetts, projected painted images of Marion's females.

2001

Director Uri Edel completed a four-hour, $20 million cable miniseries of *The Mists of Avalon,* a narrative that Kate O'Hare, critic for the Martinsville, Indiana, *Reporter-Times,* termed "likely the greatest story in Europe" (O'Hare, 2001). The Arthurian counterstory featured Anjelica Huston and Julianna Margulies in the starring roles of Viviane and Arthur's half-sister Morgaine with Samantha Mathis as Gwenhwyfar and Joan Allen as the villain Morgause. Set in 600–700 CE and filmed in April 2000 in Prague, Czech Republic, the screen adaptation by Gavin Scott appeared on TNT over two nights—July 15 and 16—and gave viewers new strands of thought on paganism and the history of the Round Table. Robert Bianco, writing for *USA Today,* proclaimed the TV version as filled with human flaws as a Greek tragedy. In the essay "Frustrating Female Heroism" for *Journal of Popular Culture,* Mary Margoulick compared the power heroines on a par with La Femme Nikita, Buffy the Vampire Slayer, and Xena, Warrior Princess. Less positive critiques complained of slow pacing, miscast actors, and a lack of energy.

2001 June

Del Rey scheduled a 25th anniversary reprint of *The Mists of Avalon* to coincide with the television series.

June 6, 2001

The Calgary *Herald* praised Diana Lucile Paxson for completing Marion's *Priestess of Avalon*. Book critic Sheldon Wiebe declared it "a memorable final addition to the Marion Zimmer Bradley library" (Wiebe, 2001, ES11). The Viking hardcover reached the public simultaneously with Davina Porter's four-cassette abridgment.

2001 August

DAW featured the entire Darkover series in an omnibus printing, *The Forbidden Circle*.

2003

Editors of Science Fiction Book Club listed *The Mists of Avalon* among the top ten significant works of sci-fi and fantasy in the previous half century. The series earned nomination for a primetime Emmy for Outstanding Miniseries.

2012 February

Ilene Kahn Power and Elizabeth Stanley purchased rights to the Darkover novels and projected turning the saga into a television adventure series revealing re-improvised gender roles. Power compared the appeal of Marion's fiction suite to that of *Battlestar Galactica* and *Game of Thrones*. While production at Amazon Studio progressed, staff hired Patrick Macmanus and Elizabeth Sarnoff to adapt the series.

2014

Moira Greyland Breen alerted the London *Guardian* to Marion's sexual abuse of her daughter between ages three and twelve. The confession launched a wave of anti–Bradley feeling among writers and publishers.

2014 April

After a twenty-year gap, a relaunch of the Darkover series honored Marion's 84th birthday. *Publishers Weekly* described the fifteen narratives as "set on Bradley's psionics-rich, technology-poor world of Darkover" ("Fiction," 2014).

2018

Recorded Books released the tape version of *City of Sorcery,* narrated by Alyssa Bresnahan.

Sources

Arbur, Rosemarie. *Leigh Brackett, Marion Zimmer Bradley, Anne McCaffrey: A Primary and Secondary Bibliography.* Boston, MA: G.K. Hall, 1982.
Bianco, Robert. "'Mists' Features Strong Women, Acting," *USA Today* (13 July 2001): E2.
Bradley, Marion Zimmer. *The Best of Marion Zimmer Bradley.* Chicago: Academy Chicago, 1985.
_____. *The Catch Trap.* New York: Random House, 1979.
_____. *The Complete Lythande.* San Francisco: Marion Zimmer Bradley Literary Works Trust, 2013.
_____. *The Dark Intruder.* New York: Ace, 1964.
_____. *Darkover Newsletter* 8 (November 1977).
_____. *Domains of Darkover.* New York: DAW, 1990.
_____. *The Door Through Space.* New York: Ace, 1961.
_____. "Exiles of Tomorrow," *Fantastic Universe* 3:2 (March 1955): 117–122.
_____. "Fandom: Its Value to the Professional," *Inside Outer Space.* New York: Unger, 1985.
_____. *The Forbidden Tower.* New York: DAW, 1977.
_____. "Foreword," *In Search of the Woman Warrior.* Rockport, MA: Element Books, 1998, viii–x.
_____. "Introduction," *Leroni of Darkover.* New York: DAW, 1991: 1–3.
_____. "Introduction," *Sword and Sorceress I* (May 1984): 1.
_____. *The Keeper's Price.* New York: DAW, 1980.
_____. *Marion Zimmer Bradley's Darkover.* San Francisco: Marion Zimmer Bradley Literary Works Trust, 2010.
_____. *The Mists of Avalon.* New York: Ballantine, 1983.
_____. "The Once and Future Merlin," *TV Guide* (April 1998).
_____. "The Parting of Arwen," *I, Palantir* 5 (1964): 1–10.
_____. *Red Sun of Darkover.* New York: DAW, 1987.
_____. *Renunciates of Darkover.* New York: DAW, 1991.
_____. *Sword of Chaos.* New York: DAW, 1982.
_____. "Thoughts on Avalon," http://mzbworks.com/thoughts.htm, 1986.
_____. *Towers of Darkover.* New York: DAW, 1993.
_____ (co-author). *Traitor's Sun.* New York: DAW, 1999.
_____. *Warrior Woman.* New York: DAW, 1985.
_____. *The Winds of Darkover.* New York: Ace, 1970.
_____. "The Word of a Hastur," *Snows of Darkover.* New York: DAW, 1994.
_____. *A World Divided.* New York: DAW, 2003.
Breen, Walter. *The Darkover Concordance.* Houston, TX: Penny-Farthing Press, 1979.
_____. *The Gemini Problem: A Study in Darkover.* Baltimore: T-K Graphics, 1975.
Craig, Paul. "Bradley's Science Fiction World a Huge Success," (Santa Rosa, CA) *Press Democrat* (15 May 1989): B5.
Crosby, Janice C. *Cauldron of Changes: Feminist Spirituality in Fantastic Fiction.* Jefferson, NC: McFarland, 2000.
Davidson, Dan. "Clear Choices Unmade," *Whitehorse* (Yukon) *Daily Star* 95 (November 1982): 24.
Davin, Eric Leif. *Partners in Wonder.* Lanham, MD: Lexington Books, 2006.
Epstein, Warren. "So You Want to Be a Science Fiction Writer, Kid?," *Tampa Tribune-Times* (14 June 1987): C5.
Evans, Richard, ed. *Prophets and Profits: Ancient Divination and Its Reception.* New York: Routledge, 2017.
Evola, Julius. *The Mystery of the Grail: Initiation and Magic in the Quest for the Spirit.* New York: Simon & Schuster, 2018.
"Fiction Reviews," *Publishers Weekly* 261:16 (21 April 2014).
Friedman, Mickey. "A Trend to Science Fantasy Books," *San Francisco Examiner* (16 November 1981): E4.
Gubar, Susan. "C.L. Moore and the Conventions of Women's Science Fiction," *Science Fiction Studies* 7:1 (March 1980): 16–27.
Hildebrand, Kristina. *The Female Reader at the Round Table: Religion and Women in Three Contemporary Arthurian Texts.* Uppsala, Sweden: University of Uppsala Press, 2001.
Howey, Ann F. "Belief and Acting on It Go Hand-in-Hand," *Edmonton Journal* (3 January 1919): F7.
James, Edward. "Marion Zimmer Bradley" in *St. James Guide to Fantasy Writers.* New York: St. James Press, 1996.
Lefanu, Sarah. *In the Chinks of the World Machine: Feminism and Science Fiction.* London: Women's Press, 1988.
Leith, Linda. "Marion Zimmer Bradley and Darkover," *Science Fiction Studies* 7 (1980): 28–35.
Margoulick, Mary. "Frustrating Female Heroism," *Journal of Popular Culture* 39:5 (2006): 729–754.
"Marion Zimmer Bradley, 69, Writer of Darkover Fantasies," *New York Times* (29 September 1999).

Mendlesohn, Farah. *Rhetorics of Fantasy.* Middletown, CT: Wesleyan University Press, 2008.

Murphy, Laura. "Marion Zimmer Bradley," *Dictionary of Literary Biography: Twentieth-Century American Science-Fiction Writers* vol. 8. Gale, 1981, 77–80.

O'Hare, Kate. "The Once and Future Women of 'The Mists of Avalon,'" *Reporter-Times* (Martinsville, IN) (14 July 2001).

Oliver, Myrna. "Marion Bradley; Writer of Fantasy Novels," *Los Angeles Times* (30 September 1999): A 24.

Orenstein, Gloria Feman. *The Reflowering of the Goddess (Athene).* Oxford, UK: Pergamon, 1990.

Paxson, Diana L. "Marion Zimmer Bradley and *The Mists of Avalon*," *Arthuriana* 9:1 (Spring 1999): 110–126.

Quilligan, Maureen. "Arthur's Sister's Story," *New York Times* (30 January 1983).

"Review: *Lythande*," *Publishers Weekly* (27 June 1986): 82.

Rosenberg, Alyssa. "Re-Reading Feminist Author Marion Zimmer Bradley in the Wake of Sexual Assault Allegations," *Washington Post* (27 June 2014).

Sadovsky, Sonja. *The Priestess and the Pen: Marion Zimmer Bradley, Dion Fortune and Diana Paxton's Influence on Modern Paganism.* Woodbury: Llewellyn, 2014.

Salmon, Catherine, and Don Symons. "Slash Fiction and Human Mating Psychology," *Journal of Sex Research* 41:1 (February 2004): 94–100.

Serpell, Namwali. "When Sci-Fi Comes True," *New York Times* (17 March 2019): 15.

Spivack, Charlotte. *Merlin's Daughters: Contemporary Women Writers of Fantasy.* Westport, CT: Greenwood, 1987.

_____. *Popular Arthurian Traditions.* Bowling Green, OH: Bowling Green State University Popular Press, 1992.

Steinberg, Sybil S. "Review: *Heartlight*," *Publishers Weekly* 245:35 (31 August 1998): 53.

_____. "Review: *Witchlight*," *Publishers Weekly* 243:34 (19 August 1996): 56.

Tichelaar, Tyler. "Children of Arthur," https://childrenofarthur.wordpress.com/tag/t-h-white/.

Unger, Rhoda K. "Science Fictive Visions: A Feminist Psychologist's View," *Feminism & Psychology* 19:1 (1 February 2009): 113–117.

Vain, Madison. "The Mists of Avalon," *Entertainment* (25 July 2014).

Walton, Jo. "'Where Did He Belong?': Marion Zimmer Bradley's *The Bloody Sun*," (3 March 2010): ttps://www.tor.com/2010/03/03/qwhere-did-he-belongq-marion-zimmer-bradleys-lemgthe-bloody-sunlemg/.

Wiebe, Sheldon. "Dance of Knives Sharp First Novel," *Calgary Herald* (16 June 2001): ES11.

Wynne-Davies, Marion. *Women and Arthurian Literature: Seizing the Sword.* London: Springer, 2016.

Genealogy

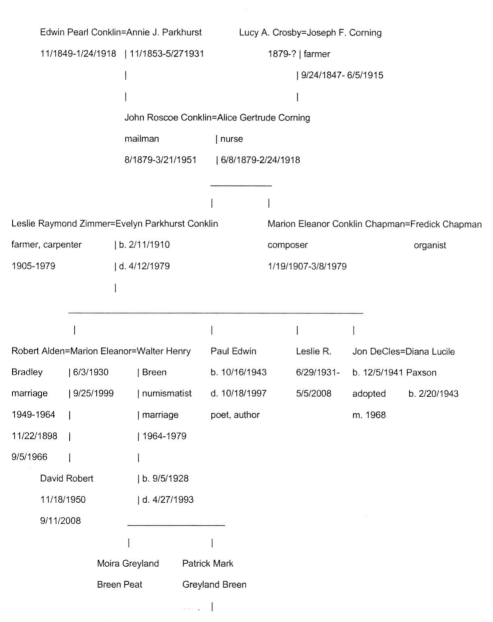

Edwin Pearl Conklin=Annie J. Parkhurst   Lucy A. Crosby=Joseph F. Corning

11/1849-1/24/1918 | 11/1853-5/271931   1879-? | farmer

               | | 9/24/1847- 6/5/1915

               | |

            John Roscoe Conklin=Alice Gertrude Corning

            mailman | nurse

            8/1879-3/21/1951 | 6/8/1879-2/24/1918

                          _____

                       | |

Leslie Raymond Zimmer=Evelyn Parkhurst Conklin   Marion Eleanor Conklin Chapman=Fredick Chapman

farmer, carpenter | b. 2/11/1910   composer   organist

1905-1979 | d. 4/12/1979   1/19/1907-3/8/1979

                   |

           _____

          | | | |

Robert Alden=Marion Eleanor=Walter Henry   Paul Edwin   Leslie R.   Jon DeCles=Diana Lucile

Bradley | 6/3/1930 | Breen   b. 10/16/1943   6/29/1931-   b. 12/5/1941 Paxson

marriage | 9/25/1999 | numismatist   d. 10/18/1997   5/5/2008   adopted   b. 2/20/1943

1949-1964 | | marriage   poet, author   m. 1968

11/22/1898 | | 1964-1979

9/5/1966 | |

   David Robert | b. 9/5/1928

     11/18/1950 | d. 4/27/1993

      9/11/2008   _____

          | |

      Moira Greyland   Patrick Mark

      Breen Peat   Greyland Breen

                 |

        Robert Jeffrey Breen

Marion Zimmer Bradley
A Companion to the Young Adult Literature

Adaptation

With an eye toward upgrading civilization, Marion stressed the significance of change and of human accommodation to newness throughout history, society, and art. In *Star of Danger,* she asserted, "A civilization changes—or it dies" (Bradley, 1965, 21). At Troy in 1200 BCE, Kassandra, the Trojan priestess in *The Firebrand,* responds to ten years of siege conditions and to her longing to join a female tribe of Amazons led by Penthesilea, a mistress of weaponry. Literary historians credit the era's lore with economic shifts in the shipping lanes between Akhaia and western Asia rather than any alteration in gender powers. When a Greek victory looms in Kassandra's prophecies for Priam's kingdom and its dynasty, she finds her fears disbelieved and mocked as female madness, a testimonial to the patriarchal confines of palace life.

The author's perusal of the choices accompanying change stress strictures and pain associated with assimilation, a realistic obligation that Magda faces in *The Shattered Chain* and Margaret accepts in *Exile's Song.* Into the Middle Ages, Marion's special ops troubadour, Lythande, complies with a male-dominant environment by dressing in hooded cloak and posing as a male rover. A cover of lies and deceptions conceals her gender from chance acquaintances at inns and saloons. Of the unique fiction cycle, in the story "Centaurus Changeling," the author commented: "I suppose all societies adapt their morals to their needs" (Bradley, 1954, 32).

For the rise of Wicca in her own era, the author adapted Thomas Malory's Arthuriana in *The Mists of Avalon* with what literary critic Carrol L. Fry called "a close tie between Neo-Pagan beliefs and western literary and folk traditions" (Fry, 1993, 67). The feminized version of medieval chivalric lore revived interest in the Great Mother, the goddess who also nurtures female intuition, healing, and musical skills in *The Fall of Atlantis* and *Tiger Burning Bright.* The paleolithic deity governed primal devotion from prehistory to the Bronze Age. Because of the decline of goddess worship during the spread of the Roman Empire in the first century CE, an androcentric ideology seizes Britannia, replacing feminine grace with patrifocal knights and the anti-woman cant of Christianity as interpreted by Saint Patricius (St. Patrick). Of the author's "full-blooded people," Steve Miller, book critic for the *Baltimore Sun,* observed: "They live in a world full of change and try to make the most of themselves and their families" (Miller, 1983, D4).

The cycle of human acclimation to isolation, environment, and available resources begins anew in *Darkover Landfall,* a fantasy study of modified life during 2,000 years of residency on pre-technological Cottman IV. Unexpected challenges force a marooned flight crew to evaluate what they know and what they need to survive in an unknown milieu, for example, land use as evaluated by geologist Rafael "Rafe" MacAran and animal life analyzed by zoologist Lewis MacLeod. The compromises to exotic animals, fierce winters, and kiraseth, a mystifying plant pollen in a ghost wind that recurs in *Rediscovery,* create differences of opinion about psychological and erotic threats to Terran lifestyle and religious beliefs, forcing the chaplain Valentine into untenable moral dilemmas. For Elizabeth "Liz" Mackintosh and David Lorne, a more serious adaptation involves postponing child conception. Their reasoning is sound: travel on spaceships forbids because of damage to a developing bone structure in "immature bodies ... more delicate and fragile than the planet bound could imagine" (Bradley, 1993, 2).

The author enhances dimensions in Darkover's Age of Chaos by equipping characters with psi powers, a multi-dimensional change in human capabilities. In *Stormqueen!,* she introduces the birth of Dorilys, a death-dealing telepath bred by reproductive manipulation. To her family's dismay, Dorilys can scan past and future events with *laran* and can control a "brilliant white flare" and magnetic fields as sources of power against the vulnerable (Bradley, 1978, 104). Characters in *Rediscovery* use the telepath as a model of the "untrained telepath ... a menace to herself and everyone about her" (Bradley, 1993, 32).

The rediscovery of Terran life on Darkover stresses characters living in the gap between planets. Despite local gender prejudice, Magda Lorne, the Terran spy in *The Shattered Chain* and *Thendara House,* attempts to supply her supervisor, Russell "Russ" Montray, with details of town talk outside Thendara. She increases her effectiveness by wearing the outfit of a Free Amazon, a woman devoid of patriarchal control, and by moving freely among socioeconomic groups. Through examination of the alien society, analyst Jane Donawerth surmises, the author can "assess the chances for growth of racial tolerance" (Donawerth, 2009, 179).

Sources

Bradley, Marion Zimmer. "Centaurus Changeling," Fantasy and Science Fiction 6:4 (April 1954): 85–123.
_____. *Rediscovery*. New York: DAW, 1993.
_____. *Star of Danger*. New York: Ace, 1965.
_____. *Stormqueen!* New York: DAW, 1978.
Donawerth, Jane. "Galactic Suburbia: Recovering Women's Science Fiction," *Tulsa Studies in Women's Literature* 28:1 (Spring 2009): 179–180.
Fry, Carrol L. "The Goddess Ascending: Feminist Neo-Pagan Witchcraft in Marion Zimmer Bradley's Novels," *Journal of Popular Culture* 27:1 (1993): 67–80.
Miller, Steve. "The Arthurian Legend: Returned to Epic Status," *Baltimore Sun* (30 January 1983): D4.
Shwartz, Susan. "Marion Zimmer Bradley's Ethic of Freedom" in *The Feminine Eye: Science Fiction and the Women Who Write It*. New York: Ungar, 1982, 73–88.

Ambition

Ambition and dreams command respect in Marion's characters, particularly Matt Ferguson's space station in "Centaurus Changeling," Manuela's guidance of pilgrims in "Chalice of Tears," acrobat Tommy Zane's command of the trapeze in *The Catch Trap*, and the epidemic fighter Jay/Jason Randall's antidote to lethal 48-year-fever in *The Planet Savers*. The lone mercenary Lythande bears paired swords in "The Secret of the Blue Star" and "Here There Be Dragons" as a dual means of righting wrongs. For prospective space pilots in *Survey Ship*, the day before selection finds 43 candidates "awake, wondering, and dreading, and fearing, and there was little sleep" after twelve years of training (Bradley, 1980, 3). In the mode of group psychology, scuttlebutt circulates more terrors and generates despair in the heart. In one of Marion's most upbeat conclusions, *The Spell Sword* ends with victory for both protagonists, with Damon Ridenow, the scholarly telepath, proclaimed a hero of the guardsmen. His compatriot, Andrew Carr, who risked freezing to death after a plane crash, realizes that "he had followed a dream, and it had brought him here" to union with the beautiful Callista, a fulfilling marriage that occurs in *The Forbidden Tower* (Bradley, 1974, 93).

The author embeds strivings in most of her characters, particularly Nimue's entry into Avalon in "The Pledged Word," Regis Hastur's rise to supreme power in *Sharra's Exile,* and Margaret Alton's search for her past in *Exile's Song.* Marion creates an unusual ambition in the wish of Cara and Ryn Kenner, an expert on atomic isotopes in "Exiles of Tomorrow." Separated by decades, they seek reunion in fluid time, the premise of Richard Matheson's fantasy novel *What Dreams May Come.* The exaltation of human love over a cruel imprisonment in different eras establishes the author's embrace of true affection as a worthy goal.

As part of *Thendara House* in the Darkover series, intelligence agent Peter Haldane schemes to replace Russell "Russ" Montray, the bigoted, inept coordinator of the Thendara spaceport. That anyone would want a lackluster administrative post shocks his Darkovan wife Jaelle, who thinks of the zealous bureaucrat as "a toady office-seeker, sniffing around for bribes and preferment" (Bradley, 1983, 212). With a twist on psychological experimentation, Frank Colby, a disgruntled human in "The Crime Therapist," incurs a cure through death. By executing Frank, Dr. Rhoum is able to end Frank's aberration and write "Discharged cured" in the office logbook. Similar in tone to Daniel Keyes's *Flowers for Algernon* and the one-act play *Wit* by Margaret Edson, the story satirizes inhumane research "in a streamlined, crime-less world" (Bradley, 1954, 100).

ADJUSTED DREAMS

Marion applies her principles of ambitions and their costs during the Roman occupation of Britannia, a stint of empire-building around 80 CE. Future aspirations enliven protagonists in *The Forest House*—the Celtic mystic Eilan and Gaius Macellius, a Romano-Celt reared among soldiers. Eilan envisions herself with "the blue robes of a priestess trailing behind her, and the veil shadowing her features with mystery" (Bradley, 1993, 4). She anticipates serenity and honor from the Vernemeton forest house at Willoughby, Nottinghamshire, where she plans to live more freely than as a wife "at some man's beck and call" (*Ibid.*, 45). Ironically, achievement rewards her with a series of unforeseen dilemmas that allow the mothering of Gaius's son Gawen to impede her satisfaction and force her to choose between a teen love match and adult motherhood.

Marion stresses that male aims have their own shortfalls, especially a choice between Gaius Macellius's career in the Roman military hierarchy and his love for Eilan and their son Gawen. Gaius admits, "Rome is not the whole world, you know," an indication of his dual upbringing as a bicultural offspring in a Roman military camp (*Ibid.*, 78). Eilan accepts promotion to the high priestess at the same time that Gaius achieves honor for his mettle against Caledonians at the Battle of Mons Graupius in pre-modern Scotland in early autumn 83 CE. He hopes the victory prefaces a senatorial or gubernatorial post, an advance on the Roman career ladder based on war readiness rather than legislative or management skills.

The novel illustrates the role of experience in Gaius's middle years. A long journey to Rome weakens his resolve to seek more promotions, leaving him "wondering if this pursuit of rank and position was really worth it" (*Ibid.*, 303). He later concludes that a rise in position forces him to support the power-mad Emperor Domitian, the last Flabian dynast, who remained in power until his assassination on September 18, 96 CE. A tragic conclusion dramatizes the cremation of the two lovers, a stately funeral honoring their lives as priestess and soldier of the empire. In the same motif as Irish author Brian Friel's play *Lovers*, naive ambitions fail to take into account the value of youth itself and living in the moment as parents of a toddler.

Gradual Re-Evaluation

Much of Marion's dramatization of achievement bears equal burdens of regret. In *The Firebrand*, twelve-year-old Kassandra, newly accepted into the tribe of horse-women, discovers liberty as a warrior and dreads return to the palace at Troy and its immurement of women. Conflict dogs her life as a priestess, a title burdened with doubt and misapprehension. At age fifteen, the princess retreats from the pampered life of Priam and Hecuba's royal family to blade and sandals by cross-dressing as a soldier for sword practice. Contrasting her knowledge of dual realms of female life, her friend Star strives only to make a name for herself in battle while Andromache, Kassandra's curly-haired sister-in-law, envisions a wealth of clothes and jewels, a lusty husband, and children. The girlish ideal echoes the thoughts of Polyxena, Kassandra's sister, and their mother Hecuba, an honored queen who lives in luxury and no longer wants the independence of a nomadic Amazon. By contrast, Kassandra stands out from the average royal female for her faith in courage.

In the critique *Rhetorics of Fantasy*, Farah Jane Mendlesohn, a British historian, characterizes quest fantasy as less allegory than "a process, in which the object sought may or may not be a mere token of reward," as with escape in the falling action of Marion's *Thendara House*, the quest of a mythic sisterhood in *City of Sorcery*, and Andrew Carr's self-knowledge in *The Spell Sword* (Mendlesohn, 2008, 4). Other possibilities of traversing "moralized cartography" range from entry into a kingdom to spiritual growth and redemption, an essential in two examples of Christian quest lore, John Bunyan's classic *Pilgrim's Progress* and Lew Wallace's *Ben-Hur* (*Ibid.*). In *The Fall of Atlantis*, the

potential of Domaris, a disciple of the power of Light, derives from the fealty of an acolyte who "holds the seeds of greatness" (Bradley, 1983, 6). With less inner direction, her
younger sister Deoris takes knowledge indiscriminately wherever she finds it, beginning in the all-woman Temple of Caratra, where she studies midwifery and healing. In
the employ of the sorcerer Riveda of the Grey Temple, she learns to hypnotize patients
for the setting of bones and the cleaning of wounds. The author presents the relationship between the priestess and the magician as a love doomed by the degeneration of
Riveda's knowledge into a lust for black magic. His depravity makes him unworthy of
Deoris's affection, a devolution that young love doesn't anticipate.

Marion views female strengths in Arthuriana as a transcendent affirmation of humankind. Like the conniving kings Lot and Uriens in *The Mists of Avalon*, Lot's wife
Morgause and the Saxon war-women tend to travel difficult, sometimes lethal terrain to
reach an aim or desire. According to literary specialist Karen Edie C. Fuog, the author
releases stout-hearted women from biological constraints: "She deliberately demystifies
female sexuality and thereby deconstructs the notion of female Otherness" (Fuog, 1991,
73). Fuog applauds the empowerment of Marion's women who extend their efficacy
"through the power structures in which they work," typically religion, healing, mothering, and household management (*Ibid.*). At the height of Morgause's grasp on potency,
her foster son Gwydion/Mordred mourns the sacrifice of Gareth to resultant violence.
He recognizes her lack of standard matriarchal devotion and charges, "When did you
ever care … for anything but your own pleasure and your own ambition?" (*Ibid.*, 858).

In contrast, King Arthur thrives on the success of his companions, whom he joins
at the Pentecost feast in reliving "those old evil days when there were Saxons and Jutes
and wild Northmen on every hand" (*Ibid.*, 544). The attitude toward past successes
primes Arthur and his knights for a universal letdown that follows their legendary
achievement.

See also Female Persona.

Sources

Bradley, Marion Zimmer. *The Catch Trap*. New York: Random House, 1979.
_____. "The Crime Therapist," *Future Science Fiction* 5:3 (October 1954): 93–100.
_____. "Exiles of Tomorrow," *Fantastic Universe* 3:2 (March 1955): 117–122.
_____. *The Fall of Atlantis*. Riverdale, NY: Baen Books, 1983.
_____. *The Forest House*. New York: Michael Joseph, 1993.
_____. *The Spell Sword*. New York: DAW, 1974.
_____. *Survey Ship*. New York: Ace, 1980.
_____. *Thendara House*. New York: DAW, 1983.
Fuog, Karen E.C. "Imprisoned in the Phallic Oak: Marion Zimmer Bradley and Merlin's Seductress," *Quondam
    et Futurus* 1:1 (1991): 73–88.
Mendlesohn, Farah. *Rhetorics of Fantasy*. Middletown, CT: Wesleyan University Press, 2008.
Palojärvi, Maija Päivikki. "Morgaine the Maiden, Morgaine the Mother, Morgaine the Deathcrone: Female
    Ageing in Marion Zimmer Bradley's *The Mists of Avalon*," Humanities thesis, University of Eastern Finland
    (1 November 2013): http://epublications.uef.fi/pub/urn_nbn_fi_uef-20131005/urn_nbn_fi_uef-20131005.pdf.
Zaerr, Linda Marie. "Women and Arthurian Literature," *Rocky Mountain Review* 51:1 (1997): 109–112.

Arthur's Genealogy

A vigorous segment of Britain's national heritage, the convoluted lineage of the
Pendragon dynasty derives conflict from incest and adultery, sexualities damned by the

new Christian faith. The beloved Arthuriad involves the king in both sins. The narrative resounds with clashes of will and onslaughts against the invading Anglo-Saxons, who began their threats in 449 CE with Vortigern's attempt to oust Picts and Scoti from Britannia. Expert Charlotte Spivack states that King Arthur's "function is to keep a torn land, a pluralist society filled with warring factions, from collapsing into civil war" (Spivack, 1992, 104). Within the span of a half century, Arthur's idealized army from Camelot reaches a bruising height at the Battle of Badon in 482 CE, the beginning of Pax Arthuriana under the newly crowned Pendragon monarch. Kevin Harper exults, "There has been nothing like it since the days of the Caesars" (Bradley, 1983, 413).

The Camelot idyll suffers a major blow after Balin seeks vengeance for his mother's death by splitting the elderly priestess Viviane's skull with an axe. The atrocity occurs in view of the royal family on the Pendragon throne. After 55 years, Pax Arthuriana comes to an end with Arthur's defeat at Camlann in 537 CE. Marion's version of the saga reduces the dominance of knights, hardihood, and chivalry by focusing on the Mother Goddess and priestesses who fight the anti-woman apostasies of Christianity and the threat to divine matriarchy. In the nineteenth-century paradigm, according to Stephen Ahern, a professor at Acadia University, women like Morgaine and Gwenhwyfar became literary "[repositories] of social values" (Ahern, 2004, 89). Nicholas John Higham, an English medievalist at the University of Manchester, acknowledged the long-lived appeal of Arthuriana and subsequent retellings: "A romanticized symbol of the Middle Ages and its contemporary cultural value, therefore, Arthur enjoyed something of a renaissance in the Victorian era, even while becoming increasingly excluded from the dominant historical enterprise of the day" (Higham, 2002, 253). Notation in the family tree indicates sexual/marital ties:

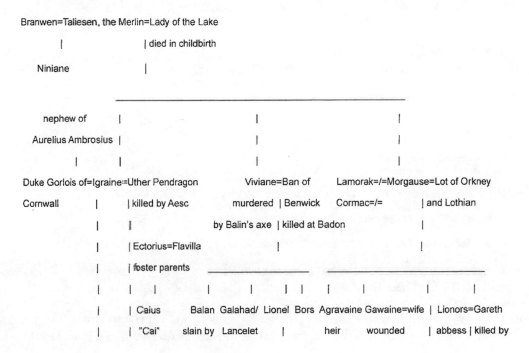

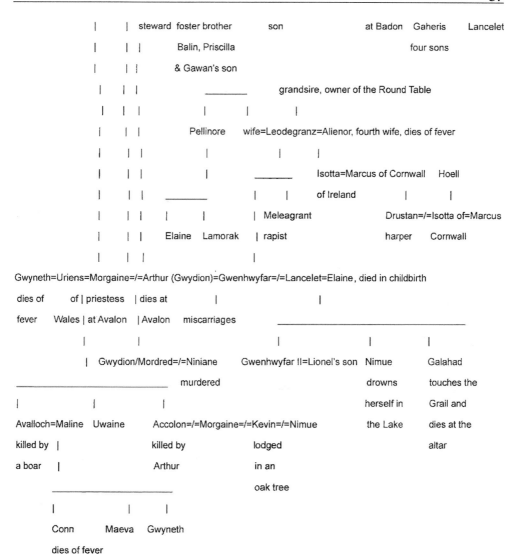

In a review for the *San Francisco Examiner,* Alix Madrigal saluted Marion's Briton epic for "[adding] a whole new dimension to our mythic history" (Madrigal, 1983, 3).

See also Knights of the Round Table.

Sources

Ahern, Stephen. "Listening to Guinevere: Female Agency and the Politics of Chivalry in Tennyson's Idylls," *Studies in Philology* 101:1 (2004): 88–112.

Bradley, Marion Zimmer. "The Pledged Word," *The Merlin Chronicles* (1995): 130–136.

_____. *The Mists of Avalon.* New York: Ballantine, 1983.

Higham, N.J. *King Arthur: Myth-Making and History.* London: Routledge, 2002.

Madrigal, Alix. "A Female Vision of the Arthurian Legend," *San Francisco Examiner* (27 February 1983): 3.

Mink, JoAnna Stephens, and Janet Doubler Ward. *The Significance of Sibling Relationships in Literature.* Bowling Green, OH: Bowling Green State University Popular Press, 1993.

Spivack, Charlotte. *Popular Arthurian Traditions*. Bowling Green, OH: Bowling Green State University Popular Press, 1992.

The Bloody Sun

Marion's rewritten novel of the second age of the Darkover landing relies on awareness of the earthly beginnings of a long colony in space. *The Bloody Sun* succeeds *Star of Danger* and *The Spell Sword* with a survey of earth exploration and cartography in space. To examine confrontations between races and societies, the author reprises social structure and the function of mystic towers and the tasks of celibate keepers. Of the rivalry at the core of interplanetary struggles, Johnny Ellers, a professional spaceman, reveals the significance of a large blue crystal: "The big secret of Darkover. The Terrans have been trying to beg, borrow, or steal some of the secrets of matrix technology for generations" (Bradley, 1964, 19).

The novel, which appeared in three translations—Dutch, French, and three German editions—and in the omnibus *A World Divided*, stresses the disappointment that often follows a lifetime of yearning and fantasy about a people's true roots. In the author's recitation of prophetic words by Bohemian-Austrian poet Rainer Maria Rilke, "The stranger who comes home does not make himself at home but makes home strange," a dire warning that dominates the contretemps of the time traveler Claire Beauchamp Randall Fraser in Diane Gabaldon's *Outlander* series (*Ibid.*, 1). Similar in tone and theme to *Sharra's Exile*, the author's survey of family dynamics focuses on Jefferson "Jeff" Kerwin, an adult earthling reared to age twelve in a Terran orphanage at Trade City, a fate he shares with Margaret Alton of *Exile's Song*.

A runaway in his teens, on his arrival at Cottman IV aboard the *Southern Crown*, Jeff labors under "the feeling that somebody had sliced a big hunk out of [my] life" (*Ibid.*, 9). As characterized by Warren Epstein, a reviewer for the *Tampa Tribune-Times*, Marion follows her own rule that "[b]oth your hero and your villain must be fallible" (Epstein, 1987, C5). The theme of search for self incorporates a series of uncertainties—unfamiliar native clothing and language, carved initials, an ascetic life in a tower, and an ancient "lucky charm" and "long-lost talisman"—a theatrical amulet crystal of unknown power and significance (Bradley, 1964, 18).

The network of characters incorporates suspense and standard Darkover surnames and dynastic links muddled by fostering and occluded birth facts:

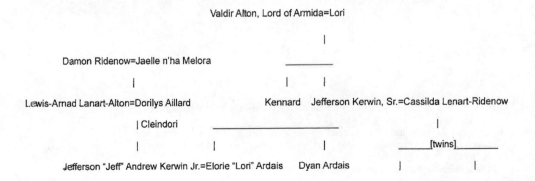

Damon Lanart-Aillard	Keeper of Arilinn		Auster	Ragan
employee of the Terran				

Space Service

Although, at age 29, Jeff is an expert with the Barry-Reade K204 computer, he gains no records of his childhood at Darkover's Spacemen's Orphanage or of his father's civil service employment. In the opening bar scene, a common meeting site for lone males, Jeff finds himself elevated by the title "vai dom," a planetary honorific meaning "revered lord" that Margaret Alton incurs in *Exile's Song* (*Ibid.*, 24). At the House of the Renunciates, Latti refuses to enlighten him about his crystal heirloom. A gothic scene offers a partial oracle, but leaves the Old Town seer dead at her table, a dread omen of the novel's resolution to an identity quest.

The author emphasizes the value of inborn traits: "Something that stood up on its hind legs and pawed the ground and said, cold and clean and unmistakable: *No*" (*Ibid.*, 54). Before deportation to the penal colony at Lucifer Delta, Jeff makes his way to Armida, the Alton Great House. His keen sensibilities alert him to a connection with the Arilinn Tower, a clearinghouse of telepathic dynamics where he trains in psychic communication. After pinpointing his original Darkovan lineage, he completes the wanderer's path to community, acceptance, matrix powers, and a future part defying "fanatics and blind superstition" to save Darkover from destruction (*Ibid.*). Appropriately, the author concludes on family acceptance of Jeff and laughter before breakfast, a verbal and gustatory gesture to the restoration of normality.

See also Prophecy.

Sources

Bradley, Marion Zimmer. *The Bloody Sun*. New York: Ace, 1964.
Epstein, Warren. "So You Want to Be a Science Fiction Writer, Kid?," *Tampa Tribune-Times* (14 June 1987): C5.

The Catch Trap

In a deviation from fantasy and sci-fi, Marion created a realistic novel of ambition, *The Catch Trap*, an engaging YA family saga set in the circus world from the Great Depression into the 1940s. By exploring commitment to an ideal of excellence, like the five-year-olds tested for the United Nations Expeditionary Planetary Survey in *Survey Ship*, the action of Marion's only circus book depicts the fourteen-year-old protagonist Tommy Zane from age five. In fantasy, he replaces his uninspiring life with the glitter and soar on the flying rig, a vigorous career that could elevate him from a mundane existence to stardom. In contrast to the flashing high bars manipulated by the three Santellis, Tommy's everyday acrobatics in aerial ballet seem illusory, sissified. His evaluation sparks a drive to excel in a circus milieu that once saw the death of Antonio "Papa Tony" Santelli in the net.

In the repressive post–World War II era, the protagonist, a teen acrobat, attempts a double lifestyle—as a trapeze catcher with the Flying Santellis and by a fully realized coming out as a homosexual. He models his dreams on the decade of success achieved by the unified Fortunatis and Santellis, Italian-American clans bonded by wedlock, mutual regard for circus careers, and dialogue sprinkled with Italian phrases as well as frequent use of the word "queer" (*Ibid.*, 113). In a dreamscape, he envisions the Lambeth Circus "packed up in the fall … and [living] like the animals in the zoo, caged in one place till the time came to go out on the road and live their real life again," an occluded reference to Tommy's closeting (Bradley, 1979, 15).

Incorporating Karl Wallenda's credo "To be on the wire is life, all the rest is waiting," the text questions the parallel commitments—to an extreme sport and to a same-sex relationship (*Ibid.*, 1). From Mario di Santalis, the legendary grandsire, the lineage acquires fame from individual creativity and success by grandson Angelo Santelli as a catcher and by two great grandsons—lion tamer Tom Zane and the in-air mystique of Matthew "Mario" Gardner, Junior, Tommy's lover, trainer, and performer of a triple flip. The text stresses that acquiring skill at mid-air somersaults and hand-to-hand catches demands acceptance of danger, crippling, possibly death. In exchange for peril, Tommy values the family's trust that he can perfect high-bar maneuvers. In a flippant acknowledgment of his daring, Angelo quips, "Okay, kid, it's your neck" (*Ibid.*, 19)

The author stresses the costs of physical daring. Lithe, sturdy, and compact, Tommy measures the cost of kinetic artistry in calisthenics on the parallel bars, skinned palms, tumbling into the safety net, and a perilous routine structured around ropes, guys, and wire rigging, thin protectors from smashed dreams. His first awareness of love emerges during a thunderstorm in Oklahoma, a metaphoric turmoil anticipating difficult choices about an attraction ""a blind man could see" (*Ibid.*, 519). Satisfaction comes from Mario, who awards Tommy a "Buon' ragazzo," Italian for "good kid" (*Ibid.*, 11).

By admitting the homoerotic attachment to Mario, a self-analysis echoing the awakening of homosexual identity of Lord Orain of Castamir in *Hawkmistress!* and of Lord Regis Hastur in *The Heritage of Hastur*, Tommy accepts a reframing of the male-with-male "ache of love," pride in trapeze skill, and Mario's unstinting friendship as the perfect future (*Ibid.*, 208). Marion graces Mario with generosity for giving Tommy "freedom of the platform and then of flight" as well as self-knowledge and "the dawning of sexuality … unsparing, uncompromising" (*Ibid.*, 506). The breakthrough in YA fiction accepted as normal the boyish crush and its physical realization.

See also Santelli-Fortunati Dynasty.

Sources

Bradley, Marion Zimmer. *The Catch Trap*. New York: Random House, 1979.
"Review: *The Catch Trap*," *Kirkus* (1 April 1979).
Ross, Deborah J. "Proofreading *The Catch Trap*," http://deborahjross.blogspot.com/2014/04/proofreading-catch-trap.html, April 9, 2014.
"Santelli Family Tree," https://www.mzbworks.com/santelli.htm.

Christianity

Through historical fiction and futuristic fantasy, Marion rejected notions that humankind and its gods dominated the earth. She viewed Christianity as intolerant, blindered, and persecutorial toward alternate faiths and their practitioners. Her canon introduced oblique comments on Christian theology, as with the programmed confession and penance in "Elbow Room" and Father Valentine's hypothesis in *Darkover Landfall* that Baby Jesus might have been the offspring of an extra-terrestrial father. The author's transformation of quest literature in *The Mists of Avalon* contradicted the Celtic gift for free-spirited fantasy in the first century CE with Lancelet's stony agnosticism and Archbishop Patricius's stern orthodoxy and warnings of damnation, a diatribe aimed at feminized evil. Her pagan glimpse paints Christianity as "gloomy, narrow and generally a bad idea" (Schweitzer, 1983, 6). The grotesque face-off in "Treason of the Blood" between the vengeance-mad Countess Teresa against the vampire Count Angelo Fieresi disputed the Christian symbols meant to stem an attack on the innocent. The rosary and crucifix emblems had no power against the totally corrupt jailer of a fiend. Thus, lack of mercy condemned Teresa, a representative of smug formalism and ferocity, the author's main grievances against the Christian faith.

In a survey of the conversion of Britannia from Druidism, Marion, according to *Washington Post* reviewer Maude McDaniel, "depicts the inevitable passing of times and religions by her use of the imagery of different simultaneous worlds, which move out of consciousness as their day ebbs" (McDaniel, 1983). Marion viewed post-pagan Christianity as "a new tyranny; not alone to make the laws but to rule the mind and heart and soul" (Bradley, 1983, 583). The story "To Kill the Undead" condemned the church custom of burying suicides in unhallowed graves, the source of vampires. Another Lythande story about cruel asceticism, "To Drive the Cold Winter Away," depicted a town devoid of joy and music, which authorities had outlawed. The plot embodied the austere laws in perpetual winter relieved by a song and the arrival of spring. The female mercenary's series continued crossing paths with Christian elements. In the story "Here There Be Dragons," Lythande bore a crucifix solely as a beneficent force rather than an icon of Christian devotion. For the story "Bitch," the author inserted folk beliefs that touching a priest's staff conjured magic.

In *The Forest House,* ironically, while the Roman military batters Britannia's obdurate far northern tribes and fears a series of crazed emperors at home, the first Christians and their black-clad "slave-nuns" anticipate a future cataclysm (Bradley, 1983, x). They ponder a universal apocalypse and the return of a savior. The fictional tribune Gaius Macellius hears criticism of the Emperor Nero, who had blamed the six-day fire at Rome of July 18–24, 64 CE, on "that odd Jewish sect," an early designation of Jesus's disciples (*Ibid.,* 306). The reference indicates a strong tie between the Judaic faith and followers of "the Nazarene—that prophet of slaves and renegade Jews" known by 70 CE as "Christians" (*Ibid.,* 356).

Speaking through Corax, who summarizes the results of the Great Fire, the author charges the reviled Emperor Nero with blaming and executing Christians "more like sheep than like men" (*Ibid.,* 306). Corax concludes that such one-sided fights of criminals, prisoners of war, women, and children in the arena amounted to "stupid slaughter" (*Ibid.*). While reflecting on the emotional release of cheering at carnage, Gaius admits that arena fights are "perverse and pointless" (*Ibid.,* 307). Part of his perspective derives from the heavy cost of war and imperialism in Britannia.

During a discussion of *pietas* (duty and obedience) at a learned gathering, Gaius muses that the dry, unemotional state religion instituted by Augustus lacks the purpose of either Christ worship or the Egyptian Isis cult to "nourish the human soul" (*Ibid.,*

310). From a different perspective, Macellius Severus calls Christians a fractious lot who persecute each other in "sectarian strife" (*Ibid.*, 354). The opposing views of father and son suggest a generation gap in early Christian Rome, when young males lost their fervor for expanding the empire by subduing alien lands. At the time, Rome ruled pharaonic Egypt, Britannia, and Judea under the Emperor Augustus's Pax Romana, which extended over two centuries, from the foundation of the empire in 27 BCE to the death of Marcus Aurelius in 180 CE.

THE FIRST CHRISTIANS

Marion summarizes the historian Tacitus's belief that the new faith appealed to slaves and women, the populations most in need of rescue and mercy. In 93 CE, Gaius comments on the proliferation of Christian hermits, an eccentric sect that had begun secluding themselves around 90 CE. Literary critic and classicist Theresa Crater, on staff at Metropolitan State University in Denver, envisioned the rise of diversity as, initially, amenable: "In Bradley's works, the first Christians who came to Britain lived in harmony with the Druids, setting up a Celtic Church alongside the sacred circles of the priestess of Avalon" (Crater, 2001, 12). Missourian Nicole Evelina, an expert on Arthuriana, differed with Crater by picturing Marion's Camelot fiction as "built on paganism with Christianity being a disruptive influence" (Tichelaar).

From a unique perspective, Marion viewed female rebellion as a source of revolt against patriarchal faith. Her paradigm of Christian indoctrination, the whiny, neurotic Queen Gwenhwyfar, was the product of an all-knowing father, Leodegranz, and all-woman cloistering for training in wifedom—cooking, sewing, herbalism, and nursing. At the heart of nunnery education in submission and dependence posed "a fear of God" that quelled curiosity, autonomy, and inquiry in young girls (Evelina, 2017, 155). The control of females from young girlhood contrasted the relative freedom of women in the Druid cult.

Marion charged Christian minions with pride and monomania, particularly Arthur for merging Pentecost with Beltane into a major holiday devoted to jousting and the Bishop Patricius and other ascetics who "make much of their fasting" (Bradley, 1983, 413). In the essay "Thoughts on Avalon" (1986), the author aimed to ameliorate early androcentric Christianity by removing patriarchs and "their completely neurotic insistence on the evil of woman," an inborn fault that patristic theologians dubbed "original sin" (Bradley, 1986). Citing fifteenth-century theorist Sir Thomas Malory for demoting the Mother Goddess and repressing females as witches, felons, and idiots who stand idle while men achieve and accomplish great deeds, Marion blamed Judeo-Christian theology for shutting women out of spiritual discourse "with their bells and their death and their Satan and Hell and damnation" (Bradley, 1983, x). While researching *The Mists of Avalon,* the author sought "ordination in one of the Gnostic Catholic churches as a priest" as a means of denying bigotry and fanaticism (Bradley, 1986). The author spoke through Morgaine a timely gibe at Christian misogyny: "You Christians are overfond of that word *unseemly,* especially when it relates to women" (Bradley, 1983, 288).

FEMALE DIVINITY

Marion concluded that feminine divinity survived in the adoration of female saints and mariology, but her prologue digressed that Christ's mother lay imprisoned in a pristine state—"ever virgin. But what can a virgin know of the sorrows and travail of mankind?" (Bradley, 1983, ix). A critique by C.W. Sullivan, a medievalist formerly on the English staff at Hollins and East Carolina universities, summarized the import of Marion's revisionist Arthuriana: the transition from the Old Beliefs (Celtic, Druidic) to Christian, with Arthur "sworn to uphold faery and Gwenhwyfar championing St. Patrick" (Sullivan, 2001, 287). Sullivan also acknowledged Marion's views on "the change from a matrilineal (and perhaps matriarchal) culture to a patrilineal and patriarchal culture [that] forces the reader to look at beliefs he or she has taken for granted, and perhaps never examined, in a new light," such as the dictum that wives follow their husbands' faith (*Ibid.*, 287–288). Viviane, the Lady of the Lake, illustrates the restructuring of myth by criticizing the Christ followers for believing "some fantastic Jewish Tale about an apple and a snake," a fable proving that all women are evil (Bradley, 1983, 11). Marion further commented on fanatic male beliefs that "the human body is the work of some devil" (*Ibid.*, 149).

The positioning of dialogue in *The Mists of Avalon* reveals the author's questioning of orthodox Christian views on repentance and redemption and her condemnation of the "increasing encroachment by the intolerant, patriarchal Christian religion" (Gordon-Wise, 1991, 141). The priest-led faith suppresses Midsummer ritual and manipulates Uther Pendragon, Duchess Igraine of Cornwall, King Arthur, and his sister-lover Morgaine of Avalon. During Uther's discussion with Igraine about the death of Aurelius Ambrosius, the new high king champions the belief of the ancients that goodness on earth receives a reward in the afterlife, which the Romans called Elysium. Duke Gorlois of Cornwall, Igraine's stern husband, speaks the evangelist's insistence that "[b]efore God all men are miserable sinners," even beloved kings like Ambrosius, whose name means "immortal" (Bradley, 1983, 48). In riposte to Uther's banner of the red dragon, Gorlois dismisses it as a wicked icon like the "lewd rites of pagandom, pandering to the folly of ignorant man" (*Ibid.*, 61). Repentant for her first husband's death, Igraine accepts Christian guilt before her wedding to Uther and withdraws from the old ways. Viviane, a vigorous worshipper of the Mother Goddess in defiance of meddling prelates, concludes that God is "greater and less bigoted than any priesthood" (*Ibid.*, 118).

Mergers of heathen with orthodox beliefs account for the celebration of Pentecost simultaneously with Beltane. The union of paganism with doctrinal Christianity dominates Morgaine's three-day project making a scabbard for Arthur's sword out of doeskin and velvet, a representation of a soft vaginal lining. During intense application of religious icons and runes embroidered with gold thread, the priestess concentrates on alliance of one philosophy with the other, a protective sheath "pregnant with magic" (*Ibid.*, 199). In danger of being identified with witchcraft, Morgaine applies her skills to dyeing, brewing ale, distilling medicinal spirits, and turning fragrant rose petals into perfume and rosewater. At the end of her patience with disputed theology, she doubts that "priests were ... tender and forgiving with sinners" (*Ibid.*, 483). In contrast to head Druid Taliesin and his gentle humanitarianism, Christian leaders lack compassion and goodness and fail to identify the Christlike character of Arthur, Britannia's rescuer. Compromise forces Morgaine to accept defeat—a peaceful Britannia, which thrives, perhaps, from the destiny chosen by the Mother Goddess.

ENHANCEMENT OF CHRISTIANITY

In the Darkover series, Marion enlarges on earthly sanctity and morality among earthlings marooned on Cottman IV, a lost colony on a planet distant from earth. Out of need for revamped mores, the characters in *Darkover Landfall* help the only prelate, Father Valentine, recover from sexual and capital crimes he commits under the control of a hallucinogenic pollen. He recognizes a shift in orthodox Christianity, which has no theology to advise a race stranded on Darkover. Unlike Ambrosius and Arthur in medieval times, survivors of the spaceship crash must evolve strictures to guide a multi-species society.

At a turning point in the creation of ethics, the *cristoforo* (literally "Christ-bearing") precepts impose a humanistic and democratic mindset among the faithful. In *Stormqueen!*, Allart Hastur rebukes Dom Stephen Hastur for his use of women as involuntary breeders. Allart asserts to his father, "I am a *cristoforo*. The first precept of the Creed of Chastity is *to take no woman unwilling*," a nonviolent approach to copulation that Allart's father brands "monkish scruples" (Bradley, 1978, 44, 54). The egalitarian acceptance of gender bans raping or drugging women—only consenting females qualify for coitus. The "Christ-bearing" oath incorporates New Testament tolerance and respect for women as offspring and sex partners unlike the past diminution of females as "instruments to breed monsters of the mind, without humanity!" (*Ibid.*, 45). However, intolerant Christ followers like Keitha n'ha Casilda in *Thendara House* revile women who love women, a form of homosexuality that breaks scriptural law.

See also Religion; Retribution; Ritual; Treachery.

Sources

Bradley, Marion Zimmer. *The Mists of Avalon*. New York: Ballantine, 1983.
_____. *Stormqueen!* New York: DAW, 1978.
_____. "Thoughts on Avalon," http://mzbworks.com/thoughts.htm, 1986.
Crater, Theresa. "The Resurrection of Morgan le Fey: Fallen Woman to Triple Goddess," *Femspec* 3:1 (December 2001): 12.
Evelina, Nicole. *The Once & Future Queen: Guinevere in Arthurian Legend*. Maryland Heights, MO: Lawson Gartner, 2017.
Gordon-Wise, Barbara Ann. *The Reclamation of a Queen: Guinevere in Modern Fantasy*. New York: Praeger, 1991.
McDaniel, Maude. "Review: *The Mists of Avalon*," *Washington Post* (28 January 1983).
Oliver, Myrna. "Marion Bradley; Writer of Fantasy Novels," *Los Angeles Times* (30 September 1999): A 24.
Schweitzer, Darrell. "Review: *The Mist of Avalon*," *Philadelphia Inquirer* (6 March 1983): 6.
Spivack, Charlotte. *Popular Arthurian Traditions*. Bowling Green, OH: Bowling Green State University Popular Press, 1992.
Sullivan, C.W. "Folklore and Fantastic Literature," *Western Folklore* 60:4 (Fall 2001):279–296.
Tichelaar, Tyler. "Children of Arthur," https://childrenofarthur.wordpress.com/tag/t-h-white/.

City of Sorcery

A salute to female cooperation during a spiritual quest, Marion's *City of Sorcery* introduces a "holy grail" motif via orienteering to the edge of civilization. Popular in

English and translations into French, German, and Portuguese and in a taped version by Recorded Books, the novel follows *The Shattered Chain* and *Thendara House* as the third and last segment of *The Saga of the Renunciates* with a display of what critic Janice C. Crosby calls "powerful women exhibiting aspects of immanent deity" (Crosby, 2000, 108). On a par with Lynn Abbey's *Daughter of the Bright Moon* and Joan Vinge's *The Snow Queen,* the narrative reveals the independence of Darkover's female mountaineers and initiation of the Bridge Society as a liaison with Earth nurses, who teach lessons in hygiene.

Giving snippets of information, Marion heightens suspense as women form a reconnaissance company, a model of self-empowerment similar in organization to the arctic expeditions in Ursula Le Guin's "Sur." On a flight to Thendara, Lexie radioed the location of a city in the Hellers Mountains near the Wall Around the World. Intelligence supervisor Cholayna n'ha Chandria concludes, "Something out there grabbed her—and then gave her back," an addendum to other inexplicable planetary phenomena (Bradley, 1984, 12). In a search for true sisterhood, intelligence specialist Magdalen "Magda" Lorne (Magali n'ha Ysabet) applies psi skills to reclaim Terran cartographer Lieutenant Alexis "Lexie" Anders, a victim of amnesia. Mental probing with a matrix stone alleviates Lexie's memory loss caused by the crash. With no knowledge of forbidding territory, she attempts to locate a remote area marked by the cawing of crows, a sound image of the raspy call of black birds, symbol of a dire sisterhood of crones.

The author outlines a journey north with Rafaella "Rafi" n'ha Doria and Alexis into the legendary snowy high country past Barrensclae toward the *cristoforo* monastery of Nevarsin. The itinerary becomes a source of character exposition and a study of female skills with first aid, weapons, and tools, such as the ice axe. In the style of a *bildungsroman,* Magda follows with two Free Amazons—travel guide Jaelle n'ha Melora and the elderly Camilla n'ha Kyria—and two Terrans, technician Vanessa n'ha Yllana and Cholayna. At the convent of Avarra, the sacred goddess, the postulant Kyntha treats the women for frostbite, chipped ankle, possible concussion, and altitude sickness, which causes nightmares, coughing, lung edema, and pneumonia. With convent harpist Marisela, the senior midwife, the group pushes on toward the robed Dark Sisterhood, a coven of wicked sorcerers.

The author heightens action with tense moments and sudden death to the undeserving. In the high peaks, an avalanche kills Dancer, Jaelle's pony. The expeditioners collapse and awaken in a cave, a perennial representation of femininity. Alexis leads Magda to the evil Acquilara, who impulsively murders Marisela. Kyntha's spirit warns that hatred of the enemy allows Acquilara to control the travelers' minds. On a second attempt at flight, combat results in Lexie's stabbing death and the lethal fall of Acquilara and Jaelle.

The abrupt losses stymy survivors, leaving them to ruminate, "Were they nowhere, lonesome spirits on the wind, or were they together, seeking something tangible?" (*Ibid.,* 272). Tempted to remain in the mythic city, the surviving company returns to Thendara, leaving Camilla and Magda to continue toward the sisterhood of the wise and the divine. The oddly truncated conclusion elucidates the truth of their hearts and their choices of a "new and unknown horizon," unknowable except to the initiated (*Ibid.,* 275). In agreement with the *New York Times Book Review,* Carol Christ, author of *Divine Deep and Surfacing*, explains the union of quest lore with spiritual identity: "If women's stories are not told, the depth of women's souls will not be known" (Crosby, 2000, 5)

See also Thendara House.

Sources

Bradley, Marion Zimmer. *City of Sorcery*. New York: DAW, 1984.
Crosby, Janice C. *Cauldron of Changes: Feminist Spirituality in Fantastic Fiction*. Jefferson, NC: McFarland, 2000.
Kimmel, Leigh. "The Saga of the Renunciates," http://billionlightyearbookshelf.com/reviews/sagaoftherenunciates.shtml, 2015.

Costume

By outfitting fictional and historic characters in garments suited to place, caste, profession, and period, Marion enhances fiction with visions of institutionalized customs, such as Mattingly's fur topcoat shielding Andrew Carr from sleet in *The Spell Sword*, the lush cloak that caresses Jeff Kerwin in *The Bloody Sun*, and matrix mechanic Lew Alton's jettisoning of Terran clothing in *The Sword of Aldones* in favor of "suede-leather breeches, low ankle-boots, and … crimson jerkin" topped by a short cloak in the medieval style of Cottman IV (Bradley, 1962, 7). Focus on female outfitting produced Lady Beauty's looped braids, a chain symbol under a hooded cloak in *The Gratitude of Kings*, Romy's hated riding skirts in *Hawkmistress!*, and the simple linen shift of the novice Nimue upon her entrance to Avalon in "The Pledged Word." In contrast to Nimue's modesty, the beribboned gown and matching sandals—"blue leather with pearls"—for bride-to-be Carlina "Carlie" di Asturien in *Two to Conquer* suit a girlish ritual occasion (Bradley, 1980, 2).

Outfits mark the difference between people of Darkover and Terrans. The bandit chief Narthen dons a fur-trimmed outfit in "A Sword Called Chaos," a reflection of the limitation of ermine and sable to nobles and, in the 1300s, to church hierarchy. Narthen's soldier wears a coarse cloak "with untanned hide covered with curly white wool on the inside, and rough brown frieze on the outer layer" (Bradley, 1982, 100). The black leathers of the Spaceforce and the garments sourced in nature in the Darkover series vary in practicality and comfort from synthetic fabrics of Terran spaceport employees, who scorn the practical Darkovan costume as barbaric.

On the colonized planet, uniforms differentiate between locals and Terrans, as with dietitian Judith "Judy" Lovat's smock and insignia and Rafael "Rafe" MacAran's leather breeches and tartan tunic in *Darkover Landfall* and Keitha n'ha Casilda and Marisela's coifs, a symbol of purity and tidiness identifying midwives in *Thendara House*. After Jaelle n'ha Melora marries Terran Peter Haldane and accepts a job in technology, she is shocked by the figure-defining tights with coded tunic and low flats, none of which protect her from a raw spring chill. To intensify opposition in *Rediscovery*, Marion characterizes gendered differences of Terran women in "breeches and some of them, earrings" (Bradley, 1993, 62). The author stresses how appearance distinguishes species, as in the dark brown complexions and "bizarre and highly unfamiliar garments … heavy rough trousers and jackets, of some kind of strange and oddly slick fabric" that Leonie witnesses on Terran spaceport builders (*Ibid.*, 58). For Margaret Alton in *Exile's Song,* a special uniform marks her as an academic; for Allart Hastur in *Stormqueen!,* a monk's habit earns him the sneer of "sandal-wearer" in garb "unfitting for a man" (Bradley, 1978, 47).

Women's Wear

Marion emphasizes the importance of climate to clothing choice on Darkover. For the title figures in *Free Amazons,* the choice of "low boots of undyed leather, fur-lined trousers, a fur smooth … with heavily embroidered leather jackets and hoods" protects wearers from the Darkover cold (Bradley, 1985, 10). The mountain outfits return on Amazon merchants at Dry-Town in *The Shattered Chain,* in which buzzcuts and daggers mark them as free from male authority. As foils to liberated females, Marion poses Dry-Town's women, "fettered with a metal bracelet on each wrist … connected with a long chain, passed through a metal loop on her belt" (Bradley, 1976, 22). Even liberation does not free the human chattel, who always bear the scars of fettering on her wrist.

In the Lythande series, silent laceless boots, Dutch boy haircut and shaved eyebrows, and unconfining mage robe, an androgynous mantle with secret pockets, suit the needs of a peripatetic female musician-mercenary. The cloak, shaped from a length of unsewn fabric, covers thigh-high boots, breeches, belt, leather jerkin, and a tunic stitched at sides and shoulders. In "The Walker Behind," the engulfing covering made Lythande "look like a piece of the night itself, or a shadow," the origin of the nickname "the shadow" (Bradley, 2013, 116). The mantle "melted into the shadows" in "The Secret of the Blue Star" like "a cloak of invisibility," the identical uniform of Rajene in "Bitch" (*Ibid.*, 2, 3). The style suits the movements of a peripatetic warrior ever on the move in dangerous places.

Marion echoes the rebellions of American and British suffragists in the late 1900s and early twentieth century. Within the planet sisterhood, Amber/Zadieyek, the female adversary in *Warrior Woman,* despises traditional T-shaped tunics and wishes for "a man's functional breeches and boots," a veiled comment on gendered costume and women's limited choices echoed by reformer Amelia Bloomer in the 1851 edition of *The Lily* (Bradley, 1985, 128). In *Thendara House,* both Jaelle n'ha Melora and Magdalen "Magda" Lorne chafe against the restrictive Terran outfits, which delineate male from female. Magda prefers the unisex dress of Darkover for its anonymity, yet finds herself threatened in a forest fire that burns her insubstantial shoe soles. Wisely, she chooses to buy work boots to replace the scorched, tattered footwear.

For Eilan in *The Forest House,* on the eve of Beltane or May Day, an outfit "woven in crossed squares of pale golds and browns and a color like budding leaves" suits celebration of the emergence of spring (Bradley, 1993, 46). The arrival of a Druid procession highlights the pristine white robes and crowns of oak leaves, sources of priestly sanctity, and contrasts survivors of rape clad in blue. As a means of expressing the duality in Gaius Macellius's life as a Romano-Celt, the author pictures him alternately in Breton tunic, breeches, and cloak or topped with a crested helmet over his Roman legionary uniform. Neither outfit defines the character, who is his own man.

CASTE AND RESPONSIBILITY

Because of frequent rituals and ceremonial processions, robing and identifications of rank dominate the outfitting of *The Fall of Atlantis,* as with the mitered hat and tabard of the magician Nadastor and Riveda's replacement of his gray uniforms with a horned crown, black cloak marked with runes, blue tunic, and red overcoat, stark indicators of black magic. Micon's luminescent robe and amulets denoting the priesthood, Domaris's shimmering gown with mantle and official gold staff and dagger, and Deoris's tonsure and single pearl, emblem of a fetus, elevate the characters in the structured socio-religious order of the Ancient Land. Marion's repeated motifs of investiture and cortege suggests tableau rather than historical fiction, especially the cincturing of Deoris in a triple red cord binding twenty-one wood links, a magic number derived from the product of magic numbers, seven times three. The author controls the effect at Domaris's initiation by describing the mechanism that admits a sun ray, like a spotlight at a dramatic moment. She comments, "It was a deception, but a sensible one" (Bradley, 1983, 184).

In *The Firebrand,* the tanning of raw pelts into leather produces Amazon armor. Hecuba, a Trojan queen from 1200 BCE, struts her engorged belly cloaked in tiered skirt and low-neck bodice. A sign of regency, the gold collar that sets off her outfit declares her more powerful than the average female in the women's quarters. Lesser women tuck up loose gowns for comfort. Alongside his mother at a wedding feast, Prince Hector dons robes over a tunic embroidered in gold. In contrast, the Amazon leader Penthe-silea, on arrival to court, embodies the nomadic horse culture that Hecuba knew in girl-hood—leather cap and knee pants and skin tanned and freckled from riding the mare Racer in the sun. Paris, a fifteen-year-old shepherd, wears similar rural garments—a coarse wool tunic tinted red with berry juice, a dye bestowed by the Earth Mother. Cheiron, a Kentaur, exemplifies his crude lifestyle by appearing naked except for a lion-tooth necklace, a representation of barbarity.

SERVING THE MOTHER GODDESS

The admission of twelve-year-old Kassandra to the stout female culture involves a uniform of breeches, a cloak, and a sword and scabbard belted at her waist. Completion of an Amazon's outfit includes a leather cap over braids, linen drawers and chemise, and an oiled-wool robe for winter, unlike the ragged hairstyles and goat hair skirts of Thracian women. The outback ensemble enhances a view of Penthesilea at her most regal—kohl eyeshadow, white doeskin boots and skirt, and the traditional horsehide tunic baring one breast, a reminder of the legend that Amazons cut off one breast to increase accuracy in archery. Setting the plot at the end of the Bronze Age, Marion depicts Queen Imandra of Colchis, a descendant of Medea, dressed in Egyptian gauze, a male wig and beard, painted eyebrows, bronze armaments, and a live snake for a belt, all elements of pharaonic Egyptian fashion to the southwest. The reptilian costuming recurs on the Colchian priestess Arikia, who wears a red sheath dyed to appear scaly and a huge snake wrapped twice around her waist, a subtle suggestion of a phallus controlled by a woman.

Evadne, the priestess who awakens Kassandra on initiation day, proffers the white robe of purity, adorned only by a green snake around the wrist. Marion repeats the basic white at Apollo's temple, where an elderly curate tops the white sheath with a saffron-yellow veil, the drape of a Roman bride. To reconnect with her joy in Amazon membership, Kassandra dresses in short tunic and helmet and masquerades as her twin Paris at the courtyard training of soldiers. Upon Hector's discovery of her camouflage, he humiliates her with a slap of his sword on her backside and dubs her a "wretched hoyden," a public diminution that infantilizes a proven warrior (Bradley, 1987, 157). Marion depicts Kassandra rejecting Odysseus's gift of amber beads, a valuable trade item throughout Europe and the Mediterranean for their luster. Once more drawn into godly service, Kassandra accepts the dictum of Charis, a 74-year-old temple authority, to wear only plain, unbleached tunic and sandals as the uniform of Apollo's virgin, which feminist critics Sandra Gilbert and Susan Gubar identify as an "absence of color … a blank page that asks to be written on" (Gilbert & Gubar, 1979, 616).

DETAILED ACCESSORIES

Marion typifies ritual via the importance of accessories and hairstyles, notably, ribbons on tunics and curls blowing freely at the spring planting festival and the polished armor and red plumes on Greek helmets. At Andromache's wedding, an extensive depiction of makeup contributes to the view of women in ancient times as dolls to be curled, oiled, gilded, and painted. In a grim simile, Kassandra thinks of Egyptian effigies buried with royal corpses. A communal dressing of the bride Creusa features knotted tresses and a flowered wreath over an embroidered veil, a parallel to Homer's memorable Achillean shield and its pictorial metal work, forged by Hephaestus, the god of fire. Another enrobing, that of the novice Chryseis, introduces her to the color scheme of Apollo's virgins, who wear a white robe tied with a silk belt. After a shift in tone and atmosphere from austerity, the text admires Kassandra for her bright colors and elaborate braids.

At a dramatic point in volume one, Marion introduces Helen, a newly seized war prize transported to Troy. To viewers amazed at her beauty, her yellow hair, resplendent veil, and gold fillet illustrate the meaning of the name Helen, the shining light. Unifying her appearance, a belt of gold disks set with lapis emulates features dominated by blonde hair and blue eyes. Her nanny, Aithra, wears the full skirt and low-neck bodice of Cretan women, whose curvaceous femininity marks Minoan statues found at Knossos. At a dramatic point of volume two, Kassandra clothes Meliantha for a dying farewell to the sun god. The aged religieuse reclines in a linen robe died yellow, the hue of the sun's rays, with makeup on lips and cheeks. Ironically, the priestly robes of the sun god allow Odysseus to draw Akhilles and Patroklos into parley with Priam and to adorn Briseis for union with Akhilles. In volume three, Marion incorporates clothing into poignant scenes, using a veil to dry Hecuba's tears, humble raiment to reduce Priam from monarch to grieving father, and the baring of feet and hacking of hair from Kassandra and Polyxena as tokens of grief.

EARLY MEDIEVAL WARDROBES

Marion excels at research into styles of the Middle Ages. The sylvan surroundings of *The Mists of Avalon* provide postulants like Morgaine a deerskin surcoat to wear over a dark blue robe to keep out the cold. Other occasions call for head drapes. The arrival of her cousin Galahad/Lancelet by barge accentuates the special colors, motions, and shapes of his costume—a swirling red cloak and red cap topped with an eagle feather, indicators of his importance to Arthuriana. At the coronation of King Arthur, Morgaine chooses to conceal her priestly function to the Mother Goddess by dressing in a black wool dress, an incognito austerity topped with a white coif suggesting affiliation with Glastonbury convent and its "housebound hens of God" (Bradley, 1983, 214).

The author contrasts religious asceticism of Morgaine's simple wool costume, silver torque, and braid wound on top of her head with the splendor of aunt Morgause, "robed richly in bright silks, with jewels and hair braided into a bright coronal on her brow," a demonstration of female exhibitionism (*Ibid.*, 209). Morgause maintains her fashion impact in the fourth stave, in which brocaded silk worked in gold thread and pearls pairs with a topaz coronet. In the background at the royal court, Romans, Angles, and Saxons jam the slopes around the crowning to view royal and aristocratic peacockery. The author singles out northern tribesmen "clad in skins and checkered cloth," a reference to the early Scots plaids emblematic of clan membership (*Ibid.*, 213). At dinner, Arthur, newly crowned king of Britannia, wears an unassuming white tunic and slender gold coronet, the same garments that mark his wedding ensemble and foretell his humility at Camelot.

Additional scenes of costuming and primping picture the young Gwenhwyfar tugging a blue gown over her kirtle. Already mature enough to gauge the effect of female beauty on men, she opts for coral beads and a cascade of hair released from braids, a symbolic advance from maidenhood to womanhood. Marion contrasts the femininity of royal children, even in youth, to girls in convents clad in regimented dark dresses, white coifs, and belts bearing crosses. On the ride to Caerleon with Queen Igraine, the bride-to-be disapproves the suggestion of wearing riding breeches, a flagrant disobedience to gendered church laws forbidding women from dressing like men. Igraine makes a joke at the expense of the apostle Paul, who "seemed to know little of the north country" (*Ibid.*, 266). Clothing dominates the wedding scene in which Gwenhwyfar wears the white and gold gown and veil that typify her natural coloring and Arthur appears in white tunic and blue cloak, the emblematic color of loyalty. Near Camelot's end, the arrival of Saxon tributaries to the court introduce hairy men in leather and fur, horned helmets, and gold arm- and headbands and torques, the garb of a triumphant race.

See also Humor.

Sources

Bradley, Marion Zimmer. *The Complete Lythande.* San Francisco: Marion Zimmer Bradley Literary Works Trust, 2013.
_____. *The Fall of Atlantis.* Riverdale, NY: Baen Books, 1983.
_____. *The Firebrand.* New York: Simon & Schuster, 1987.
_____. *The Forest House.* New York: Michael Joseph, 1993.
_____. *Free Amazons of Darkover.* New York: DAW, 1985.
_____. *The Mists of Avalon.* New York: Ballantine, 1983.
_____. *Rediscovery.* New York: DAW, 1993.
_____. *The Shattered Chain.* New York: DAW, 1976.
_____. *Stormqueen!* New York: DAW, 1978.
_____. *The Sword of Aldones.* New York: DAW, 1962.
_____. *Sword of Chaos.* New York: DAW, 1982.

_____. *Two to Conquer*. New York: DAW, 1980.
_____. *Warrior Woman*. New York: DAW, 1985.
Gilbert, Sandra M., and Susan Gubar. *The Madwoman in the Attic*. London: Yale University Press, 1979.
Kaler, Anne K. *The Picara: From Hera to Fantasy Heroine*. Bowling Green, OH: Bowling Green State University Popular Press, 1991.
Paxson, Diana L. *Costume and Clothing as a Cultural Index on Darkover*. San Francisco: Friends of Darkover, 1981.

Darkover

A polemical saga set on the planet Cottman IV, an *ad hoc* colony in the Taurus star cluster, Marion's popular Darkover novels and stories begin in trilogies, duos, and stand-alones with rational, scientific views of life on and beyond Earth. Reviewer Dave Panchyle of the Regina, Saskatchewan, *Leader-Post* compared the sprawling genealogies to a soap opera. In a light-hearted interview with reviewer Paul Craig of the Santa Rosa, California, *Press Democrat,* the author dismissed hints of intellectual technique or any clandestine reason for the name Darkover. She claimed, "I personally just started out with things I imagined and let it grow" (Craig, 1989, B5).

The saga takes the same mode as Robert Jordan's Wheel of Time series and the "In Death" police procedurals of J.D. Robb, the pseudonym of novelist Nora Roberts, who analyzes crimes and criminals in New York City against a futuristic backdrop. Marion employs the distant millennia and setting to amplify problems and possible solutions, a paradigm that fantasist Diane Gabaldon applies to the *Outlander* time travel series. Michael Hagen, a reviewer for the Wilmington, Delaware, *News-Journal,* summarized the Darkover saga as "a world of ritual and mystery, where powerful princes gifted with mysterious mental powers rule and the technology of Earth is the greatest threat" (Hagen, 1986, D4).

For *The Heritage of Hastur,* Marion opens the narrative on a map of the planet's seven domains—Aillard, Aldaran, Alton, Ardais, Elhalyn, Hastur, Ridenow—from the westward sea eastward. She expands on a controlling theme of male heirs to a dynasty that owes tribute to a Terran spaceport comprising "steel towers and stark white buildings … huge and sprawling, ugly and unfamiliar … like some strange growth" ringed "like a scab" by Trade City (Bradley, 1975, 1). Critic Walter Breen described the glimpse of might and squalor as "a mirror to our own people (past, present and developing), and to our planet" (Breen, 1975, n.p.). A more exacting comment from Zambian essayist Carla Namwali Serpell, a book reviewer for the *New York Times,* admires the sci-fi view for its "immersive simulation of the future … so that we might decide together whether we want these dreams to come true" (Serpell, 2019, 15).

Central to the author's method, plots emerge from clearly visualized character, a skill that Breen compares to the believable human engagements created by novelists Mary Renault and Sigrid Undset and mythographer Robert Graves. According to the fallacy hypothesized in *Darkover Landfall* by geologist Rafael "Rafe" MacAran: "You couldn't set down, raw and unhelped by technology, on a completely unknown world. It couldn't be done" (Bradley, 1972, 6). In reproof of Rafe's over-generalized dictum, fictional counter-evidence dazzles readers with human efforts to survive a traumatic landing. Through cooperative efforts, Terrans of the lost colony fail to return home, but manage to thrive in a foreign ecosystem amid extremes of cold and exotic beings.

A Conflicted Milieu

In a familiar setting comprised of givens and their consequences like Frank Herbert's *Dune*, the Darkover series develops overlapping conflicts. Strife springs from nature with the rockslide that crushes Dyan and Sybella's son Ardais in the story "Ten Minutes or So" and from felonious attacks, as with the arson that destroys a castle during the feud of Storn and Hammerfell in *The Heirs of Hammerfell*. In the contrasting ramifications posited by Irish critic Linda Leith, "contrary elements" determine the action:

> TERRA: Darkover
> RATIONAL: Intuitive
> TECHNOLOGICAL: Instinctive
> ESTABLISHMENT: Counter-Establishment
> ARTIFICIAL: Natural
> BOURGEOIS: Feudal
> AGE: Youth
> MALE: Female
> HETEROSEXUALITY: Homosexuality [Leith, 1980, 31].

Leith characterizes the sets of contraries as dominant motifs in each novel. The heart of dissension parallels age-old rancor on Earth summarized by the statement "The rest of you don't stand for what we stand for," a typical "us versus them" scission (Bradley, 1972, 85). By blending natural calamity with human animus, the series maintains its twofold focus on adaptation and compromise over two millennia of residency on Cottman IV. Other subjects provide subsidiary themes, such as reconciliation and empathy, called the "Ridenow Gift" in *The Spell Sword,* and the intuition that directs Kennard Alton in *The Heritage of Hastur* and *Star of Danger.*

Originally known as the Sevener cycle, Marion's extraterrestrial saga dramatizes a panoply of human ills brought on by unfamiliar milieu and environment. Novelist Joanna Russ typified the utopia/dystopia for its clannish tribes, communal anarchy, passion for nature and ecological preservation, diminution of castes, pacifism, female rescue, and nonrestrictive sexual behaviors. To stress medieval lifestyles, *Stormqueen!* pictures Alart Hastur subjugating the serfs of Syrtis Great House. *The Shattered Chain* describes women paying for well water with the copper rings that pass for currency and transporting a ransom requital of copper bars to the Scarp bandits. Through control of the elements, seven aristocratic dynasties maintain primacy over minorities and Darkover's exotic species.

The planet obtained its name a century after the first earthlings arrived from the New Hebrides Commune and may refer to the perpetual ice age that encumbers the climate. Other interpretations label as "dark" the archaic mindset that anchors castes to medieval philosophies. To the exasperation of a legate of Cottman IV in *The Bloody Sun,* Darkovan trade remains set in the Middle Ages: "We offer them planes, surface transit, roadbuilding machinery—and what do they buy? Horses" (Bradley, 1964, 33). In contrast to a civilization reliant on horsepower, Terrans "take machinery and technology for granted" (*Ibid.*, 39).

According to the author's colleague and sister-in-law, Diana Lucile Paxson, the Darkover colonies remained "feudal in structure and anti-technology," replacing invention with "a kind of magic based on the application of paranormal and psychic powers" (Paxson, 1999, 112). To comprehend transcendent elements, the author trained herself in metaphysics with scholarly readings and a course from the Rosicrucians or Brothers of the Rose Cross, a mystic fellowship founded in Berlin, Germany, and spread to Oceanside, California, and the Canary Islands. In a century that saw the rise of Arab unrest, Hungarian raiders on Venice and Lombardy, and shifts in power in Byzantium and Iberia, the mystics preserved such secret scholarship as alchemy and prophecy and practiced occult powers dating to the 900s CE.

CHRONOLOGICAL DIVISION

The author engineered catastrophe after a spaceship leaves Earth to ferry new residents to space colonies and crashes on a distant planet in an unknown galaxy. Extensive subplots in *Darkover Landfall* on human regeneration and agriculture required scientific diction, such as resinous, photosynthesis, euphoria, and narcosynthesis (Bradley, 1972, 1, 5). In a summation of the predicament, Moray, an ecologist and culture designer, predicts, "Nothing here's going to be easy" (*Ibid.,* 104). In the introduction to *The Forbidden Circle,* the novel that follows *The Shattered Chain,* Marion summarized the network of plots as "the clash of two warring cultures, apparently irreconcilable and in spite of all, closely akin" (Bradley, 2002, i). The action advanced from straightforward adventure to psychological and social issues of miscegenation, patriarchy, misogyny, human rights, nonviolence, and homosexuality. The story "Death Between the Stars" introduced speciesism, an interplanetary form of racism, and the human exploitation of other forms of life, "off-worlders" whom a superior spaceship crewman demeans as "geeks" (Bradley, 1976, 57; 1985, 135). The creation of space inhabitants enhanced the author's examination of earthly quandaries without naming specific factions of her era.

Although the writer composed segments independent of a timeline, her guide to the series divides the fiction into a chronological order of events covering 2,000 years:

The Founding
   Darkover Landfall
Chaotic Age
   Stormqueen!
   Hawkmistress!
The Hundred Kingdoms
   Two to Conquer
   The Heirs of Hammerfell
The Renunciates
   The Shattered Chain
   Thendara House
   City of Sorcery
Against the Terrans: The First Age
   (Recontact)
   Rediscovery
   The Spell Sword
   The Forbidden Tower

Star of Danger
The Winds of Darkover
Against the Terrans: The Second Age (After the Comyn)
The Bloody Sun (Marion's favorite)
"To Keep the Oath"
The Heritage of Hastur
The Planet Savers
"The Waterfall"
Sharra's Exile
Exile's Song
The Shadow Matrix
Traitor's Sun
The Sword of Aldones
Darkover Anthologies
   The Keeper's Price
   Sword of Chaos

Writer Joanna Russ epitomized Marion's science fiction genre as problem-solving, the kind that Daniel Defoe's Robinson Crusoe applied to survival on a desert Island beset by cannibals and that a marooned boys' choir in William Golding's *The Lord of the Flies* evolved for self-preservation from a murderous faction.

New Place, New Powers

For Darkover settings, Marion stressed exotic and elaborate world building that appealed to an array of readers, both male and female. In *To Save a World,* she pictured the spot "isolated at the edge of a galaxy, with a sun so dim that its name was known only in star catalogs" (Bradley, 2004, i). At closer range, newcomers see the spaceship wreckage in "a great bowl of land at least five miles across filled with low brushwood and scrubby trees" (Bradley, 1972, 5). In her words, the loosely interrelated human network relies on "a common background—the Terran Empire against the world and culture of Darkover," a dominant motif in *The Firebrand* and *The Mists of Avalon* (Bradley, 2002, iii). Literary historian Sonja Sadovsky, who trained at the University of Amsterdam, defined the author's speculative fiction in *The Forbidden Tower* as a survey of radical alternatives to the global status quo after a new civilization supersedes an established one (Sadovsky, 2014, 19). In token of Marion's respect for humankind and its complexity, William Marden, a reviewer for the *Orlando Sentinel,* acclaimed the Darkover series "one of the most beloved and best realized fictional worlds ever created" (Marden, 1999, F9).

Marion's masterly fantasy saga depicts aliens employing the potency of a blue crystal, a source of magic power she develops in *The Shadow Matrix.* The blue stone creates cultural mayhem, the cause of wars and the foundation of drama and literature. The glittering stone fuels opportunistic capitalism, the motif of *The World Wreckers,* second in the *To Save a World* trilogy. Subsequently, for *The Spell Sword* and *The Forbidden Tower,* she forges a quartet of dedicated taboo breakers and non-human enemies. A year later, the author envisioned for *Stormqueen!* the birth of Dorilys Rockraven, a mystic wielder of lightning. Of a fictional framework that succeeded for two decades, the author claimed, "I didn't invent Darkover, I discovered it" (Coker, 2011, 1). The flexible, open-ended concept encouraged new writers to post their own episodes under the canopy of Darkover and to develop past characters along with new cast members, settings, and international perplexities to negotiate.

Social Issues

The author elevated expectations for the genre by incorporating bold social consciousness of gender identification and sexual orientation alongside surveys of racial, ethnic, religious, class, and species differences. Compared to Isaac Asimov's Foundation

series, begun in 1942, and to Ursula Le Guin's *The Left Hand of Darkness,* Octavia Butler's Xenogenesis Trilogy, Marge Piercy's *Woman at the Edge of Time,* and Joanna Russ's
The Female Man, the interlinking plots foreground ethnic diversity from the isolation at
the end of the 2900s CE of Terran settlers from Earth on giant red star Cottman IV. The
intermarriage of Celtic Scots with Hispanics evens out the population with a bicultural
race that acquires telepathic capabilities by further mixing with the ancient Chieri, a
long-lived androgynous band of humanoid telepaths in *Darkover Landfall* capable of
altering their gender at will. Inspirational relics survive in *Rediscovery,* leaving identifiable melodies sung in Gaelic. Selective breeding enables Darkoverans to manipulate
the population for both good and evil purposes until the return of a shuttle from Earth.
Easing obstacles to communication in *casta* and *cahuenga,* the dominant languages,
telepathy supplants interpretation of foreign tongues, an aid to Senator Hermes-Gabriel
Aldaran, the master spy in *Traitor's Sun.*

Like a hobbyist plotting a planetarium, Marion dabbled in altering Earth atmosphere and physical restraints—seas, mountains, forests, caves, deserts, winds—by
plunging Darkover into perennial cold relieved along the equator by a horseshoe-shaped
environment that supports human travel, trapping, sheepherding, and agriculture. By
undermining reader expectations of time, gravity, atmosphere, and normal human and
animal strengths, she raised serious world-altering questions about science, notably,
control of weapons of mass destruction in *The Heritage of Hastur* and the availability
of health care to all classes in *The Forbidden Tower,* one of the least successful of the
Darkover network. In a gendered discussion of Marion and other female sci-fi writers, Jane Donawerth, an English professor at the University of Maryland, hypothesized
that females "do not see 'pure' or unapplied science as a necessary goal; instead, they
imagine application as part of the process of scientific inquiry," an element of *Two to
Conquer* (Donawerth, 1997, 27–28). Women's skill at telepathy derives from the author's
belief that females naturally empathize with creature needs, a quality found in Carlina,
Melisendra, Romy, and Melora.

In the impersonal and centralized Terran Empire, the Darkover series depicts
pragmatic policies toward coexistence with the Cralmac, an artificial race created from
changes to DNA, alongside the simian Kyrri, humanoids equipped with a taser-like
touch. An issue resulting from mixed species, zoonotic illness—a 48-year fever cycle
featured in *The Planet Savers*—endangers Terran colonists by their contiguity to forest
ruminants called Trailmen. For added conflict, the author depicts Trailwomen as waylayers of travelers. As an antithesis to mindless violence, the Old Ones of the Sky negotiate a solution to the regional pestilence, which Marion ends with the formulation of
an antidote to Trailman fever. The optimistic solution to epidemic envisions treatments
and cures of earthly ills from outer space through cooperative research.

INTRICATE PLOTS

Motifs in the fiction network revisit familiar plots from Greek and Roman myth
and epic, Aesop's fables, the *commedia dell'arte,* medieval dynasties, and crusader feats.
For humanistic value, Marion surveys sibling grief, chance meetings, martyrdom,
brotherhood, and vows of virginity and constancy. The theme of self-control in *Rediscovery* depicts Fiora as a possessor of magical powers, but little personal restraint,

the cause of a scorched earth in the myth of Phaethon and the sun god's chariot. Most time-honored patterns recall classic works: separated twins in the Roman playwright Plautus's *Menaechmi,* dueling in Robin Hood legends and the *Mahabharata,* the unacknowledged noble father in "The Sword in the Stone," daring rescues of "Aladdin" and "The Three Musketeers," and a disturbing ritual similar to the curse of Carabosse on the infant princess in the fairy tale/ballet "Sleeping Beauty." Strategies involve shapeshifting and traveling in disguise under assumed names, two ploys that the magician Lythande adopts in *The Gratitude of Kings* and Morgaine introduces in *The Mists of Avalon* by posing as a beggar at Arthur's court. *The Heirs of Hammerfell* negotiates a truce between warring regimes. With the ease of a stage comedy, Marion's text ameliorates the virulent era by joining three couples in wedlock, a social parallel to the group wedding in William Shakespeare's fantasy romance *A Midsummer Night's Dream.*

After revealing the neophyte Callina's terror of forced marriage in *Sharra's Exile* and Kyla n'ha Raineach's introduction to Free Amazons in *The Planet Savers,* the author retracts her faith in monogamy in *The Shattered Chain,* a distinctive salute to the autonomous female for pledging loyalty to self and sisterhood. Unlike the androcentric adventure tales that place Regis Hastur in charge of the Sword of Aldones and against the Sharra Matrix, *The Shattered Chain* reflects the trust in gender introduced by feminist author Charlotte Perkins Gilman in *Herland* (1915), a utopian plot that isolates women in a peaceful, orderly society free of sexist cant and male grandstanding. By reformulating gender roles, Marion's independent women make their own decisions. *Thendara House,* a sequel, overrules the oppression of matriarchy by legitimating lesbianism along with celibacy, neutering, and monogamy as female gender options.

On the return to planet Earth in the novella "The Climbing Wave," interplanetary travelers face the constraints of physics on existentialism. Marion notes, "After five years of subjective time in hyperspeeds, it was entirely possible that everyone they had known on Terra Two had already lived out a full lifetime" (Bradley, 1985, 56–57). In the analysis of Cynthia Rose Huckfeldt of the University of Wyoming, the earthlings fail because of "central isolationism and paranoia-based surveillance that is almost prophetic of George W. Bush's … domestic surveillance program in his War on Terror" (Huckfeldt, 2008, 7). The changes in Earth harden Darkover residents for permanent separation from the past. In an overview of the series, critic Roland J. Green of the (New Brunswick) *Central New Jersey Home News* declared it a standout: "For sheer skill in storytelling and word building, for wit, for strikingly intelligent development of the concept of telepathy, above all for continuous concern for people, Ms. Bradley has put some more famous SF sagas in the shade" (Green, 1982, D4).

See also Exotic Beings; Healing and Death.

Sources

Bradley, Marion Zimmer. *The Best of Marion Zimmer Bradley.* Chicago: Academy Chicago, 1985.
_____. *The Bloody Sun.* New York: Ace, 1964.
_____. *Darkover Landfall.* New York: DAW, 1972.
_____. *The Forbidden Circle.* New York: DAW, 2002.
_____. *The Heritage of Hastur.* New York: DAW, 1975.
_____. *Rediscovery.* New York: DAW, 1993.
_____. *The Shattered Chain.* New York: DAW, 1976.
_____. "Ten Minutes or So," *Towers of Darkover.* New York: DAW, 1993.

_____. *To Save a World*. New York: DAW, 2004.

Breen, Walter. *The Darkover Concordance*. Houston, TX: Penny-Farthing Press, 1979.

_____. *The Gemini Problem: A Study in Darkover*. Baltimore: T-K Graphics, 1975.

Coker, Catherine. "The *Contraband* Incident: The Strange Case of Marion Zimmer Bradley," *Transformative Works and Cultures* 6 (March 2011): 1–6.

Craig, Paul. "Bradley's Science Fiction World a Huge Success," (Santa Rosa, CA) *Press Democrat* (15 May 1989): B5

Donawerth, Jane. *Frankenstein's Daughters: Women Writing Science Fiction*. New York: Syracuse University Press, 1997.

Fayad, Mona. "Aliens, Androgynes, and Anthropology," *Mosaic* 30:3 (September 1997): 59–73.

Green, Roland J. "'Hawkmistress' Continues Darkover Saga," (New Brunswick) *Central New Jersey Home News* (26 September 1982): D4.

Hagen, Michael. "Fantasy Writers to Visit," (Wilmington, DE) *News-Journal* (21 November 1986): D4.

Huckfeldt, Cynthia Rose. "Avoiding 'Teapot Tempests': The Politics of Marion Zimmer Bradley's *Darkover*." Laramie: University of Wyoming, 2008.

Leith, Linda. "Marion Zimmer Bradley and Darkover," *Science Fiction Studies* 7 (1980): 28–35.

Marden, William, "Bradley Delves into Future of Planet Known as Darkover," *Orlando Sentinel* (28 March 1999): F9.

Panchyle, Dave. "Review: *The Shadow Matrix*," (Regina, Saskatchewan) *Leader-Post* (21 February 1998): D2.

Paxson, Diana L. "Marion Zimmer Bradley and *The Mists of Avalon*," *Arthuriana* 9:1 (Spring 1999): 110–126.

Renk, Thorsten. "Mapping Darkover," http://www.phy.duke.edu/~trenk/darkover/darkover_map.html#mental_map.

Sadovsky, Sonja. *The Priestess & the Pen: Marion Zimmer Bradley, Dion Fortune & Diana Paxson's Influence on Modern Paganism*. Woodbury, MN: Llewellyn Worldwide, 2014.

Serpell, Namwali. "When Sci-Fi Comes True," *New York Times* (17 March 2019): 15.

Darkover Genealogy

Marion chooses to end the quest novel *Darkover Landfall* with a flash forward fourteen years from a spaceship headed for Coronis Colony. The mission crashes on an unknown planet, giving rise to polyamorous relationships, propitious births, and stable foster parenting. Notation in the family tree indicates sexual/marital ties:

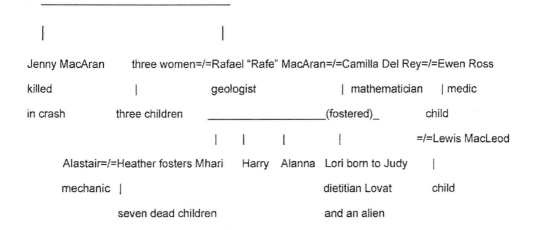

The concept of serial mates illustrates the theory of naturalist Charles Darwin, issued in 1859 as *On the Origin of Species*, that individuals vary in strength and adaptability to the environment. By reproducing and passing inheritable traits to offspring, the strong invigorate the process of natural selection. Centuries later in *The Shattered Chain*, Lady Rohana Ardais refers to a period of "selective breeding to fix these gifts in our racial heritage; it was a time of great tyranny, and not a time we are very proud to remember" (Bradley, 1976, 227). The strategy collapses because of recessive genes, "fertility lowered by inbreeding," and commoners' distrust of science (*Ibid.*).

See also Reproduction; Sex.

Sources

Bradley, Marion Zimmer. *Darkover Landfall*. New York: DAW, 1972.
_____. *The Shattered Chain*. New York: DAW, 1976.
Larbalestier, Justine. *The Battle of the Sexes in Science Fiction*. Middletown, CT: Wesleyan University Press, 2002.
Monk, Patricia. "The Future Imperfect of Conjugation: Images of Marriage in Science Fiction," *Mosaic* 17:2 (1 April 1984): 207–222.

Darkover Landfall

An organic primer for the study of civilization, *Darkover Landfall* moves characters through the basics of communal living and technology after overpopulation, exhaustion of natural resources, and pollution force earthlings to colonize space. Upon a disastrous alighting on an unknown planet, a motif of the female gladiator narrative in *Warrior Woman,* the expeditionary force of Spanish and Scots Gaels makes a detailed study of the horizon, water, biota, animals, and edibles and scans the sky for traces of known planets for use in navigation. Unlike Billy Pilgrim in Kurt Vonnegut's *Slaughterhouse-Five,* who finds luxury and pleasure in outer space, or time travelers Geillis Duncan Abernethy and Claire Beauchamp Randall Fraser, who adapt readily to eighteenth-century Scotland in Diane Gabaldon's *Outlander* series, Marion's transplants search for a "pre-technological civilization" or a possible way to survive if there is no return home, a prospect they at first reject from their discussions (Bradley, 1972, 12).

To stem defeatism, geologist Rafael "Rafe" MacAran sets an optimistic tone by quoting Jesus's Sermon on the Mount: "Sufficient unto the day is the evil thereof" (Matthew 6:34), a forerunner of the Alcoholics Anonymous maxim of "one day at a time." Marion heightens irony in the survivors' hope that there's time for Father Valentine Neville, the ship's chaplain, to hold a memorial service and raise a monument to the dead before takeoff. After a deliriant wind precipitates euphoria and group sexual frenzy, rationality wavers, leaving intelligent crash survivors, like Homer's lotus-eaters in *The Odyssey,* to wonder how they could have relished such titillating, repulsive hallucinations.

From the normality of scenes similar to Joanna Russ's *"We Who Are About to...,"* Marion's novel blazes forth eerie obstacles and dangers—a forest fire, snow, clawed birds, a humanoid lover, and exotic beings living in treehouses. Over all flow strong gusts filled with hallucinogenic pollen of kiraseth, a threat the author repeats in *Rediscovery.* While provocative strategies and regulations grow and change daily, Marion illustrates the need to expect the unexpected: "Everything they did on this planet was an interim measure," a versatility that protects the pioneers from panic and the erratic behavior of neo-agrarians, a hippie group of anti-industrialists from Scots-Irish roots (*Ibid.*, 77). Outbursts of anxiety and libido accompany spontaneous telepathy, the result of breathing psychotropic dust. The author interprets the upsurge of sensuality and precognition as a throwback to primitive humankind, who intensified psi powers to compensate for physical weakness in an ecosystem dominated by clawed and fanged beasts.

Self-Reliance

Marion defaults from technology to woods-craft and the recycling of spare rocket parts by employing the destruction of the spaceship computer, an explosion that kills 21 explorers, two of them suicides. In the explanation of Irish critic Linda Leith, survivors "learn to depend for survival on the land and on their native wit rather than on an irrelevant technology" (Leith, 1980, 28). Left to their inborn smarts in a primitive locale, the survivors diagnose temporary insanity as a "mass freakout," a nonspecific explanation of spontaneous savagery and an orgiastic rampage (Bradley, 1972, 104). The author reprises the history of human technology by authorizing search parties to locate caves for shelter and raw materials to make pottery, glass, flint, fertilizer, and cement. The need for laborers—gardeners, gravediggers, woodcutters, shelter builders—nullifies elite privileges for the commander and scientists and repudiates capital punishment, a waste of muscle power the outpost can't afford.

In the author's projections of Darkover's future, she speaks through ecologist Moray, a culture designer, the composition of soil, air, and plant life and the likelihood that neo-ruralists will be more inclined to sustain human life than scientists. The dichotomy opposes what Linda Leith describes as a "technologically advanced and liberal-cum-imperialist Terran civilization to a non- (or anti-) technological and effectively feudal Darkovan civilization" (Leith, 1980, 28). By putting a productivity value on individual laborers and artisans, Marion postulates the hierarchy of seven elite dynasties that dominates a caste system in subsequent books in the series. To the chagrin of Captain Harry Leicester, the list of future needs—glass blower, elementary teachers and textbook writers, nurses, and dietitians—outweighs the worth of highly educated space navigators, engineers, and computer analysts. To protect future generations, chief medical officer Di Asturien sets protocol for rejecting endangered pregnancies and defective infants "who really should have died, nature's mistakes" (*Ibid.*, 123). The grim regulations, which echo the orders of Nina Conti, Adolf Hitler's nurse/midwife for the Nazi super race, startle expectant mothers. The author teeters between accepting emergency triage and pitying infants and mothers, whom "protective" males expropriate for breeders.

A Structured Philosophy

Because the controlling theme scrutinizes the essence of human relations and beliefs, Marion peruses the need for moral standards that befit a pre-moral planet and its triage system. After the foundering of Father Valentine's convictions during his savage rape and knifing of fellow settlers, the series honors his humility in *Hawkmistress!* for conceiving the *cristoforos* (literally "Christ bearers") and for creating a monastery called St. Valentine of the Snows, a suggestion of the sixteenth-century Cistercian rescue center and hospice between Italy and Switzerland in the Great St. Bernard Pass. In *Stormqueen!,* followers dub the priest "Blessed Saint Valentine" (Bradley, 1978, 47). The text creates irony in the wisdom of dietitian Judith "Judy" Lovat, a nurturer of the flesh. She states a humanistic truism: "We'll all have to be priests to each other," a tenet that suits her surname (*Ibid.*, 127). The statement reduces the pecking order among academic specialties, particularly the godly confessor, who faces a future of shame and guilt for his sex romp with men and retaliatory slaughter.

The author outlines a series of positive events that counter despair by boosting spirits. Judy's wish for Captain Harry Leicester to sire her second child introduces a pragmatic method of strengthening the race by upgrading genetic combinations. The discovery of an arboreal residence discloses a peaceable race capable of empathizing with the crash survivors. The performance of Celtic lore among the farm cult at the Hall of the New Hebrides Commune directs Marion's text toward melancholy Gaelic songs and dances that celebrate an agrarian home reminiscent of Scotland. In the solacing atmosphere, Camilla and Judy recoil from the wind, a reminder of madness and potential chaos. The foundation of New Skye promises to honor memories of the mother country and its folksy mythos.

See also Exotic Beings; Healing and Death; Sex.

Sources

Bradley, Marion Zimmer. *Darkover Landfall*. New York: DAW, 1972.
_____. *The Shattered Chain*. New York: DAW, 1976.
_____. *Stormqueen!* New York: DAW, 1978.
Larbalestier, Justine. *The Battle of the Sexes in Science Fiction*. Middletown, CT: Wesleyan University Press, 2002.
Leith, Linda. "Marion Zimmer Bradley and Darkover," *Science Fiction Studies* 7 (1980): 28–35.
McIntyre Vonda N. "Review: *Darkover Landfall*," *The Witch and the Chameleon* 2 (November 1974): 19–24.
Sturgis, Susanna J. "What's a P.C. Feminist Like You Doing in a Fantasy Like This?" http://www.susannajsturgis.com/article.php?id=34.

Details

Marion turned casual readers into rapt students of fantasy and historical fiction through the deft manipulation of details, as with the swordsman's eye exploded by the skillful sling fighter in *Warrior Woman,* the puppet in "tawdry garments wearing a two-pointed fool's hat with a wobbly crown" in *Traitor's Sun,* Donal's wing-like glider and the heavy summer thunder before the birth of Dorilys in *Stormqueen!,* and the singing of wistful Celtic love plaints about Mhari in *Darkover Landfall* (Bradley, 1999, 131; 1997, 2). Various motivations underlie these specifics:

- Barry's flight to San Francisco with a man claiming to be his dad in *The Brass Dragon*
- the red cord awarded for bravery in *Two to Conquer*
- the lizard-man Aratak's color in *The Survivors*
- the dying words of the alien Theradin in Samarran dialect in "Death Between the Stars"
- the onset of pain and near freezing that threatens Andrew Carr in *The Spell Sword*
- combat strategies of Greeks and Trojans in *The Firebrand*
- the Halloween-like darkness in "Night of Nadir"

- a toymaker's shop in "Bird of Prey"
- psychotropic drug experiments in *The House Between the Worlds*
- a dancing bear at a Beltane festival in *The Forest House*
- song catcher Margaret Alton's handy recorder and transcriber in *Exile's Song*
- episodes of haunting at a San Francisco house in *The Inheritor*
- Lancelet's supervision of lighthouses in *The Mists of Avalon*
- the reprise of modern American military history in *Heartlight*.

The author's attention to precision intensifies threats, particularly the sound of the spaceport like the thunder of a waterfall in *The Heritage of Hastur,* security guard Huw's deadly cudgel in *The Forest House,* Tommy Rawlins's illicit rescue of a doomed space crew in "Hero's Moon," and Magda's slicing of a banshee's throat with a knife in *The Shattered Chain.* For unwary patients in the droll story "The Crime Therapist," Dr. Rhoum's stamp of "cured" on his logbook could equate with "killed," as in the case of Frank Colby, who dies in the electric chair (Bradley, 1954, 100).

Other details flourish in more peaceable motifs. For *The Fall of Atlantis,* the author demonstrates the importance of rank and character in Domaris's breast-to-forehead salute to Micon, a distinguished visitor to Ancient Land (Bradley, 1983, 20). The narrative anchors meaningful scenes to nature, beginning with falling stars as signs of destiny and the statue of the Star-Shaper as evidence of theft. At a cryptic ceremony involving sword and gong, a priest of light ignites pine and cypress kindling to burn incense in a brazier. The author incorporates the starved corpse of a red bird as proof of Deoris's self-absorption. A futuristic glimpse in still water at Domaris, on her deathbed, looks into the afterlife, a major theme of quasi-historical studies of the Atlantean civilization.

REWRITING HOMER

Scholarly attention to minutiae in *The Firebrand* results in imagery rich in visuals and historical accuracy, such as the blaze during the Trojan War of 1200 BCE that burns Akhaian ships and tents on the shore of the Aegean Sea. Marion's version appends the patience of Kassandra waiting for the shoemaker to sew sandals and the avuncular good will of Odysseus, a family friend. In the opening scene, the author dramatizes the importance of the migrant minstrel to households "from Crete to Colchis," a salute to the epicist Homer himself, who may have lived on the isle of Chios off the coast of Anatolia between 800 and 750 BCE and entertained audiences throughout the Aegean world (Bradley, 1987, 2). Marion's harper tunes his lyre with "tortoise-shell pegs" before launching into a folk epic that links listeners with their nation's forebears and reputation for prowess in war (*Ibid.,* 1). Outside the Trojan palace, twin lionesses adorn the gates in a dual emphasis on womanhood and the matrilineal destiny of the realm.

The novel accentuates positive and negative details—the dangers of stinking smut (rye blight) on Thracian women and their babies, recruitment of ceramicists into the Trojan army to supply materiel, and the choice of fire pots for transporting hot coals from camp to camp. At the arrival of the priest Khryse to Apollo's temple in Troy, Charis instructs him on the mathematics of tally sticks to enumerate types of offerings to the god. Khryse lauds Cretans for formulating phonics, a symbolic means of writing sounds, the invention of Hermes, the Olympian messenger and forerunner of the winged Roman god Mercury. A more ominous writing on a city map exposes the treachery of Odysseus, an old friend "full of such crafts and wiles" (*Ibid.*, 248). As a testimonial to age-old blood thirst, the author pictures seventeen-year-old Akhilles examining "a great double-bladed ax with a handle twice as long as the height of a tall man," an epic exaggeration of armaments that Priam suggests may be a relic of warfare among Titans after the world's creation (*Ibid.*, 288).

Medieval Components

For the Lythande series, the author milked the Dark Ages for tidbits of culture and lore suited to the times and its lore. Drawing on centuries of ocean misinformation, the author heightens the threats of mermaids and sea-monsters in "Sea Wrack," a standard folk motif picturing villagers in danger of starvation and extinction when their harvesting of marine wealth fails. Marion speaks of mead drinks, time-candles, sculling and net fishing, and crofts, enclosed sections of rented farmland. To heighten the menace of Roygan the Proud in "The Incompetent Magician," Lythande mentions his snaggle-toothed mouth and the covering of raw incisor edges with metal, a stop-gap method of protecting enamel before the days of more mechanized dentistry.

From intense research into the early Middle Ages, Marion filled *The Mists of Avalon* with period facets from the sixth and seventh centuries CE—Arthur's meal of apples from the trees on the shores of Avalon, the teachings of the missionary Columba, church bells in London, pigs feeding on acorns from the sacred oak grove, and Gwenhwyfar's unique scent. The servant Old Gwen, a knowledgeable herbalist, aborts Ettarr's unborn fetus, the result of a night's tryst with Duke Gorlois of Cornwall. A more permanent symbol of the era, the dragon on Uther's banner harks back to the Druidic serpent, an ancient representation of fertility, ancestry, and wisdom. Igraine legitimizes the reptilian icon for "the common folk of the countryside," the Celts who cling to the old interpretation of transformation and rebirth (Bradley, 1983, 61). A red dragon recurs in the sky along with a shooting star, a portent of the demise of High King Uther Pendragon, father of King Arthur. The historic omen echoes the death stars that heralded the assassination of Julius Caesar on March 15, 44 BCE, and the combat death of English King Harold with a Norman spear through the eye at the Battle of Hastings on October 14, 1066. The Pendragon banner remained a Welsh standard, returning to notoriety in 1400 when Welsh ruler Owen Glendower flaunted the red dragon at Carnarfon Castle during rebellion against England's Henry IV.

Woman's Work

Igraine of Cornwall's championing of army symbols and banners places her within cloistered sewing rooms. Diligent at fiber work and needlecraft, she embroiders altar linens and spins yarn to weave and design a wardrobe for her husband, Duke Gorlois. As queen, she has the leisure to refine woven borders and silk ribbons while ordinary nuns stick to the stitchery of plain wool habits and white linen for coifs and veils. On her ride to Caerleon with Gwenhwyfar, Arthur's bride-to-be requires a retinue of carts to carry her female accouterments—two looms, pots and kettles, combs and hackles for smoothing flax, and a lady's wardrobe of outfits and jewels. The juxtaposition of finery with the tools of grueling domestic labor ensure a balanced woman as future queen of the Britons.

Doubts about Gwenhwyfar's potential as a monarch and wife crumble because of her precise order to make clabber cheese (yogurt) from spoiled milk to avoid waste. The plan elicits a compliment from Morgaine: "You are a notable housewife," who later proves worthy as Arthur's nurse, cook, hostess, and caretaker (*Ibid.,* 307). On the queen's return to the unknown land called Summer Country (which Mary Stewart's *The Last Enchantment* identified as the dry lake bed of Ynis Witrin or Glastonbury), disorder prefigures Gwenhwyfar's undoing. A meticulous description of animal hides and a hall "ragged and greasy … unswept, with a sour, sweaty smell" foreshadows the savagery of Meleagrant, the half-brother, kidnapper, and rapist of Arthur's queen (*Ibid.,* 510).

Details bring the novel to its melancholy end. In a frenzy of requital, Morgaine examines her sleeping brother Arthur and ponders striking him with Excalibur or a dagger. Cognizance of the bloodletting leading to fratricide forces her mind back to his babyhood and to Igraine's dependence on Morgaine as child minder. On the ferry crossing to Avalon, sense impressions flood the action—sunrise, the shadow of Glastonbury church spire, and church bells, which disempower the enchantment that hails the barge. The shift in dominion establishes Gwenhwyfar's Christianity as a lethal threat to Morgaine and the old ways of Fairy.

See also Costume.

Sources

Bradley, Marion Zimmer. *The Best of Marion Zimmer Bradley.* Chicago: Academy Chicago, 1985.
_____. "The Crime Therapist," *Future Science Fiction* 5:3 (October 1954): 93–100.
_____. *The Fall of Atlantis.* Riverdale, NY: Baen Books, 1983.
_____. *The Firebrand.* New York: Simon & Schuster, 1987.
_____. *The Mists of Avalon.* New York: Ballantine, 1983.
_____. *The Shadow Matrix.* New York: DAW, 1997.
_____. *Traitor's Sun.* New York: DAW, 1999.
Riggs, Don. "The Survival of the Goddess in Marie de France and Marion Zimmer Bradley," *Journal of the Fantastic in the Arts* 9:1 (1998): 15–23.
Sharpe, Victoria. "The Goddess Restored," *Journal of the Fantastic in the Arts* 9:1 (1998): 36–45.
Smith, Jeanette C. "The Role of Women in Contemporary Arthurian Fantasy," *Extrapolation* 35:2 (1994): 130–144.
Volk-Birke, Sabine. "The Cyclical Way of the Priestess," *Anglia* 108:3/4 (1990): 409–428.

Diction

Out of intrinsic knowledge and appreciation for precise language from the ancient world, the Middle Ages, and futurism, Marion permeated her historical and sci-fi fiction, stories, and verse with suitable terms, for example, the noun "ragpicker" and the adjective "winter-killed" in *Stormqueen!,* the adverb "mayhap" in "Well Met By Moonlight," the insult "lackwit" in *Hawkmistress!,* the archaic exclamation "fie" in "Everything But Freedom," and the verb "gainsaid" (denied) and the nouns "paxman" (security guard) and "a tenday" (unit of time) in "The Hawkmaster's Son" and "Firetrap" (Bradley, 1980, 161, 163, 153). For *The Fall of Neskaya* and *Two to Conquer,* she invented the kenning "truthspell," a sci-fi version of truth serum. Imaginative scenarios summon period details, such as bartering at the harbor, a feudal marketing structure, raising a chant from oarsmen in ship's galleys in *The Firebrand,* and accidental hexing on "The

Wuzzles" with the phrase "May it be so," an Anglo-Saxon equivalent of the Hebrew "amen." For Zora in *Survey Ship*, the romance of two space cadets constitutes "unwisdom," while the nickname "Jimson" revisits Scandic patronyms (Bradley, 1980, 16, 28). A counterpoint to pious priestesses in *The Forest House* arises from Roman centurion Capellus, Gaius Macellius's traveling companion and escort for the wounded from field hospitals in northern Britannia. Amid cows at the Beltane fair, Capellus swears Roman style, "by Caligula's balls," a perverted, sadistic emperor nicknamed "little soldier's boots" (Bradley, 1993, 141).

Such salty "man talk" relieves some of the tedium of female temple conversation, a major deterrent to the readability of *The Fall of Atlantis*. To recount period customs, the text incorporates distinctive terms:

> *architectural*—peristyle, coliseum, tabularium, hypocaust, chantry, fretwork
> *clothing*—fibulae, toga picta, dalmatica, flamma, sigil, filleting, pectoral
> *cultural*—the greeting salve, sestercius [sic], litter, ides, genius, bellissima, barrow
> *gods*—Bona Dea, Vestal, Isia/Isis, Cybele, Nazarene, Floralia, Dionysos, Deus
> *governmental*—Titus, procurator, Pax Romana, Dominus
> *law*—conscript fathers, aedile, legatus juridicus, curia
> *literary*—codex, esoteric, scroll, cognomen
> *military*—optio, adiutrix, eagles, prefect castrorum, crest
> *musical*—sistrum, strophe, antistrophe
> *religious*—haruspex, agape, pietas, apostasy, avatar, chela, dorje, dyaus, karmic, *Sakti Sidhana*
> *socioeconomic*—eques, freedman, Aventine, Patrician, nadir, coemptio, Cornovii
> *weaponry*—trident, spatha, retarius [sic], Samnite, orichalcum

Parallel terms from Celtic culture and history—murrain, dropsy, tor, Samaine, Don, *mo chridhe* (my heart), Great Wain, spell singer, Giants' Dance, bacaudae, moonblood, Brigantia, byre-woman—set parameters of everyday behavior. A notable example, trews, names the breeches that set Celts apart from toga-clad Romans.

Words of the Times

For authenticity, the author incorporated rural diction in "The Wuzzles" and a medieval trade fair and such terms as *aer* (citadel) Donn, the burned city in *The Heritage of Hastur* (Bradley, 1997, 21, 4, 8, 10). For *The Gratitude of Kings*, she marks the narrative with "warding" (protective), "the morrow," "Yule-tide," and "You are well come" (Bradley, 1975, 2). To enhance the feel of medieval themes and idiom in *The Fall of Atlantis*, she mentions "leman" (lover), the erudite "regalie," plural of "regalia," a "crypt" used as a torture chamber, and Talkannon's directive "Be he your guest" (Bradley, 1983, 201, 23, 4, 49). For Domaris, the mother-to-be, the author equates parturition with "a childing woman," the focus of a doomed kingdom's future race (*Ibid.*, 201). At the conclusion of a reunion between Deoris and Domaris, adopting a motherly role toward her older sister, Deoris holds a handkerchief and commands "Blow" (*Ibid.*, 462). The one-word command disrupts a medieval tone and atmosphere with current vernacular.

In *The Firebrand*, lingual elements enhance the setting, for example, Queen Imandra's self-description as a "grandam" and the use of tar on Trojan fire arrows, a substance more common in medieval Scandinavia than ancient Mediterranean warfare (Bradley, 1987, 319). Unlike the city-bred Trojans, the herder Agelaus speaks a rural dialect marked by non-standard diction, a quaint argot repeated in the conversation of Odysseus, famed seaman and raconteur. Odysseus's demand for a "parley" (negotiation) with Priam and a glimpse of Paris being "cosseted" (spoiled) and packed with cobwebs to stop bleeding cite anachronisms drawn from the Middle Ages (*Ibid.*, 285, 361). At Hector's grasp on the great double-bladed ax, the author declares that he "sprange" to the floor (*Ibid.*, 289). The obsolete spelling of "sprang" enhances the feel of antique writing suited to masculine heroics in a scene pitting the Trojan Hector against Akhilles, the belligerent Akhaian teenager who becomes his nemesis.

The epic wrings humor out of plain-spoken Trojan sentries. While discussing Kassandra's return from Queen Imandra's court at Colchis, they inform her of worsening hostilities with Akhaians. Kassandra's brother Deiphobos snorts that the enemy is untrustworthy: "If one of 'em kisses you, count your teeth, thieving bastards" (*Ibid.*, 353). Marion returns to quaint understatement by speaking of a snake devouring a child as a "misadventure" (error) (*Ibid.*, 358). In a slight to Helen, Andromache observes, "No sooner has she whelped than she is in pup again," an implied comparison of the Spartan queen to a bitch dog (*Ibid.*, 626).

SUITING DEEDS TO TIMES

Marion intensifies period diction in *The Mists of Avalon* with archaic syntax ("Why came you never back?"), concepts (the feudal caste system that empowers the king over his vassals or subjects), and such items as simples or herbal cures for chilblains (chapped skin), hot possets for colds, and pillions, the pillows that prevented saddle sores on females who rode behind male horsemen (Bradley, 1983, 493). Housing formed of wattle or thatch and daub produces a tight construction out of accessible twigs and mud mixed with animal dung. Little girls learn to shape fleece into yarn with a drop spindle. In reference to folklore, Igraine calls her daughter Morgaine a "changeling," a fairy child who replaces a human infant (*Ibid.*, 78). After a lengthy dialogue at Arthur's wedding in standard language, a soldier interrupts in rural brogue, "Na, na, I see what ye mean" (*Ibid.*, 295). On Morgaine's wandering toward Avalon, a torch-bearer describes her as "benighted" (confused) and guides her to the path (*Ibid.*, 403). Lancelet addresses Gareth as "sirrah," a comeuppance to a budding knight (*Ibid.*, 425). Gossip in Britannia labels Morgause a "bawd," an archaic term for "strumpet" (*Ibid.*, 436).

Rural and seaside Lythande episodes incorporate a mix of swearing—chaos and hellfire, forsooth—and technical terms—aura, fetch, doppelgänger—with the antique pronunciations of rural folk. "Somebody Else's Magic" contains wi' (with), ye (you), havena' (have no), o' (of), hisself (himself), and gi'(give) (Bradley, 2013, 39–42, 45). Other stories feature less common archaisms:

an' n'er (and never)	"Fool's Fire," 172
f'instance (for instance)	"North to Northwander," 183–184

grand-dame (grandmother)	"The Footsteps of Retribution," 133
sha' be (shall be)	"Goblin Market," 188
t'Duke'll (the Duke will)	"To Drive the Cold Winter Away," 168
wouldna' (wouldn't have)	"Sea Wrack," 77

To facilitate information-gathering, Lythande mimics the local dialect, a clue to locale that Marion reprises in *Exile's Song*. The horror tale "The Walker Behind," features more models:

dunno (don't know)	hants (haunts)	meself (myself)
nowt (naught)	o'course (of course)	ye've (you have)

("The Walker Behind," 118, 120, 123, 125).

naw (no)	skelpin' ye (scalping you)	willna (won't)
luggin' (carrying)	dunna (don't)	yarn (tease)

(*Exile's Song*, 12, 14, 15, 17)

The local patois continues in "The Wuzzles" and "To Kill the Undead" with a wider variety of provincialisms:

could ha' (could have)	dun'na (don't)
d'ye (do you)	grandfer's (grandfather's)
I dassay (I dare say)	since'n (since then)
spell-candler (spell-maker)	spell-wright (hex-shaper)
thass (that's)	they's (they are)

("The Wuzzles," 140, 142, 143; "To Kill the Undead," 160).

Marion's facility with language introduces "maw" for jaws, "bane-wolf" for predator, "footpad" for street thief, "tapster" for bartender, and "boon," an obsolete synonym for a favor or good deed ("The Secret of the Blue Star," 27, 2, 3, 5). To elucidate the title "The Incompetent Magician," she gives the inept Rastafyre a stutter. In his first meeting with Lythande, the stammering turns to situational humor at his inability to pronounce "imbibed" and the muddling of the term "embaras–ass-assing" (Bradley, 2013, 16). Lythande gracefully relieves his discomfort by calling him "Rastafyre the … incomparable" (*Ibid.*, 17).

With a flair for American slang, Marion permeates *Castle Terror* with the Southwestern lingo "nurse lady" and "canoodling," a humorous term for "fondling" (Bradley, 1965, 9, 16). She incorporates words shortened military style in stories, as with "greenie" for paper money and "prowlies" for patrol cars in "Peace in the Wilderness," "layover" in "The Wind People," and "HQ" in "Bird of Prey" (Bradley, 1956, 57, 64; 1985, 181, 163). In "Hero's Moon," space crewmen swallow Basic Nute (basic nutrition), tend "the board" (control panel), arrive in the Twelve Bug, a shortening of "Surface Individual Transit, Model Twelve-B," and go AWOL (absent without leave), which she repeats in *The Brass Dragon* (*Ibid.*, 258). The text of "Hero's Moon" acquires a macho energy in remarks on the "bogey" (unidentified aircraft) that "came within a few hundred feet of holing their shuttle" (*Ibid.*, 260). Technology increases the need for truncated terms, as with "psych-tech" in "Elbow Room," "IS units" in "The Climbing Wave," and "DeMag" (demagnetization) in *Survey Ship* (*Ibid.*, 332, 50).

See also Glossary.

Sources

Bradley, Marion Zimmer. *The Best of Marion Zimmer Bradley*. Chicago: Academy Chicago, 1985.
_____. *Castle Terror*. New York: Lancer, 1965.

_____. *The Complete Lythande*. San Francisco: Marion Zimmer Bradley Literary Works Trust, 2013.
_____. *The Fall of Atlantis*. Riverdale, NY: Baen Books, 1983.
_____. *The Firebrand*. New York: Simon & Schuster, 1987.
_____. *The Forbidden Tower*. New York: DAW, 1977.
_____. *The Forest House*. New York: Michael Joseph, 1993.
_____. *The Gratitude of Kings*. New York: Wildside, 1997.
_____. "The Hawkmaster's Son," *The Keeper's Price*. New York: DAW, 1980.
_____. *The Mists of Avalon*. New York: Ballantine, 1983.
_____. "Peace in the Wilderness," *Fantastic Universe* 5:6 (July 1956): 55–79.
_____. *Survey Ship*. New York: Ace, 1980.
Nichols, Nichelle. "Influences of 'Star Trek' on Her Writing," *Amani* 15/16 (1976).
Schwartz, Susan. "Women and Science Fiction," *New York Times* (2 May 1982).

Divination

Marion characterizes perusal of distant or future knowledge as a valuable guide for mortals, especially Erminie, who searches her starstone in *The Heirs of Hammerfall* for proof that Alaric is still alive. For *The Spell Sword,* the author depicts Andrew Carr in search of the perfect woman in a fortune-teller's booth. Eilan in *The Forest House,* learns from the seer Merlin her role in the revival of the Pendragon dynasty. Unlike prophecy, a mystic premonition, the diviner's tool is available to the few, particularly people gifted with the Sight and its rituals involving astrology, thunder, flocks of birds, trees, bones, coins, wands, flames or smoke, dice, and cards. Typically, supernatural power can strike unbidden, confusing the thinker with inexplicable mind pictures inspired by god, an anomaly that rattles Magdalen "Magda" Lorne in *The Shattered Chain* and Morgaine in *The Mists of Avalon*. Dramatic examples picture men consulting the specter of Derik, who appears in Ysaba's smoky globe in *The Shadow Matrix*. One model in *Lady of the Trillium* introduces the Oddlings, who water-scry hidden information. The author debunks the prophesying as a "notoriously unreliable method of divination" that works best "if done on an empty stomach" (Bradley, 1995, 5).

The author sets specific forms of divining in ancient times and the Middle Ages amid period details. For *Warrior Woman,* the public procession and adornments of an animal sacrifice reflect a Rome-inspired form of predicting the future from an examination of freshly removed bull entrails. Amid garlands and ribbons, the priest kneels in the bull's blood, "digging inside; he wrenches at something red, holds it up dripping: the animal's heart" (Bradley, 1985, 40). Protagonist Zadieyek/Amber spoils the auspices by vomiting, a touch demystifying humor.

Without gory drama or regurgitation, the mage-ronin Lythande in Marion's story cycle commands charms and spells in varying amounts. Among them, in "Chalice of Tears," the protagonist displays the limited skill of reading the future in Tarot cards, intercessory tools imported from Egypt to Austria, France, Germany, Italy, and Portugal in the late 1300s CE. Her first card pair, the Ace of Cups and the High Priestess, predicts love and wisdom. Next, the Hermit card indicates a period of soul searching. From repeated card selection, the prophetic method attests that "the Guardian of the Grail is a woman," a surprise in an androcentric story of dynasty and dominion (Bradley, 2013, 154).

In *The Fall of Atlantis*, Marion inserts various means of communing with the future by both prophecy and fate projection. The guardian Rajasta's prognostication

concerning the conception and birth of Domaris's son Micail by Micon precedes selection of a birth name suited to a Scorpio, a sun sign governing lives from October
12 to November 22. Rajasta posits that proper upbringing can refine the boy's faults
of competitiveness and a sharp tongue, a useful piece of knowledge for an aristocratic
heir. Closer to the core of the plot, Deoris's trance-like study of a silver bowl of water reveals a villain of the novel and his position as student of the head magician. Such glints
of possible obstacles ahead ready characters for difficult confrontations and threats to
Micail.

PORTALS TO DIVINATION

In *The Firebrand,* Marion draws on Roman history for the methods of diviners
on a par with the *haruspex,* an official interpreter of the viscera of sacrificial sheep
and birds. The examiners select fortuitous days for ritual and the clarification of complex messages from gods. Sarmato, a priestess of the Earth Mother, interprets Hecuba's
nightmare by tossing stones shaped like dice on the floor and assessing the patterns
they form. For Queen Imandra of Colchis, the source of visions in a liquid "pool of ink"
enables her to view her youngest grandchild (Bradley, 1987, 319). During the queen's
labor before the birth of Pearl, Marion directs scrying far from Troy, disclosing to Kassandra the death of Hector and the wrath of Apollo, the god of healing who attacks both
armies with arrows, the Homeric metaphor for epidemic disease.

Out of modesty, Kassandra, who is as skilled at scrying as Haramis in *Lady of the
Trillium,* keeps simple her entrances to the otherworld. She chooses a bowl of water as
a reflective surface for looking at the near-past. The magic allows her to view the births
of three nephews, Andromache and Hector's dead baby boy and Helen and Paris's living twins. Divination also brings more bad news in the form of paralysis in her father
Priam's foot, face, and torso following a stroke. Kassandra correctly deduces that the
weakening of the doughty king will shrivel his might in war and on the throne at a time
when Troy needs leadership.

MENTAL ACUITY

Unlike straightforward prophecy, the Sight in *The Mists of Avalon* takes the form
of clairvoyance, precognition and retrocognition, or telepathy, degrees of psychic or
paranormal foreknowledge. Literature illustrates that such information was once
common to ancient oracles, such as the Pythia of ancient Delphi, Apollo on the holy
island of Delos, and the Roman sibyls, divine counselors who thrived in Etruria, Per-
sia, Libya, and Phrygia. The dreams conveyed by the Merlin of Britain, messenger of
the gods, relieve Igraine of an all-too-human despondency accompanying menstruation and cramps. At age nineteen, she feels trapped in marriage to Duke Gorlois of
Cornwall, an older man, until she surveys reincarnation in an out-of-body vision. The
trance carries her double to Stonehenge to stand in the "Land of Truth" with High
King Uther Pendragon, who calls her "Morgan," a title as well as a name (Bradley, 1983,
58). Differentiating between dreams and the "bodiless limbo" of "wandering between
worlds," she recognizes the reality of a cognizance "where the soul goes when the body
is elsewhere ... not a dream but a memory" (*Ibid.,* 92). Marion corroborates the meta-

physical past of Igraine and Uther through his narration of a similar apparition based on reincarnation.

Igraine's mounting frustration at domestic imprisonment in Tintagel castle forces the queen to seek her own form of divination, calling for the burning of juniper to invoke the divine and the cutting of hazel wands, the wood of wisdom, to summon the Mother Goddess. By strength of will, Igraine crosses "the gulf, against the laws of this world" to warn Uther of a Cornish assault (*Ibid.*, 94). Marion imbeds more prescience in Igraine's delirium, her punishment for violating limits with "forbidden sorcery" (*Ibid.*, 97). Visions of Uther recur at his death in battle at the hand of the Saxon Aesc, who ruled Kent from 488 to 512 CE. In a less ominous atmosphere, Viviane, the Lady of the Lake, experiences a "sending" (*Ibid.*, 194). For extended knowledge of the future, she gazes into the mirror pond and summons a sketchy biography of Arthur, from his fostering with Sir Ectorius in infancy to gathering supporters of his kingship and a death image of Morgaine weeping in the Avalon barge for her fallen brother/monarch. Divination returns to Morgaine's service to the mother goddess during crafting of Arthur's scabbard. For guidance, Morgaine consults a chalice of water from the Holy Well while she shapes doeskin and red velvet for embroidery with magic icons.

In book two, the Sight offers unstable knowledge that startles Morgaine and Viviane like flashes of lightning. For Morgaine, the flames that encircle Kevin Harper disclose an unthinkable death entrapped in an oak tree. The magic pool returns to use, by which Viviane tests the Sight in thirteen-year-old Niniane, who faints from the effort of concentrating her will to summon the Otherworld. The resolution requires determined action from Morgaine, who looks into brown water in a forest pool for a harbinger. A surge of foreknowledge that overcomes her consciousness exposes Accolon's future kingship, as promised by the Horned One, the primary divinity of Wicca. Because Druidic powers have atrophied in Viviane, she struggles to interpret cryptic images of Morgaine lying alongside the "grey king" and the priestess Raven lifting a cauldron, part of Avalon's regalia (*Ibid.*, 351). The effort precedes selection of a new Lady of Avalon, who guides young novices in the control of precognition.

See also Dreams; Mother Goddess; Prophecy.

Sources

Bradley, Marion Zimmer. *The Complete Lythande.* San Francisco: Marion Zimmer Bradley Literary Works Trust, 2013.
_____. *The Fall of Atlantis.* Riverdale, NY: Baen Books, 1983.
_____. *The Firebrand.* New York: Simon & Schuster, 1987.
_____. *The Forest House.* New York: Michael Joseph, 1993.
_____. *Lady of the Trillium.* New York: Bantam Spectra, 1995.
_____. *The Mists of Avalon.* New York: Ballantine, 1983.
_____. *Warrior Woman.* New York: DAW, 1985.
Evans, Richard, ed. *Prophets and Profits: Ancient Divination and Its Reception.* New York: Routledge, 2017.
Ramstedt, Martin. "Metaphor or Invocation? The Convergence Between Modern Paganism and Fantasy Fiction," *Journal of Ritual Studies* 1:1/5 (2007): 1–15.

Dreams

In fealty to the belief that "all dreams were messages from the Gods," Marion gave free play to her imaginings (Bradley, 1987, 213). The fantasy splurge haunts Lew

Alton with phantasms of a failed rebellion in *Sharra's Exile;* a vision of clairaudience or forehearing in *Traitor's Sun* alerts Herm Aldaran to treachery with enough force to cause "heart pounding and sweat streaming down his chest" (Bradley, 1999, 1). Night thoughts goad Jeff Kerwin, protagonist of *The Bloody Sun,* to trace his heritage through "the darkly beautiful world you had seen, that you still saw, sometimes, in your dreams" (Bradley, 1964, 8). More positive night apparitions inform Erminie that her missing son Conn in *The Heirs of Hammerfell* still lives in the mountains, where Conn shares visions of his twin Alastair (Bradley, 1963, 89). Paranormal images allow the fictional Max to levitate in "Phoenix." At the thought of occult powers, Max retreats from levitation: "It's too much for me! I'm not God, I don't want it, I'm too small for it" (*Ibid.*, 94). Bradley's multifaceted canon revisits other ancient concepts of night specters, their cause and significance, such as the hospital mirages that disrupt patient sleep in *The Brass Dragon,* a sore throat that causes nightmares about animals attacking the neck in *Hunters of the Red Moon,* Andy's retrogression to homesickness on Mars in "Measureless to Man," and Diana's surreal escapism into beauty in "The Day of the Butterflies."

The author emphasizes mind fancies at harrowing times, particularly for Zadieyek of Gyre, the slave in *Warrior Woman* who suffers double torment in her nightmares from abuse and rape, and for Jaelle n'ha Melora during delirium in *The Shattered Chain* from knife wounds to cheek and collarbone. Jaelle acknowledges, "It was frightful nonsense, but I have rarely been so glad to wake up" (Bradley, 1976, 173). After marriage to Peter Haldane, a Terran bureaucrat at the spaceport in *Thendara House,* Jaelle continues to experience flashbacks to the birth pangs of Melora, her mother, and to her cousin Kyril's attempts at raping Jaelle in childhood. The terrifying visions also grip Magdalen "Magda" Lorne, who relives hand-to-hand combat that appears to kill Peter Haldane. In the Gothic incense tale "The Wind People," Dr. Helen Murray, a 24-year-old scientist, accounts for her repeated dream of a sexual encounter on the green planet as "some undiagnosed conflict in her" (Bradley, 1985, 189). When her unplanned son Robin reaches age five, Helen pronounces the carnal dream a hallucination or rationalization. The dream morphs into torment when Robin reaches his teens and intimidates his mother by appearing in the form of a shadow man.

VISIONS OF LONGING

Throughout her canon, the author allies dreams with yearnings and ambitions. The struggle of Andrew Carr in *The Spell Sword* in search for the perfect female results in "a fever-dream, a ghost, a symbol of his own loneliness" of a woman "somewhere, somehow … out there waiting" (Bradley, 2002, 5). The psychic outbreaks mask his homosexual tendencies, which the author suggests with the sucking of icicles. For the mother priestess Caillean in *The Forest House,* a mental union with female victims of the Roman invasion on the holy island of Mona precipitates dreams of grabbing and tearing robes and the battery of her body by legionaries bold enough to commit sacrilege. Late in her life, "in my dreams ancient voices still cry out for revenge," a psychological depiction of unfinished business calling for requital (Bradley, 1993, 2).

Marion compounds the importance of dreams with scrying and trances in *The Forest House,* one in which the high priestess foresees the fall of Rome. Before Red Rian and the Scotti raid and burn Eilan's homestead, Caillean anticipates the cataclysm in a mirage, a form of communication with the future. During Eilan's dreams of Gaius Macellius, she views his vengeful sword practice as retribution for Eilan and her dead mother, the high priestess Rheis, and little sister Senara, murdered by the Scotti. The author applies dream scenarios to a long separation of lovers and a stoking of strong emotions, the result of Gaius's reveries of Eilan and her unborn baby before the Battle of Mons Graupius at Lughnasad on August 1, 83 CE. The couple's next meeting certifies a spiritual tryst at night through dreams. The narrative carries the love match to a tragic conclusion, but sends Caillean away from Vernemeton to Afallon, a women's hermitage on an island in Summer Country (the dry lake bed of Ynis Witrin in Somerset), a preview of the setting of *The Mists of Avalon*.

Dark Shades

Marion depicts dreamscapes as disorienting. After a venture into black magic in *The Fall of Atlantis*, Deoris struggles to maintain a hold on reality. She imagines a guided tour of icy caverns and the resultant burns requiring sedation. In delirium, she struggles to know "where reality ended and dreams began" (Bradley, 1983, 329). In her older sister Domaris's dying moments, Deoris envisions a reunion with Micon, her dead husband, who returns healthy and unharmed. Overlapping the hallucination with an afterlife, Domaris murmurs, "Now—it is beginning again" (*Ibid.,* 497). The ambiguity dominates preceding action, leaving readers to surmise what is real and what is illusory.

The novelist connects prophetic vagaries in *The Firebrand* with pain in the head and eyes, notably, the harm done to the priestess Kassandra during a vision of battling gods. The connection between cranial pain and otherworldly tidings got its start in scenes of Hermes, the winged messenger, pulling the dreamer's hair. Marion's scenario implies that knowledge revealed by angry gods foretokens human suffering, which engulfs and overwhelms Troy from a siege by Greeks that occurred around 1200 BCE. Queen Hecuba's nightmare of fire validates millennia of superstition about night specters and their meaning. The king himself fears that Hecuba's disturbing sleep visitation could be the work of an enemy deity or a beneficent god alerting her to disaster. To avert destruction from Troy, the royal couple ponder exposing son Paris in the wild, a fate authorities considered for outcast baby Demira, the child of an insane mother in *The Fall of Atlantis*.

More apparitions and trances roil the serenity of the Trojan kingdom. Paris's twin sister Kassandra has more frequent visions and dreams, which trouble the queen. Charging the maiden's sexual awakening with evoking mental turmoil, Hecuba deduces that the source of anguish is the priestess's virginity and lack of a husband. Kassandra privately rebukes her mother for stating a gendered cliché and for asserting that marital sex is "the remedy for all things that are wrong with women," a misogynistic bias still revered into the twentieth century (*Ibid.,* 258). Dream states liberate Kassandra from earthly time, body, and memory into a mystic crevice between reality and timelessness. When she shapeshifts into a specter in "the Land Beyond Death," her drift to the tents of Agamemnon and Akhilles authenticates the prophecies pent up in her psyche (*Ibid.,* 489).

Arthurian Dreams

In Marion's Arthuriana, dreams interlace visions, trance states, out-of-body experiences, and divination, indicating the impalpability of a great shift in the destiny of Britannia and the showdown of religions after Christianity destabilizes Druidism and the worship of the Mother Goddess. For Morgaine, at the threshold of empowerment over Avalon, a startling auditory clangor of alarms and church bells recalls childhood fears of Saxon raiders at Tintagel. A vision of a Christian altar, a deceased knight, and weapons foretells the rise of female empowerment at a time when male protection fails. Morgaine sees herself armed and recognizes Excalibur, the name of the blade forged by elf smiths from a meteorite. Etymologists trace the French name to a Welsh term for "solid lightning" ("Excalibur"). Marion intensifies the rare provenance by referring to Arthur's hair as "silver-gilt," a bimetallic emblem of a doubly royal conception and birth (Bradley, 1983, 200).

The author uses nightscapes as stages on which to dramatize mental vexation. For Gwenhwyfar, Arthur's snake tattoos on the wrists seem to writhe before her, aggravating her distaste at the seer Kevin's Druid symbolism and amplifying a longing to proselytize the entire army. The text pictures the gyrations of the drop spindle as the cause of Morgaine's impromptu vagaries. A year apart, one of two trances portrays the mercy killing of Cai's injured horse. The second transfixion envisions blood coating the hearth during war between Arthur's cavalry and Saxon foot soldiers. The aftereffects cause Morgaine "little lights … crawling before her eyes, pale shining worms of color," a Gothic glimpse of mortality (*Ibid.*, 306).

Marion depicts Morgaine's restlessness in contrasting milieus. After years of separation, she reunites with grandmother Viviane in a sylvan reverie. A subsequent sojourn in fairy country bemuses Morgaine with a festal hall filled with affable hosts, who treat her to food, drink, music and dance, and bedding by a gentle lover. Night phantasms continue to unsettle the priestess, notably, the image of a blond Lady of the Lake on her barge. Morgaine recoils from an unexpected substitution—a crucifix at the waist of the priestess rather than the small knife worn by an inmate of Avalon.

Marion blurs the boundary between fantasy and vision, imagination and apotheosis. In the final action, Morgaine escapes phantasms caused by depression and fasting. Her health restored, she returns to the lake in a fog of semi-consciousness, a partial explanation of "mists" in the novel's title. In a nightmare, the priestess Raven relives the loss of Excalibur. Over a series of years, news of Camelot's downfall arrives like legends that are well worn by time and verbal retellings, the author's explanation of variations in Arthuriana.

See also Divination.

Sources

Bradley, Marion Zimmer. *The Best of Marion Zimmer Bradley*. Chicago: Academy Chicago, 1985.
_____. *The Bloody Sun*. New York: Ace, 1964.
_____. *The Fall of Atlantis*. Riverdale, NY: Baen Books, 1983.
_____. *The Firebrand*. New York: Simon & Schuster, 1987.
_____. *The Forbidden Circle*. New York: DAW, 2002.
_____. *The Forest House*. New York: Michael Joseph, 1993.
_____. *The Mists of Avalon*. New York: Ballantine, 1983.

_____. "Phoenix," *Amazing Stories* 37:2 (February 1963): 88–98.
_____. *Sharra's Exile.* New York: DAW, 1981.
_____. *The Shattered Chain.* New York: DAW, 1976.
_____. *Traitor's Sun.* New York: DAW, 1999.
"Excalibur," http://www.britannia.com/history/arthur/excalibur.html.
Fuog, Karen E.C. "Imprisoned in the Phallic Oak: Marion Zimmer Bradley and Merlin's Seductress," *Quondam et Futurus* 1:1 (Spring, 1991): 73–88.
Paxson, Diana L. "Marion Zimmer Bradley and *The Mists of Avalon*," *Arthuriana* 9:1 (Spring 1999): 110–126.
Thompson, Raymond H. "Darkness Over Camelot: Enemies of the Arthurian Dream" in *New Directions in Arthurian Studies.* Cambridge, England: D.S. Brewer, 2002.

Exile's Song

The first of a trilogy encompassing *The Shadow Matrix* and *Traitor's Sun,* Marion's Darkover fantasy *Exile's Song* succeeded in French as *La Chanson de L'Exil,* a fantasy tale embedded with a "phalanx of ghosts" (Bradley, 1996, 35). Under a title plucked from the second verse of Robert Burns's Scots poem "Auld Lang Syne," the plot recasts a feminist theme, that of the resolute scholarly female who defies regimentation. At age 25, Margaret/Marguerida "Marja" Alton sets her own agenda. The story honors the author's prize protagonist, Lew Alton, by depicting his grown daughter, a talented folk music archivist who had entered a university at age sixteen.

The author reprises familiar territory in the quandaries of a lone woman who attempts to be independent in a feudal androcentric milieu dominated by father-to-son craft guilds and ruled by Regis Hastur and Uncle Gabriel Lanart Alton.

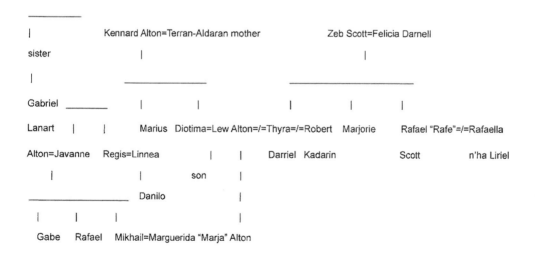

Sense impressions remind Margaret that she inherited from Lew, a senator of the Terran Federation, an allergy causing nausea and headache from re-entry drugs and disgusting smells. On a space journey from a year-long post at Relegan to Darkover with her mentor, guitarist Ivor Davidson, she receives the unexpected designation "vai domna" (highly revered noble), an honorific also applied to Jeff Kerwin in *The Bloody Sun* (*Ibid.,* 20). As a song catcher in the Kilghard Hills, Margaret retreats into her profession while avoiding duties to her aristocratic heritage and suppressing the emergence of psychic powers.

Amid a "conspiracy of silence" about the Read Orphanage for the Children of Spacemen at Thendara, a setting of *The Sword of Aldones*, the novel characterizes Margaret serving the distant Cottman IV as musicologist and mediator of controversy. Although she belongs to the lost colony's intelligentsia as heir to the Alton Domain, she has little regard for the "Alton Curse"—laran intrusions of alien voices in her head (*Ibid.*, 40). She prefers to telepath common folk songs on *ryll* and *fiol*, even violent tunes like "The Outlaw," which she appears to remember from the distant past. In conflict with herself and her stiff-necked father about the meaning of memories that fill visions and fantasies, she learns from Regis Hastur and a maternal uncle, Captain Rafe Scott, some details of her lineage and the Sharra Rebellion (*Ibid.*, 96). The telling serves the reader as a suspenseful exposition of plot and characters.

Marion details the growth of mounting self-determination in Marja as a form of late adolescent rebellion against the previous generation and their concealment of her heritage. Inquiry leaves her "frustrated at every turn, trying to get information on Cottman IV," which she left around age five after retrieval from the orphanage (*Ibid.*, 9). At entry into womanhood, she faces the perennial menace of arranged marriage. In a salute to the addition to the Darkover saga, reviewer William Marden of the Fort Lauderdale *Sun Sentinel* described the series as "perhaps the most successful blend of science fiction, fantasy, and the old-fashioned pulp 'sense of wonder' stories" (Marden, 1996, F10). Of the memorable female protagonist in *Exile's Song*, book critic Pat Wicks of the *San Bernardino Sun* declared, "Her character demands to be continued," a wish that comes true in *Traitor's Sun* (Wicks, 1996, E10).

See also Healing and Death; Violence.

Sources

Bradley, Marion Zimmer. *Exile's Song*. New York: DAW, 1996.
Marden, William. "The Darkover Series Out of Exile; Swords; Angels," (Fort Lauderdale, FL) *Sun Sentinel* (15 September 1996): F10.
Wicks, Pat. "Novel Focuses on Telepathic Woman," *San Bernardino Sun* (6 October 1996): E10.

Exotic Beings

Marion applies considerable skill at metaphor and characterization to picture human protagonists in conflict with the paranormal beings—the specter in *Ghostlight*, the evil creature in "The Malice of the Demon," and banshee birds and monkey-faced trailmen in *Star of Danger*. The classification of exotic beings results in the statement in "Death between the Stars" of harsh laws: "Few rules are stricter than the one dividing human from nonhuman" (Bradley, 1956, 70). For the story "Treason of the Blood," she draws on Bram Stoker's *Dracula* with the investigation of Cassilda's mysterious death. To the Countess Teresa, Father Milo amasses Hollywoodized proof of Count Angelo Fioresi's vampirism: the smell of grave clothes, musky coffin, a flying bat, and marks on the victims' throats, all evidence of inhuman perversity.

In the same vein as Arthur Miller's reprise of the Salem witch trials in *The Crucible*, Milo credits vicious beings to Satan—"the devil's work, done by one in league with that same devil" (Bradley, 2015, 8). Threats to simple villagers lead to classic melodrama and the decree "The creature must die" (*Ibid.*). In the opening scene of *The Planet Savers,* Dr. Jay Allison proposed genocide of Trailmen to save Cottman IV from another pandemic of 48-year-fever. Witchery in *Black Trillium* calls for detailed torments: "Lash the witch to the sword, and into the bog with her.… I hold up her severed head" (Bradley, 1990, 268). In historic episodes, "They burnt a beer-witch at the stake" for turning the brew sour (*Ibid.,* 54). In dire episodes of *The Spell Sword,* in which invisible catmen carry Callista away, her kinsman Damon Ridenow regrets that "we've made the bad mistake of underestimating them" (Bradley, 1974, 49).

A Rogues' Gallery

Not all of Marion's phantasms bear Gothic horror and death, particularly Aratak, that proto-saurian tracker aiding Dane and Rianna in *The Survivors,* the gentle salamanders that function in flames in *The Gratitude of Kings,* Rory's riding-chervine and the rabbithorn that feeds the hawk in *Hawkmistress!,* and Titania and the frolicking fairies in "Well Met by Moonlight." The list of exotic beings ranges through the author's canon with species suited to the narrative:

Beast	Title	Characteristics
Alnath	*The Gratitude of Kings*	harmless miniature pet dragon
Aratak	*The Survivors; Hunters of the Red Moon*	a gigantic philosophical lizard-man
bane-wolf	"The Children of Cats"; "To Drive the Cold Winter Away"	a lone mammal that attacks humans in the dark
banshee	*The Shattered Chain; Star of Danger; Darkover Landfall*	a shrieking miscreant bird silenced by a slit throat
bogey	"Hero's Moon"	unidentified boulder threatening a space ship
cat-hag/catman	*The Spell Sword; Thendara House; The Shattered Chain; The Door through Space; The Forbidden Tower*	dangerous human-sized nocturnal felines capable of invisibility and telepathy and killing with their claw-swords throughout the Kilghard Hills
chak	*The Door Through Space*	a golden-eyed, tailed humanoid, either normal or dwarf size, with velvety paws and muzzle that expresses its stupidity in grunts or gibbers at the sight of blood
changeling	*The Mists of Avalon;* "Centaurus Changeling"	a fairy child who replaces a human baby
chervine	*Hawkmistress!; The Heirs of Hammerfell; City of Sorcery; Rediscovery*	a saddle or pack animal like a reindeer suitable for mountain climbing and production of milk
chieri	*Darkover Landfall; The World Wreckers; Star of Danger*	a declining race of telepathic elfin humanoids who alter their gender at will
Cliff-Climber	*Hunters of the Red Moon*	a guard of the Mekhars, a cat-person with clawed hands

Beast	Title	Characteristics
cralmac	"Everything But Freedom"; *The Shattered Chain*; *Thendara House*	a leonine mammal created from altered human DNA who ride camel-shaped *oudhraki*
delfin	*The Shadow Matrix*	a leaping sea mammal similar to a dolphin
demon	"The Malice of the Demon"; *The Mists of Avalon*	a fiend that transforms a queen into an infant; an evil being that wilts at the sign of the cross
Dorilys	*Stormqueen!*; *Exile's Song*; *The Shadow Matrix*	a princess of Aldaran and mystic wielder of lightning
dragon	*The Mists of Avalon*; "The Brass Dragon"; *The Forbidden Tower*; *The Gratitude of Kings*; *The Forest House*; *The Firebrand*; "The Wandering Lute"	the horse-headed quarry of Pellinore that eats a servant; the cataclysmic power that destroys a tower
fairies/faeries	"Well Met by Moonlight"; *The Mists of Avalon*	a circle of harmless dancers delighting Titania
forge-folk	*The Winds of Darkover*; *The Bloody Sun*	half-human metalworkers and worshippers of Sharra who possess religious matrices
geek	"Death Between the Stars"	a life form exploited in outer space by humans
giants	*The Mists of Avalon*	beings forced into a permanent circle of stones
Kamellin	"Measureless to Man"	elderly Martian whose mind inhabits a chimpanzee body
kentaurs	*The Firebrand*	wild, hairy men who herd horses
kyorebni	*City of Sorcery*; *The Shattered Chain*; *Hawkmistress!*	a raptor that pecks eyes and flesh like a vulture
kyrri	*The Planet Savers*; *Star of Danger*; *The Bloody Sun*; *The Sword of Aldones*	humanoid simians that wield a laser touch and work as servants
oddlings	*The Black Trillium*	aborigines living in bogs, mountains, or rainforests
oudhraki	*Thendara House*; *The White Knight Cookbook*	a beast of burden like a camel that provides meat for soup
Pharigs	"The Stars Are Waiting"	imaginary attackers of earth
predator birds	*The Ages of Chaos*	despoilers of hanged corpses
prowlies	"Peace in the Wilderness"	patrol cars enforcing oppressive laws
rabbithorn	*Traitor's Sun*, *Darkover Landfall*, *The Forbidden Tower*	a small, edible, wool-bearing forest animal similar to a hare
Rastafyre	"The Children of Cats"	a talking shrouded corpse
Roygan	"The Incompetent Magician"	a villain whose ragged teeth bear metal coverings
sand-mice	"Measureless to Man"	harmless six-legged animals that make yeep-yeep sounds
seal woman	"The Wild One"	a fantasy ocean creature who loved a human man
sea monsters	"Sea Wrack"	an unidentified peril that wrecks ships

Beast	Title	Characteristics
Sharra	*The Heritage of Hastur; Sharra's Exile; Traitor's Sun; The Shadow Matrix; The Alton Gift; The Door Through Space*	a pseudo-human female fire demon called a matrix
snake	*The Firebrand*	Queen Imandra's religious totem in Colchis
stalker	"The Walker Behind"	an unseen phantom that terrifies travelers
Theradin	"Death Between the Stars"	an alien who speaks a Samarran dialect
toys	"Bird of Prey"	evil inventions that threaten humans
Trailmen/women	*The Planet Savers; Star of Danger*	lurking arboreal beings that carry disease and harm travelers
vampire	"To Kill the Undead"; "Treason of the Blood"	Count Angelo Fioresi takes the form of a vampire, a corpse that lives on human blood
were-dragon	*The Gratitude of Kings;* "North to Northwander"; "The Wandering Lute"	a shapeshifter under the name Lady Beauty
werewolf	"To Kill the Undead"; "In the Rift"; *Gravelight*	a roaming vampire that stalks by night and tears out throats
whispers	"The Wind People"	sources of threats on the Green Planet
witch	*Witch Hill; The Shadow Matrix; Heartlight; The Inheritor; The Mists of Avalon; Gravelight; Witchlight; Dark Satanic; Black Trillium*	a sorcerer posing as a beloved aunt
wolf	"The Wild One"; *The Mists of Avalon*	lycanthropy that turns a woman into a wolf
wraith	*The Fall of Atlantis;* "The Secret of the Blue Star"	a haggard, shadowy phantasm of Dark Powers
Wuzzles	"The Wuzzles"	small destructive animals the size of barn mice
ya-men	*Two to Conquer; The Winds of Darkover*	avian mountain species

In the opening scenario of *The Forbidden Tower*, Damon Ridenow, a triumphant soldier, celebrates "a land cleansed … the evil influence of the catmen" and the annihilation of the Great Cat in the Corresanti caves, which enlivens *The Spell Sword* (Bradley, 1977, 5). Like the "loup-garou" (werewolf) and berserker hunts in Medieval German and Old Norse fairy tales, his campaign leaves villagers free to travel the roads again. A masterly finale concludes on a fire-breathing dragon, "golden-scaled, golden-clawed, towering to the sky," the author's version of the mythic phoenix, which dates to ancient Egyptian and Greek lore and to the Russo-Slavic firebird (*Ibid.*, 357).

Terrors Await

To invite the shivers of readers, Marion, in the style of author H.P. Lovecraft, magnifies bestial terrors with sense impressions of the paranormal—Max's levitation in "Phoenix," occult secrets of witchcraft in *Dark Satanic*, disembodied footsteps in "The Walker Behind," unidentified villains of the deep in "Sea Wrack," and the talking corpse in "The Children of Cats." For effect, she adds the Man with Crossed Hands to *The Fall of Atlantis* and lurid horsemen and the lair of a dead snake to *The Firebrand*. Gothic details produce tropes of haunting in *Castle Terror*, murky bundles in a thief's cache in "To Drive the Cold Winter Away," Mike's out-of-body experiences in *Falcons of Narabedla*, Riveda's raving in chains in *The Fall of Atlantis*, and Lythande's shapeshifting into a loping hound in "Bitch." Natural threats take the form of malodorous fens and miasmas in "Here They Be Dragons," a dancing bear in *The Forest House*, and engulfing sandstorms and a doomed Martian race in "Measureless to Man," an impetus to metempsychosis and body-sharing by two intelligences. In a critique of the author's monstrosities, Irish critic Linda Leith characterized the "routing of the Catmen from the Kilghard Hills" in *The Spell Sword* as one of Marion's weakest fictions (Leith, 1980, 29). Her statement substantiates analyses that credit the author with mastery of character rather than the paranormal.

Looming in the distance in Marion's Lythande series and Darkover episodes lie the ultimate "one Great Strife," an apocalypse threatening to engulf humankind (Bradley, 2013, 23). The author stated in essays a pragmatic objective—to comment on modern fears of earthly collapse through representative terrors. Just as the lethal fever in *The Planet Savers* embodies the global threats of Ebola, Marburg fever, and epizootic Asian viruses, bestial trauma resets the classics—Grendel, medieval bestiaries, the Golem of Jewish folklore, Frankenstein's monster, the Ojibwa Windigo, and the hags of Jacob Grimm's *Deutsche Mythologie* (German mythology). Marion depicts a female slave market and alludes to terrorism, acid rain, massive blobs of pollutants floating in the Pacific Ocean, and the unknown miscreant that researcher Faye J. Ringel describes as "lurking behind the cells in petri dishes … animal and human in unholy combination: The Beast…" (Ringel, 1989, 64)

See also Darkover; Lythande; Reproduction.

Sources

Bradley, Marion Zimmer. *Black Trillium*. New York: Doubleday, 1990.
_____. *The Complete Lythande*. San Francisco: Marion Zimmer Bradley Literary Works Trust, 2013.
_____. "Death Between the Stars," *Fantastic Universe* 5:2 (March 1956): 70–83.
_____. *The Forbidden Tower*. New York: DAW, 1977.
_____. *Marion Zimmer Bradley Super Pack*. New York: Simon & Schuster, 2015.
_____. *The Spell Sword*. New York: DAW, 1974.
Leith, Linda. "Marion Zimmer Bradley and Darkover," *Science Fiction Studies* 7 (1980): 28–35.
Ringel, Faye J. "Genetic Experimentation: Mad Scientists and the Beast," *Journal of the Fantastic in the Arts* 2:1 (1989): 64–75.

The Fall of Atlantis

Marion based *The Fall of Atlantis* on the principle that "the Darkness eats ever at the Light," an appropriate motto for Ancient Land, the archaic setting that resembles the threat to monarchy in "The Ballad of Hastur and Cassilda" (Bradley, 1983, 184). To accommodate the theme of good and evil, she originally entitled the two-part manuscript *Web of Light* and *Web of Darkness*. A later reflection on sin declares, "Evil plants evil, and reaps and harvests a hundredfold, and sows evil yet again," a projection of eternal battle with and survival of dark forces that Jews study in Kabbalah (*Ibid.*, 209).

She developed concepts in the historical novel that later became literary strengths, including the layered castes of servant, fisherman, scribe, acolyte, and guardian, an early medieval social structure also prevalent in *The Gratitude of Kings,* Lythande stories, and the Darkover series.

In addition to such archaic language as *avatar* (earthly form of a god) *rune* (letter of a mystic alphabet), *chela* (apostle), and *sigil* (magic symbol), the author inserts her own arcana: *ultar* (kindling), *shaing* (flowers), *kiha* (greetings), and *saji* (apostles), who enter service to the Grey Temple priests as prepubescent students of passion and desire. For one-fourth of the postulants, training requires crossing the Black Threshold and ends in "convulsive madness which soon lapsed into drooling, staring idiocy," the price exacted for venturing too far into dark powers (*Ibid.,* 300). The peril to female pariahs and their unborn children runs counter to the training and philosophy of protagonist Deoris, who violates caste precepts by applying midwifery skills from Caratra's Temple to a parturient *saji* in the Grey Temple. Marion's extensive survey of social strictures regarding birthing mocks the current status of pregnancy in much of the world among the homeless, addicted, criminal, and insane.

NARRATIVE CONSTRUCTION

Civic organization overshadows interpersonal relations, conferring an air of regimentation. In a priestly enclave, to protect the dominion of light (goodness) over dark (evil), members have distinct ranks, assignments, and obligations, notably, to guard secrets. The metonymy of light and dark magnifies the work of the virtuous to suppress evil and inhumanity, such as the expulsion of the orphan Demira from ritual at the Grey Temple and torture by Black-robes that blinds and cripples Micon and emasculates Larmin. Emphasis on stilted, antique language and overwritten phrasing masks facts, most emphatically in Micon's revelation of his capture by the Black-robes and on the conception of the child Eilantha. Another flaw in the narrative, the pacing of group actions piles on more characters without developing their uniqueness, as with the domain of the priestess Maleina, the rule of Mother Ysouda over the shrine of the goddess Caratra, and the power of the Grey-robes to quell epidemic marsh fever.

To build suspense, Marion showcases oaths, covert languages, and gauzy garments on illusory phantoms "like dreams within a dream" (*Ibid.,* 193). The author's orchestration of mirage veils Deoris's response to the Man with Crossed Hands, a creepy touch of the occult. For atmosphere, the author conjures conical stone houses like those in the Orkney Islands and Puglia, Italy, and populates them with grotesque retardates, the phantasms of Dark Powers. She forestalls the confrontation between Micon and his heretic brother Reio-ta, an exchange suggesting the denial of Jesus by the apostle Simon Peter in John 18:13–27. The fallen brother takes on a mythic connotation of the "bent wraith," a shadow figure "haggard, haunted" lurking in the Grey Temple like a malevolent apparition rather than flesh-and-blood man (*Ibid.,* 191).

SEX AND POWER

By "contrasting power over others with inner power, or power over one's self," the novel accords female biology an added strength against the dominion of evil, a struggle illustrated by Morgaine's coming to knowledge in *The Mists of Avalon* and by the victories of the female gladiator in *Warrior Woman* (Crosby, 2000, 43). At a climactic conjury in the Grey Temple, Marion places Deoris under the hedonistic Reio-ta's control, a hint of sexual assault contravened by the magician Riveda. The smashing of a crystal sphere and resultant flash of Fire-spirit maims Riveda's hands and burns Deoris's torso in punishment for "[invoking] a great power" (Bradley, 1983, 328). Defiance enlivens the falling action, causing "a devil's rite conducted by a maniac," an ambiguous charge the author directs at either Riveda or the magician Nadastor for sacrificing the drugged child Larmin's manhood to the Dark God (*Ibid.*, 191). Without clear definition, Marion depicts the blasphemous ceremonies as a summons to the Black Star, a nebulous concept unexplored in the narrative.

The revelation of incest and the emasculation of the small boy arrive late in the novel and trigger Deoris's charges of "sorcery, distortion—black magic" against Riveda, her Svengalian lover and manipulator (*Ibid.*, 353). In the rage of Domaris, the scene bristles with her curse on the magician, whom the Guardians chain in the dungeon before poisoning him. At a crucial point in the resolution, Deoris questions the central issue: "Is there no right beyond power" (*Ibid.*, 402). A twist in the final judgment summons a euphemism—"in the days of her impurity"—a prim means of discussing menstruation and the charting of fertility and conception similar to the mystic astrology of "moonblood," "bloodsign," "courses," and "moon-times" in *The Forest House* (Bradley, 1983, 391; 1993, 4, 5, 191, 192).

To a theatrical degree, Marion permeates the text with Victorian sensibilities—cringing, fainting, collapsing, tears, dying words, and obeying patriarchal commands and all-male court judges. Rajasta's prediction of an earthquake and the destruction of both Atlantis and the Ancient Land anticipate the author's use of prognostication in *The Firebrand* to account for the collapse of Troy and Aeneas's founding of Alba Longa, the future site of Rome. Lacking specificity of crimes, broken laws, and past sins, the narrative relies too heavily on implication and emotion to clarify the cause of a civilization's ruin. The theme returns in *The Forest House* in allusions to Atlantis as the source of Druidism based on "secrets of the Wise One who had come over the sea" (*Ibid.*, 176). As a paean to virtue and obedience over sin and heresy, the novel attempts too much with too little material and thus remained unsold for a time.

See also Royal House of Atlantis.

Sources

Bradley, Marion Zimmer. *The Fall of Atlantis*. Riverdale, NY: Baen Books, 1983.
_____. *The Forest House*. New York: Michael Joseph, 1993.
Crosby, Janice C. *Cauldron of Changes: Feminist Spirituality in Fantastic Fiction*. Jefferson, NC: McFarland, 2000.
Paxson, Diana L. "Marion Zimmer Bradley and *The Mists of Avalon*," *Arthuriana* 9:1 (Spring 1999): 110–126.
Trowbridge, Serena: "Review: *The Fall of Atlantis*," http://trashotron.com/agony/reviews/2003/bradley-fall_of_atlantis.htm.

Female Persona

Marion retreated from an era of gung-ho feminism by balancing temperaments and talents at normal levels, the primary accomplishment of the priestesses Kassandra and Eilan, the Welsh rebel Brigitta, the Amazon Kindra, the emergency nurse Carlina "Carly" di Asturien, and the wandering lute player-mercenary Lythande, a series heroine. For the trilogy *Exile's Sun, The Shadow Matrix,* and *Traitor's Sun,* the author credits Marguerida Alton with wisdom and artful tastes: "She had founded a small printing house and several schools for the children of tradesmen and crafts people … and encouraged the preservation of the fine musical tradition of Darkover" by building a performance hall (Bradley, 1999, 13). In the opinion of comic and film critic Jenna Busch, Marion specialized in "powerful women who slay their own dragons, run warrior schools or travel the lands, selling their swords," for example (Busch, 2018):

Woman	Title	Role
Brigitta	*The Forest House*	Demetan fomenter of rebellion against Rome
Bruna	"The Legend of Lady Bruna"	bastion of courage, accomplishment, gallantry
Caillean	*The Forest House*	mentor, consoler, defier of Druid power
Camilla del Rey	*Darkover Landfall*	a tough, competent galactic geographer
Camilla n'ha Kyria	"Bonds of Sisterhood"	warrior who befriends fighter Rafaella n'ha Doria
Carlina di Asturien	*Two to Conquer*	empathetic survivor, devotee of the goddess Avarra
Cassiana	"Centaurus Changeling"	independent, defiant, imaginative
Cendri	*The Ruins of Isis*	astute, flexible heroine centered on marriage
Desideria	*The Winds of Darkover*	a daring sister of a handicapped lord
Domaris	*The Fall of Atlantis*	loving sister, acolyte, prophet, wife, mother
Ede	"The Dance at the Gym"	young pilot of a flyer capable of downing the enemy
Eilan	*The Forest House*	coordinator of religious devotion and earthly passion
Fiora	*Warrior Woman*	reliable tower keeper, guardian, loyalist
Floria	*The Heirs of Hammerfell*	cheery, sensible girl who welcomes outsiders
Haramis	*Lady of the Trillium*	determined mentor, benefactor
Helen	*The Firebrand*	a beauty, mother, friend-maker, and wife of Paris
Igraine	*The Mists of Avalon*	queen, wife, mother, savant, lover
Kassandra	*The Firebrand*	princess, priestess, warrior, foster mother
Kate Alderan	*Traitor's Sun*	independent native of Renney who treasures art
Kindra n'ha Mhari	"To Keep the Oath"; *The Shattered Chain Thendara House*	warrior, leader, protector of the weak
Kyla Raineach	*The Planet Savers*	tough, sturdy, independent pioneer
Lauria	*Thendara House*	composed, mannerly housemother
Leonie Hastur	*The Forbidden Tower; The Skill Sword; Rediscovery*	determined realist, career woman, vow keeper

Woman	Title	Role
Lythande	*The Gratitude of Kings;* "Sea Wrack," "The Walker Behind," "The Footsteps of Retribution," "The Secret of the Blue Star," "Chalice of Tears," "Somebody Else's Magic," "Fools' Fire," "To Drive the Cold Winter Away," "Bitch," "The Incompetent Magician," "The Malice of the Demon," "North to Northwander," "Here There Be Dragons," "To Kill the Undead," "The Children of Cats"	magician, shapeshifter, lute player, mercenary
Magda Lorne	*City of Sorcery*	expert *laran* telepath and visionary
Magdalen "Magda"	*Thendara House; The Shattered Chain*	lesbian accepting of her true self and love of women, judo
Margaret Alton	*Traitor's Sun; Sharra's Exile, Exile's Song; The Shadow Matrix*	brilliant musicologist and mediator; an *Matrix;* orphan recovered by her father Lew on Darkover
Manuela	"Chalice of Tears"	honorable, kind, welcoming leader
Marna	"Knives"	a rape victim who chooses a liberating career as Midwife
Melitta of Storn	*The Winds of Darkover*	self-determined, powerful survivor
Mhari	*A Sword of Chaos;* "The Waterfall"	seasoned survivor and avenger of her family
Morgaine	"The Heart of the Hill"; *The Mists of Avalon*	mentor, religious devotee, role model
Myrtis	"The Secret of the Blue Star"	loyal, trustworthy businesswoman
Nimue	"The Pledged Word"; *The Mists of Avalon*	a venturesome postulant to the Mother Goddess
Penthesilea	*The Firebrand*	Amazon chief, warrior, aunt/foster mother
Rianna	*The Survivors; Hunters of the Red Moon*	reliable companion, fighter, lover
Romilly MacAran	*Hawkmistress!*	a skilled animal handler who rejects arranged marriage
Taniquel	*The Bloody Sun*	autonomous, defiant secondary character
Zadieyek	*Warrior Woman*	a defiant slave who makes her own way as a Gladiator

Lythande's lengthy pilgrimage begins with youthful boredom, when she was "already restless at the life of the women's quarters, dreaming of magic and adventure," beginning with surveillance on a sea-maiden in "Sea Wrack" (Bradley, 2013, 79). Extending before two lifetimes, her training relies on espionage. In the story "The Incompetent Magician," she exults: "A woman. A woman, who in her pride had penetrated the courts of the Pilgrim Adepts in disguise," a mixed blessing that forces her to continue fooling the world with her adopted gender (*Ibid.*, 155). Marion preceded the ruse with the flight of Romilly "Romy" MacAran dressed as a man in *Hawkmistress!* to avoid an odious marriage, with Magdalen "Magda" Lorne posing as a Darkoveran in *Thendara House,* and with a spy cloaked like an alien in *The Colors of Space.* Reviewer Roland J.

Green summarized the author's focus as "the themes of choice and price…. You can't have everything" (Green, 1982, D4).

Training for a Cause

In "The Heart of the Hill," Morgaine promotes mental challenge in women through a study of ancient ritual performed Druid style. She explains, as Viviane, the Lady of the Lake, once did, "By learning the old lore we train and discipline our minds" (Bradley, 2001, 4). One aspect of study and concentration she defines as "the art of reading information from one's surroundings" (*Ibid.*, 6). In *The Forest House*, Marion restates the value of dying for a cause "so long as the ancient knowledge is not lost" (Bradley, 1993, 2). In contrast to ambitious women, Cynric, a male Briton, assumes that females work best in laundry and mending. *The Fall of Atlantis* inserts two examples of such enslaved females. For laundry and clothes folding, the author places Domaris in charge of pygmy women, a diminutive servant class. A similar less-than-human deaf-mute attends Domaris's little sister Deoris during her recovery from burns, a reprise of the character Annis, the deaf servant of Eilan in *The Forest House*. The brief mention of such underlings elevates the author's depiction of daring and achievement in ambitious heroines.

For *Warrior Woman,* loyalty guides Fiora, a tower keeper at Dalereuth in the stand-alone Darkover novel *Rediscovery*. As the result of training under Fiora, Leonie Hastur advances to Keeper of Airlinn, an accomplishment in *The Forbidden Tower* achieved through ambition and fortitude. In *The Firebrand*, the pro-woman narrative awards the rejected wife Oenone a scheme to stymy Prince Paris, her former husband. She offers him a dilemma: either claim his firstborn son Corythus or reject the boy in exchange for possession of his stolen wife Helen. For a woman so limited in ancestral and historic clout, Oenone makes good use of the two-pronged choice by abandoning Paris and taking Corythus to Mount Ida and forever out of the father's control.

On consideration of female strategizing of combat, the priestess Kassandra, a princess at Troy, dismisses male adulation of "war as a great playing field, a games-ground where the prizes are no more than laurel wreaths and honor" (Bradley, 1987, 244). The concealed weapon on Ede's partner in "The Dance at the Gym" further indicts males for swagger. Marion repeats the scenario in *The Mists of Avalon* after the feasting at Caerleon accompanying King Arthur's wedding to Gwenhwyfar. In the view of the priestess, wise females can avoid conflict by refusing to provoke an enemy such as Khryse, the priest who yearns for Kassandra. Marion builds on the priestess's fortitude with a seduction scene in which she restates fealty to Apollo and rejects Aeneas, a clever warrior whom she could easily love.

Independent Women

A more subversive stand on female disempowerment depicts females who choose their own path. In the opening scene of *The Sword of Aldones,* Diotima "Dio" Ridenow reminds the powerful Lew Alton, "The space lanes are free to women as well as men" (Bradley, 1962, 7). Part one of Marion's *The Shattered Chain* depicts Free Amazons as Renunciates who defy patriarchy by abandoning patronyms and by calling themselves by their mothers' names. Separatist feminists constitute a sisterhood of survivors who have divest themselves of reliance on males and liberate women from fearing wife abusers and rapacious raiders from Dry Towns. Marion's creation of buoyant, noble female roles like Jaelle n'ha Melora and Rafaella n'ha Liriel in *Thendara House* coincided with the rise of second wave feminism. For symbolism, the author pictures the rebel leader Lady Rohana Ardais cutting her hair, severing links to the Grimm brothers' incarcerated Rapunzel in her phallic tower and embracing the pizazz of 1920s flappers, a style flaunted in F. Scott Fitzgerald's story "Bernice Bobs Her Hair."

The author, according to reviewer Jessica Jernigan, a writer and editor in Michigan, questions "received narratives in which women are to blame for the failures of men" (Jernigan). Marion surprises the reader in *The Mists of Avalon* with the emerging combativeness of Igraine, a teen bride who grows into the role of Queen of Cornwall. After a slap from her husband, Duke Gorlois, and his threat of a beating, she flashes the bared fangs of a beast and rebukes him. Speaking as a scion of Avalon, she vows to be "no man's slave nor servant" (Bradley, 1983, 48). Her reward for defiance, marriage with High King Uther Pendragon, elevates her to Britannia's queen. The text contrasts her with wimpy daughter-in-law Gwenhwyfar, the convent-educated Christian who wards off danger with the sign of the cross. Appropriately, Gwenhwyfar's Welsh name translates as "white shadow," an ephemeral presence lacking substance and vigor.

During the ongoing appraisals of Arthurian womenfolk, key players cheapen themselves with petty motives and backbiting. Morgause, the experienced *femme fatale*, discerns Morgaine's long-lived yearning for Lancelet, the neglect of husband Uriens, and a secret affair with stepson Accolon. A shrewd evaluator of female emotion and complexity, Morgause also recognizes approach-avoidance in Gwenhwyfar, a queen lusting for her husband's best warrior. The competition with Morgaine prevents a true sisterhood from developing and reveals also-rans who fail to develop her individuality and spunk.

See also Sisterhood.

Sources

Bradley, Marion Zimmer. *The Complete Lythande*. San Francisco: Marion Zimmer Bradley Literary Works Trust, 2013.

_____. *The Fall of Atlantis*. Riverdale, NY: Baen Books, 1983.

_____. *The Firebrand*. New York: Simon & Schuster, 1987.

_____. *The Forest House*. New York: Michael Joseph, 1993.

_____. *Greyhaven*. New York: DAW, 1983.

_____. "The Heart of the Hill" in *Out of Avalon*. New York: Penguin, 2001.

_____. *The Mists of Avalon*. New York: Ballantine, 1983.

_____. *The Sword of Aldones*. New York: Ace, 1962.

_____. *Traitor's Sun*. New York: DAW, 1999.

Busch, Jenna. "Rediscovering Marion Zimmer Bradley's Sword and Sorceress Anthologies," *SYFYWire* (6 November 2018).

Green, Roland J. "'Hawkmistress' Continues Darkover Saga," (New Brunswick) *Central New Jersey Home News* (26 September 1982): D4.

Hughes, Melinda. "Dark Sisters and Light Sisters: Sister Doubling and the Search for Sisterhood in *The Mists of Avalon* and *The White Raven*," *Mythlore* 19 (1993): 24–28.

Jernigan, Jessica. "The Book That Made Me a Feminist Was Written by an Abuser," https://electricliterature.com/the-book-that-made-me-a-feminist-was-written-by-an-abuser-4c6891f548cf.

Shwartz, Susan. "Women and Science Fiction," *New York Times* (2 May 1982).

Feuds

Marion exemplifies feuds and grudges as the direct result of more serious breaches of civility, such as the threat to trade routes by feuding satellite outposts in "The Dance at the Gym." For example, the ruckus raised by Shann MacShann at the Guild House entrance in *Thendara House* typifies the possessive husband belittled by his wayward wife Keitha n'ha Casilda and the ongoing tiff between mercenary Lythande and the brigand Roygan the Proud, which energizes "The Incompetent Magician." Irish analyst Linda Leith remarks, "These [spats] had become so serious … that it became necessary to agree upon a Compact to limit the amount of damage any hot-headed renegade could cause" (Leith, 1980, 299). Civil disputes, such as Moray's challenge of Captain Harry Leicester's authority in *Darkover Landfall,* mar colonization of an unknown planet with simmering resentment. The underlying paranoia of Dry-Towners in *The Shattered Chain* generates a fractious race governed by warring and discord.

Two short stories illustrate a difference in customs and chain of command for venturers out of Earth's atmosphere. In a brief model of imbroglio in "Hero's Moon," Feniston squabbles with Tommy Rawlins over the necessity for following space flight regulations. Marion comments on chain of command discourtesy: "Rawlins' outburst hadn't been exactly the way for a first-year man to talk to his senior" (Bradley, 1985, 256). The name "Rawlins" underscores Tommy's raw demeanor on his first venture to the planet Charmides, ironically, a Greek metaphor for temperance. For the eerie story "The Wind People," the conception and birthing of Robin on the green planet by Dr. Helen Murray enrage spaceship captain Merrihew, who proposes ways of euthanizing the day-old boy before takeoff. The infanticide can prevent a gruesome death when the *Starholm's* engine reaches overdrive. In both stories, lives hang in the balance as characters allow ego to infuse their arguments.

The author began her perusal of vendettas with the blood-feud in *The Door Through Space,* "a terrible and elaborate ritual of the *code duello,*" and the pledge of the Ravens in *The Forest House* to avenge the rape of their mothers by Romans (Bradley, 1961, 10). She extends the latter novel with a Capulet and Montague division over the love of Gaius Macellius, a Roman soldier, for Eilan, a native Briton who suffers what Cheryl Fox, reviewer for the Park City, Utah, *Park Record* termed "the plight of the conquered" (Fox, 1994, B8). From a gendered angle, the author opens the story "Bonds of Sisterhood" (reprised in "Amazon Fragment") with a female dust-up between Rafaella n'ha Liriel and Camilla n'ha Kyria fed on rudeness, name-calling, and bickering, which continues in *Thendara House.* The topic of protracted animosity suits the episodic Lythande series, giving the mage-sorcerer reasons for avoiding the villain Roygan the Proud as well as anonymous marauders. Marion describes infighting among Pilgrim Adepts as an ongoing problem requiring wisdom and craft. For self-protection, Lythande studies the dark sky over Old Gandrin and chooses to avoid a scrap in any "corner or alley of that city of rogues and imposters" (Bradley, 2013, 22).

Family Animus

More serious than brawling among strangers, the author spotlights enmity between brothers. Examples of treachery and lawlessness exacerbate a senseless four-generation tong war in *The Heirs of Hammerfell*. Duke Rascard bemoans a lengthy blood vengeance "which had taken from him grandfather and father, two elder brothers, and now his only surviving son" (Bradley, 1989, 6). The rancor emanating from Storn's burning of Hammerfell's castle provokes many killings and the separation of twins Alastair and Conn Hammerfell. For decades, their mother Erminie grieves and clings to the belief that her dead husband held "grudges and old grievances against the living" (*Ibid.*, 40).

Reflecting global power struggles, Marion's depiction of a dynastic confrontation between the house of Hammerfell and the house of Storn, like William Shakespeare's tragedy *Romeo and Juliet*, reduces world mayhem to a smaller clan-oriented battlefield threatened by intermarriage. In place of nuclear bombs and missiles, the novel introduces clingfire, a hideous incendiary weapon that conflates both Greek fire, the Byzantine secret weapon formulated in 672 CE, with Dow Chemical's napalm, the Vietnam War era gelled gasoline that news photos demonized on the naked body of a young Asian girl. A reflection of the era's warfare in *The Shadow Matrix* characterizes clingfire as "a stuff that adhered to the skin and burned to the bone," an appalling means of daunting an enemy (Bradley, 1997, 12).

In Marion's historical fiction, the outrage that destroys a London coronation in 449 CE in *The Mists of Avalon* results in dangerous animosity, a time when Britannia needs to unify allies against the Saxon menace. Duke Gorlois of Cornwell, suspicious of his wife Igraine's interest in the High King Uther Pendragon, vents damaged male ego on both mate and monarch, a psychological displacement of anger and humiliation that forces the couple into a rapid flight home to Cornwall. In the exchange between Gorlois and his new king, the two discuss a divorce and the passing of Igraine from one male to another, a "woman to be given away without her own consent" (Bradley, 1983, 70). Igraine compares her situation in the quarrel to that of a horse traded at the fair, a simile later repeated by the nubile Gwenhwyfar.

INSIDIOUS TONG WARS

Quarreling overtakes the remainder of the Arthurian novel, pitting doubters of Christianity against Bishop Patricius and Celtic hill people against intrusive proselyters of Druid worshipers. In an unforeseen uproar, Viviane's mercy killing of Priscilla outrages Balin, her son. Foster son Balan confutes Balin's threats to the elderly Lady of the Lake by reminding Balin that an herbal potion saves Priscilla days of suffering from a wasting disease. Marion allows the hatred to fester until the priestess's arrival at Arthur's court, where Balin cleaves her skull with an axe, a vicious retreat to ruthlessness. The blood feud leads, predictably, to Balin's assassination as an outlaw and murderer, attesting to the unremitting nature of clan feuds.

The final clash of ambitions and yearnings concludes the Arthuriad with pitiable betrayals and fights to the death. Morgause, plotting to rule Camelot alongside her foster son Gwydion/Mordred, participates in the ambush of Lancelet in Gwenhwyfar's bedchamber. In a rush of some sixteen warriors, Lancelet's sword transfixes his beloved cousin Gareth. He blames Morgaine for directing mayhem toward securing her ambitions for Avalon. So, too, does Gawaine pledge a blood-oath against Lancelet for skewering brother Gareth. Civil war results with warriors "seeking in the darkness, swords naked, against one another," a metaphor describing enmity on a par with English poet

Matthew Arnold's "Dover Beach," in "confused alarms of struggle and flight,/Where ignorant armies clash by night." Arising from a shattered ideal of Arthur's kingship, the vendetta costs the lives of both Gwydion and Arthur and nullifies a promising future for Camelot and Britannia (*Ibid.*, 866).

See also Retribution.

Sources

Bradley, Marion Zimmer. *The Best of Marion Zimmer Bradley*. Chicago: Academy Chicago, 1985.
_____. *The Complete Lythande*. San Francisco: Marion Zimmer Bradley Literary Works Trust, 2013.
_____. "The Dance at the Gym," *San Francisco Chronicle* (17 September 1987): B3, B7.
_____. *The Door Through Space*. New York: Ace, 1961.
_____. *The Heirs of Hammerfell*. New York: DAW, 1989.
_____. *The Mists of Avalon*. New York: Ballantine, 1983.
_____. *The Shadow Matrix*. New York: DAW, 1997.
_____. *The Shattered Chain*. New York: DAW, 1976.
Fox, Cheryl. "Review: *The Forest House*," *Park Record* (Park City, UT) (4 August 1994): B8.
Hildebrand, Kristina. "The Other Cornwall Girl: Morgause in Twentieth-Century English Literature," *Journal of the International Arthurian Society* 6:1 (2018): 25–45.
Leith, Linda. "Marion Zimmer Bradley and Darkover," *Science Fiction Studies* 7 (1980): 28–35.
Robeson, Lisa. "Pawns, Predators, and Parasites: Teaching the Roles of Women in Arthurian Literature Courses," *Medieval Feminist Forum* 25:1 (1998).

The Firebrand

A matriarchal revision of the Trojan War (ca. 1200 BCE) inspired by Mary Renault's Alexandrian novels, Marion's mytho-historic fantasy *The Firebrand* relates memories of the fall of Troy following the collapse of the Minoan civilization on Crete and its worship of the snake goddess of Knossos. After the eruption of Thera (Santorini), the restructuring of eastern Mediterranean trade put Greeks on edge in the battle for passage through the Hellespont (Dardanelles), Propontis (Sea of Marmora), and Bosphorus to the Black Sea. On an esoteric plane, critic Sonja Sadovsky, author of *The Priestess & the Pen,* characterized the novel as "a parable for the loss of Goddess-centered religions and the matrilineal line of descent" that dominated Minoan society (Sadovsky, 2014, 71). In a review for *English Journal,* Sally R. Frederick, a teacher who incorporated the novel into high school classwork, acknowledged true Homeric characterization that, in Marion's hands, becomes "rounder, fuller, more personally engaging" from "convincing dialogue" (Frederick, 1989, 85). Through engaging conversation, the novel endows the Greek and Trojan cast with an appealing universality.

Incorporated in the sociopolitical mindset are standard graces of the eastern Mediterranean world—truce, hospitality to guests, kinship ritual, and gift giving—alongside the taxation of trading vessels passing through Eurasian straits, a possible cause of strife in 1200 BCE. In Sonja Sadovsky's description, the protagonist, Princess Cassandra/Kassandra, represents the dynamic woman—"the symbol of independent female authority and a living link to the Goddess she serves" (Sadovsky, 2014, xxx). She matures into the firebrand, the ardent voice alerting the royal family that Paris can and will live out a dire fate because he stole Menelaus's wife. A prescient truth-bearer, she battles frustration because people charge her with falsehood, exhibitionism, and madness. In contemplation of the Earth Mother and the Akhaian goddess Aphrodite, the priestess scrabbles for logic to explain visionary inklings of disaster to come: "Surely the Gods … would not punish a great city for the foolish transgressions of a single man and a woman" (Bradley, 1987, 217).

The classic dactylic hexameter narrative links Kassandra, Homer's career woman, with the most devastating acts of nature and humankind. During a foretaste of the priestess's fervor, she blazes through the city streets shrieking that an earthquake is imminent. In the overview of the elderly witness expunging false versions of the ten-year Trojan war with the Akhaians and their allies, Kassandra warns of restive, vengeful males during an era of culture shift from the Mother Goddess toward androcentric gods and strutting heroes. Hysterical with fear for Troy, she predicts repeatedly that fate has marked her egotistic twin Paris to be Troy's nemesis.

To express the epic in simplified terms, Marion reduces the catalog of ships and Trojans in book two and long lists of heroes and gods and their roles in funeral contests and hand-to-hand combat. The omissions remove from Greek epic Homer's contributions to genealogy through lengthy male ties with past heroes, demigods, and gods. To stress the beginnings of female power, the text omits patronyms, the confusing elements that belabor Homer's *Iliad* from the first line: "μῆνιν ἄειδε θεὰ Πηληϊάδεω Ἀχιλῆος" (Menin aeide thea Peleiadeo Achilleos) [Sing Goddess the wrath of Peleian Achilles], i.e., Achilles, son of Peleus (Jordison, 2016). According to critic Sam Jordison in a review for *The Guardian*, these rhetorical essentials are "a mark of the Iliad's great distance from us, but also of how lucky we are to be able to peer into this ancient and alien culture, to have these messages from the long vanished past, to have such enticing mysteries" (Jordison, 2016).

Anticipating womanhood at age twelve, Kassandra ponders the power of the female divine in her yearning for the freedom of Penthesilea, the chief of the dwindling Amazon culture. From the commander come reminders of the pagan, geocentric past when "before ever Apollo Sun Lord came to rule these lands, our Horse Mother—the Great Mare, the Earth Mother from whom we all are born—she was here" (Bradley, 1987, 58). Violent clashes that strip the Akhaian and Trojan armies of their leaders erupt from what Marion considers a wresting of female power by vain, power-mad men. She stated in the postscript, "The men took over their cities. I just want to look at what history was really like before the women-haters got hold of it ... [in] a mad reversal of the natural order of things" (*Ibid.*, 7).

Sources

Bradley, Marion Zimmer. *The Firebrand*. New York: Simon & Schuster, 1987.
Evans, Richard, ed. *Prophets and Profits: Ancient Divination and Its Reception*. New York: Routledge, 2017.
Frederick, Sally R. "Review: *The Firebrand*," *English Journal* 78:1 (January 1989): 85.
Hernandez, Nelson. "Greek Students Savor 'The Iliad' and the Oddity," *Washington Post* (7 September 2003).
Jordison, Sam. "Can Homer's Iliad Speak across the Centuries?," *The Guardian* (9 February 2016).
Sadovsky, Sonja. *The Priestess & the Pen: Marion Zimmer Bradley, Dion Fortune & Diana Paxson's Influence on Modern Paganism*. Woodbury, MN: Llewellyn Worldwide, 2014.

The Firebrand, Volume One

Opening with a male-female confrontation near the end of the Bronze Age, *The Firebrand* anticipates the Iron Age and the shaping of ferrous weapons and body armor by blacksmiths for ongoing wars. Marion's prologue introduces a thesis that a womanly perspective on the Trojan War rectifies the macho values in Homer's *Iliad* and *Odyssey* and Virgil's lyric *Aeneid*. A stout eyewitness testimonial from the elderly Kassandra summarizes the result of encroaching patriarchy—the dominance of "heroes and Kings, not Queens and of Gods, not Goddesses" (Bradley, 1987, 3). By setting Kassandra's telling in evening mist, Marion envisions a murky atmosphere that has enshrouded historical truth, just as divine mystery confuses Kassandra about the powers of the Earth Mother and perceptions of Akhaian ships in Troy's harbor.

The text poses the aged priestess as a reflective sounding board. Essential to her youth before entry into the priesthood, moments of communication with the sun god Apollo hint at a future of sacred service. Marion describes the dizzying mind intrusions as "the gift (or curse) of the wide-open seeing," a talent conferred by the sacred mother of all and repeated in *The Forest House* and the Darkover series (*Ibid.*, 76). Like Domaris, the acolyte in *The Fall of Atlantis,* Kassandra must advance through lessons in wisdom by traveling east to join the Amazons. Of the effort, critic Donald Michael Kraig views the journey as "an externalization of interior development … struggles to achieve self-empowerment and wholeness," a necessary coming of age for the Trojan princess (Sadovsky, 2014, vi).

In contrast to a testy Queen Hecuba and unpredictable King Priam, Kassandra's foster mothers among the Amazons nurture a postulant with patience and respect. Still learning to ride, she subsists on a nomadic diet of roast meat and mare's milk, a symbolic matrilineal feeding. As Kassandra's knowledge of goddesses increases over her three-year sojourn with the horsewomen, she ponders which immortal has omnipotence and which is most influential on her future. The narrative stresses that, over time, she acclimates to spiritual conundrums—"to knowing or hearing the unspoken and seeing the invisible" (Bradley, 1987, 124). The paranormal experiences ready the priestess for dire tests of faith and devotion.

A series of ironies permeates Apollonian prophecies, placing good fortune adjacent to impending devastation. At Andromache's birthing of Astyanax, Priam's first grandson and Hector's firstborn, Kassandra perceives that the boy's corpse will someday lie on his father's shield. Out of Andromache's knowing, the priestess imagines how soon the boy heir will die cast off and broken, the destiny of all Trojan infants at the hands of triumphant Akhaians, who toss the remains of the dynasty over the city's battlements to end the bloodline. In the falling action, the author chooses the sisterly Andromache to calm Kassandra's ravings about Paris's abduction of Helen of Sparta, wife of Menelaus. With human logic, Andromache asserts, "The Gods do not need reasons for what They do" and adds, "We are all subject to the Immortals," Marion's preface to tragedy (*Ibid.*, 197, 198).

Sources

Bradley, Marion Zimmer. *The Firebrand.* New York: Simon & Schuster, 1987.
Lewis, Jone Johnson. "Who Was Andromache?," https://www.thoughtco.com/what-is-andromache-3529220.
Miller, Kate Spitz. "Review: *The Firebrand,*" https://katespitzmiller.com/2017/03/27/book-review-the-firebrand-by-marion-zimmer-bradley/.
Sadovsky, Sonja. *The Priestess & the Pen: Marion Zimmer Bradley, Dion Fortune & Diana Paxson's Influence on Modern Paganism.* Woodbury, MN: Llewellyn Worldwide, 2014.

The Firebrand, Volume Two

Upon the arrival in Troy of Paris with Helen, his female conquest, Marion opens the second stave on Kassandra's musings about the Akhaian goddess Aphrodite, "who put such temptation into the hearts of men—and women too" (Bradley, 1987, 201). Earlier in *The Mists of Avalon*, the author referred to Helen as the woman "who had all the kings and knights of her day at strife over her in Troy" (Bradley, 1983, 862). In a perusal of anthropomorphism, the priestess debates the probity of the Earth Mother and the vanity of Aphrodite, who controverts the divine parent. The narrative applauds the princess's choice to rebel against the Olympian divine. In a discussion with the priest Khryse, Kassandra blames the Greek love goddess for sending a mad passion on humans. Convinced that males invented Aphrodite, the priestess charged men with validating sexual assault. Critic Nina Auerbach sets the character type alongside "the disobedient woman in her many guises as the heir of the ages and demonic savior of her race" (Auerbach, 1982, 25).

The priestess of the sun lord Apollo loses the trust of Trojans, who disbelieve female insights into the kingdom's destiny. A victim of the spiteful priest Khryse, Kassandra thwarts him from attempting rape. As a punishment for sexual assault on a temple virgin, Khryse suffers epilepsy, an ancient malady that the Greek doctor Hippocrates described in 400 BCE as a sacred illness caused when a god possessed the spirit. The equivocal interpretation of convulsions plunges Kassandra further into misgivings about deities and their powers, especially the anthropomorphic gods of the Akhaians. Heavy irony clings to her longing for a javelin and a position in the Trojan squadrons in place of her twin, a lack-luster soldier.

At a climactic moment, Marion reprises the rape of the Sabine women from the Roman historian Livy's *Ab urbe condita* (From the Founding of the City) in Trojan terms. The onslaught of Akhaian marauders catches Priam's warriors unaware and unarmed and allows the Greeks to seize Khryseis. The author balances bloodshed with reason in a secret council involving Priam and Hector and the Akhaian trio Odysseus, Akhilles, and Patroklos, a scenario reprised in volume three after Hector's death. In book three of *The Mists of Avalon*, Marion hints that Akhilles and Patroklos are mates adopting "the Greek fashion in love" (Bradley, 1983, 480). The palace confab dramatizes the diminution of females, even married women, as prizes for valor. Grim with dramatic irony, the meeting fills Kassandra with visions of "soldiers and chiefs here from all over the world" and a future carnage that she alone shares with the reader (Bradley, 1987, 296).

Marion breaks the intense tone and atmosphere of Troy under siege by following Kassandra on a ride east to Colchis (modern Georgia) and its pastoral tribes. Her dramatic reintroduction to Amazon society places the priestess at a harrowing divide—"bewildered, deluded, ineffectual, ... adrift in a world devoid of absolute values" (Sadovsky, 2014, 72). At a nadir in the second year of Troy's ten-year conflict with Greek invaders, the priestess commiserates with the decline of Amazonian powers after male villagers betray the horsewomen with drugged wine. Penthesilea mourns, "Those of us who treat the earth well are dying," the author's implication that urban polluters belong among the enemies of females (Bradley, 1987, 312).

According to Mary Lefkowitz, book critic for the *New York Times*, Kassandra becomes the victor, "a 'Total Woman' by having a secret love affair with Aeneas, by caring for an abandoned baby she somewhat unimaginatively calls 'Honey,' and finally by bearing Agamemnon's son" before leaving Argos at the mercy of Klytemnestra, Agamemnon's murderous widow (Lefkowitz, 1987, A27). The male clash over ownership of concubines pits the priest Khryses against the commander in chief. Perhaps because of impiety toward the gods, a major sin in Greek literature, the camp incurs an epidemic sent by Apollo in the war's ninth year around 1190 BCE. Pitting man against man, Marion ends the stave with a duel between Paris and Menelaus, a bout that settles nothing. The disappointing scenes further derogate human males for lacking rationality and respect for divinity.

Sources

Auerbach, Nina. *Woman and the Demon: The Life of a Victorian Myth*. Cambridge: Harvard University Press, 1982.
Bradley, Marion Zimmer. *The Firebrand*. New York: Simon & Schuster, 1987.
_____. *The Mists of Avalon*. New York: Ballantine, 1983.
Lefkowitz, Mary. "What the Amazons Taught Her," *New York Times* (29 November 1987): A27.
Sadovsky, Sonja. *The Priestess & the Pen: Marion Zimmer Bradley, Dion Fortune & Diana Paxson's Influence on Modern Paganism*. Woodbury, MN: Llewellyn Worldwide, 2014.

The Firebrand, Volume Three, Poseidon's Doom

A familiar trope charges the female prophet with insanity, a dominant thread in feminist lore dramatizing the degradation of verbally aggressive women. As Kassandra becomes the firebrand, she runs the streets shrieking that the gods are sending an earthquake. Hector, too, recognizes eminent mayhem as warfare turns into atrocity, demonstrated by Akhilles's violation of Hector's corpse by dragging it around Troy's ramparts. The heightened tension parallels the priestess's strife with self over her attraction to her brother-in-law Aeneas, a battle echoing Kassandra's internal turmoil over competitive deities and her duties to each. Her union with the son of Aphrodite satisfies the priestess's curiosity about passion. To Aeneas, she states her independence of patriarchal curbs: "There is no man in all of Troy to whom I must account for my doings" (Bradley, 1987, 452–453).

Although the princess achieves a breakthrough in self-determination, the palace and city walls collapse in ruins that are still landmarks in northwestern Turkey. Only the gate remains whole. After Akhilles viciously spears Penthesilea and rapes her corpse, the prophetess transfixes him in the heel with a poisoned arrow, a deviation from Homer's choice of Paris, his "hero of the dancing floor," as the unlikely, unmanly archer. The internecine era kills off Kassandra's sister Polyxena and brothers Hector, Deiphobos, and Troilus, her aunt Penthesilea and all Amazons, her three nephews sired by Paris, Paris's foster father Agelaus, and the Greek commander Agamemnon, the victim of a duplicitous wife.

In a "blame the messenger" scenario, Andromache credits Kassandra with Troy's destruction, ignoring the fact that her twin brother invoked devastation on the realm by violating the Peloponnesian guest code through intimacies with the host's wife. Following another earthquake from Poseidon, Ajax rapes both the princess and her baby daughter Honey. Allotment of female combat prizes passes Hecuba to Odysseus, Andromache to Peleus, and Kassandra to Agamemnon. Marion brings carnage to a close with the blinding light that represents the afterlife in Hades, where Kassandra views Penthesilea holding Honey. On return from Mykenae to a peaceful homeland devoid of patriarchal rule, the priestess resolves to initiate a gynocentric kingdom free of "isles where men worship Gods of iron and oppression" (*Ibid.*, 602). The conclusion, lacking in impact, leaves unexpressed the mature years of Kassandra's parenting of son Agathon and her alliance with the transvestite actor Zakynthos/Zakynthia.

   See also The Royal House of Troy.

Sources

Bradley, Marion Zimmer. *The Firebrand*. New York: Simon & Schuster, 1987.
Judge, Virginia. "'Firebrand' Tells Woman's Views of the Legend of Trojan War," (Rock Hill, SC) *Herald* (16 January 1988).
Kirchhoff, H.J. "An Old Story 'The Firebrand,'" (Toronto) *Globe and Mail* (26 December 1987).
McCash, Vicki. "A Feminist Reworking of Mythology," (Broward, FL) *Sun Sentinel* (17 April 1988).

Folklore

   Marion specialized in embroidering commoner lore with fantasy. Her canon, in the description of Charles W. Sullivan, a specialist in Celtic myth at Hollins College, takes "whole tales from the general store of legendry ... and [retells] those stories making them more fantastic in the process" (Sullivan, 2001, 279). Examples rivet the imagination such as the amulet that fails to protect Allira from the thug Brynat in *The Winds of Darkover* and a diet of "witch-food" in the dark land that the guardsman Reidel reports to Lord Damon and the mythic battle of Rafael to avenge his brother Regis the Fifth in *The Spell Sword* (Bradley, 1974, 11). Even Damon is forced to query: "Was it all superstition, rumor based on the gossip of the ignorant?" (Bradley, 1974, 12). According to *The Anatomy of Criticism* by literary specialist Northrop Frye, "Myths are the core of all literature, the kernel of truth or the seed of conception inside the realistic adaptations" (Frye, 2000, 156). The quest novel *City of Sorcery* bases its mountain expedition on "Kindra's old legends of the secret city far away in the Hellers, where an ancient Sisterhood watches over the affairs of humankind," the stories that fed the imagination of the Renunciates (Bradley, 1984, 41). Fantasy becomes the dominant quality of the lycanthropy story "The Wild One," the vampire tale "Treason of the Blood," and the death of Durraman, the fabled donkey in *Thendara House,* who starves because he can't choose what to eat.

   Marion embodies folk beliefs so natural that they seem valid, as with a red sky at morning predicting storms in *The Fall of Atlantis*, the festering evil beyond the mountains in *City of Sorcery*, and accounts of Leukas's fate in the sea from wrecking by "whatever-it-is out there" in the Lythande episode "Sea Wrack" (Bradley, 2013, 68). A second example from the Lythande series, "Fool's Fire" revisits the boneheaded villager's notion of scripture and hell, which "burns like no natural fire" (*Ibid.*, 173). Another model, "Bitch" reveals a folk release of a curse by running around a gallows. Marion heightens the occult in the flaming salamander that takes the shape of Alnath, a miniature pet dragon in *The Gratitude of Kings*. To reduce hints of evil, Marion depicts Al-nath's baby salamanders teaming to mold candles, an abridged version of their powers to survive flame.

In *The Firebrand,* Marion's resetting of epics by Homer and Virgil, narration acknowledges the ubiquity of oral lore, the source of healing skills in Kentaurs, the nomadic horse-folk from the Caucasus, and of rumors about Amazons killing their lovers and sons. The death of a twisted old rider and his horse and the dwindling strength of the horsewomen causes the author to value legends as cherished memories of past beings and their goodness. She singles out patriarchal myths about Amazons and weapons: In 1200 BCE during the Trojan War, royal midwives avow the danger caused by a woman—especially a parturient woman—touching a bladed weapon. The result, they declare, could harm her fetus or strip the weapon of its worth to the male sword owner in combat. The threat of female powers precedes the rise of Kassandra, a priestess trained as a warrior.

To intensify the ban on armed females, the Argives keep their womenfolk "from gadding about" by sequestering them indoors (Bradley, 1987, 13). More dire, suspicions about twinning imply evil that Queen Hecuba can expunge only by sacrificing her babies, Alexandros and Alexandra. Penthesilea corroborates the story with the ominous tale of Leda's twins, Klytemnestra and Helen, sired by Zeus. Significantly, Leda's girls engender mayhem in the eastern Mediterranean, where Paris's theft of Helen initiates a ten-year war. In an alpha and omega motif, her womb mate, Klytemnestra, ends the war by murdering Agamemnon, the Akhaian commander in chief.

FEAR AND DEATH

Suppositions about the dead and the almighty derive from human illogic, as Andromache's claim that "a corpse will bleed if his murderer touches it" (*Ibid.,* 475). On the day of novice initiations in Colchis, viewers of Imandra's python on the throne propose that the queen can shapeshift at will, implying that she can adapt from warm-blooded mammal to cold, slithery reptile. Kassandra's advance to serpent caretaker introduces her to stories of the priestess Meliantha's "little people" as large as the python, reputedly slain by the Greek god Apollo, and to suppositions that snakes are deaf (*Ibid.,* 269). Marion adds a poignant conclusion to the tale—the burial of Meliantha celebrating her reunion with the snakes she had loved.

Marion permeates the text of *The Forest House* with Celtic and Gaelic superstitions about garlanded novices, sacred wood burned on the eve of Beltane, and mention of the need-fire (or force-fire), a Scots ritual flame kindled by friction and installed on home hearths to protect herds from disease. After Eilan accepts a ruse to conceal her pregnancy, she ponders dire tales from childhood about the House of Maidens and accepts the possibility that the sky will collapse on her for losing her maidenhead to Gaius Macellius, a Romano-Celtic warrior. The unease and regret foreshadow Morgaine's emotional quandaries about bearing a Beltane child, Gwydion/Mordred, who engineers the fall of Camelot in *The Mists of Avalon*.

For Gaius Macellius, rescue by a Druid summons from childhood "Caesar's old horror stories of human sacrifice" and "all the old atrocity stories," a segment of Julius Caesar's *Gallic Commentaries* (58–57 BCE) describing priests weaving of huge wicker prisons for the burning of criminals (Bradley, 1993, 14, 38). Subsequent history of the invasion of Celtic Britannia reveals the purpose of stone rings as open-air shrines and regrets the loss of Druid secrets with the combat deaths of senior priests, who committed nothing to writing. The bard Ardanos fears an uprising of the Ravens, the group name for Cynric and other boys born on the Holy Island, who have reason to attack Romans to avenge the ravished mothers who had once been priestesses. Less fearful, Senara believes the superstition that a maiden gazing into spring water could see the face of her lover, a folk validation of scrying that Eilan recalls at Midsummer. The author rounds out the novel by confirming medieval folk beliefs about Joseph of Arimathea, who welcomes Caillean and her worshippers of the Great Mother to integrate female Christians at "the holy Tor" (Glastonbury) (*Ibid.*, 372).

THE ETERNAL SAVIOR

The author's bestselling Arthurian novel *The Mists of Avalon* contradicts such nonsense as the sign of the cross dispelling demons, a purring cat easing birth pangs, dragons breathing fire, fairy food endangering visitors, and witches flying. Viviane, the Lady of the Lake, dismisses such superstition as "old fables" (Bradley, 1983, 124). When Gwenhwyfar rides toward Caerleon with Igraine, the bride-to-be asks about the folk rumor that High King Uther Pendragon courted the Duchess of Cornwell in the magical form of Igraine's husband, Duke Gorlois. Gwenhwyfar charges bards with spreading an aspersion that the Merlin manipulated the maimed monarch whose atrophy caused the land to wither until the arrival of Parsifal, a lusty youthful hero in German poet Wolfram von Eschenbach's *Parzival*.

Marion speaks through Morgaine's prologue a refutation of the folk belief that King Arthur is immortal, a prediction left over from the myths of Magnus Maximus, a reputed eternal rescuer of Roman Britain, which he ruled from 383 CE to his death in 388 CE. Whatever the result of Arthur's wounding at the last great battle at Camlann in 537 CE, the episode generated multiple tales about the curative powers of Avalon "as it was before the priests of the White Christ came to cover it all with their saints and legends" (*Ibid.*, ix). Thus, Arthur's folklore remains valid to modern readers because of its quasi-historical framing. It survives alongside superstitions that bronze amulets shield children from winter fevers and the pressure of a book of masses against a cradle baby prevents rickets, a disease that stunts skeletal growth.

In the estimation of fantasy and sci-fi writer Robert K.J. Killheffer, a reviewer for *Publishers Weekly,* Arthuriana deserves its prominence in modern fiction. He declared that "[t]he legends of King Arthur and the Round Table are as much a part of our cultural heritage as fairy tales, and Arthurian novels—even when they contain a healthy helping of magic—have bridged the genre gap easily over the years" (Killheffer, 1997, 35). For corroboration, he cites Mary Stewart's Merlin trilogy—*The Crystal Cave, The Hollow Hills, and The Last Enchantment*—alongside Marion's bestsellers, which detail folk beliefs dating from prehistory. Among folk notions in the novel emerge those of the Christian era that mourners should abstain from food, drink, and coitus lest they incur the wrath of the unburied spirit.

PERSONAL FAVORITES

Marion overshadows the newer lore with long ago beliefs about Stonehenge and the moonstone, a source of "true memories of the soul" (Bradley, 1983, 62). At Arthur's wedding feast at Caerleon Castle, Morgaine recalls a magical singer who urged giants into a permanent circle of stones, a rural explanation of the construction of Stonehenge in 3000 BCE. In an extended colloquy over the precepts of Druidism and Christianity, Gwenhwyfar offers her version of the Stonehenge story as well as a fable explaining how mockers of Jesus became cawing crows. Morgaine's recital of songs from Cornwall and the Orkney Islands mesmerizes the Welsh court with melancholy laments for fishermen and the seal woman who loved a mortal, a story Marion repeats in "The Wild One." The motif of women's work—spinning, carding, herding—enthralls listeners, who call for encores.

The projection of the unknown in *Darkover Landfall* begins the deconstruction of fictional tales from earthly lore. As medical officers begin cataloging pregnancies on the uncharted planet, they record fathers or possible fathers until Ewen Ross questions dietitian Judith "Judy" Lovat. Her claim of coitus with an alien parallels Fiona Mac-Morair's Gaelic song about a human seduction of a fairy's daughter on the isle of Skye. Both acts of love result in the siring of an outré, one-of-a-kind being. Questions about the sanctity of holy writ and confession force Father Valentine, the chaplain of the expeditionary force, into wording an on-the-spot theological axiom based on Reformed Catholicism: "Every human being needs belief in the goodness of some power that created him … and some religious or ethical structure" (Bradley, 1972, 126). His assertion bridges the gap between scientific fact and intuitive wisdom.

See also Christianity.

Sources

Bradley, Marion Zimmer. *City of Sorcery*. New York: DAW, 1984.
_____. *The Complete Lythande*. San Francisco: Marion Zimmer Bradley Literary Works Trust, 2013.
_____. *Darkover Landfall*. New York: DAW, 1972.
_____. *The Firebrand*. New York: Simon & Schuster, 1987.
_____. *The Forest House*. New York: Michael Joseph, 1993.
_____. *The Mists of Avalon*. New York: Ballantine, 1983.
_____. *The Spell Sword*. New York: DAW, 1974.
Frye, Northrop. *Anatomy of Criticism*. Princeton, NJ: Princeton University Press, 2000.
Killheffer, Robert K.J. "Fantasy Charts New Realms," *Publishers Weekly* 244:24 (16 June 1997): 34–40.
Sullivan, C.W. "Folklore and Fantastic Literature," *Western Folklore* 60:4 (Fall 2001): 279–296.

The Forbidden Tower

The second of a Darkover trilogy, *The Forbidden Tower,* a longer and more complex novel than *The Spell Sword* and *The Bloody Sun,* fills the gap between them and initiates a less inhibited, more liberal society open to the concept of multiple marriage. In the post-rescue of Callista "Callie" Lanart from vicious catmen in the Caves of Corresanti, the story opens like a medieval quest tale on varied family troubles and entanglements. Keeper Leonie Hastur frees Callista from her pledge to the Keepers to marry Terran cartographer Andrew Carr, who shares her *laran* powers and earns respect as a horse trainer. Four days later, the union of Andrew and Callista at Armida coincides with the marriage of the empath Damon Ridenow and Callista's twin, Ellemir "Elli" Lanart, daughters of Lord Esteban and his deceased wife. Damon applies his psi powers to rehabilitate guardsmen suffering from frostbite and proposes extending the use of *laran* as a universal healing method.

```
Gwynn=Lord Alton=Marcella Ridenow              |                    |

Leynier  Esteban Gabriel |         Damon Ridenow       Lorenz and three other brothers

    |      Rafael Lanart  |         telepath and hero           |

    |                     |              |                 eleven sons

Desiderio "Dezi"          |              |                       |

Leynier                   |              |                  grandson

                          |              |

_____(twins)_____

        |            |              |              |         |        |

Ellemir=/=Andrew=Callista  Dorian=Mikhail=/=Ellemir=Damon  Domenic  Coryn  Valdir-Lewis

  | "Ann'dra" | tower        |                regent of                Lanart-Alton

  | Carr      | guardian   child              Alton                   novice monk

unborn son    daughter
```

In Marion's most erotic work, multiple views on coitus incorporate marital union with sexual frustration, neutering, polyamory, celibacy, same-gender love, aphrodisiacs, and group sex. Because telepathy prevents Callista from physical union with Andrew, he considers leaving his bride and shares Ellemir's bed, a contretemps with twins that fuels Esmeralda Santiago's book *Conquistadora*. By halting matrix powers from destroying Andrew's marriage to Callista, Damon intercedes with Esteban's intrusive illegitimate son Desiderio "Dezi" Leynier. In sword practice, Domenic, Esteban's son, lies inert when Dezi, like an ogre in a fairy tale, steals his matrix. Callista's intervention restores the psi crystal and splits Dezi's skull "like a piece of rotten fruit" (Bradley, 1977, 188). The multiple ownership of the matrix creates a forbidden tower, a power structure that smashes social conventions.

In the denouement, the novel bogs down in a battle of powers. Leonie, the elderly Keeper of Asilinn, holds court before the Comyn Council and hears the events that resulted in the brothers' deaths. After a Timesearch and visit with the Keeper Varzil the Good, Damon solidifies the wedlock of Andrew and Callista at the Year's End ritual by applying the aphrodisiac *kireseth*. In the Overworld, Damon announces the reclamation of old ways that release Keepers from vows of celibacy. Leonie allows Damon to retain a separate tower. Valdir inherits the rule of the Altons; Andrew becomes the first off-worlder to enter a Darkover clan. The depth of themes involving female rights and defiance of questionable traditions won Marion the 1978 Hugo Award, a Locus citation, and the Invisible Little Man Award, followed the next year by a Sense of Wonder Award and translation of *The Forbidden Tower* into French, German, and Italian.

Sources

Bradley, Marion Zimmer. *The Forbidden Tower*. New York: DAW, 1977.
del Rey, Lester. "Review: *The Forbidden Tower*," *Analog Science Fiction/Science Fact* 97:11 (November 1977): 170–171.
Jaffrey, Sheldon. *Future and Fantastic Worlds*. Rockville, MD: Borgo, 2007.
Sadovsky, Sonja. *The Priestess & the Pen: Marion Zimmer Bradley, Dion Fortune & Diana Paxson's Influence on Modern Paganism*. Woodbury, MN: Llewellyn Worldwide, 2014.
Wilder, Cherry. "Review: *The Forbidden Tower*," *Foundation* (1 January 1979): 105.

The Forest House

An historical prequel to *The Mists of Avalon* and an impetus to late twentieth-century Neo-Paganism, Marion's *The Forest House* takes shape five hundred years before the Arthurian era. The plot describes parallel movements—the Roman occupation of Britannia and the founding of Afallon, a female retreat at an island house in Summer Country (the dry lake bed of Ynis Witrin in Somerset) later called Avalon for its apple orchards. The postulation of a women's education center builds on the setting of *Thendara House*, which the author wrote a decade earlier. Literary critic Daneet Steffens, a reviewer for *Entertainment Weekly*, summarized the milieu as "a period during the Roman occupation when most people were held captive by the conquerors but were still captivated by their native priest-rulers, the mystical Druids" (Steffens, 1994).

The novel recreates in female cloistering what analyst Jan Shaw, a lecturer at the University of Sydney, calls "an escape from the oppressions of patriarchy … a community of self-sufficient women who're not beholden to men … and [who] refuse the status of marketable objects in the patriarchal economy of exchange" (Shaw, 2009, 74). A central theme of the novel, the rise of patriarchal religion and the quashing of women's natural potency, foregrounds the sisterhood at Avalon based on female agency in previous eras when women ruled tribes. Two notables included Cartimandua, an influential queen of the Brigantes from 43 to 69 CE, and Boudicca, the monarch of the Iceni who led a rebellion in 60 CE. Eilan advances the notion of women as wielders of clout with a weak argument—"because each women runs her own household" (Bradley, 1993, 58). In defiance of matriarchy, the Arch-Druid Ardanos, "greedy for power," advances to mastery of females by corrupting communication between the Great Mother and her high priestess Lhiannon (*Ibid.*, 214).

Around 80 CE before conquest of Britannia by Christianity, the narrative raises reader and academic queries about the true nature of the patriarchal Druid priesthood in what the anonymous critic at *Kirkus* characterized as "fictional tub-thumping on behalf of ancient goddess religions vanquished by male-dominated cults" ("Review," 1994). The narrative presents the Society of the Ravens as children of Druid priestesses, the offspring of torture and rape by Roman raiders of the holy isle of Mona (Anglesey) off the northwest shore of Wales. In Eilan's scrying on spring water, she views the Lady, a deity who connects her to Deoris, the priestess in *The Fall of Atlantis*. By picturing time as a current flowing through space, the scenario links mention of Caradac/

Caradoc, a Welsh ruler at Gwent after 485 CE, with Arthur and the Knights of the Round Table and melds all women, past and current, into a perpetual sorority.

RESCUE AND HOSPITALITY

The narrative illustrates the coming to knowledge of a bicultural man through his observation of the sufferings of Celts, victims of both Roman and Hibernian invaders. In contrast to the nightmare of rape on the nuns of Mona by Roman legionaries in the past, a whiff of antiseptic balsam and the actions of Eilan's father and brother to save the mixed-blood boy Gaius Macellius from infection arouse admiration for providers of Dark Age first aid and guest-host fealty. Marion confirms the worth of bicultural, bilingual people like Gaius, who grew up at a military camp in Deva (modern Chester) and can interpret the beliefs and values of disparate societies. Although reared Roman style by his father, the camp prefect, Gaius commiserates with Celts for the drafting of male levies to the Mendip lead mines and suppresses an arrogance characterized as "the lord of the world, as a Roman ought to be" (Bradley, 1993, 57).

In mid-novel, Marion places her protagonists in tests of their youth and wisdom. Eilan's weighing of devotion to the Mother Goddess and love for Gaius results in mutual affection and lovemaking at the Beltane festival on May 1. Four years after her first admission of passion for the outsider, she disproves the notion that loss of maidenhood endangers personal magic, a metaphoric opposition of earthly forces with the divine. The substitution of a double for the pregnant high priestess enables Eilan to retreat to the forest in secret to present Gaius with his firstborn son Gawen. The tissue of lies surrounding Gawen's birth becomes an approach/avoidance dilemma, granting Eilan an undisclosed motherhood without revealing her loss of virginity.

SAMAINE MARTYRDOM

To return Gaius to his paternal roots, the author must pack the narrative with cultural motifs dating to the Roman Republic. Introduction to Julia Licinia, his old-fashioned bride-to-be, and the ride north in 83 CE to meet with Agricola and his son-in-law, the historian Tacitus, before the battle of Mons Graupius grounds the novel more thoroughly in Roman philosophy and history. Marion stresses the macho legionary self-image, which descends on Gaius during combat. His valor tempers bloodlust with mercy, but he welcomes a Romanized ambition based on obeying principles of civic virtue, marriage, fatherhood, and duty to the tyrannic Emperor Domitian, who ruled from 81 to 96 CE. The suppression of Gaius's love for Eilan and son Gawen gradually bleeds Gaius dry of true affection, a loss that Marion implies haunts all Romans.

Marion's narrative teeters in its finale and the sorting out of beliefs and loyalties. Gaius's courtship of Senara, Eilan's Romano-Celtic fosterling, precedes the stabbing death of Domitian by court staff on September 18, 96 CE, and the cataclysmic rebellion of Roman occupation troops. At the end of her life at the Forest House of Vernemeton, Eilan perceives Gaius's character flaws and lack of honor toward his first love. To shield Senara, Eilan embraces martyrdom and a purifying Samaine cremation on November 1 that she shares with Gaius. In the resolution, the novelist proposes a merger of Christianity with the Mother Goddess cult and the prophecy "a defender shall come for our land" free of religious constraints (*Ibid.,* 417). Polish religious specialist Adam Anczyk, on staff at Jagiellonian University, Krakow, salutes females like Eilan for their role in cultural change: "It is the women who are the keepers of the ancient pagan mysticism, and it is because of their effort that the mystical tradition is not lost and forgotten" (Anczyk, 2015, 13).

See also Diction.

Sources

Anczyk, Adam. "Druids and Druidesses: Gender Issues in Druidry," *Pantheon* 10:1 (2015): 3–15.
_____. "The Image of Druids in Contemporary Paganism: Constructing the Myth," *Walking the Old Ways: Studies in Contemporary European Paganism* (2012): 99–118.
Bradley, Marion Zimmer. *The Forest House.* New York: Michael Joseph, 1993.
"Review: *The Forest House,*" *Kirkus* (1 April 1994).
Shaw, Jan. "Troublesome Teleri," *Sidney Studies in English* 35 (2009): 73–95.
Steffens, Daneet. "Review: *The Forest House,*" *Entertainment Weekly* (20 May 1994).

The Gratitude of Kings

Late in the author's career, she composed a gender parable complete with moral that elucidates female empowerment through magic. The narrative, a re-envisioning of a European fairy tale, depicted dueling magicians and wizards who battled each other's provinces with alternative spells and curses, a motif previously applied to "The Children of Cats." At the arrival of the musician-mercenary Lythande in the disguise of a man to Tashgan's court, Marion reprises the escape plot of Romilly "Romy" MacAran in *Hawkmistress!,* in which Romy eludes her father's plan to wed her to widower Garris of Scathfell. An aura of sex-charged sorcery pervades the atmosphere, altering the bride-to-be to the standard doll features of the day to distract the king. Between Lythande and Lady Mirwen, Marion arouses an immediate bitch fight, the stagy woman-against-woman clash common in eighteenth-century theatricals. Mirwen asserts stereotypes of males without realizing that her opponent is female.

The underlying gender humor continues between Lythande and Eirthe (Earthy?), the candlemaker of Tschardain Castle who knows about the harper's gender switch. Narrative tension builds after Lythande accepts a challenge from her nemesis, Lady Beauty, a were-dragon previously featured in "North to Northwander." Beauty travels in disguise as an itinerant minstrel to perform at the king's wedding and coronation, standard social rituals for "Sleeping Beauty" and other fairy tales. Notation in the family tree indicates sexual/marital ties:

Idriash

High King

deceased   vintner=/=mistresses

| |

Rasthan	second son	Tashgan=Velvet of Valantia		nine older sisters	three brothers
	killed by	prince of			
sons	were-dragon	Tschardain			

Marion took the title, a satire of self-important monarchy, from poet Henry Wadsworth Longfellow's Belisarius and cited by Irish nationalist Thomas Francis Meagher before the Rebellion of 1848 against the English crown.

A sex-charged tune layers more gender challenge about female lovers who court the same man. Marion guides the narrative to a feminist ending, allowing the women to mock Tashgan, who is too shallow, too self-absorbed to realize that his bride is a treasure in her natural state, freckles and all. The moral takes the form of a universal lesson in physical perfection: Women are lovely to the men who love them. To criticism of her pro-woman writing from Sarah Lefanu, author of *In the Chinks of the World Machine: Feminism and Science Fiction*, Marion asserted, "The ordinary well-plotted story is subject to the idea that plot is a masculist device" directed at men's arms and goals of domination (Lefanu, 1988, 72).

By reordering the plot to reveal such subversive traits as those of Lythande, Eirthe, Velvet and mischievous salamanders, the author upends expectations for the medieval motif of men jousting in lists or fighting in raids and combat. Instead, women shield themselves from harm through verbal misdirection and creative arts. With candles shaped to destroy malice, Eirthe enables Velvet to choose her own path. Equipping the princess for life with a narrow-minded king, Lythande and Eirthe bypass the standard quest genre and prepare Velvet for rebirth as queen. Marion returns to the motif of magic candles in "The Wuzzles," in which Lythande makes herbal lights to cleanse a barn of evil vermin.

See also Lythande.

Sources

Bradley, Marion Zimmer. *The Gratitude of Kings.* New York: Wildside, 1997.
Lefanu, Sarah. *In the Chinks of the World Machine: Feminism and Science Fiction.* London: Women's Press, 1988.
MacDonald, Margo. "Review: *The Gratitude of Kings,*" https://www.sfsite.com/04a/grat30.htm, 1998.

Hawkmistress!

Escape from a forced marriage at the end of the age of chaos, a common thread of medieval and Renaissance literature for YA readers, motivates the characters and their choices in Marion's *Hawkmistress!* A popular work in French and German and in a 1997 Czechoslovakian translation, *Hawkmistress!* won a 1983 Locus award, a nomination for a Balrog citation, and a 2007 American Library Association listing among best YA books. With a title rich in female strength and the implied association with raptors, the novel honors an adolescent girl for choosing a path suited to her true self. Fifteen-year-old Romilly "Romy" MacAran, a protector of animals like her grandfather, hawkmaster of King Carolin, answers to a vivid nickname that describes her delight in the wilderness and in her beloved flyer Preciosa.

Romy identifies with majestic hawks and falcons and their free flight and wonders, "Why is a hero always a man" (Bradley, 1982, 62). To flee an unbearable nuptial with the thrice-widowed lecher Garris of Scathfell, she lops her hair and dons masculine leather breeches, cloak, boots, and sheathed dagger, the ploy of Marion's Lythande series. On escape into the foothills on the way to Nevarsin, she introduces herself to Granny Mhari the nut farmer as Rumal, an apprentice hawkmaster "festival-got" (*Ibid.*, 53). Befriended by Lady Jandria and by Lord Orain of Castamir, a gentle homosexual, Romy finds opportunities to practice the humanism of the *cristoforo* faith.

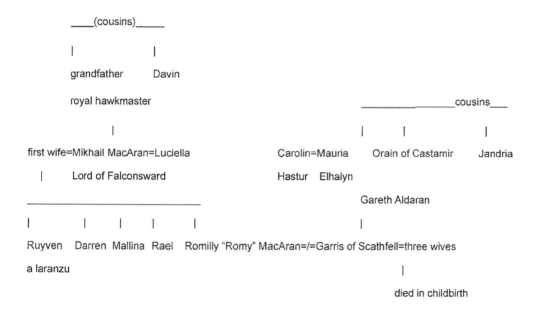

The narrative features the outdoors and flight from home as a symbol of female freedom from patriarchy and the clutches of crude blackguards like Rory, her would-be mate. Ironically, Romy seeks refuge among sci-fi Benedictines—the monks of St. Valentine of the Snows—to avoid a gendered training of girls in embroidering cushion covers, managing kitchens and dairies, and obedience to narrow-minded fathers. She enlarges the knowledge of avian veterinary, hawking, falconer's knots, and clairvoyance by hiking the wilderness, a quest she shares with Christ. The resilient theme of *laran* powers that dominates *Stormqueen!* carries over in Romy's teen years, when she violates social strictures by demanding an education and communing with horses, herding and working dogs, and raptors.

A mythic adventure set during the era of the Hundred Kingdoms, the gallop out of the stables toward Nevarsin follows Mikhail's capture and release of Romy's bird Preciosa. A visiting laronis explains Romy's dilemma: "A cagebird cannot be a falcon" (*Ibid.*, 2). On the road to Neskaya, the hawk hunts for birds to feed his mistress, who languishes in confusion. At the camp shared with the exiled company of Dom Carlo of Carcosa and his paxman (security guard) Orain, she displays avian acumen by healing three sentry birds. In a plot similar to Lythande's, Romy learns of Orain's homosexuality at the Caer Donn inn. Mind-reading of birds informs her of a coming conflict. To her credit, she becomes a valiant self-rescuer.

From shelter among girl warriors at the Sisterhood of the Sword, Romy, like Arthurian characters in *The Forest House* and *The Mists of Avalon* and the Renunciates of Darkover, profits from residence in an all-female hostel. She restores the twelve-year-old hostage Caryl Hastur to Hali city and rewards Orain's cousin Jandria with hospital necessities. A plot twist reveals Carlo's secret identity as King Carolin Hastur, whom she aids to regain his realm. The falling action requires Romy to free Orain from the capture of Lyondri Hastur. To improve her psionic gift, she chooses an education under Maura Elhalyn, a skilled telepath at Tramontana tower. In the style of literary romance, the king marries Maura and chooses Romy as hawkmaster, a conclusion that Roland J. Green, book reviewer for the (New Brunswick) *New Jersey Home News* identified with "the themes of choice and price central to Bradley's work" (Green, 1982, D4). He called these elements "the ingredients for good straight-forward space adventure with overtones of fantasy" (*Ibid.*).

Sources

Bradley, Marion Zimmer. *Hawkmistress!* New York: DAW, 1982.
Green, Roland J. "'Hawkmistress' Continues Darkover Saga," (New Brunswick) *Central New Jersey Home News* (26 September 1982): D4.
Koelling, Holly, ed. *Best Books for Young Adults.* Chicago: American Library Association, 2006.
Walton, Jo. "A Heroine's Journey: Marion Zimmer Bradley's *Hawkmistress*," www.tor.com/2010/03/05/a-heroines-journey-marion-zimmer-bradleys-lemghawkmistresslemg/.

Healing and Death

From her earliest stories, Marion identified illness, accidents, and deathbed suffering as motivations for human interaction and compassion, for example, Larry's treatment of blisters and cautery with a heated knife in *Star of Danger*, the gift of anti-frostbite lotion to the crew of a downed starship in *Rediscovery*, and the diagnosis of Queen Antonella's stroke in *The Heirs of Hammerfell*. Threats to health require pervasive bandaging of accidents, sunburn, and altitude sickness in *City of Sorcery* and *The Planet Saver*. For Marguerida Alton in *Traitor's Sun*, preparation for a family funeral causes her to long for a nap with a "sopping kerchief full of lavender on my brow," an ancient form of aromatherapy (Bradley, 1999, 68). In *Hawkmistress!*, Marion highlights Romy's rescue of birds after Davin collapses with summer fever and lauds Gwennis's salving of Romy's back after her father beats her with a crop. The pairing implies innocence in bird and human girl.

The contrast between illness and loss balances life forces in *Exile's Song.* For

Margaret/Marguerida Alton, the song catcher who faints while she shops for suitable clothes, the typical treatment consists of "a mug of strong, scented tea," the standard sugared restorative in British fiction and film that "hit her bloodstream like a drug" (Bradley, 1996, 56). The collapse introduces a crisis—the sudden death of Professor Ivor Davidson, Margaret's mentor, whom she loved like a father. Composed as a series of tests, the novel places Margaret in additional physical torment from seizures and a litter ride to Castle Ardais to seek treatment from Istvana, a leronis who salves the troubled spirit. To ease threshold sickness, Istvana applies a transderm patch on Margaret's arm to initiate healing sleep.

On a more serious issue, the crash of a survey plane in *The Spell Sword* kills all but one crewman, Andrew Carr, who protests the mass loss of a skilled pilot and cartographers Mattingly and Stanforth. In an unusual conversation with Callista, an ethereal being surrounded by blue light, Andrew charges her with sadism. He demands, "Does death by wholesale give you any pleasure, you ghoul-girl?" (Bradley, 1974, 3). Only upon conversing with her does he learn of the role of free will: "Their time is ended and their destiny was never at my disposal" (*Ibid.*). In the sequel, *The Forbidden Tower,* Damon tends his paralyzed father-in-law by making a brace for his back and a wheelchair to enable him to attend a double wedding, a ritual affirming life.

In book three of *The Mists of Avalon,* Marion refers to herbal tea for children's fever, a common cause of death that remains largely undiagnosed or identified. Morgaine, wife of King Uriens of North Wales, relies on a poultice—"hot cloths wrung in steaming herb brew"—to treat a festering sword cut in stepson Uwaine's face and digs out the roots of three fractured teeth (Bradley, 1983, 660). The narrative makes melancholy humor at Morgaine's marriage to an old man who requires from his woman foot and back rubs rather than nightly coitus. Deep into a claustrophobic winter, he struggles with lung fever (pneumonia) that depletes his body. In fear for his survival and throne, Morgaine "fought hard for his life" as well as the lives of others (*Ibid.,* 657).

While plotting spells to kill Avalloch, her lustful stepson, Morgaine applies medicinal skill at releasing a chill. Ironically, she treats him with an emmenagogue such as pennyroyal, tansy, rue, angelica, wormwood, yarrow, or mugwort, a nostrum that brings on late menstruation or an early abortion. The subsequent Pentecostal jousting at Camelot replaces more dangerous ailments with ordinary riding accidents in the lists caused by unseating during a duel. One youth suffers a twisted leg. Other knights incur smashed fingers and aches from bruising by the kick of a warhorse. In the second half of the competition, Gwydion's challenge to Lancelet produces victory for Gwydion, but only minor wounds in Arthur's chief knight. His resilience accounts for esteem from both genders.

The author emphasizes blood loss as a worse threat to women. Outflow after Morgaine's miscarriage results from herbal abortifacients, which can cause a lethal hemorrhage. Broca, the midwife, follows the treatment with a soothing liquid antidote, a pairing of herbal simples known to skilled practitioners. Marion pictures Morgaine sleeping for two days before recovering. At her lover Accolon's death, despair plunges her into madness and near suicide with her little knife, causing another bloodletting, a symbol of passion draining from the body in a necessary purgation of the new Lady of the Lake.

Brutality and Rehabilitation

The falling action depicts lethal threats to health and kingdom from combat. Arthur lies in the monks' quarters at Glastonbury to recover from sword wounds that Accolon inflicted. Morgaine diagnoses the king's weakness before she steals his scabbard, the symbolic equipage called in Latin *vagina,* the female half that completes the sword Excalibur in the Holy Regalia. During the mad dash that follows, he gallops toward Avalon "swaying in his saddle, the bandages slowly soaking through with blood," a seepage that the magical sheath had prevented (*Ibid.,* 751). Near collapse from exertion, blood loss, and cold, he returns to the sickbed with the aid of his escort.

In contrast to Arthur's bandaged combat wounds, Morgaine suffers a spiritual breakdown worsened by heartache at losing Accolon and her magical powers. Weak, wobbly, and mentally clouded, she accepts rescue by servants. Without a return to Avalon for healing, Kevin the harper fears she will die of "grief and exile" (*Ibid.,* 754). With a healer's skill, he orders food—bread and honeyed milk—to end her fasting and revives her with a diet of milk and egg, nutrients from female sources. Marion credits catharsis of grief—for Viviane and Igraine, for Elaine, for Accolon and Arthur—and water from the Sacred Well with recharging Morgaine for the job of restoring Avalon.

The epiphany of godhood at Camelot's Easter feast demands a martyr, Raven, the silent priestess who wills her strength to empower the Great Magic. The service of communion confers on each person in the Great Hall what the Merlin called "the holiest of Mysteries of the ancient world," an epiphany predating Christianity (*Ibid.,* 779). The ennui that gripped Arthur's knights in Camelot vanishes as the companions ride in search of the Holy Grail, a quest that kills Galahad for touching the mystery cup. As testimonials to their most perilous crusade, a year later, warriors still bear the traumas of combat—missing teeth, cuts and bruises, cracked ribs, and dressings on heads, legs, and arms from blows of the battleaxe, which ranged in length from one to five feet. The spate of injuries explains the ongoing need of the female touch and knowledge of herbalism. The holy chalice, receptacle of the life forces, becomes what Janice C. Crosby, a professor at Southern University in Baton Rouge, Louisiana, calls "a symbol of the Goddess" whom Christianity has tried to erase (Crosby, 2000, 43).

Space Medics

For the Darkover series, Marion adapts a mix of medieval first aid to futuristic medical care, which can do nothing to save Darren from a bolt of lightning in *Stormqueen!* For the catastrophic arrival of a spaceship on the unknown planet in *Darkover Landfall,* the author sets immediate tasks of tending the dying "while they were still digging bodies out of the wreckage of the bridge" (Bradley, 1972, 4). The connection between survival and corpse burial sets the tone for the series, which discloses generations of off-worlders living far from safe, familiar atmosphere. The crash necessitates a mix of brute labor with limited supplies—tagging the mangled remains with military precision, treating rows of unconscious patients in a field hospital, disinfecting latrines, and building shelters. The staff can offer geologist Rafael "Rafe" MacAran only headache pills as therapy for a jarring concussion, but few "human expressions of kindness" as the survivors struggle to cope (*Ibid.,* 5).

The succinct exchanges among engineers, medics, life support manager, and botanist indicate an improbable situation. The chance of encountering "any unusual illness of unknown origin" poses issues that Michael Crichton anticipated in *The Andromeda Strain* and Greg Bear in *Vitals*. Sensible solutions lessen the danger of Darkover poison ivy, which produces green vesicles and swells the eyes. Antihistamine shots for Dr. Judith "Judy" Love and Heather Stuart suppress their bodies' reaction to irritating oil on the underleaf. Medic Ewen Ross survives scorpion-ants by the action of strong stimulants. The unsteady heart rate of xenobotanist Marco Zabal causes caretakers to ponder a high death rate in an uncharted habitat. A period of euphoria—"a psychedelic wind … a ghostly wind that drove us all temporarily insane"—grips the expedition, leaving Marco to face heart failure alone. The source of psychic stimulus introduces in the author's imaginary ecosystem the possibility of a cognitive confusion not unlike temporary insanity.

Subsequent books in the saga extend the author's interest in physical ills. Mikhail receives treatment for exposure and exhaustion with bladderwort (*Utricularia*) tea and mealmush in *The Shadow Matrix*. In *Exile's Song,* new arrivals from Earth at the Thendara Spaceport require dermapatches and hyperdrome treatment to condition them for changes in gravity and climate. The threshold sickness that afflicts Margaret Alton in *The Shadow Matrix* besets Jeremiah "Jeram" Reed's friend Ulm in *The Alton Gift* until his recovery in a transient camp. Staff uses donated blood to locate a cure for the fever. On a sci-fi extreme, Lew Montray-Alton administers a small dose of *kirian,* a distillate of psychedelic blossoms, to invigorate Regis Hastur's latent telepathy, a valuable clairvoyance. For all its promise, the drug can turn the nontelepath from sleeping infant to "frenzied berserker, raging and hallucinating" (Bradley, 1975, 11–12). Such extremes resemble the Medieval nostrums pennyroyal, nightshade, and foxglove, which required caution to prevent them from shifting from curative to poison.

Managed Care

Clinical treatment on Darkover reflects earthly triage. Rafaella medicates a combat wound on Camilla in "Bonds of Sisterhood" by debriding and cauterizing with acid, a standard medieval protection from infection often applied to chilblains. Sword slashes in *Thendara House* waylay Shann MacShann and his mercenaries during the angry brawl at the Guild House door. The set-to leaves novice Magdalen "Magda" Lorne's leg bleeding heavily, requiring an icy numbing, stitches, and a restorative cordial from Marisela, an Amazon healer and midwife. After a forest fire, Lady Hilary treats Magda's burned feet with a magical blue shimmer, a healing sorcery that sets Darkovans apart from Terran techno-medical expertise. An advanced form of research in *The Shadow Matrix* depicts the wasting illness in Diotima "Dio" Ridenow-Alton as so puzzling that healers advise applying suspended animation—"a stopgap measure … [putting] her into stasis, until some new method could be discovered" (Bradley, 1997, 5).

In the sci-fi story "Outpost," first issued in *Spacewarp* in 1948, outlanders remain apart from Deneb's humanoids from landing on June 13, 2917, to the following October. After four and a half months incommunicado, Manazu, the leader of the Denebians, requests treatment for the sick by the company doctor. The reason seems to lie in planet history: "There is only one colony of people here, the rest died out in a plague years ago, and this was a dying race" (Bradley, 1949, 143). The motif of saving tribes or races from epidemic disease anticipated Marion's first Darkover novel, *The Planet Savers*. By formulating a serum from trailmen's blood, Jay/Jason Allison defeats the puzzling moon-cycles of 48-year-fever:

> A few cases in the mountain districts, the next month a hundred-odd cases ... then it skips exactly three months.... The next upswing puts the number ... in the thousands, and three months after that, it ... decimates the entire human population [Bradley, 1976, 8].

In contrast to Marion's self-effacing healers and midwives like Ferrika in *The Forbidden Tower* and Margali in *Stormqueen!*, Dr. Forth stresses the importance of ego to Jay's success, which corroborates the "much-vaunted Terran medical sciences" (*Ibid.*, 9).

During a pre-dawn gallop from Dry-Town in *The Shattered Chain*, Lady Rohana Ardais tends a wound on Nira's thigh. A detailed account of first aid lists an antibacterial wine wash as the only medicine and torn cloth strips as a coagulant until someone can stitch the tear. When Rohana completes the treatment, she awaits a challenging medical task in the delivery of Melora's infant. The peremptory healing chores illustrate a fact of life in the Darkover series that returns in the second stave when Magda stops the bleeding in knife wounds to Jaelle's collarbone, eyelid, and cheek, exacerbated by delirium, fever, and thirst. The pre-civilized milieu demands hardihood and daring.

The healer Alida applies what Janice C. Crosby terms "feminist spirituality," a religious element explored by Doris Lessing, Toni Morrison, Ntozake Shange, Margaret Atwood, Jean Auel, and Adrienne Rich and by Marion in *City of Sorcery* (Crosby, 2000, 1). Crosby declares that the female healer "[hearkens] back to a time when women's power was legitimized as a necessary force in the community as a whole" (*Ibid.*, 5). Integrating with nature, Alida invokes instant cures with a matrix stone, a blue crystal that concentrates mystical power on poisoned slashes, a nature-based treatment that defies the medical and anatomic logic of a more mechanized civilization.

See also Reproduction; *Star of Danger*.

Sources

Bradley, Marion Zimmer. *Darkover Landfall*. New York: DAW, 1972.
_____. *Exile's Song*. New York: DAW, 1996.
_____. *The Heritage of Hastur*. New York: DAW, 1975.
_____. *The Mists of Avalon*. New York: Ballantine, 1983.
_____. "Outpost," *Amazing Stories* 23:12 (December 1949): 143–144.
_____. *The Planet Savers*. New York: Ace, 1976.
_____. *The Shadow Matrix*. New York: DAW, 1997.
_____. *The Spell Sword*. New York: DAW, 1974.
_____. *Traitor's Sun*. New York: DAW, 1999.
Crosby, Janice C. *Cauldron of Changes: Feminist Spirituality in Fantastic Fiction*. Jefferson, NC: McFarland, 2000.
James, Edward. "Marion Zimmer Bradley" in *St. James Guide to Fantasy Writers*. New York: St. James Press, 1996.
Kaler, Anne K. "Bradley and the Beguines" in *Heroines of Popular Culture*. Bowling Green, OH: Bowling Green State University Popular Press, 1987.

The Heirs of Hammerfell

During the turmoil of arson and retribution that marked the Hundred Kingdoms, Darkover profited from a spirit of unity and repressed fun in Marion's *The Heirs of*

Hammerfell. A reprise of the academic conundrum nature vs. nurture, the exposition distinguishes Alastair, the pampered heir to Hammerfell, and Conn, his twin brother separated in toddlerhood and reared like a country boy by Markos in the Hellers mountains. The standard ploy, a tattooed shoulder, differentiates older from younger, a physical talisman like the racial indicators that set Honoré apart from his white half-brother in George Washington Cable's *The Grandissimes: A Story of Creole Life* and the telltale fingerprint in Mark Twain's *doppelgänger* mystery *Pudd'nhead Wilson.* On a personal level, the author dramatized separated twins "who think they're going crazy because each is telepathically in contact with the other" (Craig, 1989, B5).

A narrative filled with emotion and the potential for joy in a late medieval ballad, *The Heirs of Hammerfell* features the characterization of a large family living in exile in Thendara City. In grief, Duke Rascard cries, "My son, my son," an echo of the biblical King David for Prince Absalom in II Samuel 18:33 (Bradley, 1989, 2). The mournful scene creates an atmosphere of loyalty and gratitude between Rascard and Markos, his oldest retainer, who reared the younger twin. Erminie's grief and self-reproach for the loss of twin son Conn takes a more intrusive form in visions repeated for over a year, a time span that also impacts Conn with images of his womb mate Alastair.

The narrative mingles family heartbreak with King Aidan's need for a champion to

```
grandfather

    |

grand-uncle Ardrin, Lord Storn

    |

Rupert Storn

    |

_____(grandchildren)_____

|
|
|       Rascard Hammerfell=Erminie Leynier=Valentine Hastur      Edric Elhalyn=dead mother
|                             |                                          |
|          _____    _____
|  |        |               |           |          |         |     |     |
Lenisa=Alastair   Alaric      Conn=Floria Elhalyn   Gwynn   Nicolo  Deric
fostered by
Jarmilla
```

lead an army and recover Hammerfell from the Storn usurpers, a prime motif of such literature of conquest as Spain's *El Cid*. As a contrast to glitter and privilege in the town theater and dance floor and a chirpy little lapdog named Jewel, Marion inserts Lower-hammer, Conn's home near a barn decorated as a venue for a harvest dance. In Conn's first view of his twin, he recoils from the foppery of "a city dandy ... like a dressed doll for a little girl's dollhouse" and refuses to wear rings and elaborate ascots (*Ibid.*, 86, 89). To musician Gavin Delleray, the outstanding mannequin of the evening in red boots matching red cuffs and curls, Conn compares him to "a ball of feathers set up for the target" (*Ibid.*, 95). The mocker displays hardihood in setting out in foul weather in the dark to settle "trouble up north" by leading the fight for Hammerfell and in rescuing Alastair from Storn Heights after he is hit by a falling tree (*Ibid.*, 137).

Past literature crowds into the plotting, calling to mind the misalliances of Plautus's *Menaechmi*, William Shakespeare's *The Comedy of Errors*, Alexandre Dumas's *Corsican Brothers*, Mark Twain's *The Prince and the Pauper*, and Anthony Hope's *The Prisoner of Zenda*. Drawing on the Romeo and Juliet plot for a quick settlement, Marion introduces Lenisa, kin of the Storn arsonist who set the story in motion. By wedding Lenisa to Alastair and matching Erminie with Valentine, the author implies a carryover from Greek drama that substitutes a common enemy as a unifying point and multiple marriages for a happily-ever-after aura. Gavin, the balladeer, reduces friction by legitimizing folk dance and song and by honoring the twins equally for their musical abilities.

Sources

Bradley, Marion Zimmer. *The Heirs of Hammerfell*. New York: DAW, 1989.
Ertell, Dee. "Busy Season at McCullough," *Bennington* (Vermont) *Banner* (22 December 1989): 4.
"Review: *The Heirs of Hammerfell*," *Publishers Weekly* (29 November 1989).

The Heritage of Hastur

Marion's stilted venture into normalizing same-sex love, *The Heritage of Hastur* received French, German, and Italian translation and won a Nebula nomination in 1975 for violating conservative taboos. She identified the fiction as one of her favorites. In Darkover's second age of contact between residents of Cottman IV and their Earth ancestors, the lengthy plot opens on the journey motif and the encounter of a banner-bearing entourage on the move from Nevarsin to Thendara. Because complications incorporate social approbation of mixed races, Kennard introduces his biracial sons, Lewis "Lew" Alton and young Marius, born to a half-Terran mother.

Key to the pathos of Chapter One, Regis is born parentless and regularly "packed ... away to Saint-Valentine-of-the-Snows," a *cristoforo* monastery renowned for un-heated quarters (*Ibid.*, 17). The author stresses that he "felt queerly lonely" and useless because of his lack of laran powers (*Ibid.*, 18). On a diplomatic mission, Regis's cousin Lew contemplates rumors of illegal sexual overtures and attempted rape of Danilo-Felix Syrtis by pedophile Dyan Ardais, a sadistic act by an expert swordsman and wrestler aided by Sharra matrix powers. At its height, the conflict worsens from madness and lethal injury and the last of the Hasturs trying to accept "what he was" (Bradley, 1975, 1).

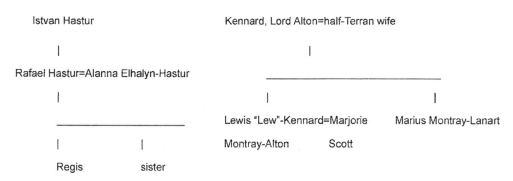

A formal challenge and reply rids the text of intimate talk about relationships. In place, the author inserts Dyan's complex problems of an heir and pledges of loyalty, a tedious, stiff medieval trope devoid of details. In open revelation, he asks, "Is it necessary to explain here, before all men, the nature of the injustice and the apology?" (*Ibid.*, 221). Danilo's acceptance of the arrangement leaves the crime unidentified. In the essay "My Life on Darkover," Marion relished fan mail from young readers who, because of the topic, "even confessed to me that they had become more willing to face (homosexuality) in themselves, without guilt or suicidal impulses" (Bradley, 1974, 12).

Critical response to *The Heritage of Hastur* disclosed support from newspaper reviewers. Roland J. Green, in a review for the *Central New Jersey Home News,* praised Marion for "(moving) from strength to strength" (Green, 1982, D4). Bill Williams, in a critique for the *Northwest Arkansas Times,* identified details as one of those strength. Of the depth of coverage, literary analyst Don D'Ammassa considered the novel a significant landmark in the Bradley canon.

Sources

Bradley, Marion Zimmer. *The Heritage of Hastur.* New York: DAW, 1975.
_____. "My Life on Darkover," *Fantasiae* 2:11 (November 1974): 1, 5, 12.
D'Ammassa, Don. *Encyclopedia of Science Fiction.* New York: Facts on File, 2013.
"From Couch to Moon," couchtomoon.wordpress.com/2016/06/15/heritage-of-hastur-1975-by-marion-zimmer-bradley/
Green, Roland J. "'Hawkmistress' Continues Darkover Saga," (New Brunswick) *Central New Jersey Home News* (26 September 1982): D4.
Williams, Bill, ed. "Mostly About Books," *Northwest Arkansas Times* (11 January 1976): 10D.

Humor

Marion earned fame for situational irony, such as Raella's stutter in "The Children of Cats," the use of herb tea as eyewash in the vignette "To Drive the Cold Winter Away," a magician's job as an exterminator in the fool tale "The Wuzzles," a phony order to Lew Fallon in "Peace in the Wilderness," and Wilidh's chuckles over snooty diners in "Centaurus Changeling." As a ruse to conceal a night escape in *City of Sorcery*, female expeditioners pretend to share lesbian embraces, an intimacy that disgusts males. A techno-joke from David Lorne in *Rediscovery* declares that spyware can "read the license plate on a car parked in the ambassadorial parking lot in Nigeria," one of Marion's more farfetched hyperboles (Bradley, 1993).

Much of the author's wit focuses on gendered situations. In *Warrior Woman,* glad-iatorial trainers make phallic jokes about Hassim's visit to his patron and "[pouring] out all your strength through the Pillar of Fire," a grandiose euphemism for "penis" (Bradley, 1985, 36). The reunion of separated twins Alastair and Conn in *The Heirs of Hammerfell* introduces the author's views on eighteenth-century male attire. Conn, a country boy, considers his brother a fancified showpiece and his brother's friend Gavin Delleray a plumed peacock. Marion details Gavin's fashionable outfit with silk knee breeches, stockings, a flame-red satin brocaded coat and firestones on the shirt neck. The rainbow tints of curled hair cause Alastair to envy a man whom Conn ridicules.

DROLL EXTREMES

Situations enhance humor beyond irony to satire, as with the rule that "it would have been scandalous for a woman of Comyn blood to travel" without a chaperone, even the powerful *leronis* Leonie Hastur in *The Forbidden Tower* (Bradley, 1977, 11). For the opening scene of psychiatrist with patient in *The Planet Savers,* the author reprises the clichéd Freudian remark, "Interesting. In-ter-est-ing" (Bradley, 1976, 2). Teague, a cadet space pilot in *Survey Ship,* makes an unfunny sally at Moira—treating her like a canary in the coal mine: "When the first keels over, something's wrong" (Bradley, 1980, 83). At the settling of a deadly quarrel between Free Amazons and debauched bandits in *The Shattered Chain,* Camilla rebukes the males for being "drunk as monks at midwinter-feast," a jab at the excesses of religious men (Bradley, 1976, 149). Wade "Monty" Montray's Terran joke about dancing in *Thendara House* pictures a gathering of three Darkovans as reason for music and frivolity. Magdalen "Magda" Lorne extends the quip into a truism about humankind: "Only men laugh, only men dance, only men weep" (Bradley, 1983, 279).

The author manages to jest about human dismemberment. For Cholayna's wish to murder Russell "Russ" Montray, a floundering supervisor in *Thendara House,* she realized "he is not even good to eat" (*Ibid.,* 322). One whimsical parable, "Toe Heaven," extends welcome to amputated parts, which occupy a separate place in the afterlife. The honored member, French actor Sarah Bernhardt's leg, succumbed to gangrene on February 22, 1915. At age 71, Sarah refused prostheses and wheelchairs and continued her stage career in a Louis XV palanquin chair transported by two porters. As an entertainer for troops, until her death on March 26, 1924, at age 78, she instilled courage and pride.

Marion's off-hand quips disclose a personality trait admired by her contemporaries. The witty "toiling away in the vineyards of statistical analysis" earned admiration from the *San Francisco Chronicle* reviewer of *Ghostlight* (Bradley, 2013, 17; 2002, 16). In barroom debate with religious know-nothings in "Fool's Fire," Lythande avoids direct confrontation by suggesting a commercial trade-off—accept the local will-o'-the-wisp as a tourist landmark. In a similar rural setting, the badinage of Gimlet the dog-barber and a gypsy at the Hag and Swine inn in "The Walker Behind" bears elements of Mary Ann Evans's yokel dialogue at Raveloe's Red Lion in the moral novel *Silas Marner.* On a noir plane, "The Crime Therapist" in *Future Science Fiction* applies precise diction and psychologist's terminology to a grimly humorous story of curing by killing.

COMEDY AND GENDER

The author shaped gender conundrums into facetious fun, notably, Ede's concern over her partner's concealed weapon in "The Dance at the Gym" and trail guide Kyla Raineach joshing about male libido at high altitudes in *Planet Savers*. At Lady Rohana's lifted eyebrows and refusal to laugh at vulgar wedding night jokes in "Bride Price," she declines to be treated "like a freak at Festival Fair" (Bradley, 1987, 87). During a self-analysis in the exposition of *Exile's Song*, protagonist Margaret "Marja" Alton jokes about her lack of skill at botany and her bent for mathematics, which might have made her "a rather successful embezzler" (Bradley, 1996, 1). The re-entry into Darkover atmosphere gives the author an opportunity to mimic the droning of the spaceship's loudspeaker and to satirize the standard inconveniences of travel. On Rohana's ride from Shainsa in *The Shattered Chain*, she hears Kindra n'ha Mhari's joke about childbirth and snow: "Both come when they will and not when it is convenient" (Bradley, 1976, 68). As a Terran linguist disguised as a Free Amazon, Magda struggles to make sense of banter from other social strata.

The writer enjoyed violating senseless strictures against same-sex unions. In "The Household Altar," the mercenary lute player Lythande, traveling incognito, reasons, "As a woman, I am one half of mankind, and therefore I feel that male pronouns can include me, too" (Bradley, 2009, 165). In "The Secret of the Blue Star," the mysterious sorcerer declares herself unlike "any man you will ever meet," an inside joke Marion repeats in "Sea Wrack" (*Ibid.,* 4). For the anecdote "North to Northwander," the protagonist talks herself into a dilemma after she promises to make a love charm for a married woman. By accident, she summons a lover, "the were-dragon Beauty," who moans Lythande's name, a threat to the musician's gender secret (Bradley, 2013, 185).

In a subsequent work, *The Gratitude of Kings,* the narrative reports the salamander Alnath's birthing of young and makes a joke out of the query "How can you tell that a salamander is in heat?," a pun on the reptile's ability to survive flame (Bradley, 1997, 22). The author speaks through the itinerant Lythande a disparagement of females who stereotype their own kind. Of the rudeness of Mirwen, a lady in waiting, Lythande thinks, "That woman would not know 'subtle' if it walked up and introduced itself" (Bradley, 1997, 13). For self-protection in "Somebody Else's Magic," Lythande "[cultivated] superb skill at own-business-minding," an adage in I Thessalonians 4:11 posed by St. Paul (Bradley, 2013, 34).

HUMOR ON THE ROAD

Survival jokes reveal the down side of a mercenary career. In "The Children of Cats," Lythande admits "taking the odd job here and there" (*Ibid.*, 230). The wanderer states a pragmatic reason: magic, "while a useful skill and filled with many aesthetic delights for the contemplation of the philosopher, in itself puts no beans on the table" (*Ibid.*, 1). For imperious royalty in "The Malice of the Demon," Lythande turns a queen into an infant. A dire fool tale, "The Footsteps of Retribution," features Lythande's bandying of the term "graveyard mould," a visual terror that forces a murderer to avoid reprisal by leaping out a window to his death (*Ibid.,* 139).

Adept at insults, Lythande spouts to a thieving wizard Beccolo, "Hedgerowsorcerer.... Defiler of virgin goats!" (*Ibid.*, 65). With a fillip toward self-gratulating womanizers, in "The Wandering Lute," she credits Prince Tashgen of Tschardain with identifying himself as "a musician who can give [women] lessons on his instrument," a penile reference he garnishes with a wink and eye roll (*Ibid.*, 90). Marion turns the tables on Tashgen's drollery by having him inform Lythande that "women have no business with the High Magic," his reference to killing dragons (*Ibid.*, 91). The comedy deepens after the countess and a farmwife fail to seduce Lythande, who believes that "no were-dragon alive could rival the rage of a scorned woman," a rewording of playwright William Congreve's proverb in *The Mourning Bride* (*Ibid.*, 96).

Fun and Animosity

Marion interlaces serious action with the sardonic turn of phrase, as in *Exile's Song* with the lovers' fallback on mushroom farming if their romance fails. At the mounting violence during the Trojan War in *The Firebrand*, the Princess Kassandra scrambles for some means of rescuing her homeland and family. The thought of returning her twin Paris to his foster father Agelaus elicits from the priestess a bitter slur: "Father should have left him on Mount Ida with his sheep, if they'd have him" (Bradley, 1987, 228). In Volume Two, Kassandra surmises that Queen Hecuba observes wifely decorum by ignoring King Priam's dancing girls, but keeps account of what they eat and how often they breed. Of Kassandra's own situation as Apollo's virgin apostle, she shuns Khryse. After a farewell hug, she smirks to herself, "I shall miss you as I would miss a toothache" (*Ibid.*, 304).

Much of the wit in *The Firebrand* accommodates an epic imbued with unrelenting combat and evil destiny, specifically, the cocky Akhilles riding a resplendent chariot "as a rooster dominates a henyard" and Prince Deiphobos's description of his brother Paris as "Aphrodite's gift to womankind" (*Ibid.*, 461, 529). According to a waggish hyperbole from the Kentaur Cheiron, "The whole world's going there for this war" (*Ibid.*, 308). He pictures the site as a place for combatants and vendors, who hope "to sell something to the fighters, one side or the other" (*Ibid.*). On a more promising occasion, Queen Imandra appears in procession during her last weeks of pregnancy. Priestess Arikia mocks her shape—"big as a python who has swallowed a cow" (*Ibid.*, 330).

Marion's adroit balance of high drama with raillery tempers the novel's militarism and comedy. At Troy, the duel between the Greek hero Diomedes and Glaucus, a Trojan ally, turns masculine vainglory into a fiasco. Their hand-to-hand encounter ends with two warriors going to dinner, a whimsical pairing of men's absorption in killing and gorging. At the climactic appearance of Kassandra in the gilded robe and mask of Apollo and the death of Akhilles from her arrow shot to the heel, the author scales down an apotheosis. Returned to the role of temple priestess, Kassandra can pretend nonchalance at the victory with the chortle, "Well, it's about time" (*Ibid.*, 519).

Drollery and Power

With less slapstick than Mark Twain's *A Connecticut Yankee in King Arthur's Court*, Marion maintains the play of grim against hilarious in her rewritten Arthuriana. Of the power of the Arch Druid Ardanos in *The Forest House*, Eilan describes his perpetual tyranny over woman as "[playing] on us all as if we were his harps," a grim jest at a fearful moment in the action (Bradley, 1993, 116). A more amusing anecdote about masculinity involves Huw, the bodyguard of the High Priestess, a "great halfwit" who faints at the sight of blood (*Ibid.*, 145). Marion rounds out the lengthy Roman wedding ritual with bride capture, ritualized playacting which the drunken groom believes "could have been held off by an old woman and a lame dog" (*Ibid.*, 269).

Comedy in *The Mists of Avalon* takes shape at the lists on Pentecost with the antics of court clowns and fools. Personal one-liners find voice in Accolon's self-effacing claims of losing to Lancelet in the jousts and in the snide worldliness of Morgause, the brash wife of King Lot of Orkney. Targeting convent dwellers, she reduces nuns to clucking hens and wonders, "If God is there, it must be hard for him to get a word in edgewise!" (Bradley, 1983, 218). At Arthur's granting of an audience to Morgaine, Morgause applies a modern cliché—wanting to be a fly on the wall to overhear their exchange. Her niece Morgaine entertains hunters on a winter's night with a bawdy put-down of Saxons, who prefer sex with sheep rather than with women. In northern Wales during a cold March, Morgaine hints that Uriens gravitates to handsome young males rather than females, to which Uriens proposes flirting with the dog.

See also Diction.

Sources

Bradley, Marion Zimmer. *The Complete Lythande*. San Francisco: Marion Zimmer Bradley Literary Works Trust, 2013.
_____. *Darkover Landfall*. New York: DAW, 1972.
_____. *Exile's Song*. New York: DAW, 1996.
_____. "Fandom: Its Value to the Professional," *Inside Outer Space*. New York: Unger, 1985.
_____. *The Firebrand*. New York: Simon & Schuster, 1987.
_____. *The Forbidden Tower*. New York: DAW, 1977.
_____. *The Forest House*. New York: Michael Joseph, 1993.
_____. *Ghostlight*. New York: Doubleday, 2002.
_____. *The Gratitude of Kings*. New York: Wildside, 1997.
_____. *Green Egg Omelette*. New York: Career Press, 2009.
_____. *The Mists of Avalon*. New York: Ballantine, 1983.
_____. *The Other Side of the Mirror*. New York: DAW, 1987.
_____. *The Planet Savers*. New York: Ace, 1976.
_____. *Rediscovery*. New York: DAW, 1993.
_____. *The Shattered Chain*. New York: DAW, 1976.
_____. *Survey Ship*. New York: Ace, 1980.
_____. *Thendara House*. New York: DAW, 1983.
_____. "Toe Heaven," *Marion Zimmer Bradley's Fantasy Magazine* 9:1 (October 1996): 32–33.
_____. *Warrior Woman*. New York: DAW, 1985.
Nastali, Dan. "Arthur Without Fantasy: Dark Age Britain in Recent Historical Fiction," *Arthuriana* 1 (April 1999): 5–22.
Sullivan, C.W. "Folklore and Fantastic Literature," *Western Folklore* 60:4 (Fall 2001): 279–296.
Thompson, Raymond. "Humor and Irony in Modern Arthurian Fantasy: Thomas Berger's Arthur Rex," *Kansas Quarterly* 16:3 (1984): 45–49.

Kenning

Marion's wordcraft reached into Old English for kenning, a transformative word juncture producing precise, dynamic figures of speech. The literary device derives from the Old Norse gerund for "knowing" and applies to myth, legend, and saga. The one-word image, a raw, impromptu convention common to Viking literature, enhances heroic and mythological narratives once broadcast by the itinerant storyteller or gleeman in courts and halls. Passage around the Saxon world of the anonymous Anglo-Saxon *The Seafarer* (ca. 975) and historian Snorri Sturluson's Icelandic *Edda* (1220) boosted pictorial accuracy:

all-father (god)	bone-yard (cemetery)	brain-box (skull)
foam-floater (ship)	life-days (age)	mind-hoard (thoughts)
raven-food (corpse)	raven-hall (crag)	ring-giver (king)
roll-steed (wolf)	stick-eater (fire)	sword-hate (war)
throne-place (hall)	valor-stone (heart)	wine-flushed (drunk)

The compiler of *Beowulf* employed 1,070 compact images from the harper's word-cache.

Kenning fan Josephine Livingstone, an Old English scholar and lecturer, characterized the sound of periphrastic word splicing as "musical, guttural, dark and rich, the aural equivalent of a pithy Scotch" (Livingstone, 2019, 24). In an essay for the *New York Times Magazine,* she equated kenning with portmanteau words and "metaphors of circumlocution" (*Ibid.,* 25). She laced her essay with models:

anstapa (lone-stepper for a "lone walker")	*banhus* (bonehouse for "body")
heathuswate (battlesweat for "blood")	*hronrad* (whale-road for "sea")
weordmyndum (mind-worth for "honor")	

Unlike standard English, which relies on word order for meaning, Old English depended on juxtaposition, "words just hovering next to each other in figurative space" (*Ibid.*).

WORD WIZARDRY

Scandic tropes, according to specialist Jonathan Davis-Secord, produced "a deeply allusive simile compressed into a single compound word or phrase" (Davis-Secord, 2016, 19). Author J.R.R. Tolkien retrieved from Old English the social term guest-kindliness in *The Book of Lost Tales,* the place names Middle-Earth in *The Silmarillion* and Swann-haven in *The Fall of Gondolin,* and the spliced name Beorn the shape-changer in *The Hobbit.* Gaelic versifier Seamus Heaney's poem "North" engaged readers with the compounded noun "word-hoard," an allusive synonym for "books" implying a wealth of language. In the twenty-first century, young adult author Gary Paulsen created his own set of riddling couplings with the titles *Nightjohn* and *Woodsrunner* and the terms "scutpuppy" and "dreamrun," his description of the psychic effects of dogsled racing.

Marion Zimmer Bradley tapped the vitality and implications of kenning with multiple versions in the titles *Darkover, Greyhaven,* "Moonfire," *Stormqueen, The Firebrand,* and the tetrad *Ghostlight, Gravelight, Heartlight,* and *Witchlight.* Examples enrich much of her canon with Scandic animation:

blood-rare ("A Sword Called Chaos")	boy-lover ("Ten Minutes or So")
Candlemas (*The Mists of Avalon*)	centerpolar (*Heritage and Exile*)
cold-sleep (*The Colors of* Space)	dot-dash ("Hero's Moon")
dreamroot ("Somebody Else's Magic")	eighthdark ("Elbow Room")
farspeaker (*The Survivors*)	fire-watch (*Stormqueen!*)
forge-folk ("Firetrap")	gene-deep (*Endless Voyage*)
goldenwash ("Secret of the Blue Star")	heart-kind ("Death Between the Stars")
herb-wife ("Fool's Fire")	hyperdrome (*Exile's Song*)
leechcraft ("To Keep the Oath")	light-lines (*The Shattered Chain*)

moonblood (*The Forest House*)   moonshadow ("Well Met by Moonlight")
mother-right (*The Firebrand*)   mouse-silent (*The Firebrand*)
need-fire (*The Forest House*)   overworld (*Rediscovery*)
paxman (*The World Wreckers*)   psychokinetics (*The Planet Savers*)
Rockraven (*The Ages of Chaos*)   slidewalk (*Darkover Landfall*)
sleep-learner (*Thendara House*)   storm-wrack (*The Fall of Atlantis*)
talesmith (*Tiger Burning Bright*)   tenday (*Hawkmistress!*)
truthspell (*The Fall of Neskaya*)   visionscreen (*The Planet Savers*)
water-scry (*Lady of the Trillium*)   we-other ("Death Between the Stars")
woolgathering (*Traitor's Sun*)   xenoanthropology (*City of Sorcery*)

One model, the late Middle English term "cutpurse" in "The Secret of the Blue Star" redoubles the menace of a knife-handed pickpocket.

A Stylized Trope

The author combed Anglo-Saxon literature for memorable writings in anonymous sources. In *The Mists of Avalon*, Lancelet's 29-line reprise of "The Wanderer" imports "fishes' road" and rephrases "whale road," both watery paths for the lone rover (Bradley, 1983, 688). Other kennings imply real or metaphysical danger:

cathag ("Bonds of Sisterhood")   catmen (*The Door Through Space*)
clingfire (*Two to Conquer*)   deadfall (*The Forest* House)
Death-crone (*The Mists of Avalon*)   dragonswamp ("The Wandering Lute")
dream-dusting (*Darkover Landfall*)   fire-spirit (*The Fall of* Atlantis)
ghost-girl (*The Spell Sword*)   hearthwitch ("The Walker Behind")
spell-candler ("To Kill the Undead")   witchfire ("The Footsteps of Retribution")
witch-food (*The Spell Sword*)

Frequent mention of hexes, fantasy beasts, and sorcery in noun compounds sets the tropes in a pseudo-dark age of folk superstition and ignorance. More positive, the pagan custom of handfasting in "Bride Price," a ritual mentioned in *The Spell Sword, The Alton Gift, Two to Conquer,* and *Stormqueen!*, honors a loving intimacy still essential to Wiccans (Bradley, 1974, 10). "Spaceman" in *Survey Ship* anticipates extensive piloting in deep space, augmented by solar operated "light-sails" (Bradley, 1980, 1, 18).

Similar to the multifaceted kennings in Dylan Thomas's religious sonnet series "Altarwise by Owl-Light," an implication both of a night-flying predator by moonlight and a harbinger of death, for *The Forbidden Tower*, Marion creates "foeman" for enemy in Callista's medieval harp song. The author continues the kenning pattern with "cat-hags" for a female pejorative, "kin-brother" as a union of blood-deep affection, and "starstones," celestial sources of the "healingspell" that recur in *Stormqueen!* and *The Spell Sword*. In each case, kenning serves the text with masterful touches of peril, gendered threat, and earthly and heavenly comfort. For *The Shattered Chain,* the author punches up animosity with the term "he-whores," a spite-filled contrast to the sharing of "grain-brew" in a "truce-hut" and forming a "shelter-truce" with enemies. The feminine images bear less hazard and risk—voluntary "oath-daughters" and "guild-mothers," embroidery of a "rainfish," and, from "Bride Price" that Rohana vocalizes in "The Ballad of Hastur and Cassilda," the hope-filled "starflower" (Bradley, 1987, 27).

Sources

Bradley, Marion Zimmer. "The Ballad of Hastur and Cassilda," *Red Sun of Darkover*. New York: DAW, 1987, 21–27.

_____. *The Forbidden Tower*. New York: DAW, 1977.

_____. *The Mists of Avalon*. New York: Ballantine, 1983.

_____. *The Shattered Chain*. New York: DAW, 1976.

_____. *The Spell Sword*. New York: DAW, 1974.

_____. *Survey Ship*. New York: Ace, 1980.

Davis-Secord, Jonathan. *Joinings: Compound Words in Old English Literature*. Toronto: University of Toronto Press, 2016.

Livingstone, Josephine. "Old English," *New York Times Magazine* (6 January 2019): 24–25.

Knights of the Round Table

Marion's identification of King Arthur's companions challenges her skills to individuate each character to be more than warrior and hero to the Pendragon dynasty. Kinship and brother bonds add to the connections between warriors, who claim lineage from the union of Taliesen, the Merlin, and the Lady of the Lake. At the table received from his father-in-law Leodegranz, Arthur seats fellow fighters without distinguishing rank. He honors his cousin Lancelet and values the loyal Gawaine, Lancelet's brother, who suffers wounding at the battle of Badon while serving as security guard to the king.

Knights	Parents	Description
Balan	Ban of Benwick/Viviane	tall, burly warrior, rational
Balin	Gawan /Priscillla	average size, sturdy, angry
Bediwere	Duke Corneus/Gundolen	the king's marshal and brother of Lucan
Bors	Ban of Benwick/Viviane	a respected knight and grail seeker
Cai (Caius)	Ectorius/Flavilla	Arthur's devoted steward and storekeeper at Caerleon and Camelot
Drustan	Marcus/Isotta	a harper and sire of Cunomorus
Ectorius	—	an aged veteran and chamberlain; Arthur's foster father
Galahad	Lancelet/Elaine	a young Christian initiate and grail seeker
Gareth	Lot of Orkney/Morgause	the youngest of four, handsome and massively built
Gawaine	Lot of Orkney/Morgause	eldest brother, grail seeker, and pagan fighter for Arthur's army
Gwydion/Mordred	Arthur/Morgaine	impudent, gifted with the Sight, ambitious, reckless
Lamorak	Pellinore	rescuer of Lancelet from insanity
Lancelet	Ban of Benwick/Viviane	a pagan jouster and pretty boy who draws women's eyes
Lionel	Ban of Benwick/Viviane	a minor figure among the companions
Lucan	Duke Corneus	veteran warrior and servant
Marhaus	Marhalt	Irish knight and brother of Iseult
Meleagrant	Leodegranz/Roman wife	crude, belligerent churl and rapist of his half-sister Gwenhwyfar
Palamedes	Esclabor	a Saracen convert to Christianity
Pellinore	Pellam	Gwenhwyfar's elderly uncle, an obsessive dragon hunter
Perceval	Pellinore	a knight killed on the Grail quest
Uriens	Cynfarch	elderly pagan knight from northern Wales and great grandson of King Cole
Uwaine	Uriens of Wales/Gwyneth	pledged at age fifteen to Arthur's companions

The ruin of Camelot results from spent idealism and dwindling kinship loyalty. Followers of the grail succumb to disillusion, adventuring, and madness, the downfall of Lancelet. His son Galahad apparently dies on the quest.

Sources

Archibald, Elizabeth, and Ad Putter, eds. *The Cambridge Companion to the Arthurian Legend.* Cambridge, UK: Cambridge University Press, 2009.
Bradley, Marion Zimmer. *The Mists of Avalon.* New York: Ballantine, 1983.
Higham, N.J. *King Arthur: Myth-Making and History.* London: Routledge, 2002.
Mink, JoAnna Stephens, and Janet Doubler Ward. *The Significance of Sibling Relationships in Literature.* Bowling Green, OH: Bowling Green State University Popular Press, 1993.

Lythande

The solitary sorcerer-ronin Lythande combines Marion's enthusiasm for conjury, mystery, curses, and spells with her knowledge of medieval sword skills and string music, both elements of hagiography and Irish wonder tales. Introduced with "The Secret of the Blue Star," a story in Robert Asprin's anthology *Thieves World* (1979), Marion's cross-dressing troubadour, the only female Pilgrim Adept in the Temple of the Blue Star, takes on the glamor of a have-gun-will-travel itinerant. With the aplomb of Angelina Jolie's film character in *Lara Croft—Tomb Raider,* she sports the throbbing blue asterisk on her forehead that marks allegiance and decks herself in cross belts, twin daggers, and a swirling dark cape that conceals a clean-shaven face.

Unlike *La Dame Blanche,* a trickster in Germanic lore, and the Gothic wailer La Llorona, a Latina wraith who steals children in the night, Lythande displays compassion to people she encounters. In "North to Northwander," she offers a sour rejection of "this vast tedium" that occupies homebound females and states in the exemplum "Chalice of Tears": "She had never had a very high opinion of women" (Bradley, 2013, 183, 155). She changes the generalization after she meets sojourner Manuela, a model of the self-determined leader of a pilgrimage. Obeying the Greek precept of φιλίος (*philíos* or group loyalty) required of all Adepts, she is too proud of the profession to ally with Manuela or, in "Somebody Else's Magic," to "make magic in the street like a wandering juggler" (Bradley, 2013, 39). Rather, in a polemical mode similar to Kindra n'ha Mhari's speeches in *The Shattered Chain,* the author views her as a rescuer. Her lore incorporates sexism and random crime against women in the sexual enslavement of Frennet in "The Walker Behind" and the kidnap and murder of Mary in "The Footsteps of Retribution," both motivators of Lythande's one-women retribution.

To maintain a crusade against evil in the episodic collection, Lysande tends to travel at dusk or dark toward a glimmer of light, an indication in "Fools' Fire" and "To Drive the Cold Winter Away" of human habitation and a feeble ray of law in the otherwise anarchical Dark Ages. Like the glow brightening the concluding scene in Lois Lowry's YA allegory *The Giver,* sources of light assure the laconic mage an evening of warmth, food, social engagement, rest, and an opportunity to do good in the world during "the great struggle of humankind" (*Ibid.,* 165). She conceals from others her consumption of food and drink and guards her true identity with "unsparing vigilance" (*Ibid.,* 42). Held at bay in her mind, friendship with Frennet, a love of music shared with

Riella in "Sea Wrack," and a failed love affair with Koira pull at Lythande's memories, dredging up past delights that hint at lesbianism.

THE LONE TRAVELER

According to the story "Bitch," Lythande, like the Wandering Jew and the Flying Dutchman, bears a curse: "an eternal solitude, with none but brief and superficial companionship," a dismal perspective typically represented by damp, foggy nights (*Ibid.*, 108). Amid the gloom of the post–Roman era, she must shroud her feminine emotions and forever play the role of the hired hitman, as demonstrated in her humorous service to Rastafyre in "The Incompetent Magician" and running with Rajene in "Bitch" after the two have morphed into dogs, a scenario Marion repeats in *The Spell Sword*. Traveling initially from Old Gandrin, a name suggesting "gandering," she remains discreet in the cautionary tale "The Malice of the Demon" and keeps her clients' confidences (*Ibid.*, 192). During years of avoiding Gandrin, the peripatetic route rewards the reader with varying Gothic settings—the Hag and Swine, Thieves' Quarter, Aphrodisia House, Gwennane, Sanctuary, Northwander, Forbidden Country, Tyrisis-beyond-the-Sea, and the Place That Is Not. Pernicious characters—Beccolo, Beauty the were-dragon, Rabben the Half-Handed, Toad-kin, Bercy, Roygan the Proud—threaten the wandering lute-player/harpist/minstrel with an additional curse or exposure of her secret. Of chance acquaintances, in "Chalice of Tears," the pilgrim Manuela informs Lythande, "Nothing is accidental," a philosophy suggesting Buddhist fatalism (*Ibid.*, 155).

The episodes vary in tone and atmosphere from comic and chilling to witty, eerie, and mystic, as in the heroine's lurking through the night in Old Gandrin like a "cat's ghost" past merchants selling slave women. She views mothers gesturing against the Evil Eye by closing the fist and raising the index and little fingers, a representation of horns to ward off ill fortune (*Ibid.*, 24). For lyrics in the vignette "To Drive the Cold Winter Away," Lythande draws on lines from the Greek poet Sappho and the Old Testament spring rhyme "Lo, the winter is past" in Song of Solomon 2:11–12, a Hebrew psalm to optimism. Anticipating the Last Battle of Law and Chaos, the "one Great Strife," each installment demands a righting of social disorder, particularly theft, a pervasive crime before the advent of community policing (*Ibid.*, 23).

THE MEDIEVAL MILIEU

In three or four normal lifetimes, Marion's road-weary mage follows a sequence of places and events on an imaginary backdrop from the Great Salt Desert to the Ice Mountains under Twin Suns Keth and Reth. The narrative accentuates elements of the times—unlighted streets and alleys, taverns and inns, hiring-fairs and bazaars, and the jobs of charcoal burning, herding sheep, and guarding caravans from brigand attack. Locales take on imaginative insights into the period, especially concrete nouns displayed on signs to direct the illiterate. The logos guide Lythande to the Blue Dragon in Tschardain and "the Fountain of Mermaids in the Street of the Seven Sailmakers" opposite the treasure room of Roygan the Proud, a suggestion of the lair in the Arabic folk tale "Ali Baba and the Forty Thieves" from *One Thousand and One Nights* (*Ibid.*, 23).

To identify past eras, the writer incorporates a chandlery and time-candles, forerunners of clocks, and taverns serving mead, a fermented honey drink created in 7000 BCE. At a cafe in "North to Northwander," the magician purchases a mortar and pestle for pounding prunes, raisins, and dates into fruit leather, a shelf-stable source of trail nutrition. The equipment marks an era when people crushed herbs and flavorings for adding to recipes for food and curatives. Lythande swaddles a newborn and leaves the little girl to the care of "pious sisterhoods" (*Ibid.,* 131). Catholic nuns predated professional childcare nurses and generously remanded unknown foundlings around 600 CE to convents and monasteries in Milan and Rome, Italy; Montpellier, France, and Trèves, Germany. Some of Marion's details violate pre-modern settings, especially whipped cream, a dairy delight invented in the 1500s and mentioned in "To Drive the Cold Winter Away," and the clavier, a Renaissance keyboard instrument from the late 1600s. "Here There Be Dragons" inserts a quip about the stock market, a concept initiated in the French *bourse* in the 1100s CE, but not completely realized until the formation of the Dutch Exchange in the late Renaissance.

The lyrical text of "The Secret of the Blue Star" refers to brigands as robbers and despoilers of women, especially working females like Myrtis the innkeeper in Sanctuary, who has gold coins worth stealing. Lythande encounters Cappen Varra, a man armed with a rapier, a thin stabbing blade common in the Renaissance. The two talk over a meal host-guest style, a revered arrangement between strangers akin to "shelter-truce" in *The Shattered Chain* that prevents random violence or theft (Bradley, 1976, 147). Characteristic of hosts, Lythande mines conversation in the inns in "Fool's Fire" and "Sea Wrack" for information and asks "What news, Friends" in the Hag and Swine in "The Walker Behind" (Bradley, 2013, 119). Wineshop customers in "To Kill the Undead" discuss the werewolf or vampire that roams by night and tears out human throats. Such evaluation of rumors is common to the modern detective fiction of author Sara Paretsky's V.I. Warshawski, Craig Johnson's Walt Longmire, James Lee Burke's Dave Robicheaux, and Lee Child's Jack Reacher.

The Medieval Woman

After a career as a court entertainer, Marion's troubadour sets out "to learn the secrets of Creation," an undertaking that introduces endless travels and an unrelenting dilemma of hiding her gender (Bradley, 2013, i). The writer posits that the life of the androgynous singer-avenger generates a gap between the settled female and redoubtable characters such as the protagonist of *Warrior Woman*: "Women who have proved themselves competing against men were not very sympathetic to the protected women's spaces and quotas" (*Ibid.,* 64). The price of satisfaction for a picara as free-wheeling as Lythande is isolation from the norm of family, children, fireside, and community and a constant battle against violators of female autonomy, especially the exploiter Rastafyre, the talking corpse in "The Children of Cats." The occasional woman-to-woman friendship, particularly the camaraderie with Eirthe the candlemaker in *The Gratitude of Kings* and Frennet in "The Walker Behind," rewards Lythande with a fleeting sisterhood, yet, even among women, she remains terse.

Much of the rover's narrative involves bouts of logic against illogic, such as Lythande's distaste for the beliefs of bible-thumpers in "Fool's Fire" and at injunctions against music, ale, and coffee in "To Drive the Cold Winter Away." She renders the prohibition on melody as a "ban on joy in men's hearts" (*Ibid.*, 167). A contemplative moment in Roygan's lair forces Lythande to ponder the virtue of regaining the magic wand of a wicked roué while leaving the jewels of vain women behind. The choice—to honor a vow to return the wand—forces Lythande into mortal combat with a bane-wolf to retrieve a tacky phallic symbol, a disgusting icon the author reprises in "The Children of Cats." Also in the narrative lies the task of carrying Rastafyre's shrouded corpse over her shoulder and digging his grave, two accomplishments that enhance her "butch" demeanor and willingness to perform grueling labor.

THE DEDICATED CHAMPION

A turning point in Lythande's saga, "Somebody Else's Magic" places her in a setting endangering her secret and survival. Stalked by Beccolo, a grudge-bearing Adept, the vagabond mercenary adapts her disguise with a skirt, which makes her a woman posing as a man posing as a woman. The return to female garb disquiets Lythande, causing rethinking of her choice of a lifestyle free of prohibitions against women's liberties that Marion details in the suffocating strictures placed on girl postulants in the Shrine of Laritha. Unlike the comic contretemps of mixed genders in William Shakespeare's *Twelfth Night,* Lythande ricochets from despair to terror until an unforeseen plot twist frees her on the spot to be whatever gender she chooses, a motif that recurs in Marion's canon. Gladdened and rid of an onerous Laritha sword, she strides toward another opportunity to fight injustice by overcoming "the helplessness of … people [who] touched her heart" (*Ibid.*, 74).

In an interview, Marion stated parameters for Lythande: "It's okay for a woman in a story to have whatever love life suits her, but the real work of the world must come first" (DuPont, 1988, 99). Because of Lythande's dedication to justice, she exterminates Roygan. The murder fills her with regret that posing as a male paladin requires the extreme acts of violence that society expects of men. Fulfilling the author's proverb in *The Fall of Atlantis,* the mercenary learns that "[i]t has never been, and never will be easy work! But the road that is built in hope is more pleasant to the traveler than the road built in despair, even though they both lead to the same destination" (Bradley, 1983, 440). In the estimation of critic Anne K. Kaler, author of *The Picara: From Hera to Fantasy Heroine,* Lythande flourishes apart from the comic book Superwoman: "As a woman, she has different goals and different obstacles to overcome; her monsters are society's disapprovals, her mountains are galactic spaces, her hunger is for self-knowledge" (Kaler, 1991, 40). As a result, she responds to human privation, avoids random killing and destruction, sings entrancing melodies of "home and fireside," and longs to "tell her story" (Bradley, 2013, 71; Kaler, 1991, 40).

See also Diction; Female Persona; *The Gratitude of Kings*; Religion.

Sources

Asprin, Robert. *Thieves' World*. New York: Ace, 1979.

Bradley, Marion Zimmer. *The Complete Lythande*. San Francisco: Marion Zimmer Bradley Literary Works Trust, 2013.

_____. *The Fall of Atlantis*. Riverdale, NY: Baen Books, 1983.

_____. *The Shattered Chain*. New York: DAW, 1976.

DuPont, Denise, ed. *Women of Vision*. New York: St. Martin's, 1988.

Kaler, Anne K. *The Picara: From Hera to Fantasy Heroine*. Bowling Green, OH: Bowling Green State University Popular Press, 1991.

Kelso, Sylvia. "The Matter of Melusine: A Question of Possession," *Literature in North Queensland* 19:2 (2016): 134–144.

Mutter, John. "Review: *Lythande*," *Publishers Weekly* 229:26 (27 June 1986): 82.

Magic

Marion characterizes supernatural and unforeseeable powers as "a fine art and of great aesthetic value" (Bradley, 1974, 8). In stagy demonstrations, she dramatizes the beguiling appearance of the matrix crystal in Damon's silk bag and of Callista to Andrew Carr via "air and fire" in *The Spell Sword*, the forgotten powers of the royal dynasty or Ruwenda in *The Black Trillium*, and the bitter curses and death-spell that fell Mayra the sorceress in *Stormqueen!* (Bradley, 2013, 171). The author exemplifies multiple sources of the paranormal—Jeremy's return from the dead to his wife Valeria and their newborn son in "The Word of a Hastur," Viviane's shimmering appearances before Morgaine in *The Mists of Avalon*, and Jaelle n'ha Melora's confusion at reading several minds at once in *Thendara House*. During Lady Rohana Ardais's telepathic conversation with Melora in *The Shattered Chain*, Rohana sings "The Ballad of Hastur and Cassilda," a folk tale laden with wonders of the blade that the god Zandru casts on his forge. In the last stave, a tangible form of magic from a blue matrix stone enables the healer Alida to extract poison from Jaelle's wounded thigh, cheek, and eyelid. The capacity to heal and read minds advances Darkovans above the mechanically inclined Terrans.

In the estimation of Ann F. Howey, a reviewer of *Heartlight* for the *Edmonton Journal*, Marion's occult plots "follow the struggles of these protagonists to accept and control their powers" (Howey, 1991, F7). Fictional events call for magic as virulent as that of Sara Latimer, hanged for a witch in the seventeenth century in *Witch Hill*, as wicked as the Dark Sisterhood in *City of Sorcery*, as mercenary as Bard's despoiling of women in *Two to Conquer*, and as graceful as the priest who inadvertently releases Lythande and Rajene from evil spells that make them hounds in "Bitch." The self-effacing candlemaker Eirthe in *The Gratitude of Kings*, a medieval artisan, claims that simple spells tell her what to avoid "if I want to stay out of trouble" (Bradley, 1997, 27). For a foil, the author inserts in "The Wandering Lute" Lady Beauty, a were-dragon disguised as a lovely minstrel sharing a meal with Lythande and later entertaining the court of King Tashgen with intricate melody. In a face-off of powers, Lythande's nose for sorcery identifies the shapeshifter and protects herself with a unique personal magic.

THE WANDERING WIZARD

By picturing the preternatural in action, Marion stresses the potency of sorcery, especially Colin MacLaren's fight against Nazism in *Heartlight* with a credo based on light. Sheldon Wiebe, a book critic for the *Calgary Herald* for parameters: "It is even more important, in fantasy, that rules be established and are consistently used; otherwise there are no stakes, no risks" (Wiebe, 2001, ES11). Of Lythande's supernatural charms, the author states, "When a wizard who wore the blue star was angered, bystanders did well to be out of the way" (Bradley, 2013, 3). Unlike Eirthe's gentle appearance and amenable work amid Alnath and other mischievous salamanders, much of the Lythande series enhances dread in onlookers. Bystanders fear her hooded mage robe and daggers, intimidating gaze, halting of time, and a ring that sparks flames on her roll-your-own herbal cigarette, a gimmick in "The Secret of the Blue Star." A brief twist—a hex chanted "Asmigo; Asmagd" under a dark moon—requires the presence of three gray mice, the author's bit of fun to lighten a too serious tone (*Ibid.*, 104).

In addition to carrying daggers and pocket snacks, the wanderer bears a book of enchantments capable of raising the dead. She uses such knowledge advisedly, tying the "magical ninefold knot" in "Somebody Else's Magic" and never activating a godlike control of life over death (*Ibid.*, 44). Instead of grandstanding, Lythande resorts to amazing onlookers by vanishing from locked rooms and, in "The Incompetent Magician," walking through stone walls, snatching three rubies from the air, and shapeshifting her body to greater heights. In "The Walker Behind," the sorcerer rescues travelers from a witchy innkeeper who turns them into pigs to cook for dinner. Marion extends sorcery against sorcery in a death struggle between Lythande and a ravening bane-wolf. Although conjured by an evil magician, the predator fights like a living beast, its flashing fangs leaving the warrior woman burned and "slimed with the magical blood" (*Ibid.*, 27). By presenting mortal pain in Lythande, the stories redeem her from supreme power.

BLACK VS. WHITE MAGIC

The author introduces a more practical incantation in *The Fall of Atlantis* with Domaris's singing to ignite a light. Unlike enemies of her domain, Domaris has no interest in black magic, which the author characterizes as the "forbidden arts of the past" (Bradley, 1983, 46). In romantic rapture, Domaris's little sister Deoris follows the magician Riveda to the Grey Temple, a forbidding edifice to the uninitiated. On her first visit, a trick of the sorcerer Craith projects a village of conical stone huts occupied by ghastly retardates who fling rocks and chase the intruder. The author delays mention that the Grey-robes burn Craith alive for endangering Deoris and her pregnant sister, a potential crime that the brotherhood deems unforgivable. At a less fearful intrusion, Deoris views necromancers in training, who learn the secrets of color, sound, and gravity, nature-based knowledge that seems more wholesome than forbidding. As though analyzing science, Riveda claims, "All unknown things are fearful to those who do not understand them," a philosophy proved repeatedly in history by such adventurers as alchemist Hermes Trismegistus, Galileo, Nostradamus, Marie Curie, and Nikola Tesla (*Ibid.*, 284).

In *The Forbidden Tower*, marvels breach the limits of time and space. Damon Ridenow's Timesearch involves the Overworld in tapping the dominion of tower Keepers in earlier times. The pseudo-human Sharra, an ancient fire demon known as a matrix, emerges in *The Heritage of Hastur* as the savior of Lew Alton, heir to the Alton Domain. In a sequel, *Sharra's Exile,* the matrix, formerly a possession of the Forge Folk, becomes a female deity and a portal to the human world. A more tangible form of hocus-pocus, Regis's transformation into the Son of Light bestows healing conjury that saves Lew from death. The author indicates the price of wielding the Sharra matrix in the change in Regis's hair, which turns white.

The author limits wizardry in *The Firebrand* to detailed scenes, primarily women's reverence toward the reptiles of the Snake Mother, the Kentaurs' soaking of arrows in toad poison, and Imandra's anticipation of a propitious naming day for little Pearl. According to Sonja Sadovsky, author of *The Priestess & the Pen,* these character uses of magic "manifest the will of the Goddess and [transmit] unique occult experience" (Sadovsky, 2014, xxx). In Helen's birthing chamber, priestesses distribute magic charms against evil and gesture holy signs to dispel mention of bad omens, especially the death of sacred snakes during an earthquake. Male magic appears in the exchange between Kassandra and the Kentaur Cheiron, who offers unique arrows in exchange for loaves of bread, an icon of female kitchen alchemy. By allying women with grain and sustenance, Marion claims the inborn female gift for nurturing. In the words of painter Kristen Olsen, "The real magic is between people and the connection with the earth" (Schneider, 2005, 106).

ARTHURIAN MAGIC

Marion launches the supernatural at a critical pass in *The Forest House* following the birthing of Mairi's daughter. To rough Scotti raiders led by Red Rian, the priestess Caillean hurls embers from the hearth without harming her hands. A gentler glimpse of female empowerment derives from the spell singer, a harpist who intones ritual enchantment in time with the melody, a form of sorcery that the author introduced in *Falcons of Narabedla.* For Eilan, study of spells advances to handling burning coals. Caillean instructs Eilan on the importance of dropping the embers at the instance of fear: "Doubt is the enemy of magic" (Bradley, 1993, 125). Eilan matures in the use of scrying and envisions the Romans and Celts warring on the Scotti, her first involvement of magic in combat.

The sequel, *The Mists of Avalon,* invites readers to savor the triumph of good over wickedness, the end result of magical intervention. Reviewer Laura Tutor, on staff at the *Anniston* (Alabama) *Star*, relives an engrossing read: "Turning each page is like entering another chamber in a storied maze;; and when you get to the end, you sit back, breathe deep and relive scenes that were vividly brought to life on the mythical and mystical holy isle of Avalon" (Tutor, 2001, 4B). According to Darrell Schweitzer, a critic for the *Philadelphia Inquirer,* Marion sets the Arthurian reprise in a time when "Christianity grows and the magic of the goddess fades…. Thus the time of legends blends into history" (Schweitzer, 1983, 6).

The author speaks through Taliesin the Merlin the waning of legendary sorcery. He warns Queen Igraine of Cornwall that magic serves special needs, but does not overcome everyday obstacles. Morgaine makes a similar pronouncement to Gwenhwyfar that "[c]harms do not their magic as men and women would have it, but by their own laws" (Bradley, 1983, 443). The priestess further denigrates charms and spells "for concentrating the will of the ignorant" (*Ibid.*, 523). The action demonstrates her warnings with the silent summons of Viviane, the Lady of the Lake, to the magic barge, a supernatural transportation within sight of St. Michael's tower above the spiral approach up Glastonbury Tor, all known landmarks.

Again, Marion indicates that doubt can override the magic by which Viviane disperses mist to reveal an idyllic haven set in oaks and apple trees above the water's edge, where swans glided among the reeds. To strengthen Morgaine for rigorous training, Viviane limits her to a piscatorial diet of fish, fruit, bread, and water from the Holy Well, aliments that heighten consciousness and the control of superhuman potency. At the initiation of Raven and Morgaine into a higher level of telepathy, heavy dose of herbs leaves them bleeding, vomiting, and depleted, the price exacted from the seer for a sweeping vision of Britannia's history. The antidote—water of life, also called aqua vitae or whiskey—revives Morgaine.

Women's Magic

Composed as fantasy rather than a chivalric saga on the Middle Ages, Marion's version of Arthuriana upholds the sisterhood of the mist-shrouded island of Avalon, where intuitive women converge to honor the Lady of the Lake and practice the Sight. In a motif of incipient kingship developed in *The Shadow Matrix* and *The Gratitude of Kings,* Viviane assigns Morgaine to protect King Arthur—the pairing of his sword Excalibur with a scabbard to prevent bleeding, a yin/yang symbol of phallic blade with ripe uterus. Morgaine invests the sheath with "blood-stanching spells" and icons of paganism and Christianity, a merger of the two faiths vying for control of Celtic Britannia (Bradley, 1983, 205). The task represents a promotion of the postulant and an expectation of supreme power after Morgaine replaces her aging aunt.

In intimate scenes, the author reveals detailed forms of enchantment. After giving birth to Arthur's son Gwydion/Mordred, Morgaine maintains her role as protector by halting the hex that Morgause places on the infant, casting into flames "secret herbs" and bits of Arthur's hair and blood, two elements of voodoo curses (*Ibid.,* 250). Upon revelation of Gwydion's siring and birth, his grandmother Viviane, the Lady of the Lake, values his doubly royal line allying Avalon with the Pendragon dynasty. The dilemma of the legend lies in acceptance of Gwydion/Mordred among the hill people and the Christian rejection of a child conceived by incest. In subsequent action, to shield herself from scoldings by Father Eian, Morgaine distances her consciousness from the Sight, except when she spins wool, a vortex that "opened the gates too quickly to trance" (*Ibid.,* 656). To prevent the paranormal from seizing her thoughts, Morgaine foregoes the spinning wheel and distaff and favors the loom.

In Marion's resolution of the Arthuriad, primeval enchantment resurges in the form of seduction and spying. Nimue, a young beauty determined to punish Kevin Harper for profaning his sacred oath, observes moon lore for the timing of her plot. Because the moon lay in the crescent stage, she chose "moon-dark, the slack time when the Lady sheds none of her light on the world" as the ideal time for concealed retribution (*Ibid.,* 787). The seduction causes double deaths—Kevin's and Nimue's by suicidal drowning in the Lake. With more guile and heartlessness, Morgause uses fresh dog blood to investigate her manipulation of Gwenhwyfar and the future of Gwydion/Mordred. The ruthless control of a cat's paw, the servant Morag channeled by Becca, yields proof that Arthur's queen is no longer fertile. Witchy with greed for rule after she "found the way to sorcery," Morgause declares herself "Queen of Darkness," the dire side of necromancy (*Ibid.,* 822, 821).

Sources

Bradley, Marion Zimmer. *The Complete Lythande.* San Francisco: Marion Zimmer Bradley Literary Works Trust, 2013.

_____. *The Fall of Atlantis.* Riverdale, NY: Baen Books, 1983.
_____. *The Forest House.* New York: Michael Joseph, 1993.
_____. *The Gratitude of Kings.* New York: Wildside, 1997.
_____. *The Mists of Avalon.* New York: Ballantine, 1983.
_____. *The Spell Sword.* New York: DAW, 1974.
Da Silva, Bridgette. "Medieval Mindsets: Narrative Theory and *The Mists of Avalon,*" *Strange Horizons* (1 October 2007).
Farwell, Marilyn R. *Heterosexual Plots and Lesbian Narratives.* New York: New York University Press, 1996.
Howey, Ann F. "Belief and Acting on It Go Hand-in-Hand," *Edmonton Journal* (3 January 1991): F7.
Sadovsky, Sonja. *The Priestess & the Pen: Marion Zimmer Bradley, Dion Fortune & Diana Paxson's Influence on Modern Paganism.* Woodbury, MN: Llewellyn Worldwide, 2014.
Schneider, Wolf. "My World," *Southwest Art* 35:6 (November 2005): 106–107.
Schweitzer, Darrell. "Review: *The Mist of Avalon,*" *Philadelphia Inquirer* (6 March 1983): 6.
Tutor, Laura. "Back to Avalon," *Anniston* (Alabama) *Star* (15 July 2001): 4B.

The Mists of Avalon (1983)

The first of the six-book Avalon series, Marion's bestselling novel takes the form of a quest narrative in "fairyland, eternal peace," a romanticized tapestry of the post–Roman rescue of Britannia from Saxon marauders (Bradley, 1983, 145). According to Kate O'Hare, critic for the Martinsville, Indiana, *Reporter-Times,* the story remains Europe's best narrative in part because "it remains shrouded in mystery and open to interpretation" (O'Hare, 2001). She lauded Marion's version for spotlighting "five women who represent the emotional core of the tale and the struggles between competing world views," that of "earth-centered, polytheistic" paganism and Christianity (*Ibid.*).

Beset by waning control of the Sight, Viviane, the Lady of the Lake and high priestess of Avalon, ponders the grand scheme she and Taliesin the Merlin devise to suppress Saxon invasions. To ensure unity among tribes in Britannia, the two plot to elevate the boy Arthur to replace his father, High King Uther Pendragon. Inspired by love for the Mother Goddess and the priestesses of the House of Maidens, Viviane consoles herself that she intends to "save this land and its people from rapine and destruction, a reversion to barbarism, a sacking greater than Rome suffered from the Goths," e.g., the German leader Odoacer's replacement of Romulus, Rome's last emperor, on August 23, 476 CE.

Critical opinion identified *The Mists of Avalon* as Marion's masterwork for what Steve Miller, literary critic for the *Baltimore Sun* characterized as a "story [that] combines honor, duty, and love in an irresistible way" (Miller, 1983, D4). Editor Mike Ashley applauded the novel for "[capturing] the imagination and [catapulting] the genre onto another plane" separated from reality by mist, a metaphor for political and religious anarchy (Ashley, 1995, 130). With more detail, researcher Don Riggs characterizes the awareness of milieu and self in the author's setting as "an alteration of consciousness … a floating, indefinite space where the world's standard divisions of time, space, and even causality are suspended" (Riggs, 1998, 22). The events of the sixth century occur in a nebulous prehistory when "the gates between the worlds drifted within the mists," before the Christian priesthood closed the magic gap (Bradley, 1983, ix). Diana Lucile Paxson, Marion's sister-in-law and colleague, summarized the human interaction as a "family saga, in which relationships mutate from one generation to the next, and secrets can be more deadly than swords" (Paxson, 1999, 118).

THE OTHER HALF OF THE STORY

The source of reader appeal, Marion's storytelling about women's lives, drew generations of fans to the series much as feminist narrative boosted reception of Toni Morrison's *Beloved,* Kim Chernin's *The Flame Bearer,* and Alice Walker's *The Temple of My Familiar.* Literary expert Marilyn Farwell, on the English staff at the University of Oregon, describes Marion's framework saga as "one of the great heroic legends of white, Western culture, the Arthuriad" (Farwell, 1996, 21). In a speech on January 19, 1989, at Trinity College in Hartford, Connecticut, Marion named Cadbury Castle in Somerset as the foundation of the legendary Camelot, which flourished in the fifth and sixth centuries CE. She justified the subject matter and concluded that there was indeed a monarch at Cadbury "real enough to hang a novel on" (Vain, 2014). The prequels, *The Forest House* and *Lady of Avalon,* cover identifiable historic periods. The three staves of *Lady of Avalon* begin in 96–118 CE, advance to 285–293 CE, and conclude in the familiar King Arthur time span, 440–452 CE, which Marion covers in *The Shadow* in the ethical reshaping of policy by Varzil the Good banning weapons that kill from a distance.

By revealing the maturing of Viviane, the Lady of the Lake, the second stave of the trilogy exults in "the most powerful and awe-inspiring High Priestess" of the Mother Goddess cult, the focus of *The Mists of Avalon* (Shaw, 2009, 74). Through what Harvard-trained critic Susan Shwartz terms "a woman's and pagan's eye-view of a very traditional mythology," the narrative showcases fertile, assertive female action figures— Viviane (the wisewoman), Morgaine (the maiden), Igraine (the maternal figure), and Morgause (the wild card woman warrior). The quartet become forerunners of Raven, Gwenhwyfar, Niniane, and Nimue, the enchantress who heals Lancelot's insanity.

Eric Mink, a fiction critic for the *New York Daily News,* calls the original quartet "the strong-willed, manipulative, magical and sometimes malevolent women who pulled the strings behind the scenes before, during and after the age of Camelot" (Mink, 2001, 120). Paralleling Marion's "The Ballad of Hastur and Cassilda," the narrative exalts the births of two shining boy-children, King Arthur of Camelot and Jesus of Christendom, the dual champions of Arthur's wife. For background, the author researched fifth- and sixth-century history by Jeffery Ash and Jamie George, perused parish records, and visited Cadbury Castle, Glastonbury, and Tintagel, England, the Cornish outcrop in the Atlantic Ocean that became Arthur's birthplace. The historical novel flourished for four months on the *New York Times* list of bestsellers and in translation into Dutch, Italian, French, and German.

ARTHUR'S CAMELOT

In *The Atlantic,* journalist Alyssa Rosenberg saluted the author for constructing a complete royal court and for "drawing on established myth and real geography" while shrouding magic in mystery (Rosenberg, 2010). Literary historian Jeremy Rosen noted that the author introduced a wave of fiction exploring heroic figures alongside a cast of minor female characters that include Queen Morgause of Lothian, Lancelet's wife Elaine, and Priscilla, Balin's mother and Balan's surrogate mother. Of Marion's pro-woman motifs, she proclaimed "that the emergence of women in our time is more important than the flight to the moon" (Vincelette, 1989, 1). To establish chutzpah in

Arthurian characters, the author set the self-willed, authoritative Morgaine, a Druid priestess, against a Christianized foil—Gwenhwyfar, a "sniveling idiot," the antithesis of the liberated female (*Ibid.*). For the first time, in the prologue, Morgaine/Morgan le Fay speaks for herself and reveals a distinctive personality beset by jealousy of her beloved baby brother Arthur. To account for conflicting passions in Morgaine, critic Madison Vain defined a dominant strand of "female adolescence and the desire to fit into a world that constantly wants to constrict your role" (Vain, 2014).

According to Jan Shaw, on staff at the University of Sydney, Marion rewrote the Arthurian classic to "[take] the marginalised mysterious feminine otherworld and [reclaim] it, developing it as a feminine narratological space that has been elided by mainstream masculine literatures" (Shaw, 2009, 73). The novel achieved a significant place in British legendry. In the overview *Once and Future Queen,* Arthurian expert Nicole Evelina proclaimed Marion's effort "a major feminist reinvention" of Arthuriana (Evelina, 2017, 151). To that end, the plot resets macho-dominant lore from the late 400s and early 500s CE from the male perspective to the struggle of Celtic priestess Morgaine against Christian encroachment by the sour, controlling Bishop Patricius (St. Patrick), who may have reached Ireland in 432 CE. Maureen Quilligan, book critic for the *New York Times,* compared the gynocentric view of early Medieval Camelot to novelist Jean Auel's rewriting of prehistory in *The Clan of the Cave Bears,* the first of the Children of Earth series. Quilligan praised Marion's "massive narrative that is rich in events placed in landscapes no less real for often being magical" (Quilligan, 1983). Myrna Oliver, a medievalist writing for the *Los Angeles Times,* applauded Marion's attention to detail from "meticulous research … on the dress and architecture of the period, as well as food and herb lore," two sources of wellness and healing controlled by women (Oliver, 1999, A24).

A WOMEN'S ACADEMY

The author anticipated the subject of cloistering in *Two to Conquer* (1980) with the character Carlina "Carlie" di Asturien, a devotee of Avarra, the goddess of the death/rebirth cycle, who longs to avoid marriage and to serve the sick and needy. Protected from a vicious wizard-mercenary, she lives on the Island of Silence and promotes the Sisterhood of the Sword. Marion prefigured the medieval Beguine and Beghard visiting nurse corps of Ghent and Paris by Carlina's aid to victims of catastrophe and her adoption of the name Sister Liriel, the Hebrew word for "God's lyre." The female cadre takes the fictional form reflected in the women's education center in *The Forest House* and the House of the Maidens and a priestly enclave in *The Mists of Avalon.* Among teachers in a womblike setting, young females learn to read and write, refine precognition and prophecy, collect herbs for preparation into tonics and medicines, and tend the suffering.

Key to the all-female motif lies Marion's idealized society of Avalon, a blend of womanly spirituality and Christian esotericism. In the clarification of Sonja Sadovsky, author of *The Priestess & the Pen,* the fictional cast emerges from the author's "theory of the Triple Goddess, or Maiden, Mother, and Crone," a feminist foregrounding of the Christian concept of Father, Son, and Holy Ghost (Sadovsky, 2014, 2). Sadovsky credits female energy, sisterhood, and innovation with promoting women's artistry. Their contributions include minstrelsy, hymnology, gardening and herbalism, nurse care, fiber work, astronomy, child welfare, elder care, and peace.

　　See also Mother Goddess; Religion.

Sources

Ashley, Mike, ed. *The Merlin Chronicles.* New York: Carroll & Graf, 1995.

Bradley, Marion Zimmer. *The Mists of Avalon.* New York: Ballantine, 1983.

Evelina, Nicole. *The Once & Future Queen: Guinevere in Arthurian Legend.* Maryland Heights, MO: Lawson Gartner, 2017.

Farwell, Marilyn. *Heterosexual Plots and Lesbian Narratives.* New York: New York University Press, 1996.

Gordon-Wise, Barbara Ann. *The Reclamation of a Queen: Guinevere in Modern Fantasy.* New York: Praeger, 1991.

Miller, Steve. "The Arthurian Legend: Returned to Epic Status," *Baltimore Sun* (30 January 1983): D4.

Mink, Eric. "'Avalon' Gradually Improves Its Caliber," *New York Daily News* (13 July 2001): 120.

O'Hare, Kate. "The Once and Future Women of 'The Mists of Avalon,'" *Reporter-Times* (Martinsville, IN) (14 July 2001).

Oliver, Myrna. "Marion Bradley; Writer of Fantasy Novels," *Los Angeles Times* (30 September 1999): A24.

Paxson, Diana L. "Marion Zimmer Bradley and *The Mists of Avalon,*" *Arthuriana* 9:1 (Spring 1999): 110–126.

Quilligan, Maureen. "Arthur's Sister's Story," *New York Times* (30 January 1983).

Riggs, Don. "The Survival of the Goddess in Marie de France and Marion Zimmer Bradley," *Journal of the Fantastic in the Arts* 9:1 (1998): 15–23.

Rosen, Jeremy. "An Insatiable Market for Minor Characters," *New Literary History* 46:1 (Winter 2015): 143–163, 188.

Rosenberg, Alyssa. "The Rules of Fictional Worlds," *The Atlantic* (24 September 2010).

Sadovsky, Sonja. *The Priestess & the Pen: Marion Zimmer Bradley, Dion Fortune & Diana Paxson's Influence on Modern Paganism.* Woodbury, MN: Llewellyn Worldwide, 2014.

Shaw, Jan. "Troublesome Teleri," *Sidney Studies in English* 35 (2009): 73–95.

Shwartz, Susan. "Marion Zimmer Bradley" in *St. James Guide to Science Fiction Writers.* New York: St. James Press, 1996.

Vain, Madison. "The Mists of Avalon," *Entertainment* (25 July 2014), https://ew.com/article/2014/07/25/mists-of-avalon-marion-zimmer-bradley/.

Vincelette, Bob. "Bradley Lectures on Morgan LeFey," *Trinity Tripod* 86:11 (24 January 1989): 1.

Mists of Avalon, Book One: Mistress of Magic

　　From the outset, Marion flourishes at clan relations. In the view of Alyssa Rosenberg in an article for the *Washington Post,* "She sustains a sprawling narrative with a huge, intergenerational cast of characters over almost 900 pages" (Rosenberg, 2014). The author blurs the kinship lines between parent, sibling, and child, the same smudging of relationships of Micon and his half-brother Reio-ta, an underlying conflict in *The Fall of Atlantis,* and of Kassandra's mothering of the foundling Honey in *The Firebrand.* The author repeats the system of fostering by Priscilla of Balan, son of Viviane, the Lady of the Lake, an adoption scheme that allies Eilan with stepbrother Cynric in *The Forest House.* In Igraine's discussion with Viviane and the Merlin about the encroachment of Christianity into the old ways, the sisters shift relationships to a mother-daughter pairing. At a height of disagreement, Viviane silences Igraine, who ripostes, "You shall not treat me as if I were a babbling child" (Bradley, 1983, 17). The squabble humanizes the drama with normal sisterly resentments and feuding, but maintains the gift of foresight that enables Viviane to anticipate Igraine's role in the birth of a great warrior-king who will revive worship of the Great Mother.

　　The terse dialogue between Igraine and her husband, Duke Gorlois of Cornwall, extends from his return home to Tintagel to a state visit to the crowning of High King Uther Pendragon in Londinium, a pageantry suited to the early Middle Ages. War talk at table underscores the obsessions of militaristic men—power, land, violence, booty, dynasty. Uther Pendragon caps the exchange with a personal credo: "I am a man of battle, I have been so all my days, and I pray to live all my life in war, as befits a man…. I want war and plunder and women" (*Ibid.,* 38). Marion wrings irony out of Gorlois's patronizing of his nineteen-year-old wife Igraine, whom he calls "Child," the future mother of the great leader of the Celts (*Ibid.,* 40). After their virulent clash at Londinium, Igraine compares her wifely incarceration to "[chattel] like a horse or a milk goat" (*Ibid.,* 71). Typically vainglorious and domineering, Gorlois dies without realizing the future greatness of Igraine.

TRANSCENDENT FEMALES

On the approach of age twenty, Igraine develops self-determination and rebukes both her tyrannic husband and Columba, his priest and the evangelist who initiated the Hiberno-Scottish mission on the island of Iona. In widowhood, she unites with Uther as his confident wife and queen. Her abandonment of childrearing to concentrate on conceiving another son turns daughter Morgaine into the unwilling caretaker of baby brother Arthur. Rescued from jealousy and misery by her aunt Viviane, Morgaine travels to Avalon and, fostered by Viviane, begins training in the House of the Maidens, a curriculum that she summarizes as "the making of a priestess" (*Ibid.,* 136).

Rosemary Skinner Keller's *Encyclopedia of Women and Religion in North America* characterizes Marion's views of the period as a time "that humanity lived at peace with itself and in harmony with nature during a Goddess-worshiping, woman-led prehistory" (Keller, 2006, I, 19). The narrative names skills of telepathy and magical fire-making, followed by summoning of mist and rain, learning ritual songs and harp playing, and studying herbal therapies. Morgaine's seven-year education concludes in a self-study through hallucinogenic drugs and lone wandering of the lake before her magical return through the mist, a pilgrimage on a par with Christ's wandering in the desert during a spiritual struggle, and the plains Indian vision quest, a means of clarifying self-knowledge.

Marion's revelation of conflict in chapter 13 contains the aim of the Merlin Taliesin and Viviane to provide England with a warrior-king. Viviane's intent to introduce the boy Arthur to Avalon and equip him with a sword of victory foreshadows a visual tableau of king making and a ritual encounter of the King Stag with the Maiden Huntress to conceive a royal child. Binding the scene in memory and regret, Marion alludes to a line from François Villon, a fifteenth-century French poet who asked, "Mais où sont les neiges d'antan?" (Where are the snows of last year?). The night ritual involving Morgaine and Raven, the silent priestess, compresses the history of Britannia into waves of migration following the collapse of Atlantis. Raven's vision of the running stag, the king of the forest, concludes with three owl calls, a tripartite evocation of blood and death and a salute to female wisdom, symbolized by Raven's sickness, Morgaine's heavy, dark menstrual flow, and Viviane's wrinkled face, the appearance of the Old Death-crone or third and last stage of womanly existence.

A RITUAL UNION

While Morgaine recovers from the herbal drink, Viviane outlines the primeval concept of martyrdom and installation of the Horned One in nature through carnal union with the Mother Goddess. Common in archetypical patterns of worship, the ritual alters over time to an atavistic sacrifice only in times of danger. The tone mellows from Marion's heart-pounding post-coital cave scene to Morgaine's encounter with the harper Kevin, a hideously crippled musician recovering from burns incurred during a Saxon raid. Introduction of a secondary character destined to replace Taliesin as the next Merlin gives Marion an opportunity to outline Arthur's promise of might and kingship, which she can assure by giving him the legendary sword of Avalon.

In an underground chapel, Marion shrouds in mysticism the presentation of sacred Druid regalia—cup, platter, spear, scabbard, and sword. The ceremony commits Arthur to both paganism and Christianity and "the sacred magic of those who have set you on this throne" (Bradley, 1983, 203). The oath directs the young monarch toward gratitude and justice, a reflection of the last words of David in II Samuel 23:3: "He that ruleth over man must be just, ruling in the fear of God." The theme of uprightness and virtue overturns in the final scenes, which picture Morgaine willfully digging an abortifacient root. In a frenzy to abort the unwanted pregnancy conceived by her brother, she ends a relationship with Viviane, her overbearing foster mother.

See also Mother Goddess.

Sources

Bradley, Marion Zimmer. *The Mists of Avalon.* New York: Ballantine, 1983.

Keller, Rosemary Skinner, Rosemary Radford Ruether, and Marie Cantion, eds. *Encyclopedia of Women and Religion in North American.* Vol. 1. Bloomington: Indiana University Press, 2006.

Rosenberg, Alyssa. "Re-Reading Feminist Author Marion Zimmer Bradley in the Wake of Sexual Assault Allegations," *Washington Post* (27 June 2014).

Vaim, Madison. "The Mists of Avalon," *Entertainment* (25 July 2014).

Mists of Avalon, Book Two: The High Queen

Marion energizes book two with significant character interaction and dialogue, from the arrival of the bride to a wedding and Lancelet's fall from a horse startled by a goose to Gwenhwyfar's grief at losing a pregnancy. In the evaluation of critic Jessica Jernigan, "Bradley shows us real people struggling against their destiny" (Jernigan, 2017). The author intensifies focus on womanhood and its vulnerabilities while Morgaine struggles to give birth, the second phase of her transformation of what Charlotte Spivack calls "the archetypal fourfold feminine—maiden, mother, wise-woman and warrior" (Spivack, 1992, 21). Morgause applies knowledge of maternity by denying the new mother her babe Gwydion to prevent immediate imprinting, a psychological identification between an infant and its parent. Nonetheless, parturition matures Morgaine, activating a dynamic of the self-sacrificing female versus the "new woman," a figure set free of outdated expectations and gestalts.

Morgaine, the unfettered female, foreshadows issues of adulthood and self-control in her literary foil, a young and fretful Gwenhwyfar, whose irrationality and emotional intensity pose new obstacles to Arthur's dream kingdom. The opposites, in the evaluation of critic Melinda Hughes, constitute "an example of the nineteenth-century American Dark Lady/Pale Maiden antagonism with each sister having the obvious physical differences as well as antithetical cultural and religious beliefs" (Hughes, 1993, 24). Both women derive familiar characteristics from Myth. While Gwenhwyfar channels the stories of the huntress Artemis/Diana, the Virgin Mary, and Saint Brigid, Morgaine gains strength from the lore of Aphrodite/Venus, Circe, and Eve. Love becomes the wedge that separates the two: they both adore Arthur but compete for Lancelet's affection. Critic Leslie Fiedler, author of *Love and Death in the American Novel,* recognized a more rigid pattern in the blonde Gwenhwyfar's moral purity and the brunette Morgaine's aggressive self-definition and anti-patriarchal values, "The standard form in which American writers project their ambivalence toward women" (Fiedler, 1960, 197). For a model, he cited Cora and Alice Munro, the half-sisters in James Fenimore Cooper's *The Last of the Mohicans.*

Interwoven in a revealing stave, motifs of Druidic humanism and Christian zealotry permeate the before and after of Arthur's wedding. Like Aeneas in *The Firebrand* and Gabriel Ardais in the Darkover story "Bride Price," Lancelet stands out among other military men for approving of intelligent women, including his mother Viviane, a wisewoman of Avalon and the current Lady of the Lake. Marion contrasts the educated followers of the Mother Goddess with the stunted creativity in Christianized females, especially Igraine, who abandons the Sight of her youth "as the work of the fiend," even though clairvoyance could ease her worry about Morgaine's whereabouts (Bradley, 1983, 257). Igraine despairs at women's trials and concludes that, with "all the tears women shed, they leave no mark on the world," a dramatic irony of her role as mother of the next high king (*Ibid.,* 259).

Arthur's Marriage

At the post-nuptial celebration, Kevin's invitation to Morgaine to play his harp elicits comments on the importance of music to Celts and the degradation of female Christian musicians for performing before males in public. Marion impacts the scene with opinions from Ectorius, Archbishop Patricius, Lancelet, and the Merlin. At the height of a theological wrangle, Morgaine wonders why Arthur remains silent, but more unpropitious appears a waning moon, a metaphysical indication that the high king's behavior before Gwenhwyfar bodes ill for their union. Arthur views the harbingers from the aspect of his army, which gains cavalrymen as a dowry from Leodegranz. The military enrichment contrasts the king's need for the ideal wife, the paragon of purity and character, the female version of chivalry that T.H. White depicted in *The Sword in the Stone.*

Marion orchestrates a homecoming of soldiers as a reprise of character status. At a gathering at the Round Table, Arthur proposes the Apollonian notion of Camelot as a relief from crowding at Caerleon's main hall. In the post–Saxon era, he plans to build a roomier castle near Glastonbury big enough to house the Round Table in comfort. In the mold of Aristotle's philosopher king, he foresees Celtic boys reared for more than fighting and harpers soothing the spirits of his people. To keep his knights in condition, he proposes war games with laurel wreaths as prizes. His Camelot idyll reflects the themes of Arthurian art, song, opera, and poetry in the verse of Tennyson's *Idylls of the King*, the operas of Wagner and Purcell, and paintings produced by Dante Gabriel Rossetti, Edward Burne-Jones, Arthur Hughes, William Holman Hunt, John Everett Millais, and other members the mid–Victorian Pre-Raphaelite brotherhood.

Style and Action

The writer creates stirring drama that retrieves the Arthuriad from stiff, monochromatic legend. She spotlights Morgaine's lyric veneration of the Mother Goddess, "without [whose] beneficent mercy none of us could draw a living breath" (*Ibid.*, 398). The narrative amplifies motifs of conception and death by depicting reactions to Priscilla's merciful release from suffering and Igraine's preoccupation with her daughter Morgaine and daughter-in-law Gwenhwyfar, who recognizes the first trimester of a pregnancy. Igraine's death initiates heightened responses to loss. After burying the Cornish queen at Tintagel, Gwenhwyfar gallops through dangerous country and enters Caerleon in battle mode.

A hiatus among fairies celebrates medieval hospitality at Castle Chariot, where kind folk welcome Morgaine, honor her title, and invite her to wear a flower garland, dance, and feast at the high table. The manifestation of generosity takes shape with a tankard of sweet beverage, possibly wine drugged with a sedative. A profusion of fruits and bread heap her plate while harp music fills the hall. The author incorporates an indirect blessing from the Mother Goddess in a necklace feminized by shells that replicate female genitalia. The blend of festivity with enchantment implies that Morgaine's drink lulls her into a timeless semi-dream state indigenous to fairyland, where she spends five years. A symbolic act—the discarding of her iron dagger—strips away her only tool and weapon.

Marion rounds out the themes of Morgaine's story with a blend of two Greek terms for love—ἀγάπη (agape or loving affection) and ἔρως (eros or passion). By coupling with the crippled singer Kevin Harper, Morgaine reveals a maturation that overrides self-pity and anger for conceiving a child by her brother Arthur. Her compassion for Gwenhwyfar encourages confession of the conception and birth of Gwydion. Against the strictures of Avalon, Morgaine chooses to assist Arthur's marriage to Gwenhwyfar by offering an amulet to ensure conception of a Beltane child. The chapter closes on the sexual encounter between the queen and Lancelet, whom Arthur encourages as surrogate sire. The drunken *ménage à trois,* like the ritual copulations in Margaret Atwood's feminist fable *The Handmaid's Tale,* distort the concept of monogamy and insert a blasphemous violation of dynasty for Camelot's heir.

Sources

Ahern, Stephen. "Listening to Guinevere: Female Agency and the Politics of Chivalry in Tennyson's Idylls," *Studies in Philology* 101:1 (2004): 88–112.

Bradley, Marion Zimmer. *The Mists of Avalon.* New York: Ballantine, 1983.

Engelking, Tama Lea. "Renée Vivien and the Ladies of the Lake," *Nineteenth-Century French Studies* 30:3–4 (2002): 363–380.

Fiedler, Leslie. *Love and Death in the American Novel.* New York: Stein & Day, 1960.

Higham, N.J. *King Arthur: Myth-Making and History.* London: Routledge, 2002.

Hildebrand, Kristina. "The Other Cornwall Girl: Morgause in Twentieth-Century English Literature," *Journal of the International Arthurian Society* 6:1 (2018): 25–45.

Hughes, Melinda. "Dark Sisters and Light Sisters: Sister Doubling and the Search for Sisterhood in *The Mists of Avalon* and *The White Raven*," *Mythlore* 19 (1993): 24–28.

Jernigan, Jessica. "The Book That Made Me a Feminist Was Written by an Abuser," https://electricliterature.com/the-book-that-made-me-a-feminist-was-written-by-an-abuser-4c6891f548cf, 2017.

Spivack, Charlotte. *Popular Arthurian Traditions.* Bowling Green, OH: Bowling Green State University Popular Press, 1992.

Mists of Avalon, Book Three: The King Stag

The third stave restates significant factors in the action—the arguments for and against Gwenhwyfar as the high king's wife, cryptic threats to Arthur's throne, and criticisms of his friendship with Lancelet. Marion introduces the faults in young Gwydion/Mordred, an impudent, demanding boy genius who conceals his command of the Sight. Kevin Harper speaks Morgaine's secret—that Gwydion is a scion of Avalon and "son to the son of the Great Dragon," making him Arthur's child and Uther Pendragon's grandson (Bradley, 1983, 474). In the same dilemma as Marcus Aurelius, Rome's philosopher-emperor and his megalomaniac heir Commodus, Arthur views an unseemly, emotionally stunted son to name as heir. The decision to educate Gwydion among Druids comes to Morgaine in a dream as a solution for rearing a doubly royal child, a dynastic motif that also affects the youth of Lancelet and his brothers Balan, Lionel, and Bors as well as Agravaine, Gawaine, Gaheris, and Gareth, the four sons of Morgause and Lot of Orkney and Lothian. The massing of Arthur's companions at court illustrates the enmeshed kinship among them and the decline in Morgaine's spirit from blunted magic and self-doubt.

In the cataclysm of Druidism vs. Christianity, the author electrifies court action with the unforeseen attack on Viviane, the Lady of Avalon, a white-haired crone and wisewoman. With one blow, Balin splits her skull with an axe, leaving her soaked in blood, one hand clutching the emblematic sickle knife of the Mother Goddess. Because the craven act demands kindred reprisal from Galahad/Lancelet, Viviane's son, and her nephews Gaheris and Gawaine as well as from niece Morgaine, Taliesin the Merlin, Viviane's father, demotes the loss from blood-price for the mercy killing of Balin's mother Priscilla to a "sacrifice to Avalon" (*Ibid.*, 500). The slaughter of the aged female leader results in Kevin's rise to the status of the Merlin and a vacancy in Avalon's Lady of the Lake. Marion turns the Christian calendar to irony by depicting the atheist Lancelet's ill-planned marriage to Elaine on Transfiguration, a feast day each August 6 celebrating Jesus's return in glory to his apostles.

A Confrontation of Beliefs

In the opinion of critic Marion Wynne-Davies, a professor at the University of Surrey, Marion's radical reshaping of the matriarchy in Arthurian lore jumpstarted more complex epiphanies of medieval conquest and gendered treachery. During the rise of Christian prudery and control of female options, the Avalon sisterhood remains "free to have sex with whatever man they choose ... [and] to choose whether or not to end a pregnancy" (Wynne-Davies, 2016, 180). As women's liberation loses ground to post–Roman patriarchy, male libido surges from an era of fighting, a biological fact of warfare that novelist Pearl S. Buck demonstrates in *The Good Earth*. Arthur cites renewed vigor as his excuse for taking the part of the Horned One and siring a son with his sister Morgaine. Marion states, "An encounter with death sends a man ready for rutting," an appropriate term for the King Stag's role in the Beltane ritual that conceives Gwydion/Mordred (Bradley, 1983, 540).

Marion orchestrates a masterful denouement in the third book. The theological dialogue between Arthur and Gwenhwyfar creates tragic irony by enacting an Adam vs. Eve debate, with Eve's advice on sin convincing Adam to do wrong. Couched in a mid-life crisis, Arthur's penance and fasting dismay the queen, who had not foreseen the burden her piety had placed on him. In North Wales, where Morgaine stokes her regrets, a reunion with the fairy folk ends her penance for abandoning Avalon. Back at Camelot on Pentecost, a bumptious clan reunion draws typical comments on relationships, marriages, and children, the real future of Arthur's kingdom and all of Britannia. Amid a whorl of gossip, attention returns to Gwenhwyfar, whose toxic judgments and backbiting ill suit her pious airs.

A RETURN OF WAR

The demand for tribute from the mythical Roman emperor Lucius ignites a new war to rescue Bors from captivity. Arthur's success at rule draws a mix of factions—"Romans, Welsh, Cornish, West-countrymen, east Anglians, men of Brittany, the Old People, the men of Lothian" (*Ibid.,* 648). Marion presents the reopening of conflict as a boon to the Knights of the Round Table, left complacent and bored by the Pax Arthuriana. Although older by seventeen years, they maintain loyalty to the king and stoke their lust for fighting "from Cornwall to Lothian" (*Ibid.,* 650). In the pattern of the Western hero tale, the text illustrates how a nation that wins its way to sovereignty by military clashes grows stale from inaction and a lack of victories.

In the final monologue, Gwydion, a Druid priest, indulges in self-pity that he has not seen his mother since babyhood and that destiny requires him to defeat Arthur, his cousin, whom he lionizes. Wearied by his fate, he chooses alcohol as an escape while musing on a line from Herodotus's *Histories*: Solon, an Athenian lawgiver and philosopher, refused to admire the grandeur of the Sardis palace, the home of Croesus, king of Lydia. Solon gave as his reason, "I cannot respond until I know the manner of your death. Count no man happy until his life is ended." Gwydion, completing stages of the stereotypical *bildungsroman,* opts to accept death with dishonor for himself and Arthur. The boy's coming of age, paralleling Morgaine's *Reifungsroman*, prefigures the tragic events in the final stave.

Sources

Ahern, Stephen. "Listening to Guinevere: Female Agency and the Politics of Chivalry in Tennyson's Idylls," *Studies in Philology* 101:1 (2004): 88–112.
Bradley, Marion Zimmer. *The Mists of Avalon*. New York: Ballantine, 1983.
Palojärvi, Maija Päivikki. "Morgaine the Maiden, Morgaine the Mother, Morgaine the Deathcrone: Female Ageing in Marion Zimmer Bradley's *The Mists of Avalon*," Humanities thesis, University of Eastern Finland (1 November 2013): http://epublications.uef.fi/pub/urn_nbn_fi_uef-20131005/urn_nbn_fi_uef-20131005.pdf.
Wynne-Davies, Marion. *Women and Arthurian Literature: Seizing the Sword*. London: Springer, 2016.

Mists of Avalon, Book Four: The Prisoner in the Oak

The author turned fantasy into a prime mode for modernizing Arthuriana. Critic Barbara Ann Gordon-Wise, author of *The Reclamation of a Queen: Guinevere in Modern Fantasy*, characterized the genre shift from Renaissance quest lore as an encouragement of "the transgression of the limits of realism, and provides an ideal medium for the revision and empowerment of the female figure—in this case, Gwenhwyfar"

(Gordon-Wise, 1991, 23). An outgrowth of second wave feminism, the events lament a Dark Age matriarchy on the wane, transforming the wife of the High King. From her introduction, Arthur's queen fulfills the archetype of the *puella aeterna* (eternal girl), an enchanting golden girl who hovers within safe space. In the estimation of Gwenhwyfar's father Leodegranz, his motherless daughter is a "pretty little featherhead" who is "afraid of everything, anyway. That's why you need a man to take care of you" (Bradley, 1983, 154, 265).

In summation of Marion's overhaul of the traditional Guinevere, critic James Noble declares, "A timid girl, a shrewish wife and lover, a religious fanatic, and a queen who has no interest in ruling, Gwenhwyfar is … the villain of Bradley's novel" (Noble, 2006, 199). Just as the Glastonbury convent stifled her urge to play the harp and practice calligraphy, a barren marriage turns her life-long renunciation into tragedy for herself, Arthur, the kingdom, and the Mother Goddess. By internalizing the patriarchal myth of Eve, the corrupter of Eden, Gwenhwyfar becomes the reactionary anti-feminist who surrenders to total male domination. While on staff at the University of Oregon, literary critic Marilyn R. Farwell noted, "As if in punishment for woman's previous ascendancy, the priests and especially a viciously portrayed Archbishop Patricius (St. Patrick), insist that women are sinful, weak, unreasonable and, at best, passive helpmates to their husbands" (Farwell, 1996, 99). Farwell pictured the queen as "the patriarchal enforcer of Christianity's negative view of women" (*Ibid.*). In an updated quip, critic Diana Lucile Paxson dubs the queen "the Phyllis Schlafly of the fifth century," a diehard conservative who opposed women's rights in the 1960s and 1970s (Paxson, 1999, 119).

THE SELF-SUFFICIENT WOMAN

Marion's denouement depicts the cost to wisdom from errors in judgment by the trio of protagonists—Morgause, Gwenhwyfar, and Morgaine. Arthur's queen shudders at the audacity of Morgause as co-ruler with King Lot and "willed herself into semi-consciousness" (Bradley, 1983, 145). Liberating pent-up rage in the form of religious frenzy, Gwenhwyfar entreats Arthur to quash the commoners' devotion to the Mother Goddess in Camelot and, around 480 CE, to take up the guidon of the Virgin Mary. In a conflict between love and duty, he makes the difficult choice. Under a Christian banner, he successfully leads his men against the Anglo-Saxon host in February 482 CE at the Battle of Mount Badon near Bath or Swindon.

In a pattern common to post-menopausal women, Morgaine regains serenity and forgives herself for past errors in judgment. As she ripens into the humble, confident crone, the novel counterposes Morgause, a former helpmeet to King Lot who caroms into plots and power grabs. The pacing of home scenes in northern Wales with Morgaine reveals the chutzpah of Gwenhwyfar's literary foil, who refuses to be relegated to "whispers of women's things—embroidery, servants, who at the court was breeding" (*Ibid.*, 714). Her story lurches unexpectedly into passion for Accolon and a death spell against Avalloch, the would-be despoiler of his stepmother. In the surreal flick of Morgaine's shuttle into loomed sections of brown and green warp and woof, lethal pains and snorts shapeshift her into the dying sow while Avalloch becomes "blood sacrifice, spilled to the Goddess" (*Ibid.*, 674). The result of Morgaine's divination in the woods predicts death for Accolon. In a faulty evaluation of her powers, Gwenhwyfar downsizes the future Lady of the Lake to "a little thing after all, and the queen of an unregarded kingdom" (*Ibid.*, 685).

THE FALLING ACTION

In a critique of the novel's conclusion, critic Jessica Jernigan warned, "Doom hangs over Arthur's glorious reign, just as fate rules many a legend and fable. There is no happy ending for anyone at Camelot—there never has been" (Jernigan, 2017). Orchestrated like grand opera, Marion's novel casts the spotlight on Lancelet as he sings a resetting of *The Wanderer,* an Old English poem in the Exeter Book, stressing his solitude during a lengthy sojourn away from court. At a melancholy moment, Morgause introduces Gwydion, a sly, mendacious jester armed with a "cat-smile" who milks the scene for attention (Bradley, 1983, 689). Named Mordred ("bite" or "evil counsel") by his Saxon companions, he predicts a short life for Galahad, his rival for the Pendragon throne.

As evidence of lost control, Marion escalates Morgaine's anger at a theatrical confab in Arthur's private chambers into near hysteria. In a diatribe for Avalon, she charges the king with blasphemy for turning Excalibur into a crucifix, a symbol of torture and death. Her outburst morphs into a prediction of Arthur's downfall and a demand for the return of Avalon's sword. After repeating the prophecy of Galahad's death, Gwydion/Mordred receives promotion as royal advocate among the Saxons, the future rulers of Britannia. The plot to kidnap Arthur to Avalon and place Accolon on his father's throne leads the company to the Castle Chariot, where they part amid the controversies that unsettle Camelot and betray its ideal of harmony and unified action.

On return to Camelot, Morgaine searches for abortifacient herbs and sinks into a stupor while using the Sight to view Accolon wounding Arthur with Excalibur. The vision concludes with the duelers entering Glastonbury for medical care by monks and nuns, who contributed to the historical growth of hospitals during the crusades. Marion stresses the engulfing madness that goads Morgaine to steal Arthur's scabbard and hurl it into the Lake, a visual retrieval of women's magic from an apostate male as an offering to the Mother Goddess. The tense gallop of king and guards provides Arthuriana with a fantasy of magic and shapeshifting. To retrieve Morgaine from prostration, Kevin performs a song of Orfeo, the tragic Greek harper who retrieves himself from the Underworld, leaving his wife Eurydice behind. Potent melody corroborates the strands of the Arthurian saga that claim powers of enchantment for medieval balladry.

THE FEMALE VIEW

Marion voices the resolution of Arthur's struggle against Druidism through the words of poor women huddled in the Great Hall. Pocked with peasant lore and gossip, the commentary illustrates how the uneducated interpreted a major alteration in English religion and pageantry. Analyst Gloria Orenstein termed the "wresting the Grail from the hands of patriarchy" as a return "to the Goddess in order for life on Earth to flourish again" (Orenstein, 1990, 182). Magnified into a shimmering presence bearing a chalice, Morgaine serves a communion—a love feast with the Mother Goddess—and reinstates monotheism with the command "Know ye that I am One" (*Ibid.*, 771). The "Great Magic" demands sacrifice: Raven's death and Morgaine's life of solitude (*Ibid.*,

773). In parity, the transfiguration of the Great Mother into the Virgin Mary begins the merger of disparate faiths and a quest for the Holy Grail, a bract of Arthuriana introduced by Chrétien de Troyes.

In a salute to independent scholarship, Rosemarie Arbur, a teacher at Lehigh University, honored the research and literary success of Marion's masterwork. Charlotte Spivack, on staff at the University of Massachusetts, declared the novel "the most ambitious retelling of the Arthurian legend in the twentieth century" (Spivack, 1987, 149). Medievalist Nicole Evelina credited the novel with "[turning] Arthurian legend on its head by marrying it with feminism and focusing on the female stories" (Tichelaar). Of its importance to Arthuriana and women's literature, critic Marion Wynne-Davies, a professor at the University of Surrey, stated, "Bradley's contribution must be recognized as a catalyst … [challenging] the dominant male discourse of the legends" (Wynne-Davies, 2016, 176). Wynne-Davies predicted further gendered retellings of Arthur's story.

Sources

Farwell, Marilyn R. *Heterosexual Plots and Lesbian Narratives*. New York: New York University Press, 1996.
Godwin, Parke. "The Road to Camelot: A Conversation with Marion Zimmer Bradley," *Science Fiction & Fantasy Review* (April 1984): 6–9.
Gordon-Wise, Barbara Ann. *The Reclamation of a Queen: Guinevere in Modern Fantasy*. New York: Praeger, 1991.
Jernigan, Jessica. "The Book That Made Me a Feminist Was Written by an Abuser," https://electricliterature.com/the-book-that-made-me-a-feminist-was-written-by-an-abuser-4c6891f548cf, 2017.
Noble, James. "Guinevere, the Superwoman of Contemporary Arthurian Fiction," *Florilegium* 23:2 (2006): 197–210.
Orenstein, Gloria Feman. *The Reflowering of the Goddess (Athene)*. Oxford, UK: Pergamon, 1990.
Paxson, Diana L. "Marion Zimmer Bradley and *The Mists of Avalon*," *Arthuriana* 9:1 (Spring 1999): 110–126.
Spivack, Charlotte. *Merlin's Daughters: Contemporary Women Writers of Fantasy*. Westport, CT: Greenwood, 1987.
Thompson, Raymond H. "The First and Last Love: Morgan le Fay and Arthur," *The Arthurian Revival*. New York: Routledge, 1992, 230–247.
Tichelaar, Tyler. "Children of Arthur," https://childrenofarthur.wordpress.com/tag/t-h-white/.
Wynne-Davies, Marion. *Women and Arthurian Literature: Seizing the Sword*. London: Springer, 2016.

Mother Goddess

Because of the onslaught of rigidly patriarchal sects and religions late in the twentieth century, multiple narratives by Marion Zimmer Bradley revisit the paleolithic female divine, a primal deity whose worship flourished from prehistory into the Bronze Age, causing the refugee Mikhala in *Warrior Woman* to pray "Goddess guard us" in protection of her newborn daughter (Bradley, 1985, 104). At a dangerous moment in *City of Sorcery*, Jaelle takes on the grandeur and mystique of the sacred lady in "dark robe glittering with stars, jeweled wings overshadowing the dark spaces" (Bradley, 1984, 100). Upon young Nimue's entry into Avalon in "The Pledged Word," the ruling priestess takes the child on her lap, consoles her fears, and refutes the anti-female teachings of Christian priests. More than words, the physical closeness epitomizes a loving deity who welcomes rather than brainwash in the style of abbesses with novices. Revered by the philosopher Starhawk, the Great Mother offers a return to the spiritual wholeness: "To invoke the Goddess is to awaken the Goddess within, to become, for a time, that aspect we invoke" (Starhawk, 1979, 85).

In Marion's fiction, models in the Lythande cycle and the Darkover series elevate devotion to the Great Mother, the giver of visions in *Traitor's Sun*. Carlina "Carly" di Asturien, a chaste beauty in *Two to Conquer,* adheres to the goddess by being virtuous despite double rape by the brute Bard di Asturien. An exemplary priestess in *The Mists of Avalon*, Morgaine defends the primal matriarchy with a stout denial of casual witchery: "I am no village wise-woman, to meddle with birth charms and love potions and foretelling and spells. I am a priestess" (Bradley, 1983, 306). The author's reclamation of early medieval theology rids it of current misconceptions and restores resilience and dignity.

An online critic for *The Heretic Loremaster* points out Avalon's mistreatment of the female devout in Marion's version of Arthuriana, which discloses the burden that falls unequally on holy women. Viviane, the religious elite, assigns Igraine and Morgaine tasks to acclaim the Great Goddess and further her veneration. A gendered protocol does not apply the same control of volition in either Lancelet or Gwydion/Mordred, both priesthood trainees. After Morgaine's pilgrimage in the wilderness and a revival of her faith, she achieves greater cognizance of suffering, an indispensable part of mortal life. She reviews the avatars of the Great Goddess as "Green Lady of the fruitful earth," "Dark Lady of the seed," and "Our Lady of rot and desert lion and death at the end," a triad of birth, maturity, and demise (*Ibid.,* 399). The three-in-one deity echoes the inflexible apotheoses of the Hindu Shiva and the Christian god.

Renewed Devotion

Through fiction, the author proposed to freshen and rejuvenate womanly connection with the Mother Goddess, the dominant theme of her adapted Arthuriad, *The Fall of Atlantis,* and *Tiger Burning Bright.* The motif also enriches "The Pledged Word" and the Lythande stories "Goblin Market" and "Somebody Else's Magic," a tale of stalking and multiple gender identities. Critic Victoria Sharpe applauded the feminized concept on the basis of feminist theorist and sculptor Merlin Stone's "archeological evidence ... [which] proves that the notions of great goddess and earth mother were actually appropriate concepts for the earliest objects of worship in past societies" (Sharpe, 1998, 36). In a pro-woman age, women bore value as embodiments of fertility and reproduction, tenets that connected the female side of humankind with all creation. As symbols of their union with the Great Mother, priestesses adorned their heads with a crescent or sickle moon and bore a sickle-shaped knife at the belt. The emblems reflect exaltation of Artemis/Diana, the virgin goddess of the moon and the hunt, and expanded to esteem the Virgin Mary and the Wiccan goddess of all life.

Timeless and bountiful, the outpouring of ἀγάπη (agapē or divine love for humankind) took metaphorical form in the holy spring, a breast image that "had been flowing since the beginning of the world, and ... would flow forever, generous and magical, and free to all people" (Bradley, 1983, 114–115). According to Lithuanian-American archeologist Marija Gimbutas, author of *The Language of the Goddess,* worship of the primal mother deity flourished in Europe in 7000–6000 BCE until Indo-European invaders forced it underground in Galicia and Brittany "roughly between 4300 and 2800 BCE." (Gimbutas, 1989, xx). Critic Don Riggs referred to the overthrow of the earth mother and her devotees as "a devolution from their original supernatural status to that of demigods ... and finally to subhuman characters" under the pejorative "Faerie" (Riggs, 1998, 16, 20). The regression generated eras of anti-woman bias that emboldened witch branding and burning to rid the Earth of female-provoked evil.

Communing with the Holy One

Marion avoided the historical discord of the genders by depicting the sustaining, mothering aspect of females. For entry into the realm of the mother goddess, Nimue, a child postulant in "The Pledged Word," learns from Niniane that followers must "try to do the will of the Goddess, and that is all anyone can do" (Bradley, 1995, 136). From a more abstract vision of obedience, Riggs characterizes communion with the deity as "an alteration of consciousness" on a par with hypnosis (*Ibid.*, 22). He stresses the transportive mechanism of the trance state, which suspends time to amplify the moment of apotheosis or oneness with sanctity. Enhancing the liturgical chant in *Tiger Burning Bright,* a red-rayed heart graces the dome of the temple of One Who Dwells Beyond the Stars. Below, lighted candles "drew the attention of the worshipers toward heaven, where the Goddess dwelt" (Bradley, 1995, 1). In a half-trance, Gemen Elfrida views an angel, "sexless and inhumanly lovely ... glowing with its own light" (*Ibid.,* 2). The service the worshippers share "made them true daughters of the Goddess for as far back as the records went" (*Ibid.,* 20).

For Domaris, the acolyte in *The Fall of Atlantis,* acceptance of a love offer from Micon precedes the freeze-framing of a metaphoric baptism—a dip in the sacred pool and kneeling at the mother's shrine. Communion with the hallowed invokes hazy visions and serenity, a calm the author connects with Domaris's full maturity and acceptance of responsibilities. For a dying swordsman in "Somebody Else's Magic," a last thought of the deity Larith asserts the power of choice: "The Goddess does not forgive—those who submit—," a rewording of Benjamin Franklin's "God helps them that help themselves" (Bradley, 2013, 35). As a result of free will and receipt of godhood, Magdalen "Magda" Lorne, a Terran postulant posing as a Darkovan at the Guild House in *Thendara House,* receives surprise visions of majesty and righteousness. Unbidden, the goddess Avarra in her elegant and sparkling attire reassures Magda and confers peace and contentment. On the down side of mortality, the midwife Marisela struggles with the "Dark Lady ... a very ancient and friendly adversary," the side of godhood that demands human life, the counterbalance of conception and childbirth (Bradley, 1983, 257).

The Goddess at Troy

In *The Firebrand,* Marion elevates the earth mother to the Great Goddess and Serpent Mother, the protector of the House of Troy and of women who "all come under Her Wing" (Bradley, 1987, 335). Like her daughter Kassandra, Queen Hecuba reveres the ancient female divine. At Prince Hector's reach for an antique double-headed ax, the queen warns that such bravado commits sacrilege against the Mother Goddess, an embodiment of peace. By predicting in a dream that the birth of Prince Paris bodes doom for the kingdom, the deity warns of a male-generated catastrophe that will devastate the city. Kassandra, upon initiation into the matriarchal tradition at Colchis, identifies with horrific truth, the visions she has borne from girlhood of fire, blood, and death caused by warriors from the fleet of Akhaian ships in Troy's harbor. In reference to an era of disaster, critic Nina Lykke corroborates the concept of "the goddess metaphor, which for many years has functioned as a common landmark for the international wave of spiritual ecofeminism, [that] seems to point us ... toward a return to 'the natural'" (Lykke, 1996, 23). Equating matriarchal with beneficent and life-affirming, Marion embraces late twentieth-century nostalgia for a clean, sustaining, organic world free of war.

The Firebrand enhances communion with the Mother Goddess in Penthesilea's voicing of a command to ride east. The mystic revelation to Kassandra of the Dark Lady of the Underworld poses a koan, a Zen Buddhist paradox: "You are I and I am you" (Bradley, 1987, 127). The bemusing claim characterizes Kassandra's attempt to balance a mortal self with godly possession and to determine whether to obey the Earth Mother or Apollo, the Sun Lord introduced by the Akhaians. The rift in loyalty deepens when Kassandra puzzles over Apollo's failure to protect her from entanglements with mortal men. Her fealty to the Great Mother increases with the answer to her rhetorical question "Would the Goddess she had served during her time with the Amazons have taken the part of a man against Her sworn priestess?" (*Ibid.*, 253). The answer seems obvious.

THE GODDESS AND DRUIDS

Inklings in Marion's *The Forest House* trace female oracular lore to northwestern Europe in prehistory, after the sinking of Atlantis in the Bronze Age and before the arrival of Celtic Druids to Britannia in 600 BCE. Because Celts revered the Earth Mother, priestesses esteemed Druidic lore "and added the ancient knowledge to their own," a synthesis of compatible sources of wisdom (Bradley, 1993, 129). Marion affirms syncretic scholarship, especially herbalism and Merlin's understanding of "the stars and of the standing stones," an allusion to Stonehenge, which Mary Stewart's *The Crystal Cave* claims as Merlin's engineering (*Ibid.*, 130). In a respectful moment, the mentor Caillean proclaims the goddess "the Mother of all women, the maker of all things mortal" (*Ibid.*, 222). In the falling action, the Earth Mother speaks through Eilan, the high priestess, a midsummer comfort: "I will remain. I *am*," a rephrasing of Exodus 3:14 in which God speaks to Moses through the burning bush the constancy of Yahweh (*Ibid.*, 353).

Critic Theresa Crater substantiates the timeline of goddess worship with historical evidence: Reverence of the Mother Goddess "continued into Celtic times and was suddenly cut short by the Roman invasion of England [in 43 C.E]. The Great Mother was challenged by Roman Christianity and her cycle was forced underground" (Crater, 2001, 20). According to analyst Janice C. Crosby, on staff at Southern University in Baton Rouge, Louisiana, female devotees reversed the immurement: "The historical conflict between God and Goddess worship [draws on] a perspective made possible by feminist scholarship" (Crosby, 2000, 43). Marion characterized a conciliation through the religious adoption of the Mother Goddess into Christianity, a prequel of early medieval mariology from 431 CE. In an interview with Parke Godwin, the author asserted, "If men reject her in one form, she will appear in another.... She just changes her name" (Godwin, 1984, 7). Through the character of Viviane, the Lady of the Lake in *The Mists of Avalon*, the author declares, "When you pray to Mary, mother of Jesus, you pray, without knowing it, to the World Mother in one of her many forms" (Bradley, 1983,

134). In comparison to the anti-woman Christian patriarchy, the "Goddess is gentler with women," but Morgaine acknowledges the whim of sacred dominion: "She will do with us as she will" (*Ibid.*, 525, 740).

For *The Mists of Avalon,* set in the semi-pagan fifth and sixth centuries CE, Marion based action on detailed research. Steve Miller, book reviewer for the *Baltimore Sun,* noted the fairness of representation: "We see no band of evil pagans attempting to fight off the good of Christianity here. Rather, we see worshipful people seeking to save their land from alien invaders and alien religions" (Miller, 1983, D4). Miller describes the religious complexities of "an unremitting Christian malice toward those who believe in the old ways" (*Ibid.*).

Marion's Arthuriad transcends time in the worship of a universal mother whom Viviane, the Lady of the Lake, calls by the Welsh name Mother Ceridwen, meaning "transfiguration." Critic Marilyn R. Farwell insists that Avalon remained "the sanctuary of strong feminist values" (Farwell, 1996, 99). In the critique of Arthurian enthusiast Nicole Evelina, in the early pagan era, "Women were held in the highest esteem and even venerated as the embodiment of the Goddess" until the culture "[left] behind the Goddess and [moved] toward the patriarchal belief systems of the Christian church" (Evelina, 2017, 152, 199). An outgrowth of second wave feminism, the novel's setting epitomizes a late Dark Age matrifocus at a climax when, according to Marion, "the ancient matriarchal religion was making its very last appearance" (Godwin, 1984, 8).

THE DECLINE OF GODDESS WORSHIP

According to researcher Don Riggs, Marion provides a "detailed and psychologically nuanced" version of the Mother Goddess when characters are unable "to integrate the fey experiences and powers successfully into life at King Arthur's court" (Riggs, 1998, 16). At the novel's climax, the Great Mother compromises with Christianity by sweeping Arthur to victory in February 482 CE at Mount Badon, even though he abandons the Pendragon standard. Kevin Harper explained the deity's accommodation of Arthur's perfidy: "Like enough the Goddess herself knew that she would be the worse if the land was ruled by the Saxons" (Bradley, 1983, 414). In the first-person prologue, Morgaine, a disenfranchised alien in Camelot, admits the expedience of concealing her devotion to the Great Mother after King Arthur's death. To placate a society beset by misogynistic Christian zealots, epitomized by clanging church bells, Morgaine poses in a dark robe easily misconstrued as a nun's habit. In a critique of Marion's matrifocal view of historic change, Jan Shaw, a lecturer at the University of Sydney, charges the deceiver Morgaine with fantasizing "feminine learning, autonomy, and agency" to produce a "break in realism" and vicarious fulfillment of "repressed desires" (Shaw, 2009, 463, 465). The text refutes Shaw's claim in the words of an adamant priestess: "I am Niniane of Avalon, and I account to no man on this earth for what I do with what is mine" (Bradley, 1983, 849).

Critic Marion Wynne-Davies, an authority on Arthuriana, noted another of the writer's radical reworkings of the quest legend. She interpreted the inclusion of Excalibur "as part of the holy regalia of Avalon and therefore as specifically belonging to the pagan world of the Mother Goddess," a placement anticipated in the Lythande series story "Here There Be Dragons" (Wynne-Davies, 2016, 177–178). Forged of a miracle metal that fell from heaven, Arthur's sword "negates the violent images of rape, male aggression, war and the phallus" (*Ibid.*, 178). In balance to the penis symbol, the narrative advances the magic scabbard, a relic that prevents excessive blood loss, a fact of female biology that is sacred to goddess ritual. By reverencing primal regeneration, the novel's conclusion, spoken by Morgaine, exalts the Great Goddess, "the Worldmother to whom all return" (Paxson, 1999, 125).

The novel makes an ambiguous concession to British history. In the denouement at the all-night vigil of a new companion, Galahad lauds devotion to the high king. The statement anticipates the concept of divine right of kings, an assertion of dynastic legitimacy originally made by James VI of Scotland, the first Stuart king under the name James I of England. The notion echoes Old Testament deference toward the "anointed," whom God himself consecrates, and the New Testament title of Jesus taken from the Greek Χριστός (Christos, the anointed Messiah). In a thrust against Christian theology, Morgaine quietly redirects respect for the Great Mother, "token of the land the king shall rule" (Bradley, 1983, 691). Her son Gwydion/Mordred, a priest of Avalon, predicts, "The Goddess shall endure forever" (*Ibid.*, 691).

Marion proves Gwydion correct in the Darkover series. The concept takes on a futuristic note in *The Shattered Chain*, in which Lady Rohana Ardais prays to a maternal deity, "Blessed Cassilda, Mother of the Seven Domains" (Bradley, 1976, 32). In childbirth, Rohana implores aid from "Evanda, Goddess of light and Goddess of birth," a concept of aid to the parturient that translates readily into an extraterrestrial deity (*Ibid.*, 72). In the opening episode of *Two to Conquer*, Carlina di Asturien, an unwilling bride-to-be, approaches the handfasting ritual to cousin Bard di Asturien with repugnance because of his rape of Lisarda, a twelve-year-old house maid. Urged by family pressures, Carlina turns to a female deity and prays, "Avarra, merciful Goddess, Great Mother, pity me, spare me this marriage somehow" (Bradley, 1980, 1978). The soulful plea reveals Carlina's dependence on a power that shields females, especially the very young and vulnerable.

See also The Forest House; Divination; The Mists of Avalon; Religion.

Sources

Bradley, Marion Zimmer. *City of Sorcery*. New York: DAW, 1984.
_____. *The Firebrand*. New York: Simon & Schuster, 1987.
_____. *The Forest House*. New York: Michael Joseph, 1993.
_____. *The Mists of Avalon*. New York: Ballantine, 1983.
_____. *The Shattered Chain*. New York: DAW, 1976.
_____. *Thendara House*. New York: DAW, 1983.
_____. *Tiger Burning Bright*. New York: William Morrow, 1995.
_____. *Two to Conquer*. New York: DAW, 1980.
_____. *Warrior Woman*. New York: DAW, 1985.
Crater, Theresa. "The Resurrection of Morgan le Fey: Fallen Woman to Triple Goddess," *Femspec* 3:1 (December 2001): 12–22.
Crosby, Janice C. *Cauldron of Changes: Feminist Spirituality in Fantastic Fiction*. Jefferson, NC: McFarland, 2000.
Evans, Richard, ed. *Prophets and Profits: Ancient Divination and Its Reception*. New York: Routledge, 2017.
Evelina, Nicole. *The Once & Future Queen: Guinevere in Arthurian Legend*. Maryland Heights, MO: Lawson Gartner, 2017.
Farwell, Marilyn R. *Heterosexual Plots and Lesbian Narratives*. New York: New York University Press, 1996.
Gimbutas, Marija. *The Language of the Goddess*. San Francisco: Harper Collins, 1989.
Godwin, Parke. "The Road to Camelot: A Conversation with Marion Zimmer Bradley," *Science Fiction & Fantasy Review* (April 1984): 6–9.

Lykke, Nina, and Rosi Braidotti, eds. *Between Monsters, Goddesses and Cyborgs: Feminist Confrontations with Science, Medicine and Cyberspace*. London: Zed Books, 1996.

Miller, Steve. "The Arthurian Legend: Returned to Epic Status," *Baltimore Sun* (30 January 1983): D4.

Paxson, Diana L. "Marion Zimmer Bradley and *The Mists of Avalon*," *Arthuriana* 9:1 (Spring 1999): 110–126.

Riggs, Don. "The Survival of the Goddess in Marie de France and Marion Zimmer Bradley," *Journal of the Fantastic in the Arts* 9:1 (1998): 15–23.

Sharpe, Victoria. "The Goddess Restored," *Journal of the Fantastic in the Arts* 9:1 (1998): 36–45.

Shaw, Jan. "Feminism and the Fantasy Tradition: *The Mists of Avalon*" in *A Companion to Arthurian Literature*. Oxford, UK: Blackwell, 2009.

Starhawk. *The Spiral Dance: A Rebirth of the Ancient Religion of the Great Goddess*. San Francisco: Harper & Row, 1979.

Wynne-Davies, Marion. *Women and Arthurian Literature: Seizing the Sword*. London: Springer, 2016.

Music

The author viewed melody and minstrelsy as adaptable to a wide range of human emotion and motivation, from the rowdy student drinking song in *The Shadow Matrix*, Bard's lullaby to his baby brother in *Two to Conquer,* and an opera house cantata in *The Heirs of Hammerfell,* a Thetan voyager's rhythm, the kind that echoed the plunge and lift of oars to the ring dances at midsummer in *Hawkmistress!* At the Guild House in *Thendara House,* women relax from their day with stringed instruments— harp, lute, dulcimer, guitar. The mercenary and tracker Devra sings to Rafaella n'ha Doria's strumming of the *rryl* in *The Shattered Chain.* For Elizabeth Mackintosh, the cultural anthropologist and musician aboard a spaceship in *Rediscovery,* the sighting of a Terran colony on Cottman IV sounds like a great subject for a ballad because "an awful lot of primitive history was contained in songs and ballads," such as the twelfth-century tune "The Meeting of the Waters," supposedly "the oldest English or Irish melody in existence" (Bradley, 1993, 2, 61). Prophetically, the sound of a Gaelic ballad provides the link between the starship crew and "one colony which was Gaelic-speaking" (*Ibid.,* 59).

Marion respects the depths of melody for assuaging human fears. For earthlings stranded on an uncharted planet, music salves the anxiety caused by hallucinogenic dust and the prospect of a winter of unknown bouts of cold . Geologist Gabriel "Gabe" MacAran asserts, "Even savages had music and he couldn't imagine life without [musical instruments]" (Bradley, 1972, 110). He predicts, "Music just might keep us all sane," a testimonial to both need for solace and a faith in its healing powers (*Ibid.*). In a dirge for fishermen in *Darkover Landfall,* singing echoes emotions at life's end.

Styles range from the iambic trimeter-dimeter of a pagan processional in *Lady of Avalon* rhyming aaabcc to the monk's morning invocation and harper Aliciane's querulous love song "Where Are You Now" in *Stormqueen!,* a ballad similar in yearning and loss to the Czech folk plaint "Waters Ripple and Flow." For Margaret Alton, a musicologist in *Exile's Song,* love takes the form of culture and music training passed on by her foster parents, Ida and Ivor Davidson, a musicologist who practices with flexed fingers on an invisible keyboard. After an unnerving flight to Darkover, arrival at the Street of Musicians, marked by signs picturing musical instruments, brings out Margaret's contented laugh, an element of the confidence she gains while studying at a university and from her affection for her foster family. Fittingly, funereal music eases her parting with musician Ivor Davidson, who dies suddenly.

The Lythande series contributes a ballad of sisterhood to the strumming of the pilgrim's harp in "Goblin Market," the humming of sea chanties at the shore in "Sea Wrack," and sounds of her enchanted lute at inns to mimic "sunlight, the shore winds, the sounds of the soft, splashing waves" (Bradley, 2013, 71). In a hostile town, the background of "To Drive the Cold Winter Away," the wandering paladin asserts that "music distinguishes men from beast" (*Ibid.*, 166). Melody offers a dissimilarity in tone from her red-bound dagger and the magical pocket-lined robe in "Somebody Else's Magic" that shields her from fire through three or four lifetimes. The enchanter-mercenary encourages the royal storyteller Prince Tashgan of Tschardain in "The Wandering Lute" to discuss his love of music, which his parent chose for him to give him "some semblance of purpose" (*Ibid.*, 89). Lythande esteems the gifted minstrel, who possesses "honor higher than a prince" (*Ibid.*).

CELTIC MUSIC

In *The Forest House*, Caillean's harp music revives centuries-old plaints that Marion reprised throughout her canon. The sound soothes a woman in labor; tinkling bells accompany new moon worship; and, in 83 CE, the spear-shaking chants of Caledonian warriors rouse spirits before the Battle of Mons Graupius. Marion permeated the novel with song and libretti from the hymns adapted from Vincenzo Bellini's tragic opera *Norma,* which debuted in Milan's La Scala on December 26, 1831. At the return of Dieda from Hibernia in the gold-edged cloak of the bard, Eilan requests lessons for the youngest priestesses of Forest House. The author magnifies the ancient lays for "the ancient learning, the lore of the gods and heroes" (Bradley, 1993, 287). She values Hibernian songcraft, which women teach their children as "the last sanctuary for the old wisdom of our people," a tenet of Australian aborigines, Gypsies, and Native American tribes as well (*Ibid.*). Dieda complies with her niece's request by singing a descant to the new moon, a high note that facilitates bardic magic.

From the opening paragraphs, *The Forest House* thrums with dreams of battlefield acoustics—the ululations and shrieks of women and "the Druid war harp [which] throbbed with a dreadful music," a subversion of the clichéd view of harpers as gentle and soothing (*Ibid.*, 1). After the bad dream dissolves, Marion depicts combat sounds giving place to the strains of maidens singing at a sacred well. On Beltane eve at midnight, flutes announce the arrival of the Mother Goddess. At an apotheosis, the Merlin sings a prophecy to Eilan: "Daughter of Druids, through you the Dragon will be reborn," the culmination of her initiation into the priesthood and the establishment of the Pendragon dynasty (*Ibid.*, 174).

MUSIC AS POWER

Unlike the ephemeral enchantment of Lady Beauty's lute music in *The Gratitude of Kings,* Marion conjured potency from the mercenary-sorcerer Lythande's magic instrument in "The Wandering Lute." The tethering of Koira to the lute in "The Incompetent Magician" creates regret that "while this lute survives, I am enslaved to it" (Bradley, 1983, 157). Lythande acknowledges that "a slave's counterfeit of love is not love" and smashes the instrument over her knee, plunging herself into more decades of pilgrimage "on her solitary way" (*Ibid.*, 158, 159). A symbol of passion and community, the wood fragments remind Lythande that mastery of the strings comes at a price.

In *The Fall of Atlantis,* the crooning, rhythmic pulsations and the oar-chant of galley slaves channel strength. In a series of processions and ceremonies, melody seems disembodied from singing, which floats like incense. At a ritual in the Grey Temple, participants carefully form a circle and use their instruments to raise "the softest of pipings, a whimper of flutes, the echo of a gong" accompanying "strange monodies and throbbing cadences [and] a single whining wailing dissonance" (Bradley, 1983, 194, 196). By forming an ensemble of ancient music makers, the narrative complements and enhances costumes, architecture, mosaic, and ceremonials of the dim past.

Melody in Ritual

The author lists communal singing and chanting in *The Firebrand* as elements of entertainment in Aeneas's childhood memory, a source of lore and learning recast as the sounds made by the harper Ardanos in *The Forest House.* Melody eases camaraderie among the Amazons and accompanies a ritual of good fortune for the bride and groom at Andromache's marriage to Hector and the union of Creusa with Aeneas. During petitioning of the Great Goddess, the horsewomen rattle gourd shakers and pat the skins stretched over hoops for percussive tempos, the sound that thrums again in harmony with a reed flute during Kassandra's initiation. At Andromache's bridal chamber, "joyous hymns" honor the union of Priam's heir with the daughter of Imandra, queen of Colchis (Bradley, 1987, 155). Trojan shipbuilders revive the epic of Jason and the Argo by singing to the bard's notes. The song of the Maiden rings out from processions until the arrival of Helen, a scorned queen whom Kassandra refuses to venerate as Paris's lawful wife.

The narrative weaves chants and canticles into everyday life, as with Kassandra's dawn hymn to the sun and the song and winding labyrinth dance from Crete at Hector's funeral feast known as the γερανός (*Geranos* or Crane Dance), a ritual altar performance described in Greek mythology. Dithyrambs to the Mother Goddess return each spring at planting time, when worshippers dance to extol her control of nature and sing "Bring the grain…. Bring it with songs and feasting and joy" (*Ibid.*, 261). The annual salute to agriculture precedes Helen's labor and delivery, when Creusa strums soothing tunes on a lap-harp, a member of the lyra family known as a *kithara,* zither, or psaltery that originated in Anatolia. As a part of communal birthing during Imandra's lying-in at Colchis, women intone customary birth-songs and croon welcome to the soul of the unborn child. Choreography depicts reincarnation of "the soul making its way past the guardians of the World Before," a hint of reincarnation in Trojan theology (*Ibid.*, 358).

Marion accounts for Homer's epics as well as others in the bardic creativity at Troy. One song lists Akhaian ships; another names Trojan allies, a significant outtake from the *Iliad.* At a dreaded one-on-one match-up between Paris and Menelaus, Helen pleads for sacred recitation to call down sea fog to shield Paris from harm. After a night of keening and mourning for Troilus, a harper performs a mythic dirge that likens the boy's beauty to that of Ares/Mars, a grim reminder of the price of war. In a buoyant finale, the author introduces Kassandra to the beloved dead—a martyr safe in an atmosphere of brilliant light and harp music.

REFLECTIONS OF CONFLICT

In a classic perusal of religion in *The Mists of Avalon,* the author contrasts liturgical music, coronation hymns, and the peal of London's church bells, which epitomize the smugness and conceit of Christian philosophy. The passage of rule at the funeral of Aurelius Ambrosius begins with doleful Christian psalms that give place to praise anthems for the selection of his brother Uther Pendragon as the new high king of Britannia. Similar in tone to the monks' chant to the Divine in *Stormqueen!,* Marion describes Britannia's Celtic music as a source of priestly power, "one of the keys to the laws of the universe," a mathematical concept of "harmony of the spheres" that the Greco-Roman polymath Ptolemy of Alexandria developed in his treatise *Harmonics* (ca. 135 CE) (Bradley, 1983, 151).

At a plot shift after Morgaine's union with the Stag King, Marion indicates that Morgaine will become high queen simultaneous with the advance of Kevin the harper to the next Merlin. The range of Kevin's skills take shape in Irish style—an emotive refrain preceding a bawdy tune. At Arthur's wedding, Kevin recognizes Morgaine by offering his harp to entertain guests with her lyric voice. Her belief in the sanctity of singing clashes with Gwenhwyfar's pious comment that "it is unseemly for a woman to raise her voice before the Lord," a rephrasing of Paul's command in 1 Corinthians 14:34–35: "Let your women keep silent in the churches, for they are not permitted to speak; but they are to be submissive, as the law also says ... it is shameful for women to speak in church" (*Ibid.,* 288). Because Gwenhwyfar shrinks from violating Paul's dictum, Kevin the Merlin challenges, "Why yes, madam, music is sacred—did you not learn the harp in your nunnery?" (*Ibid.*). With more affability, Arthur returns from combat with a hunger "for harps and all the things of civilized men," a gesture of respect for humanism (*Ibid.,* 313).

Marion reverences Kevin Harper and his song of Orfeo, the Greek singer Orpheus who fled the Underworld in a failed attempt to return his wife Eurydice to the light. The ballad renews enchantment and hope in Morgaine as despair saps her will, turning her into "a bridge between earth and sky" (*Ibid.,* 756). The vocal urging creates an apotheosis—an appearance of the Great Goddess. In Nimue's defense of sacred hymns, she compares Kevin to "the psalmist," an allusion to David, unifier of desert tribes and founder of a capital at Jerusalem (*Ibid.,* 784). In regard for the author's fiction and the singer's "loss of self" in song, Celtic harpist Alan Stivell of Rion, France, anthologized Breton, English, and French melody inspired by *The Mists of Avalon* (Dell, 2011, 172).

Sources

Bradley, Marion Zimmer. *The Complete Lythande.* San Francisco: Marion Zimmer Bradley Literary Works Trust, 2013.
_____. *Darkover Landfall.* New York: DAW, 1972.
_____. *The Fall of Atlantis.* Riverdale, NY: Baen Books, 1983.
_____. *The Firebrand.* New York: Simon & Schuster, 1987.
_____. *The Forest House.* New York: Michael Joseph, 1993.
_____. *Greyhaven.* New York: DAW, 1983.
_____. *Lady of Avalon.* New York: Viking, 1997.
_____. *The Mists of Avalon.* New York: Ballantine, 1983.
_____. *Rediscovery.* New York: DAW, 1993.
Dell, Helen. "'Yearning for the Sweet Beckoning Sound': Musical Longings and the Unsayable in Medievalist Fantasy Fiction." *postmedieval* 2:2 (2011): 171–185.

Fry, Carrol L. "The Goddess Ascending: Feminist Neo-Pagan Witchcraft in Marion Zimmer Bradley's Novels," *Journal of Popular Culture* 27:1 (1993): 67–80.

Nastali, Dan. "Arthurian Pop: The Tradition in Twentieth-Century Popular Music," *King Arthur in Popular Culture* (2002): 138–167.

Names

Marion paired names for her cast and settings that enhanced characterization and motivation, a clue to the naming of the planet Megaera, one of the Greek Erinyes (Furies), in "Centaurus Changeling," Novenus (Latin for "new") for the emerging town on planet Deneb in "Outpost," the rugged the Hellers Mountains in *The Winds of Darkover,* and rescuer Cliff-Climber, a renegade Mekhar in *Hunters of the Red Moon.* For Senator Hermes-Gabriel "Herm" Aldaran, a clairvoyant in *Traitor's Sun,* the author selected a name for a Roman *herma* (Latin for "signpost"). For *Bluebeard's Daughter,* Marion named the protagonist "Sybil," suggesting a prophet or oracle. Early in her career, she published "Exiles of Tomorrow" in *Fantastic Universe,* the story of a couple separated in time. To intensify the tender reunion of Ryn and Cara Kenner, Marion names the wife the Latin for "dear" and a Gaelic Scots surname for "perceiver."

The author connected a variety of languages to her characters and places, as with the Latin Max ("Maximus" for "greatest") for the protagonist's name in "Phoenix," Acquilara (from the Latin for "eagle") for the pompous hostess in *City of Sorcery,* the late Latin Nevarsin for "city of snow" in *Stormqueen!,* the Greek Callista for a beautiful apparition in *The Spell Sword,* and the French Dorilys (gold lily) for a motherless infant in *The Bloody Sun.* Raella, the child wizard in "The Children of Cats," carries the Hebrew for "ewe." The connection between Davidson and MacDoevid in *Exile's Song* reminds readers of the Scots ancestry of Darkover residents. For *The Catch Trap,* she gave Italian-American circus star Matthew Gardner, Jr., the nickname "Mario," a retrieval of the Italian name of his great grandfather, a legendary Italian circus trapeze artist bearing the Roman honorific to the god Mars. For Earth exploration of the planet Mars, she chose German for *Erdenluft,* a spaceship in "Measureless for Man" named "Earth Air" in German. In a pairing of opposites, the story "Ten Minutes or So" features Gareth (Welsh for "gentleness") Lindir, a stammering mollycoddle bearing the name of one of King Arthur's Knights of the Round Table. She revisits Gareth in *The Mists of Avalon* to mourn his accidental death at a young age.

For *Witchlight,* the author contrasts the quandary of Winter Musgrave, a former dabbler in magic and victim of amnesia, with that of a psychic researcher, Truth Jourdemayne, a name redolent with the honest journeyman's day labor and a fifteenth-century English sorcerer, Margery Jourdemayne of Smithfield, whom authorities burned at the stake in Westminster on October 27, 1441. For the suspenseful sequel, *Gravelight,* Marion revives parapsychologist Jourdemayne, but splits action between a past feud of neighbors and ongoing animosity at Wychwood and LittlerHeller Creek in Morton's Fork near Watchman's Gap in Lyonesse County, place names suggesting sorcery, deviltry, puncture, surveillance, and bestiality. The occult saga, set in Appalachia, incorporates the names Wycherly Ridenow Musgrave, Luned Starking, and Thorne Blackburn, Magister Magus (Master Teacher) of the Church of the Antique Rite. By referring to Nicholas Taverner's book *Haants, Spooks, and Fetchmen* and clipping Melusine's honeyed first name to "Sinah," the narrative implies a sinister culpability.

NAMES FOR LYTHANDE

The Lythande series demanded clever names for people and destinations. The Greek sounds of "Lythande" imply two common words—"stone" and "man," a deeply buried suggestion of the hardening of female feelings to hide a wanderer's true gender. For the picara story "Sea Wrack," the author shields "the Shadow" behind an adopted name but conceals her birth name, which the reader never learns. The inept sorcerer Rastafyre in "The Incompetent Magician," bears a patronym suggesting Rastafari, an Ethiopian cult that emerged in Jamaica in 1930, the beginning of the 24-year reign of Ras Tafari Makonen, the Emperor Haile Selassie. The Abrahamic sect failed to achieve its intent to return Caribbean blacks to Africa, their motherland.

The author edged identifications with humor and whimsy. For the setting of the grotesque revenge tale "Treason of the Blood," she chose the ludicrous name Castello Speranza (Castle of Hope); for "The Walker Behind," she named the dog-barber Gimlet, the Dutch term for "drill." The name implies the dog groomer's ability to cheat his clients. The inn servant Frennet bears an altered pronunciation of "friend," a designation worthy of its use in the worker's rescue of Lythande from pig charmers at the Hag and Swine saloon. The Greek "Myrtis" in the Lythande series refers to the victor's myrtle wreath in classic athletic contests. In "Chalice of Tears," Manuela, a pilgrimage leader whose name means "God with us" or "hand of God," proves useful to Lythande with a lesson in humility and an alert to bias against women.

MAKING CONNECTIONS

The medieval anchoring of people to clans and professions marked characters in the Darkover series, which initiates interplanetary settlement with Hispanic and Scots colonists. Critic Anne K. Kaler made a valuable leap in connecting the patronym of Scots geologist Rafael "Rafe" MacAran with the agrarian roots of the Aran Islands, which preserve fields and meadows with limestone walls surviving from the Bronze Age. By writing the surname in French, Kaler deduces that Rafe is the genetic source of *l'aran*, the mystic psi power that both enables and weakens planet dwellers. For the Amazons, the creation of "daughter of" to indicate a maternal line results in female names Jaelle n'ha Melora and Keitha n'ha Casilda, a corollary of her husband's Scots patronym Shann MacShann (Shann son of Shann) (Bradley, 1983, 125).

A Gothic touch marks Marion's characters with innuendo. Magdalen "Magda" Lorne's Terran name identifies a forlorn character who strips herself of the need for men and retreats to a cave to commune with the Dark Sisterhood. A desert figure, Jaelle n'ha Melora, an allusion to the Hebrew assassin lauded in Judges 5:17–22 who drives a tent stake through the temple of the cruel Sisera, supplies tent dwellers in Dry Towns. The name Jaelle recurs in *Thendara House,* in which Felicia, Latin for "lucky," seems a cruel designation for the mother of an unwanted son.

Alaric di Asturien, a noble in *The Heirs of Hammerfell, Two to Conquer,* and the story "To Keep the Oath," recalls the Visigoth chieftain who sacked Rome on August

24, 410 CE. References to Roman history continue in *Darkover Landfall* with the mass said by Father Valentine, bearing the name of a martyr to the Roman emperor Claudius on February 14, 269 CE, and the identification of a survivor "Camilla," a Volsci princess-warrior in service to the goddess Artemis/Diana in Virgil's *Aeneid*. An inside joke in *Landfall* anticipates repair of a wrecked spaceship for the journey to Coronis Colony, a Latinized name for "Crown Colony," a hint of British rule over land acquired by conquest and war.

COMIC AND HALLOWED

In *The Forest House*, Marion renders humor and irony from identifiable names, especially the Arch Druid Ardanos, an Irish word meaning "high aspiration." Julia Licinia names her daughters Roman fashion Secunda, Tertia, and Quartilla (Latin for "second," "third," and "little fourth"), an obvious diminution of girl babies. The introduction of Romano-Celtic tribune Gaius Macellius to Rome places him in varied company among the empire's elite. One senator, Marcellus Clodius, bears the cognomen "malleus" (the hammer); the aristocrat Flavius Clemens, Domitian's cousin, earned the name "clemens" (mild, calm, merciful) for his demeanor; the legate Lucius Domitius Brutus carries the designation of "muscular" (Bradley, 1993, 304, 309, 331). Among the Celts, similar symbolism acknowledges mythic significance, as with Bethoc (life), mother of the king of Celts Ambigatus (fighter on both sides).

The author's revival of the antique renaming ritual confers significance on both ceremony and recipient. For characters in *The Fall of Atlantis*, the pairing of sacred with common names enhances an aura of holiness in mortal life acknowledged by such nomenclature as Micon, whom his wife honors as "Son of the Sun," and Eilantha, dubbed Tiriki (Little Singer) for her voice in infancy (Bradley, 1983, 497). Both Domaris and her little sister Deoris adopt adult identification by accepting Isarma (sensitive soul) and Adsartha (warrior child) as temple identities. The Atlantean Prince Micon's courtship of Domaris begins with sweet compliments to his "Flower of the Sun," "Heart of Flame," and "lady of Light," gestures of love and respect for her beneficence and passion (*Ibid.*, 78, 207, 234). Before the birth of their son Micail (the Slavic spelling of "Michael," meaning "god-like"), priests choose a propitious designation for the child—O-si-narmen, a prodigy who eventually marries Deoris's daughter Eilantha/Tiriki and founds a new realm. At the infant's formal blessing, Michael receives more bynames: "Royal Hunter, Heir-to-the-Word-of-Thunder" (*Ibid.*, 236). Marion's apparent preference for "Micail" appears to have spawned a repeat in *Traitor's Sun* as Mikhail Lanart-Hastur, regent of Darkover.

CLASSIC NAMES

In *The Firebrand*, the renaming of Alexandra (Greek for "defender") as Kassandra (Greek for "shining") coincides with the time that Alexandros (male form of "defender"), renamed Paris, departs Troy to live on Mount Ida with a shepherd. In introducing the Amazon outriders, Marion names them Charis (Greek for "Grace") and Elaria (Egyptian for "Joyful"). Other names promote prosperity and future greatness, as with Astyanax (Greek for "king of the city"), Priam and Hecuba's first grandson. To assuage Oenone's fears about her son Corythus (helmet), Kassandra informs her that the male children of Amazons bear their mothers' names. Oenone reminds the priestess that only the children of Trojan prostitutes bear matronyms. Because Oenone's mother was the river god Scamander's priestess who died young, Oenone retains only a first name, Greek for "wine server."

The Arthurian strand of Marion's writing follows the lead of British literature, as with Priscilla in *The Mists of Avalon*, a Christian foster mother bearing the name of a follower of the Apostle Paul mentioned in Romans 16:3. A group of the legendary characters shares names: Galahad Lancelet and son Galahad, Isotta of Ireland and Isotta of Cornwall, Gwenhwyfar I and II, and Gwydion/King Arthur, father of son Gwydion/ Mordred. The infant Arthur takes a blended name, "Uther's bear," from the Celtic term *artos* for bear. His surname, Pendragon (Anglo-Saxon for "chief leader"), proves prophetic for both father and son. The traitor Mordred acquires his name from the irregular Latin verb *mordeo* (to bite). His rival, Galahad, abandons a childhood name from the Latin for "helmet" and takes the military identification "Elf-Arrow" from the Saxons (Bradley, 1983, 252). The former Galahad prefers Lancelet, a derivative of the Latin for "spearman." His distaste for the first name causes Morgaine to chide him for a belief from fairy times "that one who knows your true name can command your spirit if he will" (*Ibid.*, 150).

Sources

Bradley, Marion Zimmer. *The Fall of Atlantis*. Riverdale, NY: Baen Books, 1983.
_____. *The Forest House*. New York: Michael Joseph, 1993.
_____. *The Mists of Avalon*. New York: Ballantine, 1983.
_____. *Thendara House*. New York: DAW, 1983.
Jones, Libby Falk. "Gilman, Bradley, Piercy, and the Evolving Rhetoric of Feminist Utopias" in *Feminism, Utopia, and Narrative*. Knoxville: University of Tennessee Press, 1990, 116–129.
Kaler, Anne K. "Bradley and the Beguines" in *Heroines of Popular Culture*. Bowling Green, OH: Bowling Green State University Popular Press, 1987.

Olympian Gods

A shortened version of the vast Greek panoply of deities stresses the most common names, the ones that Marion chose for rewriting Homer's Trojan War epic. The anthropomorphic nature of the Greek/Roman pantheon contrasts the Mother Goddess, a single, more ethereal, comforting presence devoid of human frailties. Notation in the Greek family tree indicates sexual/marital ties:

|	|	|	|	|	|	|	|	|	|	|
| Hermes	Pallas	|	Apollo	Vesta (Hestia)	Artemis	|	Ares (Mars)	Aphrodite	Hades
| (Mercury)	Athene	|	(Helios)	goddess	(Diana)	|	war god	(Venus)	god of the
| messenger	(Minerva)	|	sun lord	of the	huntress	|		goddess of	Underworld
Poseidon	goddess	|		hearth	_____	(siblings)____		passion	

(Neptune)	of war and	Demeter (Ceres)				
lord of the sea	wisdom			Hera (Juno)=Zeus (Jupiter)
		Hades=/=daughter	protector		thunderer
		(Pluto) (Proserpina	of wedlock		Sky Father
		or Persephone)			
				Pan
				nature god

Marion designates no name to protect the refugee Mikhala in *Warrior Women,* in which she prays to a generic female presence to shield her infant daughter. The author chooses Artemis/Diana, the nature goddess and hunter, to identify the protagonist of "The Day of the Butterflies." To the Greek princess Kassandra, a devotee of the Great Mother in *The Firebrand,* the Greek Aphrodite/Venus is a "foreign Goddess of lawless love" who promotes promiscuity and forbidden passion (Bradley, 1987, 253). Both Ares/ Mars and Hera/Juno display vicious, narrow interests in the Trojan War. In contrast, in *The Forest House,* Caillean refutes the Roman notion of multiple deities charged with a variety of powers, such as Hestia/Vesta, goddess of the hearth, whose name recurs on a starship in "Death Between the Stars." To Caillean, "The Light of Truth is One," a tenet similar to the monotheistic faiths of Atenism, Judaism, Sikhism, Islam, and the Wakan Tankaism of the Sioux in the insistence on a single creator and supreme being (Bradley, 1993, 166).

See also Mother Goddess; Religion.

Sources

Bradley, Marion Zimmer. *The Firebrand.* New York: Simon & Schuster, 1987.
_____. *The Forest House.* New York: Michael Joseph, 1993.
_____. "Thoughts on Avalon," http://mzbworks.com/thoughts.htm, 1986.
_____. *Warrior Woman.* New York: DAW, 1985.
Evola, Julius. *The Mystery of the Grail: Initiation and Magic in the Quest for the Spirit.* New York: Simon & Schuster, 2018.
Thompson, Diane P. *The Trojan War: Literature and Legends from the Bronze Age to the Present.* Jefferson, NC: McFarland, 2013.

Patriarchy

An active proponent of women's rights, Marion declared male-dominant societies dictatorial, the source of Mikhail's cry to his daughter, "You haven't heard the last of this, damn you" in *Hawkmistress!,* of sexual bondage of refugees in *Warrior Woman,* and of Radan's dirty soldier talk and chaos in *Stormqueen!* (Bradley, 1982, 12). According to critic Jessica Jernigan, "It's not just impersonal fortune to blame for … downfall. Instead, it's systems of oppression" (Jernigan). The author blames women as well for yielding to androcentrism in matters of chaperonage, courtship, and marriage, for example, Lorill's goading of his twin sister Leonie Hastur in *Rediscovery*. In *The Heirs of Hammerfell,* she depicts the widow Erminie lightly rebuking her son Alastair for declaring bridal negotiations a man's prerogative. To herself, the mother admits, "She had brought him up to the habits and customs of their mountain kinsmen" (Bradley, 1989, 41).

Reviewer Roland J. Green admired Marion for "her eloquent concern with the way men have of making women do the paying" (Green, 1982, D4). In *Thendara House,* Jaelle n'ha Melora falls prey to a grasping husband, Peter Haldane, who wants "to own me, me and the baby, like things, like toys" (Bradley, 1983, 387). A rejection in *Two to Conquer* causes the lusty Bard di Asturien, a model of the Roman stereotyped *miles gloriosus* (Latin for "boastful soldier"), to curse the "general damnableness of women," his term for independence (Bradley, 1980, 197). For Ellemir Lanart in *The Forbidden Tower,* her lack of a father, older brother, or reliable mate causes her to pass to the "wardship of Lord Serrais" and three female chaperones (Bradley, 1977, 332). In reference to ending male suzerainty, the author prioritized autonomy: "I think women's liberation is the great event of the twentieth century, not space exploration" (Bradley, 1984, Introduction). Ignoring advancing techno-wizardry, which bored her, she championed the "great change in human consciousness" energized by second wave feminism (*Ibid.*).

The arrogance of Marion's fictional males takes shape in dynastic glory and in commands to women, a future that Lady Rohana expects in "Bride Price" along with loss of her patronym at marriage to Gabriel Ardais. A fearful wife, Keitha n'ha Casilda, escapes in *Thendara House* by fleeing her abusive husband Shann MacShann, who raids the shelter and demands her return. In "Knives," Marna remains illiterate because her husband believes "there was no point in teaching a woman to read more than enough to spell out a public placard, or sign her name to a marriage contract" (Bradley, 1993, 60). Male dominion historically violated female self-determination for millennia, as demonstrated by the fisherman's taunt in "Sea Wrack" that "[l]asses stay home and bake bread where they belong" (Bradley, 2013, 67). The rover mercenary Lythande encounters men's stories about domesticating free sea folk and making them "servant to man" until they fled domesticity and resumed free swimming in the ocean, a subtle hint to discontented women (*Ibid.*, 81).

The Oppressors

The macho view of female impotence and worthlessness in *The Shattered Chain* generates "old dirty stories" alleging that strong women fight unfairly, make love with other females, and travel in packs like wolves (Bradley, 1976, 150). The suppressed females earn contempt in Dry-Town for being "helpless, harmless chattels. Victims" (*Ibid.*, 39). Hayat, a sour-toned misogynist, scorns rebellious free Amazons for refusing to be male possessions: "Shameless bitches, that's what they are, running around like that with no man to own to 'em" (*Ibid.*, 12). Taken as a diatribe against gendered society, the citations capture an odium that simmers like a fever.

Even though women have superintended healing and midwifery from prehistory, the orders of Bendeigid Vran to his daughter Eilan in *The Forest House* to leave the room or else "don't scream or faint" at first aid to an injured man disclose biased thinking that girls bear innate frailties (Bradley, 1993, 15). In a later scene, Eilan realizes how thoroughly she has internalized masculine judgments: "It had never occurred to her to question the wisdom of men like her father and grandfather" (*Ibid.,* 100). The priestess Caillean takes a more cynical view of men's control of weaponry and harp music "and everything else save for the suffering of childbirth and the toil of the cooking pot and the loom," a terse summary of women's remaining domains (*Ibid.,* 124). To Eilan's question "Why did things change?," her mentor Caillean cites an age-old male ploy: "For our own protection," a well-meaning platitude cloaking tyranny (*Ibid.,* 190). While the Head Druid Ardanos secretly disdains priestesses as "these silly hens," women at Forest House conceal their discontent and suppress complaints about priests who override the opinions of the High Priestess in the style of Roman Catholic popery that stifles activist nuns (*Ibid.,* 196). Caillean predicts that only in a magic realm—"a place outside time"— can women express their own truth, an allusion to the havens of Thendara House and Avalon (*Ibid.,* 191).

ASSETS AND LIABILITIES

In *Gratitude of Kings,* Marion overturns the stereotype of the dimpled maiden betrothed to a handsome prince. For Princess Velvet of Valantia, a provincial marriage arrangement to Tashgen, prince of Tshardain, bodes well for her father's wine sales, thus reducing her to a secondary commodity. In the trade-off of girl for profits, Velvet's welfare bears little importance to father or prince. For rescue, the author turned to an artisan, Eirthe, the savvy candlemaker and abettor of the mercenary Lythande, who foils a court conspiracy. In a review of Bradley's rebellion against the bride swap, critic Marleen Barr declared the author's chutzpah "disconcerting to the patriarchy" (Barr, 1990, 21). She extended her disgust for self-important monarchs to the "patriarchal literary establishment" for devaluing "speculative fiction," a subgenre proposing top-to-bottom restructuring of the gender hierarchy. Barr proposed her own term, "feminist fabulation," to "[address] woman's place within the system of patriarchy" (*Ibid.,* 22).

Marion intensified realism in *The Fall of Atlantis* with situations reflecting modern times. Talkannon, the arch-administrator, rejects Karahama, his illegitimate daughter born to a servant, with the ease that Tashgan ousts a bedmate from his quarters in "The Wandering Lute." In token of Talkannon's lordly preeminence, society exiles the mother and her daughter Demira, who hangs herself. Literary historian Ronald Hutton summarized such female pariahs as "kicked around by men, imprisoned in hopelessly dreary and self-denying domestic labor, and allowed no opinions, no adventures, no true existence of their own" (Hutton, 1999, 355). To prevent social stigma from shaming Domaris, her lover Micon confers on their unborn son the paternal "name, station, and estate," three assets that elevate the fatherless child from bastardy (Bradley, 1983, 137). In evidence of her refusal of male devaluation, Domaris states a necessary self-classification: "I am a person before I am a woman" (*Ibid.,* 262). The axiom reflects the author's defiance of misogyny that banishes a single mother from respectful parenthood, a social distinction that marks computer technician Ysaye Barnett in *Rediscovery*.

Historic Barrers

In *The Firebrand,* the writer redefines the male-female animosities of the classical period. In the eastern Mediterranean, toxic masculinity retains unquestioned ascendancy over women, the reason for Paris's choking of his unmarried twin Kassandra to stop her hysterical prophesying. Marion redirects the crux of the *Iliad* from the kidnapping of females to the price that nations set on the loss of stolen women. In support of male hegemony, Queen Hecuba of Troy admires the horse-folk, who reward concubines with gold trinkets for producing males and groom their sons for adulthood. Marion notes the patriarchal validation of daughters as assets "as valuable as any son, for a daughter could be married" for political reasons to rivals (Bradley, 1987, 11). The comment explains the logic of Julius Caesar's arranged wedlock between his only child, 17-year-old Julia Caesar, to 47-year-old Pompey Magnus, Rome's star general, a common form of placating rivals in Republican Rome.

Of the androcentrism of 1200 BCE, when iron-shapers replaced the outdated technologists of the Bronze Age, *The Firebrand* illustrates restrictions on female agency. The priest Khryse justifies Cretan rules against teaching females to write, a stricture still in effect against Japanese women until the Heian period in 794 CE and against all American slaves before the Civil War. In debate with Kassandra about female autonomy, Khryse declares that the gods validated male sexual desire as a message from the divine. He asserts that "woman is made for man," a declaration rife with objectification of the female primarily as bedmate (*Ibid.,* 213). Kassandra calls Khryse a liar, fool, blasphemer, and hypocrite and rightly rebuts, "Every seducer has spoke so since time began" (*Ibid.,* 214).

Even in the Trojan palace, Hecuba accedes to Priam's dicta. He demands that she not touch weaponry before the birth of his heir, Prince Hector. His prioritizing of shipping profits over the rescue of his sister Hesione from kidnap confirms the queen's private thoughts about male pomposity and avarice. After eight years of marriage, Hecuba eludes the king's ill temper and admits that sleeping alone in their bed appeals to her, even if her mate couples with a concubine. In ordering the abandonment of Hecuba's doomed son Paris, Priam asserts, "I have spoken; let it be done!," a majestic imperative that results in devastation from a ten-year war, the focal catastrophe in the works of Homer and Virgil (*Ibid.,* 18).

The Coming Revolution

In redirection from Akhaia and Troy to the history of Britannia, Marion's Arthuriana replaced the sexual politics and culture of chivalry in Alfred, Lord Tennyson's, *Idylls of the King* with renewed interest in femininity and women's agendas. In the explanation of reviewer Dawn D'Aries, the author "answered questions of motivation for the female characters that were not explored as deeply in more traditional myths" (D'Aries, 2014). One rebel, Queen Morgause of Lothian, charges anti-woman prejudice among Christian fathers and husbands for denying females any real work or responsibility, therefore leaving them to demean themselves with jealousy and tittle-tattle. Critic Bridgette Da Silva adds another devaluation of women as collectibles for their beauty. Because fair-skinned, blue-eyed women like Gwenhwyfar tend to remain indoors, they appeal more to men as stereotypical trophy wives. In contrast, Morgaine, a petite, out-doorsy brunette, follows "conceptions of womanhood, spirituality, and beauty that were not available on mainland Britain that allowed them a greater sense of power [and] a healthier sense of self" (Da Silva, 2007).

With a hint of satire, critic Lee Ann Tobin summarizes the nostalgic story line as "male bonding, rivalry over women, and the impossibly conflicting demands of church and chivalry ... a hypothetical golden age when lovers were more noble and knights more heroic" (Tobin, 1993, 147). Like Buddhism, Islam, and Judaism, Christianity based its sanctity on an all-powerful, judgmental father-god. As a result, the age championed Gwenhwyfar's tyrannic father Leodegranz, chider of his "pretty little featherhead," who studied in a convent where nuns kowtowed to priests (Bradley, 1983, 309). His patri-archal marriage arrangements and a dowry of mounted horsemen make her feel like furniture, or a "brood mare" (*Ibid.*). Because of Catholic indoctrination, she accepts her lot as the result of original sin, a patriarchal construct based on an anti-woman interpretation of the myth of Adam and Eve.

According to expert Charlotte Spivack, the Arthurian narrative *The Mists of Avalon* "[attacks] patriarchal and phallocentric concepts ... to replace them with a non-patriarchal understanding of power" (Spivack, 1992, 93). Marion faults the Ro-mans with reducing female identity to "chattels of their menfolk" and speaks through Gwenhwyfar a fear that "God cares nothing for women" (Bradley, 1983, 312, 442). In the interpretation of literary expert Karen E.C. Fuog, the author must battle male su-periority by repositioning pre-existing traditions of fifth- and sixth-century legends of "men and their deeds" (Fuog, 1991, 73). When Gwenhwyfar begins displaying symp-toms of agoraphobia, the house priest belittles her concerns about venturing onto open land. Her father interprets the anomaly as a personal annoyance invoked by "womanish nonsense in his house" (Bradley, 1983, 252). Fuog exemplified tales of women's foolish-ness as examples of aspersions that "have been retold by patriarchies for centuries" as though they bore gospel truth (Fuog, 1991, 73).

Reviewing male grousing over overt female sexuality, the narrative reprises the double standard of men who regularly bed females of all types—free women, slaves, and servants. At the chirpy female eyeing of soldiers at Tintagel, Duke Gorlois of Corn-wall charges his thirteen-year-old sister-in-law Morgause for being "a puppy bitch with eyes hot for anything in the shape of a man" (Bradley, 1983, 26). He slaps his own wife, Igraine, for conversing with High King Uther Pendragon, a known womanizer. The author indicates that the decline of manhood arouses the aging Gorlois to wartime excesses that cause his death. After Igraine's marriage to Uther, he accuses her of "(play-ing) the shrew" and commands "obey me" (*Ibid.*, 47). The marital situation worsens with Uther's impotence, which he blames on Igraine's witchery, an imaginary threat to male hierarchy.

See also Christianity; Female Persona; *The Firebrand*, Volume One; *The Shattered Chain*.

Sources

Barr, Marleen. "Food for Postmodern Thought" in *Feminism, Utopia, and Narrative*. Knoxville: University of Tennessee Press, 1990, 21–33.

Bradley, Marion Zimmer. *The Best of Marion Zimmer Bradley*. New York: DAW, 1984.
_____. *The Complete Lythande*. San Francisco: Marion Zimmer Bradley Literary Works Trust, 2013.
_____. *The Fall of Atlantis*. Riverdale, NY: Baen Books, 1983.
_____. *The Firebrand*. New York: Simon & Schuster, 1987.
_____. *The Forbidden Tower*. New York: DAW, 1977.
_____. *The Forest House*. New York: Michael Joseph, 1993.
_____. *Hawkmistress!* New York: DAW, 1982.
_____. *The Heirs of Hammerfell*. New York: DAW, 1989.
_____. "Knives" in *Marion Zimmer Bradley's Darkover*. New York: DAW, 1993.
_____. *The Mists of Avalon*. New York: Ballantine, 1983.
_____. *The Other Side of the Mirror*. New York: DAW, 1987.
_____. *The Shattered Chain*. New York: DAW, 1976.
_____. *Thendara House*. New York: DAW, 1983.
_____. *Two to Conquer*. New York: DAW, 1980.
D'Aries, Dawn. "Books We Can't Quit: The Mists of Avalon, by Marion Zimmer Bradley," *Pank Magazine* (3 June 2014).
Da Silva, Bridgette. "Medieval Mindsets: Narrative Theory and *The Mists of Avalon*," *Strange Horizons* (1 October 2007).
Fuog, Karen E.C. "Imprisoned in the Phallic Oak: Marion Zimmer Bradley and Merlin's Seductress," *Quondam et Futurus* 1:1 (1991): 73–88.
Green, Roland J. "'Hawkmistress' Continues Darkover Saga," (New Brunswick) *Central New Jersey Home News* (26 September 1982): D4.
Hutton, Ronald. *The Triumph of the Moon: A History of Modern Pagan Witchcraft*. New York: Oxford University Press, 1999.
Jernigan, Jessica. "The Book That Made Me a Feminist Was Written by an Abuser," https://electricliterature.com/the-book-that-made-me-a-feminist-was-written-by-an-abuser-4c6891f548cf.
Spivack, Charlotte. *Popular Arthurian Traditions*. Bowling Green, OH: Bowling Green State University Popular Press, 1992.
Tobin, Lee Ann. "Why Change the Arthur Story? Marion Zimmer Bradley's *The Mists of Avalon*," *Extrapolation* 34:2 (1993): 147–157.

The Planet Savers

One of Marion's most engaging character studies, the novella *The Planet Savers* positions Dr. Jay Allison/Jason Allison, a troubled schizophrenic, as rescuer of Darkover from rampant disease. Set a century and a half after *Rediscovery* amid the arboreal habitat of Trailmen, the story contrasts the academic hauteur of 34-year-old parasitologist and surgeon Jay Allison with the candor and bonhomie of Jason, age 22.

Jason Allison, Sr.

explorer-cartographer

deceased

|

Dr. Jay Allison/Jason Allison=/=Kyla Raineach

free Amazon

Questing for a remedy for 48-year-fever pandemics in exchange for training in matrix mechanics, the protagonist enlists Lord Regis Hastur to scale the Hellers Mountains to recruit 100 Old Ones as medical guinea pigs to combat a plague marked by 87 percent mortality. In a rush to save Terran pride, cooperation among unarmed men over five months of lab work results in a synthetic serum developed from the volunteerism of "*homo arborens*: nocturnal nyctalopia humanoids" (Bradley, 1976, 18).

The narrative moves sure-footedly through Dr. Randall Forth's exploration of multiple personalities and his delineation of differences between Jason and Jay:

Jay	Jason
retiring, studious physician	gregarious expert on Trailmen
cautious, repressed	adventurous, cocky
taciturn	talkative
selfish	intrinsically motivated
conservative	flashy
racist	compassionate

The experiment involving Jason as central agent releases details of eight years in a Trailmen's nest in the trees and five years in the Spacemen's Orphanage in Trade City spent by Jay, his alter ego. Among the company of "mountain roughnecks," no one recognizes Jason as Jay (*Ibid.*, 17). His greatest fear is reversion to his original persona: "If I slept, who would I be when I woke?" (*Ibid.*, 18).

Formulation of a serum requires strenuous work and cooperation. The exploratory crew prepares for snow blindness, sleet, and crossing swinging bridges over high country torrents through rocky chasms. Jay impresses the crew because he "worked tirelessly and unsparingly; scarcely sleeping, but brooding; silent, prone to fly into sudden savage rages, but painstaking" (*Ibid.*, 44). Less certain about personal relations than medical obstacles, he must atone for slugging Lord Regis because of "slipping mental gears" that obscure the permanent third personality that eventually emerges (*Ibid.*, 47).

Male-female dynamics bring the novel to a tentative close. Conversation between Jason and guide Kyla Raineach require explanations why Jason has multiple personalities and why Jason considers Jay the better man. Marion solves the anomaly by crafting the warring personae into "a man who'd balanced his god and daemon for once" (*Ibid.*, 46). Out of his labors, he is able to reward himself: "This work—this would be something which would satisfy both halves of myself" (*Ibid.*, 47). A romantic touch illustrates the value of a loving companion to consolidation of the final and hopefully permanent persona.

Sources

Bradley, Marion Zimmer. *The Planet Savers*. New York: Ace, 1976.

Clark, Mary Higgins. "Review: *The Planet Savers*," https://webcache.googleuser content.com/search?q= cache:KqTaaNfTkFoJ:https://www.tisec.org.uk/6d188f/the-planet-savers.pdf+&cd=18&hl=en&ct=clnk &gl=us.

Prophecy

Marion's canon reverences prophecy for its orphic mysticism and divine guidance, for example, the prognostication in *The Bloody Sun* that Jeff Kerwin "will find the thing you desire" (Bradley, 1964, 47). Typically obscure, the oracle concludes on a conundrum: he will both destroy and save his heart's desire. Literary augury reveals to the few the destiny of nations, the task of the Pythia at Delphi and the controlling metaphor of the author's fairy tale *Black Trillium,* a favorite of young readers. To the troubled Mhari in *A Sword Called Chaos,* folkloric predictions carry some hope of relief from post-rape grief encompassing assaults to her mother, sisters, and self. She recites the proverb, "What is done under four moons … need never be remembered nor regretted" (Bradley 1982, 86). Shucking thoughts of slitting her own throat with a dagger, Mhari grasps the prospect that the Gods saved her for some important task, an uplifting projection of her future.

The Darkover series interweaves premonitions as normal, even propitious facets of human thought. In *Darkover Landfall,* characters experience ominous precognition before Lieutenant Camilla Del Rey's ill-advised venture from the shelter tent. Zoologist Lewis MacLeod confesses, "I've never taken ESP very seriously … I thought I was the only one having freaked-out second sight," a suggestion that some people require confirmation of their mystic glimpse of fate (Bradley, 1972, 35). Later in the series, more pronounced psi powers affect human knowledge and behavior. At the moment Valerie gives birth to a son in "The Word of a Hastur," she acquires ghostly corroboration when the wraith of her deceased husband Jeremy returns to kiss mother and infant. In a blend of warning and support, he states, "There will be ill news for you in the days to come; so you must be strong," an encouragement that prepares her for misfortune (Bradley, 1994, 198).

The Invisible Divider

To explain the location of second sight and the gift of seeing beyond reality, in *The Fall of Atlantis,* Marion pictures the telepathy of the priestess Domaris in metaphor: "She stands very close to an open door which views beyond the framework of one life and one time" (Bradley, 1983, 495). The wording echoes Edward Fitzgerald's translation of Quatrain 53 in Omar Khayyam's *Rubaiyat* in which the poet views earthly life as an unyielding floor and heaven as a closed door. Quatrain 64 defines the metaphoric door, a melancholy trope for a direct passage from life to death. In Plato's fictional story of a doomed Atlantis, prognostication of an earthquake precedes total ruin. Marion's Atlantean version depicts human life as a "single scene of an ending drama" bound up in karma (*Ibid.*).

Dreams, visions, and revelations ground Marion's resetting of the Trojan War in *The Firebrand,* a modernized Greek epic about divine control of human destiny. Reducing the sanctity of Princess Kassandra, a priestess and omniscient oracle of the god Apollo, her brother throttles her to stop an outpouring of visions in which invaders burn and plunder the Trojan realm and expunge its royal family. During a parley between Trojan leaders and a trio of Akhaian invaders, Odysseus cites the significance of Akhilles's role as the star warrior. The old seafarer states that, so long as the boy wonder stays *hors de combat,* the two nations may seek detente, "So the oracles have said" (Bradley, 1987, 290). As is common in ancient oracles, the wording conceals the fact that Akhilles actively seeks warfare and pads the total of kills. After the combat death of his friend Patroklos, Akhilles's out-of-control response precipitates the disaster that Kassandra foretold.

In Marion's overview of medieval Britannia in *The Forest House,* the reading of omens provokes dread after Caillean gives little hope of Rhodri's return to his wife

Mairi after Romans capture him. Having delivered Mairi and Rhodri's daughter, Caillean envisions a veil, the metaphor for "far-seeing," a portent of sorrow in Eilan's adult life (Bradley, 1993, 127). Subsequent omens indicate raids by the Scotti, the Gael forces from Ireland and Scotland. Arch-Druid Ardanos recognizes disaster in the croak of a raven, a Gothic sentry from nature that Shakespeare summons in *Macbeth*. To call Cynric, the "Raven-son," the old man scries into a silver bowl and commands an image "by the powers of earth and oak and fire," the pillars of Druidism (*Ibid.*, 117). In the novel's resolution, Marion swathes Caillean in prophecy that foresees a female shrine, "not … in her own lifetime; but it would come" (*Ibid.*, 372).

ACCEPTING FOREKNOWLEDGE

The Sight energizes *The Mists of Avalon* with a sense of urgency, a common aura in Arthuriana. Marion describes both a fetch (apparition) alongside vast shifts in armies after Saxons oust Celts from Britannia. Viviane, the Lady of the Lake, and Taliesin the Merlin foretell British history as disclosed in "the Holy Well"—the fall of Rome, rise of Christianity, and raids by Saxons and wild northmen (Bradley 1983, 14). In search of peace, Viviane interprets the anxious times as a divine call for "our own leader, one who can command all of Britain," an allusion to King Arthur Pendragon (*Ibid.*). She anticipates an ecumenical ideal—"a world with room for the Goddess and for the Christ, the cauldron and the cross" (*Ibid.*, 15). The author justified such grandiose prognostication as "a fiction whose sole *raison d'etre* is to think about the future of the human race" (Bradley, 1984, Introduction).

At the novel's climax, Marion orchestrates a tangle of prophecies. Raven, the mute priestess of Avalon, predicts that Arthur will betray Avalon and the hill folk by adopting a banner featuring the Christian cross in place of the Pendragon standard flashing a red dragon. The event fulfills a matchup of Celts against Saxons at Mount Badon in February 482 CE, "the great battle that had been prophesied" (Bradley, 1983, 414). On a mock battlefield at Gwydion/Mordred's first duel at Arthur's Pentecost games, the newly knighted son refuses to join a scrimmage battle because he has intuited Gareth's death. After Balin's assassination of Viviane with an axe to the skull, Morgaine identifies the attack from a previous inchoate oracle "Blood on the foot of the King's throne. Blood, poured out on the hearth" (*Ibid.*, 500). Arthur charges the crazed killer with "private vengeance to be taken by the sword before his throne of justice" (*Ibid.*, 501). Marion's tone melds extra-sensory perception with God's will, especially the allotment of punishment for slaughter of a hapless old woman.

See also dreams; *The Fall of Atlantis; The Firebrand;* Mother Goddess.

Sources

Benko, Debra A. "Morgan le Fay and King Arthur in Malory's *Works* and Marion Zimmer Bradley's *The Mists of Avalon*" in *The Significance of Sibling Relationships in Literature*. Bowling Green, OH: Popular Press, 1992, 23–31.

Bradley, Marion Zimmer. *The Best of Marion Zimmer Bradley*. New York: DAW, 1984.

_____. *The Bloody Sun*. New York: Ace, 1964.

_____. *Darkover Landfall*. New York: DAW, 1972.

_____. *The Fall of Atlantis*. Riverdale, NY: Baen Books, 1983.

_____. *The Firebrand*. New York: Simon & Schuster, 1987.

_____. *The Forest House*. New York: Michael Joseph, 1993.

_____. *The Mists of Avalon*. New York: Ballantine, 1983.
_____. "The Word of a Hastur," *Snows of Darkover*. New York: DAW, 1994.
Quilligan, Maureen. "Arthur's Sister's Story," *New York Times* (30 January 1983).

Rape

A repeated theme in Marion's canon, the overpowering of females motivates girls and women to keep perpetual watch against assault, the task of Mallina in the presence of pedophile Garris of Aldaran in *Hawkmistress!*, of computer technician Ysaye Barnett in the clutches of Ryan Evans in *Rediscovery*, and of preteen Dorilys of Aldaran against her fiancé Darren in *Stormqueen!* Depicted in *The Shattered Chain* by the seizure and sexual concubinage of Melora Aillard by Jalak of Shainsa, the threat of gang rape of Magdalen "Magda" Lorne in a roadside hut and Kyril's grasp on Jaelle n'ha Melora in the Hellers result not from lust but from a perverse blend of pride, cruelty, and vengeance. For Callista, a hostage of catmen in *The Spell Sword*, much comfort lies in the feline species, which kidnaps but cannot rape her. Fortunately, catmen can only steal her jewels and lock her in the dark. In response to the logic, earthling Andrew Carr mutters, "What a hell of a world, where this kind of war against women is taken for granted" (Bradley, 1974, 43).

Feminist theorist Susan Brownmiller, author of *Against Our Will: Men, Women and Rape*, concluded that "one of the earliest forms of male bonding must have been the gang rape of one woman by a band of marauding men" (Brownmiller, 1975, 2). According to theorist Anna Angeli, on staff at the University of New Mexico, five forces motivate sex crime: class struggle, aesthetic drive, military prowess, a test of morality, and evidence of patriotism. Rape accounts for women's suspicions of male affection and emotion, particularly that of sorcerers and exploiters like the kidnapper of Mary, a rural girl in "The Footsteps of Retribution," the greedy company personnel in *The World Wreckers*, the third in *The Saga of the Renunciates*, and the Dry Town bandits who seize Melora in "Bride Price."

The author's perception of danger includes varied scenarios in the wild, at work, and at home. For Marna, the fatherless girl in "Knives," apprenticing as a midwife is the only escape from Dom Ruyvil, her lustful stepfather. At the sale of a female slave in *Warrior Woman*, the author dramatizes the terror of powerlessness by turning physical harrying into a surreal cycle of grappling hands: "An animal biting, sobbing, suffocating, without breath to scream, fighting to run, claw, tear, bite, survive" (Bradley, 1985, 1). Mauled by a "fierce face, ugly, ugly, bearded," she survives "split, torn, bleeding" (*Ibid.*) The unfocused lines of verbs project the unstinting bashing of Zad'yek, a gladiatorial trainee, but the overall effect could be any victim's story.

Marion's narratives stress the difficulty of making decisions, particularly the requirement for Free Amazons in *Thendara House* to bear no child that is not wanted, even a baby conceived by violence. Mother Lauria, the head of the Guild House, envies Terrans their drugs that suppress ovulation and menstruation to protect women from unplanned pregnancies while they travel or labor among such unprincipled coworkers. Camilla n'ha Kyria, a neutered female, relives her capture and rape by raiders and her insistence on being free of sexual allure while working among men. Considerations of women's fears and vulnerability include Kassandra's interaction with Kyntaurs in *The Firebrand* and the inclusion of Kyla Rainreach as guide to eight uncouth mountain trekkers in *The Planet Savers*.

SELF-PROTECTION

The author centers combat plots with misogyny and anti-female violence. At the capture of the realm of Merina in *Tiger Burning Bright*, Leopold admits the outrages committed by "scum-troops" intent on "a bloodbath … looting and rape," a pairing that equates slaughter and plunder with sexual battery (Bradley, 1995, 212). At an extreme of violence, Mhari murders the guard who tries to seduce her in "The Waterfall." Marion returns to the rape theme in "A Sword Called Chaos," in which tears flow and thoughts of suicide and insanity devastate the victim for forty days after a bandit "usurper and ravisher" commits "the unthinkable … the unendurable" (Bradley 1982, 87, 86). In *Hunters of the Red Moon*, the author indicates that females like Mhari "are routinely taught … [to avoid] would-be thieves and rapists" (Bradley, 1973, 68). As though summing up women's struggles for security, Aliciane, Donal's widowed mother in *Stormqueen!*, explains to her fatherless son, "Life is not easy for a woman unprotected" (Bradley, 1978, 2). Ironically, Aliciane dies from giving life to a daughter, Dorilys (Gold Lily), another female in the endless parade of predators' pillage.

The price of female safety in *Thendara House* and its sequel, *City of Sorcery*, is constant vigilance. The interest of drunken men in fellow drinkers on a festival night in *Thendara House* results in offers of a dance or an evening's dalliance. In the opening chapter of *City of Sorcery*, a female messenger to Thendara feels secure because of her respectable status. She reminds herself that women wouldn't encounter molestation "if they minded their own business, acted and looked as if they had somewhere to go; did not loiter, kept moving" (Bradley, 1984, 1). Missing from the Thendaran axiom are the perils of strolling for exercise, impromptu encounters with fellow pedestrians, and such harmless pleasures as window shopping, any of which could subject the innocent to a sexual predator.

In *Darkover Landfall*, the introit to the grueling Darkover series dramatizes the fate of the warrior princess Camilla, who bears the identity of the Volsci huntress and wartime ambassador from Virgil's *Aeneid*. In a milieu lacking children, Marion's Camilla falls into the hands of orgiastic males and suffers rape-induced conception. In defiance of colonial law, she retorts, "Damn you, I'm not going to accept forced childbearing" (Bradley, 1972, 112). Her retort leads to a uterine assault to kill her fetus. Because she survives a ghoulish sexual predation that mutilates her reproductive organs, she becomes barren and loses status as a tower priestess. The savagery reprises the ninth episode of the TV series *I, Claudius*, which dramatized the Roman emperor Caligula's slicing of a fetus from his 21-year-old sister Julia Drusilla's body in June 38 CE. Caligula ate the baby's remains, a bizarre demonstration of depravity in the Julio-Claudian line.

VIOLATING THE VULNERABLE

The Lythande series approaches the issue of sexual assault as an expected reaction of males to unprotected or deceased females. In "Somebody Else's Magic," Marion excoriates male lust for the corpse of Laritha, which Lythande encounters on a street in Thieves' Quarters. The wandering magician realizes that the women of Old Gandrin avoid walking outdoors because of fear of unspeakable defilement. A brutal ravishing of a Druid priestess on the Holy Isle of Mona in *The Forest House* opens the narrative, dramatizing war as an opportunity to profane females. The author depicts the potential of the mind to withdraw from physical desecration into a mental refuge. The capacity for repression returns to the narrative in the fire trance of the Irish midwife Caillean, who relives rape at age twelve in an outlaw's hut on the shore. She recalls the odor of his shack—"filth, bracken, seaweed, and being pushed down on it"—and the punishment of burning in a wicker cage to any woman charging a rapist (Bradley, 1993, 99). The narrative indicates that sexual aggression causes Caillean to take a radical stance by avoiding marriage.

Marion evaluates the multiple outcomes of trauma. In the science fantasy *The Winds of Darkover*, the ravishing of the timid Allira Storn by Brynat Scarface, a brigand from Dry Town, reveals the arid soul of a bandit chieftain and sexual abuser. The solution to the crime is a forced wedding of rapist to victim to validate his invasion of Storn Castle, a parallel to Allira's young body. For a glimpse of the recovery period, the intensity of post-traumatic stress in *A Sword Called Chaos* probes the personality disorder that assails Mhari, the rape victim. After four decades of "thinking about the unthinkable … enduring the unendurable," she philosophizes on destiny of "any woman married for political reasons to some stranger, and unwilling" (Bradley, 1982, 86). The two situations attest to the hell of coercive wedlock.

Mixed Signals

The author particularizes deception as a subgenre of lecherous felonies. For Deoris, a priestess in *The Fall of Atlantis*, friendship with her kinsman Chedan incites his lust for her, which he masks as camaraderie. In rapid order, Marion contrasts the lengthy, convoluted seduction of Deoris by Riveda, a magician who demands full control of his wanton conquests. The lewd relationship, like that of the iconic Elmer Gantry in Sinclair Lewis's satiric novel, reflects the appeal of priests and ministers to the naive, who trust without differentiating between religious devotion and erotic opportunism. The incestuous nature of the Grey Temple also despoils the virginity of Demira, who doesn't know her black-robed ravisher is her father Riveda.

In *The Firebrand*, a resetting of Homer's *Iliad* from the eyewitness account of the Trojan princess Kassandra, a devotee of the god Apollo, Marion underscores seduction, trickery, and sexual assault. In the opening scene of volume one, Leda recognizes the lordly approach of Zeus and, fearful of his thunderbolts, submits to his carnal touch, cold and devoid of humanity. Molestation results in the birth of Helen of Troy, the focus of the Trojan War. Marion sets the portent of rape in twelve-year-old Kassandra, who envisions the aquiline, black-bearded profile of Agamemnon, the Akhaian warrior chief who makes her feel like bestial prey. After he wins her as a combat trophy and transports her from Troy, she views wartime captivity as no worse than patriarchal marriage.

Primal Fear

The author reviles the duplicitous man of God. She charges Khryses, a thirty-year-old priest obscured by the mask of Apollo with clutching, kissing, and groping Kassandra, a fellow temple servant of the sun god. A scenario re-enacting the basics of Greek drama, the maiden's disparagement of Khryse causes her to violate religious decorum. By rejecting Khryse and the god Apollo, she falls victim to hubris, a source of *hamartia*, a missing of the mark and introit to tragedy. For her successful opposition, Apollo blames her for calling on the Earth Mother and curses Kassandra's predictions, causing citizens to disbelieve her. On return from Colchis, the princess assures her mother that no one "[offered me] an insult," Hecuba's euphemism for rape (*Ibid.*, 358). The crime takes on monstrous proportions on the battlefield when Akhilles commits necrophilia against Penthesilea. To Kassandra, the overt "act of contempt" becomes "the final insult to a warrior who dared challenge him" (*Ibid.*, 516). The narrative indicts the Akhaian mad dog for indecency, the boorish Ajax for raping Kassandra in the presence of the goddess, and a pedophiliac for lusting after Honey, still a toddler.

The Amazons corroborate the pervasive female fear of kidnap in "lands ruled by men" (Bradley, 1987, 49). Marion advances the focus of the horsewomen on independence with the decree that attempted rapists must die. The threat of a knife to the throat subdues shaggy Thracian brutes who are unfamiliar with liberated women. At Kassandra's duplicity in joining sword practice in the Trojan courtyard, Hector warns her of a standard truth: Men at war believe unprotected women are fair game, a truism she had already learned in Thrace. In volume two, his brother-in-law Aeneas, a liberal thinker, concludes, "A man faces nothing worse than an honorable death; but women must face rape, capture, slavery," a list that omits pregnancy with an unwanted child (Bradley, 1987, 244). Tragically, bondage at war's end awaits his mother-in-law, Queen Hecuba, and his sisters-in-law Andromache and Kassandra, both of whom bear offspring as the result of sexual assault.

Dark Ages Patriarchy

At her best in the dialogue of *The Mists of Avalon,* Marion dramatizes the rise of a tiff between husband and wife, Duke Gorlois of Cornwall and Duchess Igraine, into a threat of beating and spousal rape, a subject much debated in the United States in the mid–1970s and in England, Australia, and Wales in 1991. Interwoven in the sparking animosities, Marion lobs a charge against Christianity for castigating defiant brides while exonerating vengeful husbands for carnal assault and battery posed as proof of marital love. In Igraine's musings on intercourse at age fifteen with Gorlois, she thought "the act of marriage seemed terrifying and even grotesque" (Bradley, 1983, 75). The description captures the affront of old men's hasty coupling with tender, nubile girls.

The author chooses Morgaine to state disproportionate risks in warfare, which Susan Brownmiller identifies as the "male ideology of rape" against helpless victims who "could not retaliate in kind" (Brownmiller, 1975, 1–2). In a discussion of cavalry strategy in book two, Morgaine explains to Lancelet why women have a great stake in war against Saxon invaders. She cites a raid on villagers "from little girls of five years old to old grandmothers in their nineties with no teeth and no hair had been raped"

(Bradley, 1983, 293). Her female perspective articulates the fears of men versus women: women dread ravaging, while men worry only about a quick combat death.

Assault on a Queen

Preceding the premeditated intimidation of Gwenhwyfar by Meleagrant, Morgaine refrains from prophecy and declares, "It needs no sorcery to know that a villain is a villain" (*Ibid.,* 507). Marion reverts to the Gothic entrapment cliché and omens common to Victorian bodice rippers, from greasy rags and stale mildew in the air to Meleagrant's yellow teeth, foul breath, and "big meaty phallus" (*Ibid.,* 514). The attack, in Brownmiller's words, "became the vehicle of his victorious conquest over her being, the ultimate test of his superior strength, the triumph of his manhood" (Brownmiller, 1975, 2). Marion details retaliation for his crime: his head explodes under Lancelet's attack. Even with the monster dead, the author depicts the self-recriminations and shame felt by female victims, some of whom consider suicide. Although Gwenhwyfar is Arthur's queen, she lives out the miserable cycle with fears of pity and scolding.

Focus on "sexual imperialism" against the high king's wife reveals the impact of patriarchy and Christian orthodoxy on female self-assertion (Gale, 1975). In one of her rare surges of independence, Gwenhwyfar discovers the result of living under a demanding father, Leodegranz, and a royal husband, and of attending the Glastonbury convent academy where young women absorb the anti-woman screed of Christian doctrine. Duty and indecision frame her thinking, negating positive action to defend herself because, in the words of reviewer Mary Ellen Gale, "Rape is the hidden foundation for too much of our social order" (*Ibid.*). Reared in a tradition demanding compliance and martyrdom, Gwenhwyfar sacrifices herself to the males who squelch her very being.

See also The Forest House; Reproduction; Retribution; Royal Houses of Akhaia and Sparta; *Two to Conquer;* Violence.

Sources

Angeli, Anna. "Rape and Male Identity in Arthurian Romance, Chrétien de Troyes to Marion Zimmer Bradley," digitalrepository.unm.edu, 2010.

Bradley, Marion Zimmer. *City of Sorcery.* New York: DAW, 1984.

_____. *Darkover Landfall.* New York: DAW, 1972.

_____. *The Firebrand.* New York: Simon & Schuster, 1987.

_____. *The Forest House.* New York: Michael Joseph, 1993.

_____. *Hunters of the Red Moon.* New York: DAW, 1973.

_____. "Knives" in *Marion Zimmer Bradley's Darkover.* New York: DAW, 1993.

_____. *The Mists of Avalon.* New York: Ballantine, 1983.

_____. *The Spell Sword.* New York: DAW, 1974.

_____. *Stormqueen!* New York: DAW, 1978.

_____. *Sword of Chaos.* New York: DAW, 1982.

_____. *Tiger Burning Bright.* New York: William Morrow, 1995.

_____. *Two to Conquer.* New York: DAW, 1980.

_____. *Warrior Woman.* New York: DAW, 1985.

_____. *The Winds of Darkover.* New York: Ace, 1970.

Brownmiller, Susan. *Against Our Will: Men, Women and Rape.* New York: Simon & Schuster, 1975.

Donawerth, Jane. *Frankenstein's Daughters: Women Writing Science Fiction.* New York: Syracuse University Press, 1997.

Gale, Mary Ellen. "Rape as the Ultimate Exercise of Man's Domination of Women," *New York Times* (12 October 1975).

Rediscovery

The reconnection between Darkovans and their home planet in *Rediscovery* completes the arc launched by *Darkover Landfall* and examines the double motif of skills and ambition. The narrative amplifies the fate of the mythic pre–Empire "lost colony, one of those founded from one of the pre–Empire Lost Ships" (Bradley, 1993, 7). The suspenseful action alternates chapters in which Terrans aboard the star craft *Minnesota* approach Darkovans in hopes of a landing and break from light-years in the ship. Over a two-year period, the novel reached European markets in French, German, and Italian.

Dialogue features the teen telepath Leonie Hastur, the first perceiver of coming change and an important figure in *The Spell Sword*. She shares a vivid friendship with fellow music buff Elizabeth "Liz" Mackintosh, an anthropologist, meteorologist, and collector and performer of folk ballads whose daughter Magda has a major part in subsequent Darkover plots. Leonie intuits a threat from the heavens: "Something very important is about to happen," the second wave of Earth's galaxy exploration aimed at Cottman's Star and intended to establish a spaceport or weather station (*Ibid.,* 13).

MAKING CONTACT

Through the manipulation of precognition, Leonie eavesdrops on the crew of the starship that crashes in the mountains near Aldaran, a disaster motif that Marion reprises from *Darkover Landfall, Thendara House Part Three: Outgrowth, The Forbidden Tower, The Spell Sword,* and *City of Sorcery.* The character list emphasizes Leonie's twin, Lorill, heir to Hastur, whom she alerts to a starship downed in a snowstorm. Local people, in a spirit of hospitality, treat the survivors to food, drink, and a lotion antidote to frostbite. The ship captain, Commander Britton, values Elizabeth's skill at sharing music with Darkoverans: "You seem to have found a way to communicate with them, even if you don't speak the language" (*Ibid.,* 61). He assumes that dialogue between races is "an excellent way to lessen potential hostility" (*Ibid.*).

Terrans recognize the valuable remains of a past exploration party and, against Elizabeth's advice, initiate a spaceport near Caer Donn. With advanced training, Leonie establishes a *laran* link with Ysaye Barnett, a computer technician with ESP who teaches Leonie about Earth music. The stress on female intellectual acuity reprises the theme of sisterhood that dominates the author's canon.

DIPLOMACY IN SPACE

The falling action contrasts definitions of civilized ethics, another subject the author valued. Ryan Evans threatens the two women with kireseth pollen, source of the ghost winds in *Darkover Landfall.* Ysaye ruins Ryan's laboratory propagation of the blue aphrodisiac bell flower for its profitability in brothels and drug houses. In retaliation, Evans, a potential rapist, murders Ysaye, the "star woman," and dies of internal flame, a symbol of the cruelty that guides his actions (*Ibid.,* 180). At a discussion of strategies to liberate Elizabeth and David Lorne from captivity in a tent among bandits, Dr. Aurora Lakshman, a physician, reminds the others that war in previous times involved assaulting pre-industrial nations with grenades and major explosives.

Earth-made weapons free the two kidnap victims by igniting a fire that burns 24 leagues of forest. Irate at the loss, a bandit declares, "You cannot be civilized. A brute animal has more morals and ethics than you people" (Bradley, 1993, 229). Lorill concludes that Darkovans should avoid contact with Earthlings and their savage war-making. After a serious debate, the Comyn Council agrees. For its revelations about contrasting societies in space, William Marden, a book critic for the *Orlando Sentinel*, considered the novel "pivotal to the series" (Marden, 1993, D11).

See also Darkover Landfall.

Sources

Bradley, Marion Zimmer. *Rediscovery*. New York: DAW, 1993.
Marden, William. "Otherworldly Entries in Fantasy Fiction Genre," *Orlando Sentinel* (8 August 1993): D11.
"Review: *Rediscovery*," *Kirkus* (14 April 1993).
"Review: *Rediscovery*," *Publishers Weekly* (29 March 1993).

Religion

Through scholarly perusals of myth, worship, and philosophy, Marion drew conclusions about the spirituality of ancient eras, for example, the choice of Carlina "Carly" di Asturien to elude marriage to her cousin in *Two to Conquer* and to "live out the rest of her life in chastity and prayer" on the fog-bound Isle of Silence (Bradley, 1980, 101). The author's survey of sanctity predated the Judeo-Christian tradition of absolute virtue and sinlessness, beliefs of survivors of a spacecraft crash in *Darkover Landfall*, and the twentieth-century intolerance of Wicca, a theme dominating *In the Rift*. Of Marion's respect for human differences, Steve Miller, book critic for the *Baltimore Sun*, admired the even-handed depiction of varied beliefs.

Journalist Alyssa Rosenberg, on staff of the *Washington Post*, admired Marion for "[establishing] a deep sense of respect for the deities," making them "easier to accept" (Rosenberg, 2010). At a time of personal need, Damon Ridenow, the protagonist of *The Spell Sword*, cries out in terror "Aldones! Lord of Light deliver us!," a shouted prayer against invisible assailants (Bradley, 1974, 12). In his search for kinswoman Callista, he pleads of the Mother Goddess, "Blessed Cassilda, mother of the Seven Domains, be with me now" (*Ibid.*, 48). Farther reaching than Christian ecumenism, the author's tolerance toward the gods of the future derived from her respect for all hallowed places and beings. The photo album *The Faces of Science Fiction* quoted her love of science fiction for "[encouraging] us to explore … all the futures, good and bad, that the human mind can envision" (Oliver, 1999, A24).

In *The Fall of Atlantis*, the bedside prayer of Domaris with little sister Deoris implies sanctity in innocent sisterhood, a foreshadowing of Marion's prayer to the "Woman Eternal," who rescues Deoris from damnation "life to life forever" (Bradley, 1983, 367). Runes and cryptic icons embroidered on the vestments of elders venerate ancient lore. With subtler symbolism, Domaris's blue robe of motherhood retains the artistic cloaking of the Virgin Mary in blue, a standard color in Renaissance art of guilelessness and constancy. The plot deepens Domaris's religious instincts by following her through a self-baptismal pool to the shrine of the Mother Goddess and by attending her at the laying on of hands conferring knowledge. With wisdom comes a sense of "rising, expanding to touch the far-flung stars," a mystic union that bestows "a sustenance ... around her and in her and of her" (*Ibid.*, 99). At a parallel ritual for Micon, Domaris pledges that their son is a "child of virginity," a vow not required of expectant fathers (*Ibid.*, 137).

Rampant sin dominates the author's chastising of magicians, who abuse the female novices in their service. The cleansing of a holy brotherhood of corruption in the novel requires a six-month investigation and a dozen lashings for "blasphemies and infringements: misuse of ceremonial objects, the wearing or display of outlasted symbols" (*Ibid.*, 145). Two cases of sexual profanation require the banishment of culpable Grey-robes. Marion contrasts the male order with female healers and midwives, such as the practitioners in *Warrior Woman,* who avoid charms and spells by treating living women with established methods, not magic. At a pensive moment for Domaris and her newborn son, she prays, "Help me—O Thou Which Art" (*Ibid.*, 238). Use of the verb "to be" as statement of godhood resembles Yahweh's call to Moses from the burning bush: "I am that I am," a statement of the ineffable (Exodus 3:14). Marion actualizes the novel's title with the sinking of the temple in the Ancient Land and the demise of the Unrevealed God, a deity no more.

Greco-Roman Epic

From Greek mythology and the epics of Homer and Virgil, the author reset *The Firebrand* to narrate the story of the Trojan War, fought in western Asia in 1200 BCE. The era generated quandaries about Amazon, Trojan, and Akhaian pantheons and their influence on human destiny. Marion interwove such customary ritual as communal birthing of royal children to the sound of chanting, strummed harp, and spells. Because of Hecuba's nightmare about the birth of Paris, King Priam relates a common belief about the inscrutability of deities: "The ways of the Gods are not for us to question" (Bradley, 1987, 17). His apothegm attests to an anti-enlightenment position, the retreat of the dogmatist to orthodoxy.

Throughout the narrative, Marion examines the individual seeker and ongoing changes in credos. In training as a priestess in the Earth Mother cult at Colchis, Priam's daughter Kassandra restructures her convictions, She learns from riding with the Amazons that fasting is uncomfortable, but a necessary gesture of fealty to the earth goddess. Before initiation into the cult, Queen Imandra reminds her of a universal truth: "The soul is always alone before the Gods," an existential determiner of Kassandra's position as protagonist and apostle/victim of Apollo (*Ibid.*, 119). In feminine company at the Serpent Mother's shrine, Kassandra feels a kinship with the assembly and ease in scrying before witchfire, a mystic proof of celestial presence.

Priestly Service

Returned to Troy, Kassandra enters the instructive level of Apollonian service: interpreting omens and oracles, making offerings, caring for holy reptiles, and interpreting commands of the sun god during one year of training. Marion summarizes the atmosphere of virgins awaiting union with Apollo, a parallel of Catholic novitiates, where postulants become brides of Christ. With strictures akin to those of Rome's Vestal Virgins and medieval nuns, newcomers accept sequestering from men and visits from male relatives only under chaperonage. During elucidation of oracles, Kassandra relates pre-formulated answers to ordinary questions about betrothals, crop rotation, and the legitimacy of a newborn son. She commits her service to the pyre of Agelaus, Paris's foster father, and to the inurnment of his bones as a demonstration of respect. In private, she ponders the conflict between Apollo and the Great Goddess and her place in the middle of the competition: "Am I no more than a fleeing animal before the strife of these Gods?," a statement common to lore of anthropomorphic pantheons (*Ibid.*, 262).

To characterize obeisance to agrarian-based religion, the author details visual and aural elements of the planting ritual, which begins with song and processions. Both Hecuba and Andromache advance in red robes; their bare feet retain direct contact with the Earth Mother. The fearful day, ended in an Akhaian raid and kidnap of the priestess Chryseis, prefaces the dying moments of the aged priestess Meliantha. The virgin servants of Apollo honor her counsel and purity with garlands and honey cakes, a celebration that resembles ancient Egyptian services to the dead. Kassandra tries to arouse Khryse from his sorrow and apathy, but scolds him instead with a reminder of divine autonomy: "You cannot bargain with a God" (*Ibid.*, 279).

Marion stresses the authoritarian control of the Olympian pantheon over humankind. Aeneas, in a measured evaluation, concludes that "[g]ods do not need reasons for what They do" (*Ibid.*, 402). The gap between mortal and divine widens for Kassandra after her venture into the afterlife. She muses, "I do not think funeral rites matter at all … to the Gods, but only to us" (*Ibid.*, 490). As ambivalence erodes her piety, she views Apollo and other divinities as "petty and cruel" and "not for mankind to venerate" (*Ibid.*, 540). At a nadir in devotion, she projects animus toward Apollo, ironically, a wellspring of truth, mental health, and enlightenment.

DRUIDS, ROMANS AND THE MOTHER GODDESS

In the author's scrutiny of Celtic religion, she epitomizes Druidism from variant perspectives. With esteem for nature worship, *The Forest House* honors a belief system based on worship in the open air and the entrusting of sacred laws to memory rather than writing. Critic Theresa Crater accounts for threats to the Old Way as a post–Roman revolution: "After the Roman conquest of Europe, patriarchal science and religion replaced the pagan cyclical way of thinking with the idea of the linear march of progress," which decentralizes native Briton myth and ritual (Crater, 2001, 20). At Camelot in *The Mists of Avalon*, court ladies and priests diminish Britannia's prehistoric worship style to "tribes who paint their faces and wear horns and run with the deer like animals" (Bradley, 1983, 401). Contempt for antique ritual threatens the survival of seasonal festivals. In northern Wales, aborigines still venerate the Old Ways, causing King Uriens to propose razing the sacred oak groves before Beltane on May 1.

The novel indicates that postulants of the Mother Goddess recognize a shift away from women's power toward artificial strictures on females. Still loyal to pre–Roman philosophy, Eilan studies the Celtic science of herbalism by collecting plants under sun or moon, which infuse leaves and stems with curative strengths. She scans the heavens to learn astronomy, but avoids the harp, which is limited to male clergy. Her mentor

Caillean confides, "A great deal that the priests do makes no sense; and they know it" (Bradley, 1993, 124). She compares priestly tyranny to a stone wall, a barrier imported with Roman patriarchy in 43 BCE to the detriment of matrifocal worship.

Marion amplifies male perfidy in the collusion between the dwindling high priestess Lhiannon and the bard Ardanos, who defies the mystic election of a successor. Before the elderly mother superior retires, she withdraws into solitude and eats oatmeal with nuts, her replacement of meat in the diet with food from plant sources. Preparations for passage of dominion to a younger women incite jealousies and speculation about "tantalizing hints of power" (*Ibid.*, 42). Speaking for goddess cultists, Lhiannon extols the past and its master magicians from Atlantis, "a lost land now sunk beneath the sea" and mourns the lapse in magic after the Romans slaughtered female trainees on Mona, a sacred isle named in Gaelic for nobility and goodness (*Ibid.*). The author details the lengthy inauguration of Eilan as Lhiannon's successor. Eilan's aura shimmers with the transformation of the new high priestess into an embodiment of the Mother Goddess.

A Clash of Creeds

Analyst Gloria Orenstein faulted the gendered erasure and bias of Druidism in Western culture for "[masking] the historical verities of female empowerment … and denied and degraded the human connection to the spiritual and natural world" (Orenstein, 1990, 130). Marion makes sporadic remarks about the smugness of Christians, particularly the "fundamentalist mentality that can arise in any religion, the antithesis of enlightenment" (Paxson, 1999, 124). In the fool tale "Fool's Fire," after a local busybody avows, "No man is righteous of himself but only by the wisdom that is written in the Good Books," Lythande, the wandering magician, declares the statement illogical (Bradley, 2013, 172). She proposes stripping science of subjective allegations that paranormal forces hold a grudge that humans can oppose with prayer and fasting. Rather than debate biblical wisdom, she proposes turning a will-o'-the-wisp into a tourist attraction, a joke on simple villagers who replace hell-minded fears with a natural marvel derived from marsh gas. In the opening of the story "Bitch," the author speaks through Lythande a tendency toward agnosticism on a par with French religion expert Ernest Renan's prayer, "O God, if there is a God, save my soul if I have a soul."

According to Arthurian specialist Nicole Evelina, Marion shifted *The Mists of Avalon* "from the Malory-influenced medieval Christian court that so informs early iterations of the legend to a semi-historical pagan Britain" (Evelina, 2017, 152). In reclaiming female spirituality and rebuilding Celtic theology, Marion's version inspired reevaluations of Celtic Wicca and Camelot's myth. By educating women, the priestesses of Avalon sought to halt the crippling of young girls' minds like that of Gwenhwyfar, who believed during her studies at a convent that reading the mass book was "all I needed of learning" (Bradley, 1983, 255). In a liberal evaluation comparing Druidic postulants to Catholic nuns, Lancelet concludes, "It is all one. The priestesses of the House of Maidens are much like to the nuns of holy church, living lives of chastity and prayer, and serving god in their own way" (*Ibid.*, 685).

CHRISTIAN PREEMINENCE

The regeneration of Arthur lore focused on the early medieval Christian mission to smash paganism and supplant devotion to Druidism and the Great Mother with orthodoxy and dogma. The aged Taliesin, known as the Merlin, states, "The Christians seek to blot out all wisdom save their own" (*Ibid.*, 12). He believed

> It is God's will that all men should strive for wisdom in themselves, not look to it from some other. Babes, perhaps, must have their food chewed for them by a nurse, but men may drink and eat of wisdom for themselves [*Ibid.*, 260].

To achieve the aim of liberating the world from overbearing doctrine, according to theorist Joy Dixon, a history professor at the University of British Columbia, the author reconstituted the political milieu "as sacred space," a fictional location for testing reformist ideals, such as Taliesin's hope to use Avalon's sacred regalia for serving the Eucharist "in token that all the Gods are as One" (Dixon, 2001, 205; Bradley, 1983, 206). At Arthur's coronation, placement of the Merlin alongside the Archbishop of Glastonbury indicates some progress toward detente between religious authority figures. In a later scene, the archbishop snubs Taliesin's version of Christ's humanistic example and urges the Druid and his followers "to listen to their priests for the true interpretations" (*Ibid.*, 260). At the archbishop's promise to close Glastonbury's sacred well, Marion describes his glow as "the austere fire of the fanatic" (*Ibid.*, 263).

Because Viviane, the Lady of the Lake, embodies both human and Earth Mother "in a way the man-priests of male Gods could never know or understand," she bows to no human (Bradley, 1983, 200). At the House of the Maidens, the sisterhood absorbs her majesty like nourishment. Critic Mimi Winick depicts the sacred activities as opportunities to "embody the deity, participate in joyous and sacred sexual rites" (Winick, 2015, 589). Marion Wynne-Davies notes a "significant shift" from traditional Arthuriana in the reclamation of Excalibur "as part of the holy regalia of Avalon and therefore as specifically belonging to the pagan world of the Mother Goddess" (Wynne-Davies, 2016, 177–178). A model of the unearthly, the sword, shaped by elf smiths from a meteorite, "negates the violent images of rape, male aggression, war and the phallus" and incorporates Arthur and Morgaine in the timeless worship of the all-mother (*Ibid.*, 178). An opposing view blames Viviane, the religious elite, for coercing Igraine and Morgaine into specific tasks for the Mother Goddess and for driving Nimue to drown herself in the Lake after a harsh penalty for sacrilege imprisons Kevin Harper in an oak. According to a review on *The Heretic Loremaster*, Marion discloses "the short-sightedness of religious institutions, no matter what name they use in worship, and the dehumanization to which they are inclined when they believe that larger spiritual matters require it" ("Review: *The Mists*," 2009).

FUTURISTIC FAITH

In the Darkover and Lythande series, Marion used medieval concepts to examine religious abstracts, such as Allart Hastur's suitability for living at Nevarsin Monastery in *Stormqueen!* The characters in "To Kill the Undead" conclude that the refusal to bury Haymil, a suicide, unleashes a vampire that devours sheep, dogs, and a shepherd. In a rare preachy moment in the Lythande series, the mage-ronin states that "even a priest should err on the side of mercy" and bury the unfortunate in hallowed ground (Bradley, 2013, 164). In 1982, *Hawkmistress!* progressed from feudal mayhem to the mellowing of religion from black-and-white beliefs to humanism. For its gracious philosophy valuing all people and their creeds, in 2007, the American Library Association listed the novel in *Best Books for Young Adults*.

In addition to forgiving suicides and opening opportunities to minors and women, Marion ventured into tolerance of diverse sexuality, which Catholicism blasts as a sin. Contrasting the gentle 15-year-old Romilly "Romy" MacAran with her pig-headed father, Mikhail of Falconsward, *Hawkmistress!* ponders the role of education in freeing women from patriarchal beatings, training in needlework, and forced marriage. The universal transdressing motif allows Romilly to flee an ogrous union with Dom Garris of Scathfell, a lust-filled widower. Like the chained hawk, she longs for "a chance to fly, and to feel again the soaring ecstasy of flight and freedom" (Bradley, 1982). The author introduces the heroine to the monastery St. Valentine of the Snows, a version of the Benedictine order and its vow of hospitality whom the narrative reveres as "Holy Bearer of Burdens" (*Ibid.,* 28). Marion refines the term *cristoforo* from Christopher Columbus's respelling of his name as *Christoferens* "Christ bearing," an indication of the Catholic intent to proselyte residents of the New World. Freed at last from authoritarian religion, she, like Christ, wanders in the wilderness and refines hawking skills, ESP, and animal care. Marion's affection for the character suggests her regard for all who live with Christ-like grace and tolerance.

See also Christianity; Mother Goddess; Ritual.

Sources

Bradley, Marion Zimmer. *The Complete Lythande.* San Francisco: Marion Zimmer Bradley Literary Works Trust, 2013.
_____. *The Fall of Atlantis.* Riverdale, NY: Baen Books, 1983.
_____. *The Firebrand.* New York: Simon & Schuster, 1987.
_____. *The Forest House.* New York: Michael Joseph, 1993.
_____. *Hawkmistress!* New York: DAW, 1982.
_____. *The Mists of Avalon.* New York: Ballantine, 1983.
_____. *The Spell Sword.* New York: DAW, 1974.
_____. *Stormqueen!* New York: DAW, 1978.
_____. *Two to Conquer.* New York: DAW, 1980.
Crater, Theresa. "The Resurrection of Morgan le Fey: Fallen Woman to Triple Goddess," *Femspec* 3:1 (December 2001): 12–22.
Dixon, Joy. *Divine Feminine: Theosophy and Feminism in England.* Baltimore: Johns Hopkins University Press, 2001.
Evelina, Nicole. *The Once & Future Queen: Guinevere in Arthurian Legend.* Maryland Heights, MO: Lawson Gartner, 2017.
Fox, Cheryl. "Review: *The Forest House,*" *Park Record* (Park City, UT) (4 August 1994): B8.
Hildebrand, Kristina. *The Female Reader at the Round Table: Religion and Women in Three Contemporary Arthurian Texts.* Uppsala, Sweden: University of Uppsala Press, 2001.
Koelling, Holly, ed. *Best Books for Young Adults.* Chicago: American Library Association, 2006.
Miller, Steve. "The Arthurian Legend: Returned to Epic Status," *Baltimore Sun* (30 January 1983): D4.
Oliver, Myrna. "Marion Bradley; Writer of Fantasy Novels," *Los Angeles Times* (30 September 1999): A24.
Orenstein, Gloria Feman. *The Reflowering of the Goddess (Athene).* Oxford, UK: Pergamon, 1990.
Paxson, Diana L. "Marion Zimmer Bradley and *The Mists of Avalon,*" *Arthuriana* 9:1 (Spring 1999): 110–126.
"Review: *The Mists of Avalon,*" *The Heretic Loremaster,* http://themidhavens.net/heretic_loremaster/2009/05/the-mists-of-avalon-reviewed/, 2009.
Rosenberg, Alyssa. "The Rules of Fictional Worlds," *Atlantic* (24 September 2010).
Winick, Mimi. "Modernist Feminist Witchcraft," *Modernism/Modernity* 22:3 (September 2015): 565–592.
Wynne-Davies, Marion. *Women and Arthurian Literature: Seizing the Sword.* London: Springer, 2016.

Reproduction

Marion articulates scenes of conception, labor, and delivery, a common link to women's motifs in the stories "Exiles of Tomorrow," "Women Only," "Jamie," and "The Word of a Hastur" from the Darkover series. In the last moments of life, Melora, the concubine of Jalak of Shainsa in *The Shattered Chain*, gives birth to a son and experiences "a moment of joy, when the face changed, alight and glowing ... so happy, so happy" (Bradley, 1976, 76). The possibility of death during labor and delivery looms when Lady Melora cuddles her newborn son before expiring from hemorrhage. Of the giving and taking of life, Lady Rohana Ardais treasures "this moment of joy" that precedes the weeping of motherless babes (Bradley, 1976, 76). The contemplation of a difficult birthing dismays Kindra n'ha Mhari, an Amazon in "To Keep the Oath" bound to aid "any woman who asks me in the name of the Goddess" (Bradley, 1985). Her problem is hemophobia (Greek for "fear of blood"), whether the result of combat or childbirth. She declares her terror of suffering: "I would rather fight men, or beasts, than for the life of a helpless woman or baby" (*Ibid.*). Her regard for the endangerment of two lives refutes the casual dismissal of Damon Ridenow, who has no first-person knowledge of the process.

Departing from *Thendara House,* Jaelle n'ha Melora checks her beads calculating moon phases that tabulate female cycles. A possibility of conception makes her dread "some small parasite within her body, sickness, distortion, the appalling ordeal of birth which had killed her own mother" (Bradley, 1983, 138). As Byrna labors to give birth at the Guild House, she compares the early stages to hard menstrual cramps before she delivers "something red, slick, wet, streaked with blood" (*Ibid.*, 117). The wiggly boy creates a surge in Magdalen "Magda" Lorne, the midwife's helper: She "suddenly wanted to cry, she wasn't sure why," a visceral response to intense emotion (*Ibid.*). The narrative balances joy with Keitha n'ha Casilda's memories of her baby girl, who died of fever, and the maternal instincts of Camilla n'ha Kyria, a rape victim and neutered woman still thrilled to snuggle a newborn.

In *Stormqueen!,* the author links childbirth with dread as well as family affection. Mikhail of Aldaran unites the disparate emotions at the birth of daughter Dorilys: "Birth is an ordeal of terror; there must be someone to reassure her, someone who awaits her with love" (Bradley, 1978, 28). On the forcing of a fetus into life, Alicia agrees, "How could any woman bear a child without fear?" (*Ibid.*, 4). For the story "Well Met By Moonlight," the author envisions Titania and Oberon as mates from the fairy world and the dangers of "Time and Mortality and Death" suffered by human children (Bradley, 1998, 32). Titania admits from the female perspective "that the mother bore more risk," but she eagerly binds herself soul-to-soul with the sprite who fathers her child (*Ibid.*, 32–33). The remark indicates the priority of childbearing to wedlock.

A FUTURE IN SPACE

Emphasis on later generations undergirds authorial views on interplanetary travel and the furtherance of outer space settlements, such as Deneb in "Outpost." A more pressing situation in "Measureless to Man" causes Kamellin, a survivor of an ancient Martian race, to occupy a chimpanzee's body. By continuing to place disembodied minds in chimps, the dying space people plan "to reclaim their race a little, gain back their culture [as] a colony of intelligent beings, monkey-like in form but not monkey-ish" (Bradley, 1962, 105). The bizarre reproductive plan, suggesting Charles Darwin's conclusions about human descent from primates, offers hope for a new beginning.

Because of conditions in the outer universe, the author stresses alterations to women's reproductive plan, as with the pregnancy and morning sickness of Elizabeth "Liz" Macintosh, lover of David Lorne in *Rediscovery*. A previous spaceship crash in *Darkover Landfall* disrupts hormonal cycles that once relied on anticeptin, an injectable contraceptive. For scientist Camilla Del Rey, the prospect of high IQ and mathematical abilities in her offspring prohibit abortion, thus demanding "forced childbearing" for the sake of the pioneers' gene pool (Bradley, 1972, 112). Australian writer Justine Larbalestier summarizes the male seizure of female sexuality as "a decision to treat the women's wombs as communal property to ensure successful propagation of the race" (Larbalestier, 2002, 150). Camilla panics at morning sickness at the same time that Scots-Irish neo-ruralist Fiona MacMorair celebrates coming motherhood of a child fathered by Captain Harry Leicester. Because of the endangered future for earthlings, medical experts limit parturient women like Alanna, Alastair's woman, to light labor and pampering, a loss of freedom that violates Article Four of Earth laws. Ruth Fontana's miscarriage falls within the 50–50 chance that Darkover newborns will survive.

ACCEPTING RISKS

Marion's stories unearth additional problems for women. The specter of death during labor and delivery haunts her fiction, including the stillborn boy of Andromache in *The Firebrand* and the demise of the Lady of the Lake in *The Mists of Avalon,* who dies giving life to daughter Morgause. Viviane, the subsequent Lady of the Lake, states the peril of motherhood: "No woman knows, when she lies down to childbirth, whether her life will not be demanded of her" (Bradley, 1983, 23). Restructuring of the family leaves girls like Morgause unmoored from a birth mother. The haphazard pairing of motherless child and surrogate in *The Ages of Chaos* forces 15-year-old Romilly "Romy" MacAran to battle her stubborn father, Mikhail of Falconsward. Equally daunting is his new wife, Domna Luciella MacAran, a ruffled, flounced stepmother in the Victorian sense who "simpers and twitters" to please her new husband and dresses Romilly in green velvet as a showpiece (Bradley, 2002, 402).

In *The Forbidden Tower,* wounds, birthing, and pain enhance drama in Damon Ridenow's unease at his wife Ellemir's first pregnancy. To offset tensions, the narrative commends the regional midwife, Ferrika, who attends village mothers. Like the apprentice Marna and Maestra Reva n'ha Melora, the Amazon midwife in "Knives," Marisela in *Thendara House,* and Broca in *The Mists of Avalon,* Ferrika respects her profession: "It was a tremendous responsibility indeed" well suited to the "calm, firm, round-bodied" daughter of a midwife (Bradley, 1977, 77). Because of her training at the guild-house, she provides competent emergency treatment and nurse care, an omnipresent comfort in feminist literature. In an eruption of misogyny, Damon disparages the healing art as "work any stupid housewife could do," yet, the action indicates his need of help during Ellemir's labor (*Ibid.,* 93).

Mixed Species

Space travel and occupation threaten the unborn with unknown handicaps. From an unplanned conception in "The Wind People," physician Helen Murray gives birth to abnormal boy Robin because "four years in space made me careless" (Bradley, 1985, 181). For off-planet conception amid polygamists in "Centaurus Changeling," the author inserts the Victorian custom of secluding expectant mothers and the concealment of freakish offspring compromised by the planetary gravity and climate. As Terran wife Beth Ferguson struggles to understand a strategy for merging species without knowing the result, her Megaeran friend Cassiana states a womanly truism: "A baby is the passport to the one big sorority of the universe," a salute to parturition and mothering in whatever form (*Ibid.*, 48).

The author's interest in human-with-human, human-with-humanoid, and animal-with-animal reproduction takes numerous forms, as with the rare synthanthroid infant in the story "Women Only," the hybrid human-*cheri* paxman Raman Kadarin in *Rediscovery,* and child thievery by space nomads in *Endless Universe.* The mating of a Chieri with a human from Terra in *Darkover Landfall* precedes interspecies reproduction, one parent normal and the other a telepathic mortal who alters gender at will. The theme of hybrids dominates *The Sword of Aldones,* in which Terran Kennard Alton's bi-species son Lew labels himself a "freak ... a half-caste boy, a bastard" born to a mother from an "early feudal culture" (Bradley, 1962, 41, 14, 13). The series earned respect for acknowledging inter-primate, illegitimate, hermaphrodite, gay, heterosexual, bisexual, celibate, sterile, and lesbian relationships as suitable for the individual practitioner.

By introducing hybridization, Marion set up two millennia of Darkover plots that result in a third race that possesses variant degrees of psi receptivity, a complication of the balance of power. The quandary of mixed parentage in *Thendara House* depicts the childbed death of Lady Melora, a captive breeder whom the barbarian Jalak of Shainsa kidnaps to pass along mystic gifts to her children. In *Stormqueen!,* the author introduces selective breeding of humans to enhance the innate skill of *laran,* an extra-human psychic weapon that can range from simple weather misdirection to calamities that upset delicate ecology. The author advances the possibilities of meteorological chaos in *Thunderlord!,* which incorporates magical skills with dynastic rivalry between the domains of Aldaran and Scathfell.

A broader view of planned reproduction in *Darkover Landfall* incensed feminists. Critics targeted the female author for betraying her gender and forcing women to continue bearing the burden of gestation and childbirth. Authorial interest reached a pinnacle of the outré in *The World Wreckers,* a novel based on economic imperialism engineered by Andrea Closson, head of Planetary Investments Unlimited. By pairing pioneers of the Taurian planet Cottman IV with the bi-gender *chieri* Missy Gentry and Keral, the narrative discloses the uncontrollable elements of speculative reproduction and the threat that Terrans will add Darkover to its space empire. Marion worsens the anti-child stance in *World Wreckers* through interplanetary sabotage of three Aillard gestations. Before authorities can question the coincidence, the midwives die of poisoning.

Natural Cycles

The author's choice of compromised protagonists raised issues of sexuality and conception common to the age. In *Two to Conquer,* Melisendra exonerates the need for abortion "if the woman does not wish to bear a child into squalor, or on campaign, or fatherless, or she knows she will have no milk for it" (Bradley, 1980, 99). For the immature Deoris, a scribe and reader in *The Fall of Atlantis,* the thought of strenuous labor and bloody delivery seems horrible. In rebuke, the acolyte Micon reminds her, "To live is to suffer, and to bring life is to suffer…. Pain is the law of life," a bleak statement of women's role in the mortal struggle (Bradley, 1983, 116). The pronouncement captures the lyricism of Mary Stewart's consoling axiom in *The Hollow Hills:* "Every life has a death and every light a shadow. Be content to stand in the light and let the shadow fall where it will." Contributing an existential conclusion, Micon informs Deoris that each person alone learns mortal truths, a life passage that haunts Deoris because of the deaths of her mother and her friend Arkati in childbirth.

Speaking through Domaris, Micon's lover, the author instructs Deoris on nature and female fulfillment: "The cycles of womanhood and of the universe itself are attuned" (*Ibid.,* 128). In a light moment before giving birth, Domaris jokes to Micon, "This one privilege you cannot have!" (*Ibid.,* 211). As the fetal crowning approaches, she finds the waiting tiresome and personal questions annoying and compares contractions to torment on the rack. For Deoris, the birthing attendant, the struggle arouses a furious rhetorical question about the arrival of her tiny nephew Micail: "Why should such an indefinite scrap of flesh be allowed to cause such awful pain" (*Ibid.,* 226).

The novel pictures birthing through the experience of Eilan, a young girl who aids her mentor Caillean, the Irish priestess/midwife. In joy at a safe delivery, Caillean remarks, "always it is a miracle" (*Ibid.,* 87). The scene follows washing, delivery of the afterbirth, and swaddling. Caillean fastens an amulet to protect the baby girl from fairies who would steal her and leave a changeling in her place, a European folk explanation of diseased or disabled infants. Eilan's conversation with the Merlin about celibacy informs her that she may initiate seduction by the Sacred King so "life may be renewed in the land," a holy ritual dramatized in *The Mists of Avalon* (*Ibid.,* 173). For a balance, Marion dramatizes Gaius Macellius's introduction to his newborn son, a scenario softened by his protection of a helpless infant and a radiance identifying him as "the Father-face of the God" (*Ibid.,* 255). The duality of the Mother Goddess as both parents lessens the harsher separation of Romans by gender-—military men to the soldier's god Mithra and women to the Bona Dea. The longing for a son threatens Gaius's wife Julia Lucinia, who sickens from hemorrhage after delivering a stillborn male in 93 CE. Marion stresses the Roman solution—adoption of a male child as a replacement, the choice of Julius Caesar according to the reading on his will on March 15, 44 BC.

Medieval Motherhood

In *The Mists of Avalon,* Marion presents multiple views of maternity, as with Morgaine's memories of her infant "full-fed and sweet-smelling, when she had sat holding him and crooning to him, thinking of nothing, her whole body filled with mindless happiness" (Bradley, 1983, 401). References to Queen Igraine show her late in life mourning for a dead baby son meant to satisfy Uther Pendragon's longing for a legitimate heir rather than a delight for his birth mother. In a lugubrious Christian atmosphere, authorities blame the infant's demise on the queen's sin, a common fallback for anti-woman priests bent on damning all women for repeating Eve's error. Speaking through Taliesin the Merlin, Marion dismisses guilt-obsessed Christianity as "a simpler faith than [Druidism]" (Bradley, 1983, 162). Ironically, Morgaine attempts to conceal the first weeks of pregnancy while in company with her stiff-necked mother and other cloistered "brides of Christ" (*Ibid.*, 260). Her aunt Morgause recognizes the symptoms of morning sickness and intercedes with a wet towel and wine. Typically light-hearted, she blames "something in the belly" for the dizziness, queasiness, and vomiting and advises Morgaine on abortion, a topic that recurs in *The Age of Chaos* (*Ibid.*, 221).

Marion chooses Gwenhwyfar, Morgaine's foil, as the model of Christian muddle-headedness toward women. In contrast to independent women who claim the rights to their own bodies and to service of the Mother Goddess, Gwenhwyfar rejects sorcery or the Sight as wickedness that has "no place in this house of holy women" (*Ibid.*, 356). She maintains that "a woman's proper business [is] to be married and bear children … she must obey her father's will as if it were the will of God" (*Ibid.*, 268). In addition to failed motherhood and two miscarriages, Arthur's queen accepts as a universal duty "to atone for that Original Sin of Eden," a belief that erroneously elevates Eve to the fount of mortal evil (*Ibid.*). When enchantment swirls Morgaine out of her senses at the queen's fireside, herbs end her pregnancy with a flow of blood and vomiting. Broca, the midwife, recognizes the herbal smell and congratulates Morgaine on avoiding a late-in-life delivery by aborting the fetus early. Because of her experience and stature at court, Broca has the clout to assail Uriens for impregnating a wife too old to bear a child safely.

Sources

Bradley, Marion Zimmer. *The Best of Marion Zimmer Bradley.* Chicago: Academy Chicago, 1985.
_____. *Darkover Landfall.* New York: DAW, 1972.
_____. *The Fall of Atlantis.* Riverdale, NY: Baen Books, 1983.
_____. *The Forbidden Tower.* New York: DAW, 1977.
_____. *The Forest House.* New York: Michael Joseph, 1993.
_____. *The Gratitude of Kings.* New York: Wildside, 1997.
_____. "Knives" in *Marion Zimmer Bradley's Darkover.* New York: DAW, 1993.
_____. "Measureless to Man," *Amazing Stories* 36:12 (December 1962): 74–107.
_____. *The Mists of Avalon.* New York: Ballantine, 1983.
_____. *The Shattered Chain.* New York: DAW, 1976.
_____. *Stormqueen!* New York: DAW, 1978.
_____. *The Sword of Aldones.* New York: Ace, 1962.
_____. *Thendara House.* New York: DAW, 1983.
_____. *Two to Conquer.* New York: DAW, 1980.
_____. "Well Met by Moonlight," *Marion Zimmer Bradley's Fantasy Magazine* 11:1 (October 1998): 32–33.
Breen, Walter. *The Darkover Concordance.* Houston, TX: Penny-Farthing Press, 1979.
Larbalestier, Justine. *The Battle of the Sexes in Science Fiction.* Middletown, CT: Wesleyan University Press, 2002.
Leith, Linda. "Marion Zimmer Bradley and Darkover," *Science Fiction Studies* 7 (1980): 28–35.
Volk-Birke, Sabine. "The Cyclical Way of the Priestess," *Anglia* 1990:108 (1990): 409–428.

Retribution

Marion depicts grievances as irrational and identifies vengeance as an evil stripe on human character, a mark on civilization such as the punishment of the seducer of a Keeper in *The Forbidden Tower,* who "would have been torn on hooks" in past times (Bradley, 1977, 13). Payback is a fault of Frank Colby in "The Crime Therapist," who wants to murder wife Helen because she annoys him, and Rumail Deslucido, who nurses a grudge into old age in *The Fall of Neskaya,* the first of the Clingfire Trilogy. To a lesser degree, the vignette "The Dance at the Gym" pictures Ede, a young flyer pilot, who would rather join a space feud between outposts than dance with an enemy partner. In *Thendara House,* Shann MacShann demands return of his wife Keitha n'ha Casilda on pain of mercenary onslaught at the Guild House entrance.

Payback in Marion's canon does not flourish without punishment. For the philosopher Micon, the victim of Black-robes in *The Fall of Atlantis,* torture leaves his hands bent and his eyes blinded. He accepts cruelty as the unchangeable past: "The deed will carry its own vengeance" (Bradley, 1983, 37). In *The Firebrand,* the author dramatizes Oenone's pent-up hatred for Paris and her refusal to heal his festering arrow wound, the result of a sacrilege against "Father Scamander," a river god (Bradley, 1987, 535). In contemplation of revenge in "Treason of the Blood," Countess Teresa torments Angelo Fieresi, a vampire who kills her family. For the sake of her soul, Father Milo urges, "Revenge belongs to God alone," a restatement of the biblical injunction in Romans 12:19: "Vengeance is mine; I will repay, saith the Lord" (Bradley, 1985, 222).

In picturing the bloodlust of Mhari, a rape victim and Narthen's kept woman in "A Sword Called Chaos," the author dramatizes a cannibalistic meal with Gothic overtones—"feeling her teeth grinding and chewing on the tough seared meat as if they worried Narthen's very throat" (Bradley, 1982, 94). Armed with a talking sword, Mhari expresses less vengeance than the enchanted blade, which demands, "my price of blood, blood, bloodbloodblood" (*Ibid.,* 102). The resulting slaughter reveals to Mhari the horror of nemesis gone mad from a thirsty sword chanting "I thirst! Blood, more blood, more blood, morebloodmore" (*Ibid.,* 106). Marion's monstrous weapon parallels a truth of violence, that retribution tends to exceed a fair requital.

The author links animus with barbarity, the source of citizens burning Princess Narice and her lover alive in *Black Trillium.* In *The Shattered Chain,* a punitive nature causes Jalak of Shainsa to torture and kill potential rescuers of Lady Melora and her daughter Jaelle n'ha Melora. Marion contrasts the male imperative toward payback to female nonviolence: "Blood-feud and revenge are for men" (Bradley, 1976, 77). Varied motivations compel raiders to destroy castles in *Two to Conquer* and *The Heirs of Hammerfell* and nurses to plot the extermination of a mixed-species infant in "Women Only." Women take "grisly revenge" on mercenaries attacking the realm of Merina in *Tiger Burning Bright* (Bradley, 1995, 431). In response to gory scenes of recompense, Marion borrows from David's Psalm 137:1 for the lament, "Weep, weep, O my city! By the waters of the river, lie down and weep!" (*Ibid.,* 142).

ENLIGHTENMENT VS. DEPRAVITY

In other scenarios, Marion showcases wisdom or experience that defeats the competitive urge to retaliate, the theme of Ray Bradbury's end to racism in the space fable "The Other Foot." For Javanne Hastur, a malcontent in *Traitor's Sun,* "rancorous arguments ... during Comyn Council meetings ... tended to be emotionally heated and often vindictive" because of her dislike of Senator Lew Alton (Bradley, 1999, 6). Lew's

choice to agree with Javanne quells her keen hatred, a strategy that encourages consensus and peace. The compromise parallels the acts of King Arthur's Round Table, a
consortium of rational knights who debate the future of Camelot.

Lythande, the wandering mercenary, encounters reprisal in daily dealings with
pursuers. In "The Walker Behind," animus stalks the rover, who fears that her tracker is
an assassin. Rabben the Half-Handed, the evil sorcerer of "The Secret of the Blue Star,"
wreaks his revenge on his rival Lythande by working a spell on the child-woman Bercy.
The magic casts sadness on all the characters, leaving Myrtis the innkeeper ineffective
in comforting her old friend Lythande. For the anonymous necrophiliacs ravishing the
corpse of a Laritha priestess slain in "Somebody Else's Magic," Lythande discovers too
late that the victim's sword is empowered to murder the unnamed men. Because her
actions stir the vengeance of Beccolo, whom she previously bested in a hand-to-hand
combat, she faces a dual challenge. In a gendered no man's land, she exposes Beccolo's
homosexuality, a surprise twist on an episode of rape and reprisal.

In *The Forest House,* set in 80 CE during Roman occupancy of Britannia, vengeance
separates two secondary characters, Dieda and Cynric, an orphan born to a priestess of
the sacred isle of Mona whom Roman legionaries raped. The bard Ardanos fears a call
for revenge from the Ravens, the Celtic name for the children of sexual assault picturing
cawing blackbirds crying for recompense. A major clash between cultures threatens the
bard and Lhiannon, the mother superior, both of whom represent "ancient ways" and
the continuity of Briton history and Druid ritual (Bradley, 1993, 39). By scrying into a
bowl of water, at a mystic communion at Vernemeton, the Forest House, the Druids
identify Red Rian as the arsonist and murderer of a Celtic household and vow redress
"for the sake of vengeance against those devils" (*Ibid.,* 119). In retrospect of the Raven
Cynric's joining the Roman pursuers, Gaius Macellius mutters, "Revenge made strange
bedfellows" (*Ibid.,* 151).

WAR AND REPRISAL

The author ponders the soldier's conscience in *The Mists of Avalon* as a natural
outgrowth of cutthroat combat. Although not a Christian, Gorlois, Duke of Cornwall,
looks ahead to settling the score with a higher power "for all the things I have had to
do in a life as a soldier" (Bradley, 1983, 28). Among Arthur's companions, individual
malice and arguments result in Lancelet's attack on Gawaine for hinting that Lancelet
is a pretty boy and despoiler of Gwenhwyfar. The most dramatic eruption of festering
hatred, Balin's murder of the defenseless Lady of the Lake before the throne at Camelot,
attests to lingering ruthlessness in knights who ostensibly fulfill the Pax Arthuriana. The
axe-wielder justifies his attack on the ancient priestess Viviane as recompense for her
mercy killing of his mother, Priscilla, but his excuse does not rid him of blood-crime.

Trauma follows trauma in the novel's resolution. The return of Accolon's corpse
from Glastonbury arrives with a message from Arthur that he discovered Morgaine's
evil spell and theft of Excalibur. The pursuit of sister by brother through the forest
results in physical collapse for Arthur and a consuming malaise for Morgaine, who
convalesces at Tintagel in Cornwall. Both lessened by nemesis, they return to their
realms. In a grisly reprise of requital, Nimue remains the unknown party who forms
a friendship with Kevin Harper and "[works] the vengeance of the Goddess on this

man who had betrayed them all" (*Ibid.*, 784). Before a tribunal by the Lady of the Lake, Kevin faces slaying and burial under an oak. On a par with the fate of the Wandering Jew, a legendary apostate who mocked Jesus on the way to crucifixion on Golgotha, the future promises one hundred rebirths for Kevin marked by futile roving, the curse of Mary Shelley's unredeemed monster in *Frankenstein*.

See also Dreams; Feuds; Treachery.

Sources

Bradley, Marion Zimmer. *The Best of Marion Zimmer Bradley*. Chicago: Academy Chicago, 1985.
_____. *The Fall of Atlantis*. Riverdale, NY: Baen Books, 1983.
_____. *The Firebrand*. New York: Simon & Schuster, 1987.
_____. *The Forest House*. New York: Michael Joseph, 1993.
_____. *The Mists of Avalon*. New York: Ballantine, 1983.
_____. *The Shattered Chain*. New York: DAW, 1976.
_____. *Sword of Chaos*. New York: DAW, 1982.
_____. *Tiger Burning Bright*. New York: William Morrow, 1995.
_____. *Traitor's Sun*. New York: DAW, 1999.
Haught, Leah. "A Moment in the Field: Voices from Arthurian Legend by Margaret Lloyd," *Arthuriana* 17:4 (2007): 125–126.
Lifshitz, Felice. "Destructive Dominae: Women and Vengeance in Medievalist Films," *Studies in Medievalism* 21 (2012): 161–190.

Ritual

In the same vein as Mary Stewart and Starhawk, Marion favors ceremonial acts and behaviors, music, liturgy, and sacred objects and garments as proof of the holiness of a custom or sacrament, notably, the sacred dances of monks in *Hawkmistress!*, Esteban's blessing of Damon, his future son-in-law in *The Forbidden Tower*, and Eduin's reverence of Lord Alton for saving Eduin's life in battle in *The Spell Sword*. Out of gratitude, Eduin recites the ancient formula, "There is a life between us" (Bradley, 1974, 53). A protracted eulogy to Regis Hastur in *Traitor's Sun* incorporates blessings on the wood casket in the names of three Darkover gods, Evanda, Zandru, and Avarra. The somber passage concludes with respect for Avarra the Harvester: "In her dark womb you shall lie, and be transformed" (Bradley, 1999, 217). Ironically, or perhaps purposefully, Marion issued the novel in January 1999, nine months before her own death, proclaiming Regis's spirit a guide to "illuminate the way for those who follow you!" (*Ibid.*).

Illegitimate offspring in *The Forest House* heighten tensions between Roman rapists and Celtic victims. Because of the desecration of the Isle of Mona and ravishing of priestesses from the ages of nine to grandmothers, a cadre of Ravens, the surviving boy babies, grows up in a culture of militarism and requital. In contrast, celebration of Beltane eve on April 30 dramatizes aroused libido and coitus as couples retreat to the darkness. Eilan reverences the custom because "children were born after they so honored the Lady," even if their parents were unwed (Bradley, 1993, 60). The arrival of the Earth Goddess at midnight contains Marion's skillful dramatization of trance and ecstatic dance induced by the renewer of life.

The author set rites in a royal or social context, such as the bare-breasted pledge by firelight of Magdalen "Magda" Lorne to the Free Amazons in *The Shattered Chain*, Father Valentine's graveside rites for crash victims in *Darkover Landfall*, and the "*cristoforo* sign of prayer" that a mercenary makes after a sword fight in *Thendara House* (Bradley, 1983, 127). She opens *Two to Conquer* on handfasting, a Celtic commitment ceremony betrothing Carlina "Carly" di Asturien to her cousin Bard di Asturien. As described in *Rituals and Ceremonies in Popular Culture* by Ray B. Browne, a distinguished professor at Bowling Green State University, these rites articulate and codify attitudes. Examples range from the respect for Romilly "Romy" MacAran's *cristoforo* faith in *Hawkmistress!* to Allart Hastur's prayer in *Stormqueen!* to the "Holy Bearer of Burdens" for self-control against a vicious father (Bradley, 1978, 47).

Much of the author's canon epitomizes the pure and sacrosanct ceremony, for example, the greeting between travelers at a shelter in *The Shattered Chain* and postulants' worship at the all-female Shrine of Laritha in "Somebody Else's Magic." With sinister significance in *The Fall of Atlantis*, the author dramatizes the pious alongside the corrupt—"a devil's rite conducted by a maniac," which sacrifices the manhood of the drugged child Larmin in honor of the Dark God (Bradley, 1983, 191). Before the marriage to Gabriel Ardais in "Bride Price," Rohana objects to another distortion— the perversion of matrimony into the patriarchal cementing of two dynasties. After preliminary handfasting, Rohana claims to "have learned my part as well as any lyric performer on any stage … to queen it for a day" (Bradley, 1987, 82).

STAGING RITUAL

At ceremonies timed to coincide with moon phases and equinoxes in veneration of the Earth, the author epitomizes male ritual in *The Mists of Avalon* as a bestowal of dominion rather than a commitment to faith. Viviane's kingmaking requires young Arthur to revert to atavism, cover himself in deer hides, and stalk and kill the King Stag, a symbolic rise to dominance anticipating the high king's loss to his illegitimate son Gwydion/Mordred.

In multiple references, Marion focuses on Beltane, a female-initiated ritual on May Day at which Arthur's disguise as the new King Stag represents both savior and sacrifice. In ritualized sex called the Great Marriage, performance unites god with goddess rather than brother with sister. Celtic orthodoxy exonerates the incestuous act, which analyst Carrol L. Fry termed "a very subversive ceremony, in the sense that the woman in the ritual becomes the Goddess … the Great Mother" (Fry, 1993, 69).

In a frenzied trance state brought on by herbs, the priestess Raven predicts, "The Horned One must be crowned … the Virgin Huntress must call the king to her, she must lay down her maidenhead to the God" (Bradley, 1983, 193). Masked before the Maiden Huntress, the costumed stag sires Morgaine's son Gwydion/Mordred. In the opinion of Theresa Crater, an expert on world power locations at the pyramid at Giza and Glastonbury Tor, "As the High Priestess and Priest, the representatives of the Goddess and the Horned God at Beltane, it is their duty to perform the Great Rite, a ritual of sexual magic ensuring the fertility of the land. That a child is born from this union is a blessing," a theological concept parallel to Egyptian marriage customs and Buddhist tantric union in Bhutan, India, Nepal, and Tibet (Crater, 2001, 2). Because maternity is more verifiable than paternity, the female participant who bears a child gains stature in the religious community.

Liturgical Show

Arthurian expert Charlotte Spivack acknowledges Marion's dramatization of women's rituals that emulate Wiccan mysteries and initiation: "The creation of a female liturgy and rituals for women has been an important issue both in traditional and Neo-Pagan religions" (Spivack, 1992, 102). At a meeting with Cornwall royalty in *The Mists of Avalon*, the blessing of the guest cup at Tintagel elevates Viviane for sanctifying the wine, an allusion to the Holy Grail and the offering of the Eucharist, a rite that priests deny to female Christians. More crucial to veneration of the Mother Goddess, the Spring Maiden ceremonial blessing of the fields at Midsummer stirs differences of opinion in North Wales. The procession and masked dancing with phallic wands please Uriens's sons, Accolon and Uwaine, but outrage Father Eian, who castigates the custom as "evil and idolatrous" (Bradley, 1983, 577). The reaction illustrates the fundamental differences between native Briton piety and Christianity.

Of King Arthur's Pentecost procession and pageantry, Morgaine recognizes the value of "making great display," a form of drama common to Druid celebrations of Beltane and to Arthur's mock battles, jousts, and duels blessed by Christian mass and feasting. To welcome Saxon tributaries to the court, Arthur raises Excalibur. Because it casts a cruciform shadow down the hall, the liturgical position violates Avalon's sacred sword, the onset of Camelot's ruin. A poignant formality, the Merlin Taliesin's "ancient prayer of passage," sets a funereal standard after Balin murders Viviane, the elderly Lady of the Lake. The sacrament concludes with Kevin Harper's plaintive postlude (Bradley, 1983, 501). Compounding the heinous death of the old priestess, Arthur dispatches her remains for burial in Christian ground at Glastonbury, a placement that violates Morgaine's preference for holy interment in Avalon.

Knighthood Rites

Marion expands on androcentric power at the vigil of young Gareth the night before his investiture in Arthur's knights of the Round Table, a ceremony repeated in *The Heritage of Hastur* at the commitment of Danilo Syrtis as paxman (security guard) to Regis Hastur. Regis acknowledges a solemn vow: "Now you've only had formally what we both knew all along, *bredu*" (Bradley, 2002, 170). In the Arthurian setting, repetition of Acts 2:1–17 jolts Morgaine into an alternate view of Pentecost as a visitation of the Sight on Christ's apostles. Concluding the epicenter of the Arthurian pledge of loyalty with holy communion and the promotion of Gareth to Arthur's companion and worthy warrior, the passage leaves the priestess of Avalon wondering at the syncretic nature of the Roman Christianity and the Old Ways of Britannia's hill people. The ritual recurs in the falling action with the investiture of Galahad, Arthur's heir, and the boy's promise to "Be always faithful and just, and serve the throne and the righteous cause always" (*Ibid.*, 696). The ongoing opposition of faiths shows Morgause yawning during communion and castigating rituals as expedient, unrealistic "games which men and women played with their minds…. One religious lie was as good as another" (*Ibid.*, 695, 696).

In summation of the position of ritual in liturgy, the author cites familiarity and erosion as the enemies of dogma. The surprise knighting of Gwydion/Mordred in the second half of the Pentecost games omits the overnight vigil, an indication of his illegitimate claim to knighthood. At Accolon's death, his lying in state in the chapel involves softly chanted prayers rather than a formal encomium. Morgaine's flight from Camelot revives memories of hymns sung for the interment of Igraine and Viviane and of the mute figures of Raven and Nimue, both serving the Mother Goddess in silence. As Christianity advances with its masses and church bells, the Old Ways retreat to Cornwall and North Wales, the most authentic Celtic environs in Britannia.

See also Christianity; Mother Goddess; Patriarchy; Religion; Wicca; Womanhood.

Sources

Bradley, Marion Zimmer. *The Best of Marion Zimmer Bradley*. Chicago: Academy Chicago, 1985.
_____. *The Fall of Atlantis*. Riverdale, NY: Baen Books, 1983.
_____. *The Forbidden Tower*. New York: DAW, 1977.
_____. *The Forest House*. New York: Michael Joseph, 1993.
_____. *The Gratitude of Kings*. New York: Wildside, 1997.
_____. *The Heritage of Hastur*. New York: DAW, 2002.
_____. *The Mists of Avalon*. New York: Ballantine, 1983.
_____. *The Other Side of the Mirror*. New York: DAW, 1987.
_____. *The Spell Sword*. New York: DAW, 1974.
_____. *Stormqueen!* New York: DAW, 1978.
_____. *Thendara House*. New York: DAW, 1983.
_____. *Traitor's Sun*. New York: DAW, 1999.
_____. *Two to Conquer*. New York: DAW, 1980.
Browne, Ray B., ed. *Rituals and Ceremonies in Popular Culture*. Bowling Green, OH: Bowling Green University Popular Press, 1980.
Crater, Theresa. "The Resurrection of Morgan le Fey: Fallen Woman to Triple Goddess," *Femspec* 3:1 (December 2001): 12–22.
Fry, Carrol L. "The Goddess Ascending: Feminist Neo-Pagan Witchcraft in Marion Zimmer Bradley's Novels," *Journal of Popular Culture* 27:1 (1993): 67–80.
Łaszkiewicz, Weronika. "Religious Conflicts and Their Impact on King Arthur's Reign in Marion Zimmer Bradley's *The Mists of Avalon*," *Acta Neophilologica* 19 (2017): 133–143.
Pagès, Meriem, and Karolyn Kinane. *The Middle Ages on Television: Critical Essays*. Jefferson, NC: McFarland, 2015.
Spivack, Charlotte. *Popular Arthurian Traditions*. Bowling Green, OH: Bowling Green State University Popular Press, 1992.

Roman-Celtic Dynasty

Marion dramatizes the results of imperialism in *The Forest House* with a teen romance. Gaius Macellius, the bicultural son of a Roman prefect, embodies a proud family relationship with his uncle, a Silurian chieftain of the hillforts in southeastern Wales, and ties to the bardic arch–Druid Bendeigid Vran and high priestess Rheis and their daughter Eilan, also a postulant of the Mother Goddess. Both ethnic groups, Roman and Celtic, valued fostering as a means of providing homes for children like Cynric, the offspring of a former postulant of the Mother Goddess raped by Roman invaders of the sacred isle of Mona. Notation in the family tree indicates sexual/marital ties:

plebeian	Arch-Druid Ardanos
farmer in	bard
Tarentum		

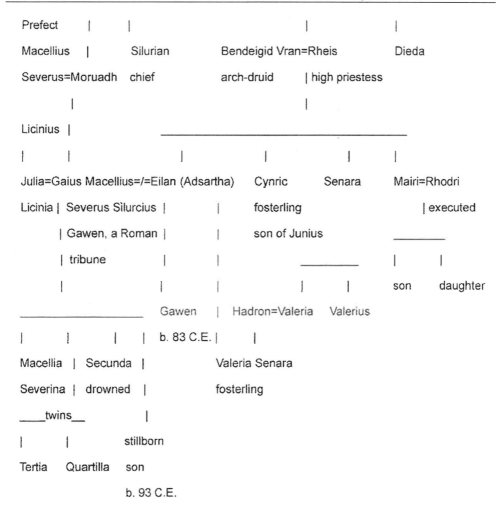

The genealogy reveals some of Marion's standard motifs—orphaning, fostering, twinning, blended cultures, stillbirths, child deaths, and widowhood.

Sources

Anczyk, Adam. "Druids and Druidesses: Gender Issues in Druidry," *Pantheon* 10:1 (2015): 3–15.
_____. "The Image of Druids in Contemporary Paganism: Constructing the Myth," *Walking the Old Ways: Studies in Contemporary European Paganism* (2012): 99–118.
Bradley, Marion Zimmer. *The Forest House.* New York: Michael Joseph, 1993.
Filmer-Davies, Kath. *Fantasy, Fiction and Welsh Myth: Tales of Belonging.* New York: St. Martin, 1996.

Royal House of Atlantis

Marion's outline of the dynasties kin to the Atlantean priesthood and a Sea Kingdom sisterhood produced a warren of sibling jealousy, parenting, and fostering complicated by clan tragedies. The narrative holds out hope for surviving island realms in the accomplishments of the younger generation. As a token of promise, the resolution anticipates marriage between Micail and Tiriki, cousins borne by sisters Deoris and Domaris. Notation in the family tree indicates sexual/marital ties:

```
grandmother     servant=/=Talkannon=priestess                    Atlantean grandsire

    |               |Arch-priest   |died in childbirth                    |

 peasants           |          |                              wife=Mikantor=second wife

  |      |          |       _____          |priest   |

         |          |      |                        |        |         |
_____  |          |      |                        |        |         |

Rajasta Riveda=/=Karahama   |     Mani-toret=priestess |   _____

guardian wizard | insane    |     Atlantean  |       |       |             |

 _____              |               |       |       |             |

  |        |                |               |       |       |             |

Larmin  Demira=/=Riveda=/=Deoris  Chedan=Elis=/=Arvath=Domaris=Micon=princess  Reio-ta=Deoris

        hangs   apostate |scribe  acolyte   |        |acolyte |adopted      Lantor |

        herself poisoned |                Lissa     |exiled to |by Rathor    priest |

                  Nari                              |Atlantis  |                     |

                    _____             O-si-nar-men Micail=Eilantha Tiriki

                    |             |

                    infant girl   boy

                    dead at       mutilated

                    birth         at birth
```

In 1999, the book received attention in Diana Tixier Herald's *Fluent in Fantasy,* a guide to young adult reading, followed by commentary in 2005 in *Genreflecting.*

See also *The Fall of Atlantis.*

Sources

Bradley, Marion Zimmer. *The Fall of Atlantis.* Riverdale, NY: Baen Books, 1983.
Herald, Diana Tixier. *Fluent in Fantasy.* Englewood, CO: Libraries Unlimited, 1999.
_____. *Genreflecting.* Englewood, CO: Libraries Unlimited, 2005.
Paxson, Diana L. "Marion Zimmer Bradley and *The Mists of Avalon*," *Arthuriana* 9:1 (Spring 1999): 110–126.

Royal House of Troy

The family tree of King Priam and Queen Hecuba of Troy illustrates the patriarchal bias of the Iron Age, which traced its founding to male power wielders to the detriment of mothers and female influences. Vicki McCash, a journalist for the (Broward, Florida) *Sun Sentinel* stated, "These stories have been revered for centuries, but in *The Firebrand* they are retold to become one epic novel, not only of heroes and gods, but of heroines and goddesses and of change in the very fabric of society" (McCash, 1988, 10F). Notation in the family tree indicates sexual/marital ties:

```
Erechtheus

King of Crete

   |

Ilos
```

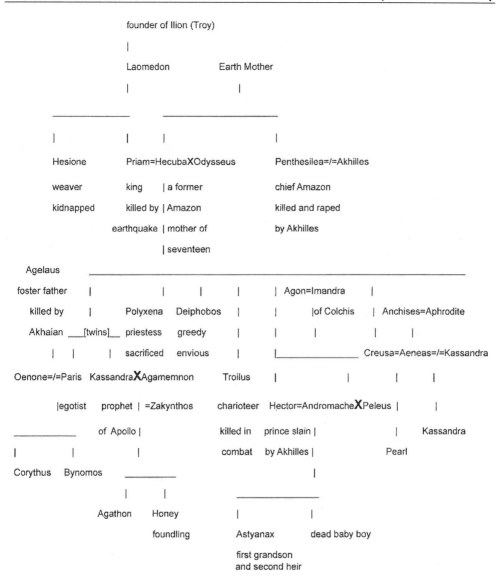

Of the change in godhood, clans, and civilization to a war-torn shambles, Queen Imandra of Colchis blames women for enabling men in establishing woman-less dynasties and for allowing Apollo to kill the Serpent Mother, an incarnation of the Mother Goddess. The queen summarizes the error as "the fault of the women who did not keep their men in their place" (Bradley, 1987, 323). The generalization reflects twentieth-century feminist charges that mothers favor sons, fail to teach them respect for females, and encourage macho stereotypes through toys, play, and visual media.

Sources

Bradley, Marion Zimmer. *The Firebrand*. New York: Simon & Schuster, 1987.

Judge, Virginia. "*Firebrand* Tells Woman's Views of the Legend of Trojan War," (Rock Hill, SC) *Herald* (16 January 1988).

Kirchhoff, H.J. "An Old Story 'The Firebrand,'" (Toronto) *Globe and Mail* (26 December 1987).

McCash, Vicki. "A Feminist Reworking of Mythology," (Broward, FL) *Sun Sentinel* (17 April 1988): 10F.

Royal Houses of Akhaia and Sparta

Marion's structured review of the interrelated Greek clans in *The Firebrand* draws on the mythology based on a set of twins, Helen and Klytemnestra, who result from Zeus's rape of their mother Leda. The twins marry brothers Menelaus and Agamemnon. Because the brothers' rule Sparta and Akhaia, respectively, they embroil two armies in the recovery of Queen Helen, the prize of Prince Paris of Troy. Notation in the family tree indicates sexual/marital ties:

```
        grandmother

        |

        mother

        |

Zeus=/=Leda=Tyndareus

        | northern invader

_____twins_____

        |               _____brothers_____        |    Hecuba=Priam

        |             |                        |    |        |

Aegisthos=/=Klytemnestra=Agamemnon X Kassanda  Menelaus=Helen=/=Paris

                | murdered    |                | Queen |  X Deiphobos

                          Agathon             | of Sparta |

_____                | 

  |        |        |                          |        |

Iphigenia Orestes Elektra=swineherd         _____      twin sons

sacrificed                                     |    |        three killed in

                              Hermione        Nikos    earthquake
```

The conclusion characterizes the violation of female war prizes, Kassandra by Agamemnon and Helen by the warrior Deiphobos. Vengeance also repays Agamemnon for his crimes by the scheming Klytemnestra and a murderous trap.

Sources

Bradley, Marion Zimmer. *The Firebrand*. New York: Simon & Schuster, 1987.

Judge, Virginia. "'Firebrand' Tells Woman's Views of the Legend of Trojan War" (Rock Hill, SC) *Herald* (16 January 1988).

"Review: *The Firebrand*," *Publishers Weekly* (1 October 1989).

Santelli-Fortunati Dynasty

The union of the Fortunati and Santelli clans in *The Catch Trap* yields sixteen professional flyers for the circus milieu at its height in the 1940s and 1950s. Their Americanized nicknames—Jim, Lionel, Liss, Johnny, Tony, Joe, Mark, Tessa, Clay—free the ethnic Italians from ties to the Old Country. Only Matthew Gardner, Jr., chooses to honor his roots with the nickname "Mario," the name of his Italian great grandfather, Mario di Santalis.

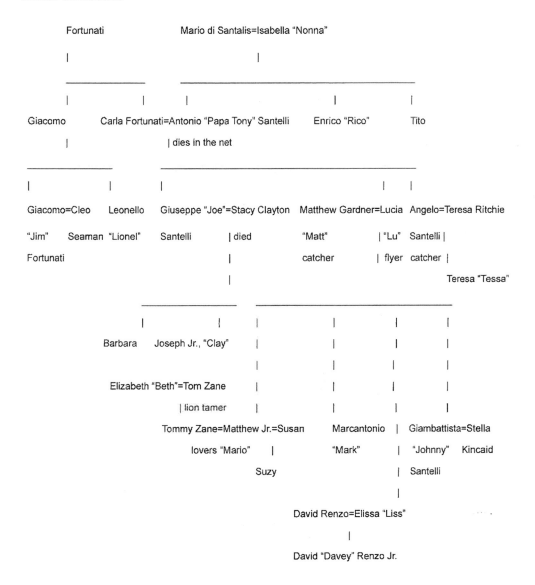

The author earned regard for introducing same sex love themes to YA fiction. Reviewer Deborah J. Ross admired the narrative for its images of clan and commitment: "It's about all the ways families destroy and save us. It's about that rare bond of a shared vocation, a calling, the thing that makes us most fully alive" (Ross, 2014). According to *Kirkus Review,* "The narrative soars with love of the high stuff. A grand, overlong spectacular—but not for kids" ("Review," 1979).

Sources

Bradley, Marion Zimmer. *The Catch Trap.* New York: Random House, 1979.
"Review: *The Catch Trap,*" *Kirkus* (1 April 1979).
Ross, Deborah J. "Proofreading *The Catch Trap,*" http://deborahjross.blogspot.com/2014/04/proofreading-catch-trap.html, April 9, 2014.
"Santelli Family Tree," https://www.mzbworks.com/santelli.htm.

Sex

Marion elevated sexuality from casually carnal teen couplings in *Survey Ship* to the dramatic and transcendent, an ambition of Terran cartographer Andrew Carr in *The Spell Sword* "for perfection in a woman to protect yourself against a real relationship ... because it wasn't really women he wanted at all" (Bradley, 1974, 6). The motif of Ἔρως (Eros, passion) anchors much of her characterization, particularly in wisps of lesbianism described in the Lythande novella *The Gratitude of Kings* and a gladiatorial school in *Warrior Woman,* the sexual domination of the scribe Deoris by the priest Riveda in *The Forest House,* and androgyny in *The World Wreckers.* In addition to the coming of age misgivings of teen acrobat Tommy Zane in *The Catch Trap,* the author explores the failure of his lover Mario at living a bisexual cover for homosexuality with wife Susan and attempting to rear daughter Suzy. Preparations for a mountain trek of eight men and a female guide in *The Planet Savers* involves standard warnings to amazon Kyla Raineach that most of the company consists of "mountain roughnecks" given to horseplay and "funny stuff," a veiled threat of rape (Bradley, 1976, 42, 79). For an extreme perversion of normal sexuality, Terran Ryan Evans in *Rediscovery* attempts to lengthen the street life of child sex slaves with an aphrodisiac pollen extracted from *kireseth* blossoms.

At the fount of conflict in *The Mists of Avalon,* the author's Arthuriad surveys universal libidinous behaviors—the ritualized union in nature that analyst Janice C. Crosby, on staff at Southern University in Baton Rouge, Louisiana, connects with the Greek ἱερὸς γάμος—"*hieros gamos* or sacred marriage" (Crosby, 2000, 45). The long-range purpose of a masked ritual union of the King Stag with a priestess chosen by the Lady of the Lake invests the Pendragon dynasty with the domain of Avalon, the old Celtic faith that promoted fertility in crops, herds, and people. In contrast to prehistoric ritual, the author presents Christianity as the hostile, sterile cant of the authoritarian Bishop Patricius (St. Patrick), who condemns intimate liberties at agrarian folk festivals of Beltane and Samaine.

In deference to Celtic conventions, Marion approached human attraction and desire as natural responses requiring integrity and self-restraint. The priestess Morgaine's hunger for her stepson Accolon causes her to take chances in northern Wales by slipping into his bed at night down the hall from her ailing husband, King Uriens. The ache for intercourse provokes her to reassess Queen Gwenhwyfar and her endangerment of King Arthur's throne with a sex scandal involving Lancelet, captain of the horse. By daylight, Morgaine admits, "I have never known what it was to be only a woman" (Bradley, 1983, 663). Marion completes the scene with Avalloch's prowling in the corridor and his attempt at seducing his stepmother Morgaine to satisfy his lust.

The text builds irony from Avalloch's accusation of harlotry and his offer to Morgaine of more of the same. He applies a common double standard—he is innocent of the yen for a beautiful woman because Morgaine bewitched him. The charge proves true at the forest divination by a brown pool, where the Horned One reveals to Morgaine Accolon's future. The swirl of precognition discloses a magical copulation of Morgaine with Accolon like lightning, which coincides with a heavenly eclipse. For Accolon, union with the priestess/stepmother reveals her duality with the Mother Goddess, the source of male-female attraction.

To Arthur's prudish entourage, any woman capable of overpowering a man with her will must be a sorceress. The salacious banners that introduce Camelot's fall involve naked caricatures engaged in disloyalties and lascivious gratification, notably, Morgaine's suspected coupling with the devil. Morgause, Queen of Orkney and Lothian, parallels Morgaine's self-confidence in her faith in women's skill at the sexual favors that controlled males, who are "foolishly dependent on that thing a woman could offer to them" (*Ibid.*, 454). The narrative creates irony when Arthur orders an evergreen fire and incense to purify the air. Marion taunts the dual use of nature to conjure spur-of-the-moment copulation and to cleanse the court of prurient mockery of the king's sister.

Momentary Madness

According to Rosemarie Arbur in *Twentieth-Century Science Fiction Writers,* the author excelled in her study of "the very nature of human intimacy" (Oliver, 1999, A24). At a fearful pass in *Darkover Landfall,* Marion views unrestricted passion as it arises from alien nature. On the unknown planet of Cottman IV, Lieutenant Camilla Del Rey and geologist Rafael "Rafe" MacAran flinch from the banshee wail of a beast in the night. To prevent Camilla from advancing into hysteria, Rafe slaps her, then snuggles his head against hers. Realizing the perils of climbing above 8,000 feet on the unknown planet, he chastises himself for a stir of desire: "This was one hell of a time to start something like that" (Bradley, 1972, 41). On return to camp after peaceful lovemaking by moonlight, Rafe still feels "a deep gnawing hunger for her" (*Ibid.,* 61). Because a rising wind distributes *kireseth* pollen, a mysterious surge of ardor infiltrates the camp, throwing security guards into a mass of groping and romancing that "proceeded, totally without discrimination—man and woman, woman and woman, man and man— to more direct and active satisfactions" (*Ibid.,* 89). Rafe describes the hyper-stimulated orgy as "unreason … panic … lust and wild sensual euphoria" (*Ibid.,* 93, 94). The spree produces typical human regrets—shame, guilt—as well as some conceptions.

Marion reviews the problem of sexual profligacy from the perspective of female outcomes—coping with pregnancy and childbearing, a focus shared by Lady Deonora in

Stormqueen! To keep survivors safe on the planet, Medic Ewen Ross elaborates on contraception: "Sex is voluntary ... but information is mandatory" (*Ibid.,* 78). The problem of disrupted hormonal cycles in females creates worry that sexually active women like Camilla may conceive. Emergency directives aim to prevent impregnation that may require abortion, a surgical procedure for which the survivors of a crash landing are not prepared.

Unlike the more fastidious scruples of the crew from Earth, the permissive society that evolves at the domain of Hastur in *Stormqueen!* considers female serfs in Syrtis worthy bedmates for Hasturians. To guests, hosts offer sexual dalliances like appetizers and aperitifs. To avoid extensive smutty talk from Dom Marius, Allart rejects the gift, earning from the host implications that the former monk "[prefers] the pleasures to be found among the brethren" (Bradley, 1978, 54). Enlarging on the overlord's inhumanity, Marius claims to have modified beautiful boys "to be almost without response to pain" from penile penetration (*Ibid.*). The change in human mores since the arrival of earthlings suggests that departure from the home planet requires Darkovans to formulate their own morality.

Passion in Paradise

To suppress realism and fear of society's gendered restrictions, sci-fi authors like Marion create alien worlds loaded with possibilities. Essayists Nicola Griffith and Kelley Eskridge term speculative fiction "a different kind of coming-out story—more of coming-in stories at heart, about people coming into themselves," a specialty of Bradley, Robert Heinlein, and Theodore Sturgeon (Griffith and Eskridge, 2008, 42). In the analysis of scholar Deborah L. Zanghi, Marion, like Gothic novelists Anne Rice and Octavia Butler, unleashes women readers to enjoy escapism. Beyond social decorum, they can examine oppression by a male hierarchy vicariously one victim at a time, including Camilla n'ha Kyria, the neutered Amazon in *Thendara House* who relives gang rape and breast removal by raiders at age fourteen. Unlike past and current history, when women served as prostitutes, war prizes, and sex slaves for sale and trade, the utopian female enjoys autonomy to negotiate a life story offering satisfaction as well as compromises, the lifestyle of neutered Free Amazons like Camilla who abandon womanliness and motherhood. To the benefit of both genders, unrestricted women function equally with males in sexual relationships as well as in labor, finance, research, science, medicine, and religion.

Carnal Complexities

Marion made her most compelling studies of gender and sex in the Darkover series. In *The Shattered Chain,* Magdalen "Magda" Lorne, a Terran linguist and translator at the spaceport in Trade City, masters nuances of costume and the vernacular that identify obedient women, prostitutes, and homosexuals. To achieve a thorough knowledge of Darkovan meanings, she, like Terran spies and anthropologists, disguises herself as a local resident and meanders the marketplace. At repeat of a punishment meted out at the Golden Cage, an audience laughs at the tarring of entertainers pantomiming the lesbianism of Free Amazons. Because vulgarity is limited to men, she learns "women's talk" about menstruation, but hears no dirty jokes, a gendered realm left to males

(Bradley, 1976, 110). Among the jests are standard degradation of Amazons for reputed lesbianism, a common misconception of men who condemn the woman-to-woman loyalty of sisterhood. By scrutinizing individuals, the author characterizes libido as an unavoidable outgrowth of stress, especially when people face terror or a death sentence, as Peter Haldane does during imprisonment in Sain Scarpa. His reunion with Magda, his ex-wife and rescuer, releases yearnings that he misreads as a revival of their old romance. Her oath to the Amazons confuses him, causing him to judge her as lesbian rather than independent.

In an article for the *Washington Post,* journalist Alyssa Rosenberg lauded Marion for understanding psychosexual urges like those of Peter and Magda. Rosenberg declared, "Zimmer Bradley's descriptions of the awakening of sexual design, the devastating power of sexual assault and the psychic damage wrought by constricting women's roles in society remain beautiful and evocative" (Rosenberg, 2014). In one example from *Survey Ship,* a story of six graduates from training for space exploration, Ravi opts for "frantic sex with Moira" to relieve stress and further self-discovery (Bradley, 1980, 76). For models of female dilemma, the author chose such events as the rape of holy women of Mona island in *The Fall of Atlantis,* Helen's defaming as a slut by her husband Menelaus and the Trojan forces in *The Firebrand,* and the arranged nuptials of teenager Rohana in "Bride Price" to Gabrial Dyan, Warden of Ardais, a much older mate. From these women's stories come what Rosenberg terms "tremendous insight into pain and transcendence" (Rosenberg, 2014).

See also The Forbidden Tower; Rape; Santelli-Fortunati Dynasty.

Sources

Bradley, Marion Zimmer. *Darkover Landfall.* New York: DAW, 1972.
_____. *The Mists of Avalon.* New York: Ballantine, 1983.
_____. *The Planet Savers.* New York: Ace, 1976.
_____. *The Shattered Chain.* New York: DAW, 1976.
_____. *The Spell Sword.* New York: DAW, 1974.
_____. *Stormqueen!* New York: DAW, 1978.
_____. *Survey Ship.* New York: Ace, 1980.
Crosby, Janice C. *Cauldron of Changes: Feminist Spirituality in Fantastic Fiction.* Jefferson, NC: McFarland, 2000.
Griffith, Nicola, and Kelley Eskridge. "War Machine, Time Machine" in *Queer Universes: Sexualities in Science Fiction.* Liverpool, England: Liverpool University Press, 2008, 39–49.
Oliver, Myrna. "Marion Bradley; Writer of Fantasy Novels," *Los Angeles Times* (30 September 1999): A24.
Rosenberg, Alyssa. "Re-reading Feminist Author Marion Zimmer Bradley in the Wake of Sexual Assault Allegations," *Washington Post* (27 June 2014).
Zanghi, Deborah L. "An Exploration of Alternate Realities: Women's Contemporary Speculative Fiction," master's thesis, digital commons.brockport.edu, 1997.

Sharra's Exile

Following events in the groundbreaking novel *The Heritage of Hastur,* Marion opens the first book of *Sharra's Exile* on male camaraderie, spirited tavern insults and brawling, and boy-girl attraction. More serious action quickly segues to a compressed realignment of domains. In Book Two, through energetic dialogue, she presents Arthurian-style power struggles against Sharra, a dangerous female daemon on a par with the mythic Medusa and the Erinyes, the Greek goddesses of vengeance and reprisal. The text coordinates *doppelgängers,* Midsummer festival masking, hawking, and a magic weapon, the Sword of Aldones, housed in *rhu fead,* a hallowed shrine like the chapel that stored King Arthur's Excalibur.

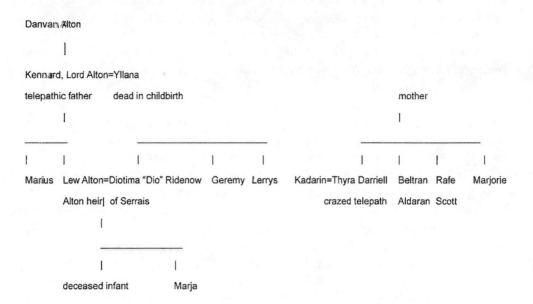

Danvan Alton
|

Kennard, Lord Alton=Yllana
telepathic father   dead in childbirth   mother
| |

| | | | | | | | | |
Marius Lew Alton=Diotima "Dio" Ridenow Geremy Lerrys   Kadarin=Thyra Darriell Beltran Rafe Marjorie
        Alton heir| of Serrais   crazed telepath Aldaran Scott
        |

        | |
        deceased infant   Marja

A legendary advance on the 3,000-year Darkover saga and *Exile's Return* trilogy, the popular novel won a 1982 Locus award for its dynamic clashes and flourished in French, German, and Italian.

A holdover from the Age of Chaos, the Sharra matrix—"the image of a woman of flame, chained, restless, tresses of fire rising on a firestorm wind, hovering … rising, ravening"—frees herself from the forge and threatens Darkover (Bradley, 1981, 2). Her menace thrusts to prominence Lew Alton, a tower mechanic and Marion's favorite hero. Hounded by telepathic messages from his father, Lew repeatedly weighs the sufferings of a half-caste Terran/Darkoveran and batters the fearful Sharra in his nightmares, fearing he "will never be free" (*Ibid.,* 4). His thoughts mull over the loss of his beloved Marjorie, the lopping of his left hand, and a return to Cottman IV from exile.

To set Darkover on a promising trajectory, Marion manages more than one protagonist. Contrasted with Lord Dyan Ardais, the hawk-faced antagonist, Regis Hastur, the ultimate ruler of Darkover, matures considerably by accepting that "the Heir to Hastur has come of age" (*Ibid.,* 12). Marion's somber resolution recounts the heroic death of Dyan and the losses of Lady Aillard and the Alhalyn. Grandfather Danvan Alton indicates that Regis has "the right to define what Darkover will become" (*Ibid.,* 236).

Marion's metamorphosis elevates the novel to one of her more unforgettable Darkover segments. In a brilliant apotheosis, Regis blazes into the "son of Aldones, who was the Son of Light" (*Ibid.,* 231). Of the complexities and challenges, Keith Roysdon, a reviewer for the *Muncie* (Indiana) *Evening Press,* declared the intense maze of character "just a bit too complex a look at Darkover power and politics, and I couldn't tell the players even with a scorecard" (Roysdon, 1981, T8). In defense of the labyrinthine fantasy saga, Marion declared, "People who are interested in fantasy are interested in human values—the basic confrontations that get down to the gut" (Friedman, 1981, E4). She typified Darkover themes of good versus evil as "archetypes of the human psyche … inner space" (*Ibid.*).

Sources

Bradley, Marion Zimmer. *Sharra's Exile*. New York: DAW, 1981.
Friedman, Mickey. "A Trend to Science Fantasy Books," *San Francisco Examiner* (16 November 1981): E4.
Roysdon, Keith. "Good Female Writers Abound in Science Fiction Category," *Muncie* (Indiana) *Evening Press* (14 November 1981): T8.

The Shattered Chain

A sequel to *Darkover Landfall* and prequel to *Thendara House,* Marion's novel *The Shattered Chain,* a female *Bildungsroman,* reassesses earthly society by exploring alternate worlds. As a model of what theorist Janice C. Crosby terms "magical incantation, a calling into being … in the eternal present," the narrative examines the Darkover Renunciates, a band of outlaw females who rid themselves of patriarchal control to rescue a woman and her daughter (Crosby, 2000, 41). Like Sally Miller Gearhart's *The Wanderground,* according to Victoria Hollinger, an analyst for Liverpool University Press, *The Shattered Chain* employs "sex-role reversals" that "privilege the feminine order over the masculine" (Hollinger, 1990, 230). To anchor their lives, females choose among matrimony with a suitable mate, an authoritarian paradise where men make all decisions for women, or autonomy as Free Amazons.

The narrative, divided into three characterizations of liberated women, opens on the pledge of Free Amazons promising to fight off potential rapists and to identify the self by a matronym, a pledge reviewed by Joan Gordon in *Science Fiction Studies.* The choice of neutered female Camilla n'ha Kyria to abandon sex and motherhood receives legitimation in her maternal surname, meaning "daughter of Kyria." Additional vows free each Amazon of patriarchal childbearing and promote the social refuge of sisterhood. Marion surveys liberated women who refute feudal notions of uniting with men and living *di catenas* (in chains). To disputes about the motif of marital chains on women, Australian critic Lenise Prater of Deakin University, Melbourne, replied that the metaphor relates to women's wedding rings "to signify their 'ownership' by a man; given that her texts were written in the USA in the 1970s … this extrapolation from common heterosexual practices suits the historical context" (Prater, 2013, 150).

Situating themes in a medieval setting, the author creates in readers what Janice C. Crosby calls "a magical product … a state of consciousness that brings about transformation" through spiritual renewal (Crosby, 2000, 41–42). Marion cites an oath to sodality that unites the Free Amazons much like King Arthur's Knights of the Round Table, who bind themselves to fealty and chivalry. Echoing archaic lifestyles and transportation, the novel pictures saddled mounts and travelers dressed in tunics and cloaks and armed with daggers as they arrive in Dry-Town to raise their tents. For its blend of speculative fiction with the sword-and-sorcery genre, the *Wilson Library Bulletin* gave the novel a top rating. A posthumous omnibus volume, *The Saga of Renunciates,* issued the novel along with *Thendara House* and *City of Sorcery.*

See also City of Sorcery; Thendara House.

Sources

Bradley, Marion Zimmer. *The Shattered Chain*. New York: DAW, 1976.

Christ, Carol. *Diving Deep & Surfacing: Women Writers on Spiritual Quest*. New York: Beacon, 1995.

Crosby, Janice C. *Cauldron of Changes: Feminist Spirituality in Fantastic Fiction*. Jefferson, NC: McFarland, 2000.

Gordon, Joan. "Review: Playing the Field," *Science Fiction Studies* 36:1 (March 2009): 161–163.

Hollinger, Veronica. "Feminist Science Fiction: Breaking Up the Subject," *Extrapolation* 31:3 (October 1990): 229–239.

Prater, Lenise. "Monstrous Fantasies: Reinforcing Rape Culture in Fiona McIntosh's Fantasy Novels," *Hecate* 39:1/2 (2013): 148–167, 218.

Tolmie, Jane. "Medievalism and the Fantasy Heroine," *Journal of Gender Studies* 15:2 (2006): 145–158.

Williams, Lynn F. "Everyone Belongs to Everyone Else: Marriage and the Family in Recent American Utopias 1965–1985," *Utopian Studies* 1 (1 January 1987): 123–136.

The Shattered Chain, Part I: Lady Rohana Ardais, Comynara

In fealty to choice, the feminist mantra, Marion's speculative sci-fi novel *The Shattered Chain* introduces her most liberated female society in a suspenseful dead-of-night rescue scenario. In a culture where married women wear veils, cumbersome skirts, and "fetters of possession" on the wrists anchored to their belts, Kindra n'ha Mhari's band of Amazon mercenaries pledges to retrieve Jaelle n'ha Melora, the twelve-year-old child of pregnant concubine Lady Melora, from Jalak of Shainsa in Dry-Town (Bradley, 1976, 26). Notation in the family tree indicates sexual/marital ties:

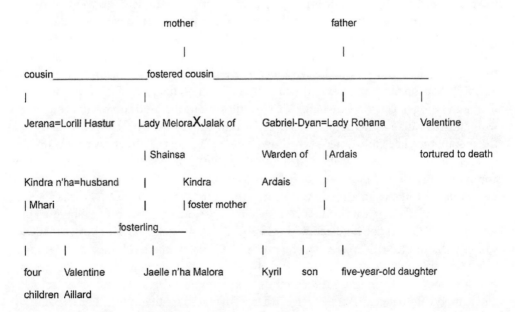

Close to the enemy, the girl mercenaries apply their training in ignoring fear and slipping silently toward guards, with Gwennis playing the hapless bait. To requite Jalak for his barbarity toward girls and women, the narrative follows the style of male commando raids, awarding the followers of Kindra n'ha Mhari respect for their cunning and risk of rape, imprisonment, sex slavery, or death.

Marion makes use of a noontime rest to reveal character attitudes toward gender, sisterhood, and freedom. Kindra's band shares clothing, bread, wine, and information about the unfettered life that awaits Jaelle. The narrative emphasizes choice as the foundation of liberation, especially for women like Camilla n'ha Kyria who opt for neutering. At the chapter climax, Melora reveals the impetus to her cry for help—her daughter's game of mock chaining by tying ribbons to her wrists. Among free women, Melora, in the early stages of labor, calls others *"Breda,"* a Darkover word meaning "sister" or "darling" (*Ibid.*, 70). More than food or drink, sisterhood vitalizes and reassures the parturient mother during "breaking, tearing, splitting, coming apart … dying" (*Ibid.*, 75). With ironic understatement, Gwennis sums up the female destiny to provide the world with a future generation: "It is troublesome to be a woman" (*Ibid.*, 62).

The novel acquires thematic thrust from decisions about Melora's childbed death from hemorrhage and the hardy baby boy she delivers. In defiance of Kindra's demand for retribution, Rohana snuggles the infant and declares, "Blood-feud and revenge are for men" (*Ibid.*, 77). To assuage Jaelle, the twelve-year-old orphan, Rohana launches into storytelling by repeating the Darkover origination myth of Cassilda and Hastur. The story of Thendara shifts toward female heroism, which shames Lord Lorill Hastur for failure to retrieve Melora from the Dry-Towners. To symbolize Jaelle's liberation to make a unique life and career, Marion concludes with a request for a haircut, a representative shearing of external controls, an introit to more complex conflicts and accomplishments.

Sources

Bradley, Marion Zimmer. *The Shattered Chain*. New York: DAW, 1976.

Jones, Libby Falk. "Reading/Writing/Creating Feminist Utopian Communities," *Journal of Education* 172:1 (January 1990): 38–46.

Vaughn, Sue Fisher. "The Female Hero in Science Fiction and Fantasy: 'Carrier-Bag' to 'No-Road,'" *Journal of the Fantastic in the Arts* 4:4 (1 January 1991): 83–96.

Wehrmann, Jürgen. "Jane Eyre in Outer Space: Victorian Motifs in Post-Feminist Science Fiction" in *A Breath of Fresh Eyre*. Amsterdam, Holland: Brill Rodopi, 2007, 149–165.

The Shattered Chain, Part II: Magda Lorne, Terran Agent

For maximum contrast, Marion departs the picara's life of the Free Amazons and the royal throne that dominates Rohana's existence to shape a separate stave. At the Terran spaceport outside Thendara, Magda Lorne, like Terran cartographer Andrew Carr in *The Forbidden Tower* and Dan Barron in *Winds of Darkover*, adapts to a Darkovan life as a spy. She translates the local argot and informs Russell "Russ" Montray, her bumbling superior, of ethnic data gleaned from surveillance in town. By having Magda fill in gaps in his knowledge, the author uses dialogue to enlighten the reader about the Comyn and Hastur dynasty. The exchanges also reveal that Terrans maintain gender-based standards banning women from advancement on the job. Magda considers moving to a less prejudiced planet. Notation in the family tree indicates sexual/marital ties:

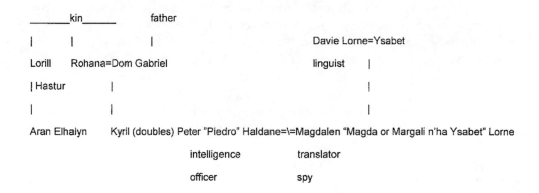

```
_____kin_____        father

|      |              |                  Davie Lorne=Ysabet

Lorill  Rohana=Dom Gabriel              linguist  |

| Hastur        |                                 |

|              |                                  |

Aran Elhalyn   Kyril (doubles) Peter "Piedro" Haldane=\=Magdalen "Magda or Margali n'ha Ysabet" Lorne

                       intelligence          translator

                       officer               spy
```

To rescue intelligence officer Peter Haldane, her ex-husband, from the Sain Scarpa bandits, Magda conspires with Lady Rohana to employ the disguise of a Free Amazon, an anticipation of guile and pragmatism in the Lythande stories and the resolution of *The Mists of Avalon*. The chance meeting under shelter-truce with Jaelle n'ha Melora introduces Magda to the hospitality of the trail, a parallel of welcome at Troy in *The Firebrand* offered to Greek envoys Odysseus and Akhilles by King Priam. Marion elevates the consequence of trail hut rules by appending punishments for crimes: three years of outlawry for assault and castration for rape plus an additional threat of emasculation if a felon violates peace at the shelter. The gendered motif identifies the penis as the weapon of choice for sex crimes.

Marion evens out strengths and outlook for both women, forcing Magda to slay two bandits with her knife and to nurse Jaelle through delirium and thirst. The deeds convince Jaelle to pledge aid to Magda's mission. Throughout their friendship, Magda realizes that Terran society restricts women more than she had thought. A successful negotiation with Rumal di Scarp builds self-confidence and identity as a Free Amazon, even though Magda doubts the applicability of the guild oath to her circumstances. The attraction between Jaelle and Peter suggests a romantic tie, which Marion leaves to the third stave. The pairing enhances the author's typical suspense—the future of relationships between Darkovans and Terrans.

Sources

Bradley, Marion Zimmer. *The Shattered Chain*. New York: DAW, 1976.
Gordon, Joan. "Review: Playing the Field," *Science Fiction Studies* 36:1 (March 2009): 161–163.
Leith, Linda. "Marion Zimmer Bradley and Darkover," *Science Fiction Studies* 7 (1980): 28–35.
Vaughn, Sue Fisher. "The Female Hero in Science Fiction and Fantasy: 'Carrier-Bag' to 'No-Road,'" *Journal of the Fantastic in the Arts* 4:4 (1 January 1991): 83–96.

The Shattered Chain, Part III: Jaelle n'ha Melora, Free Amazon

Marion develops the final stave as a test of an oath of sisterhood vs. physical attraction between Peter and Jaelle n'h Melora and marital loyalty from Lady Rohana to Dom Gabriel. The cure that Gabriel's sister Alida directs against poisoned wounds gradually removes the toxins inflicted by bandits on Jaelle and Magda. By focusing inner strengths at her own cut arm, Magda discovers potent control over maimed flesh. Both women's recovery enables them to attend a midwinter feast, a model of medieval banqueting, torchlight, music, and sword- and ring-dancing.

Notation in the family tree indicates sexual/marital ties:

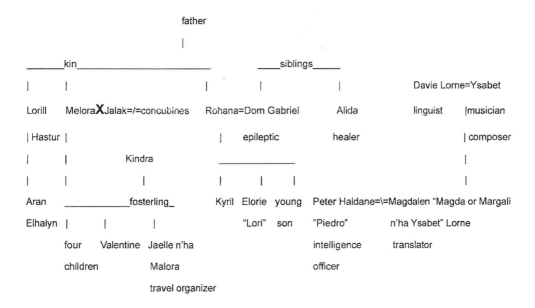

The narrative severs Magda's identity into thirds—the girl reared in Caer Donn under "straitlaced sexual taboos," the Terran linguist and spy among Darkovans, and the Free Amazon (Bradley, 1976, 221). Like academy graduates in Marion's *Survey Ship* and off-planet students in Orson Scott Card's *Ender's Game*, Magda missed the socialization of her peers while she trained off-planet in language and culture espionage. The intimacies of the midwinter festival in the Hellers district emphasize her alienation from a childhood home, but they clarify her indifference to Peter Haldane, her ex-husband. Magda activates the will "to know what I am to myself," a key tenet in Second Wave feminism (*Ibid.*, 227). While identifying personal wants and needs, she encourages Jaelle's romance with Peter and longs for the ideal one-world alliance with all planets.

The novel's moot conclusion contrasts the loyalties of married women with the oath-bound sorority of the Guild House, an alternative lifestyle to Comyn andro-centrism. As noted in Susan M. Shwartz's essay "Marion Zimmer Bradley's Ethic of Freedom" in *The Feminine Eye: Science Fiction and the Women Who Write It,* "For every gain, there is a risk; choice involves a testing of will and courage ... any attempt at change or progress carries with it the need for pain-filled choice" (Shwartz, 1982, 73). Jaelle's lengthy debate with Rohana draws out glimmers of regret for loving outsiders like Peter and Gabriel, whom Rohana shields from public curiosity the Dom's epilepsy. Both women accept compromise in exchange for affection and belonging.

Magda forms a triad with Jaelle and Rohana in conceding her fear of living among the Free Amazons and distaste for the angry outbursts of her son Kyril and Gabriel. Gravitating toward a new identity as an Amazon, Magda gains relief from a Terran job that denied her advancement and respect for her talents. By discussing feminist issues as Marion does in *The Ruins of Isis*, the three-woman colloquy airs secrets and hidden fears and desires, thus opening all three women to self-actualization and a relaxation of differences and prejudices between Terrans and Darkovans. In the estimation of analyst Susan Shwartz, the improvement "[enabled] them to become keepers of their own consciences and charters of their own course" (Shwartz, 1996, 102).

Sources

Bradley, Marion Zimmer. *The Shattered Chain*. New York: DAW, 1976.
Jones, Libby Falk. "Reading/Writing/Creating Feminist Utopian Communities," *Journal of Education* 172:1 (January 1990): 38–46.
Shwartz, Susan. "Marion Zimmer Bradley" in *St. James Guide to Science Fiction Writers*. New York: St. James Press, 1996.
_____. "Marion Zimmer Bradley's Ethic of Freedom" in *The Feminine Eye: Science Fiction and the Women Who Write It*. New York: Ungar, 1982, 73–88.
Vaughn, Sue Fisher. "The Female Hero in Science Fiction and Fantasy: 'Carrier-Bag' to 'No-Road,'" *Journal of the Fantastic in the Arts* 4:4 (1 January 1991): 83–96.

Sisterhood

A critical issue among females in Marion's fiction, the bonding of women gener-ates aspects of peace, mutual support, and affection through sisterhood, a source of strength among female mercenaries rescuing a sex slave in *The Shattered Chain* and the tie between Mikhail Aldaran's wife Deonara and his mistress Alciane in *Stormqueen!* Researcher Anne Kaler linked a mystic women's guild with the Beguines, a monastic society of Holland in the 1200s that introduced community nursing through the fellow-ship and collaboration of visiting healers, midwives, and nutritionists. Scholar Deborah L. Zanghi described the sodality as "something denied women in patriarchal literature and societies" (Zanghi, 1997, 31). The triad of friendship, fealty, and nonviolence safe-guards Nimue, the child postulant to Avalon in "The Pledged Word," shields animal protector Romilly "Romy" MacAran of the Sisterhood of the Sword in *Hawkmistress!*, and in "Bonds of Sisterhood," commits Camilla n'ha Kyria to Rafaella n'ha Doria during three days of lying in chains. For *Darkover Landfall,* the author dramatizes the emotional paralysis from a disaster in Lieutenant Camilla Del Rey's inability to weep for her beloved friend, Jenny MacAran, who dies mangled in a rocket ship crash. Pressed to perform professional duties, Camilla suppresses sorrow until a later time, when she can mourn without interruption.

Marion highlights the communion of females in times of need or terror. Communal affection welcomes Ellinor Wade and Paula Sandoval on the return flight from Darkover to Earth in "The Climbing Wave." For physician Helen Murray, Dr. Chao Lin's acceptance of day-old Robin Murray eases the mother's fears that her son may be euthanized before the spaceship *Starholm* leaves its layover on the green planet. By politely countering the angry proposals of Captain Merrihew to kill the boy, Lin reinforces Helen's choice to remain alone on the planet to raise her baby. The reinforcement patterns of these two examples display what critic Melinda Hughes calls "doubling … a woman-to-woman dyad in both books in order to show the potential for recognition of identity through positive sisterhood relations" (Hughes, 1993, 24).

SOCIAL SERVICES

Marion's bold, stout-hearted females rescue girls threatened by mother hunger, patriarchal fathers, and expedient marriages. Female counselors defy sexual predators as insidious as men who murder a female traveler and rape her corpse in the Lythande story "Somebody Else's Magic" and the Roman legionaries who rape and impregnate priestesses on the holy island of Mona in *The Forest House.* At a terrifying raid by Red Rian and his feral Scotti, the Irish priestess Caillean banishes them from harming her, Mairi, and Eilan, Celts whom she claims as siblings. Caillean asserts a feminist vow, "All women are my sisters," a common rallying cry in the author's writing (Bradley, 1993, 94). The sentiment returns during Eilan's initial vows to the Mother Goddess, which require the initiate to "treat every woman in this dwelling as your sister, mother and daughter, as your own kin" (*Ibid.,* 120). The camaraderie of other girls and women reduces the newness of cloistering and comforts Eilan at a signal change in her life. Her mentor Caillean reassures Eilan that "the Face of the Goddess [exists] in the face of every woman" (*Ibid.,* 167).

In an essay on J.R.R. Tolkien's *The Lord of the Rings,* Marion validated close relationships between people of the same gender and cited as an example the camaraderie of Sam and Frodo, which epitomizes the philosophies of Greek teacher Aristotle, Jewish sage Moses ben Maimon, and Muslim cleric al-Ghazali in their esteem for friendship as the greatest of human relationships. The concept of a lasting interpersonal commitment with the other self invests a story-within-a-story in the ballad Lythande sings in "Goblin Market." For siblings Domaris and Deoris in *The Fall of Atlantis,* mother hunger causes the sisters to turn to each other and to create a mother-daughter closeness, at times marred by jealousy and petulance. In *Hawkmistress!,* Orain, a considerate homosexual, retrieves fifteen-year-old Romilly "Romy" MacAran from a dangerous plan to dress as a boy and escape an awkward marriage. At the Sisterhood of the Sword hostel, Romy finds shelter, camaraderie with Lady Jandria Hastur, and strength in numbers.

The value of female unity continues in *Zandru's Forge* as swordswomen march on villainy. Typical of female confederates, Romy rewards the hostel staff with three sacks of bandage linen and jelly as first-aid for burns caused by clingfire, which the empathic Renata scrapes from the burned flesh of Dorilys. Romy's altruism and Renata's quick action testify to women's solicitude toward the wounded and sick.

WOMANLY TEAMWORK

The author's respect for female collaboration echoes Ursula Le Guin's salute to female collegiality in "Sur," a short story of an international women's team of expeditioners to the South Pole. In typical reactionary style, doubters of the exploration condemn it as insane or satanic, a lacklogic charge against female engagement as demonic. A similar censure of the birth mother in Marion's story "Women Only" elicits sympathy from nurses, who privately doubt the ethics of a syntho female conceiving a child by a human male. More poignant, in "Sea Wrack," Lythande, the mercenary lute player, cuts down a mermaid with her dagger before realizing that the two share a musical kinship: "The mermaid had called her 'Sister,' speaking to a womanhood renounced forever" (Bradley, 2013, 85). The instant empathy for the same gender illustrates Aristotle's concept of φιλία (*philía*, a friendship based on affection between equals), particularly the affinity Lythande shares with Frennet, the servant at the Hag and Swine in "The Walker Behind" and with candlemaker Eirthe in *The Gratitude of Kings*.

In contrast to Homer's focus on military might and courage, Marion follows the motifs of Euripides's Τρῳάδες (*Trōiades,* The Trojan Women) by venerating the kingdom's female strength. She expanded in *The Firebrand* on the variant needs of women during catastrophes. Social commentary on Princess Kassandra, a priestess of Apollo at Troy, results in twofold censure for association with the Amazons and for her prophetic ravings of doom. The creation of a female community enabled the author to focus on friendship and sisterhood as springboards to spirituality and, in the estimation of critic Hannah Nelson-Teutsch, to avoid the stereotype of females "exploring the power of their beauty and refinement while waiting for the menfolk to save the day" (Nelson-Teutsch, 2015). Because a siege engulfs Troy, Andromache wraps Kassandra in loving arms and soothes her frenzy, a divine madness that Andromache misinterprets. Despite their opposing perspectives on the future, the generous display of succor elevates the royal household shortly before its dissolution and the allotment of women as battle trophies.

The Lythande series allows the cross-dressing mercenary to bond with other females, such as Madam Myrtis the innkeeper, in secret without revealing her gender to others. In "Somebody Else's Magic," the suffering of a dying postulant from the Shrine of Laritha causes the wandering singer to break a vow to mind her own business. In "Sea Wrack," the beauty and naiveté of a sea-maiden weakens Lythande's intent to remain objective. To seal the fate of the mermaid who lures fishermen to their deaths on the rocks, Lythande stabs her mercilessly and sings a rowdy tavern ditty, leaving the stinking corpse on the beach. In a subsequent venture in "North to Northwander," the sounds of women enjoying "a cozy cafe" reminds the roving poseur that she once was female (Bradley, 2013, 183).

Arthurian Sisterhood

In Marion's *chef d'oeuvre, The Mists of Avalon,* an early fifth-century CE shuffling of influence and domains between Celts and Saxons stirs the relationships of four primary characters—Viviane, Igraine, Morgaine, and Gwenhwyfar. At the wedding of High King Arthur Pendragon at Caerleon, Morgaine, the king's half-sister, broadens the kinship she shares with Igraine and Gwenhwyfar, devotees of the Great Mother. In a salute to the earth deity, Morgaine concludes, "All women, indeed, are sisters under the Goddess" (Bradley, 1983, 285). The quartet, reduced by two after the deaths of Igraine and Viviane, varies in devotion, substituting where necessary Morgaine's disguise as a nun and Gwenhwyfar's fervor for the Christian Virgin Mary and her retreat into cloistering at Glastonbury.

Models of sisterly zeal counter ongoing disputes over the sanctity of Avalon and the overarching theocracy of Christians as represented by the hard-handed Archbishop Patricius (St. Patrick). On Pentecost morning, Morgaine refuses to take holy communion, but gently braids Queen Gwenhwyfar's hair and pins it into place before the sacred holiday. Morgaine insists that the queen "is as likely to do mine, or to lace my gown, as sisters do" (Bradley, 1983, 493). In agreement on womanly bemeficence, her aunt Morgause declares, "A woman must depend on the goodwill of other women" (*Ibid.,* 708). Arthurian specialist Barbara Ann Gordon-Wise, an English professor at Mount Saint Vincent University in Halifax, Nova Scotia, noted the ironic conclusion of a tragic saga: "While the companions and the Round Table have disappeared, it is the sisterhood on the Isle of Glastonbury which endures" (Gordon-Wise, 1991, 147).

See also The Forest House; The Gratitude of Kings; The Mists of Avalon; The Shattered Chain, Part I: Lady Rohana Ardais.

Sources

Bradley, Marion Zimmer. *The Complete Lythande.* San Francisco: Marion Zimmer Bradley Literary Works Trust, 2013.

_____. *The Forest House.* New York: Michael Joseph, 1993.

_____. *The Mists of Avalon.* New York: Ballantine, 1983.

Gordon-Wise, Barbara Ann. *The Reclamation of a Queen: Guinevere in Modern Fantasy.* New York: Praeger, 1991.

Hughes, Melinda. "Dark Sisters and Light Sisters: Sister Doubling and the Search for Sisterhood in *The Mists of Avalon* and *The White Raven*," *Mythlore* 19 (1993): 24–28.

Kaler, Anne K. "Bradley and the Beguines" in *Heroines of Popular Culture.* Bowling Green, OH: Bowling Green State University Popular Press, 1987.

Nelson-Deutsch, Hannah. "Nine Books That Have Subtle Feminist Sneak Attacks in Their Pages," https://www.bustle.com/articles/63025-9-books-that-have-subtle-feminist-sneak-attacks-lurking-in-their-pages (6 March 2015).

Smol, Anna. "Oh … Oh … Frodo!: Readings of Male Intimacy in *The Lord of the Rings*," *Modern Fiction Studies* 50:4 (Winter 2004): 949–979.

Zanghi, Deborah L. "An Exploration of Alternate Realities: Women's Contemporary Speculative Fiction," master's thesis, digital commons.brockport.edu, 1997.

The Spell Sword

The brief introduction to a Darkover trilogy, *The Spell Sword* precedes Marion's *The Forbidden Tower* and *The Bloody Sun* with information on expeditions from Earth to explore and map space colonies within a galactic empire. Cartographer Andrew Carr encounters the mysticism of Cottman IV after his survey plane crashes in crosswinds during a sleety storm over the Hellers mountains. Trapped by one ankle in twisted wreckage, "tearing skin and flesh ... cut to the bone," he has a vision of the Keeper Callista, a gauzy "fever dream" from the Overworld who directs him to escape the cold (Bradley, 1974, 3, 6). At the same time, matrix specialist Damon Ridenow leaves his job after dismissal by telepath Leonie Hastur. On his departure to Armida at the call of his kinswoman Ellemir Lanart, invisible forces ambush his party. The unseen waylayers slash Guardsman Reidel's throat, leaving Damon the only man alive. The killers depart to "the darkening lands uninhabitable to mankind," a Gothic aspect of the mystic planet that sets it apart from Earth (*Ibid.,* 43).

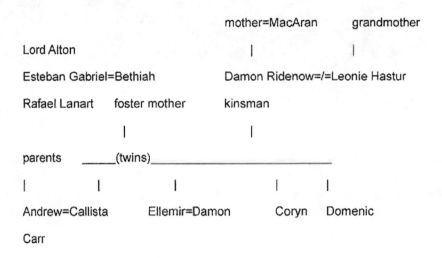

Marion packs the novel with maximum action and violence. At Damon's destination, Ellemir reports another assault and the seizure of her twin sister Callista from her room. The kidnappers leave her starstone behind. While Damon probes the murky Overworld to locate Callista, Andrew arrives to ask for aid and believes Ellemir is Callista. A third attack wounds Caradoc, Eduin, Istvan, and Esteban Gabriel Rafael Lanart, father of the twins. A spinal cut leaves Esteban a paraplegic, cheating the household of "the best swordsman and commander in all the Domains" (*Ibid.,* 50). Damon requests marriage to Ellemir, which Esteban allows. By equipping Damon with a matrix crystal in his sword hilt, Esteban enables him to mount a search for Callista and to ward off vicious catmen who "fell out of the air" (*Ibid.,* 51).

Much of Marion's plot hinges on the willingness and ability of characters to master telepathy and out-of-body travel, a surprising experience for Andrew. With the advice of Leonie, he teleports himself into the Caves of Corresanti to locate Callista. A battle with the Great Cat destroys the catman's magic while boosting Damon's self-confidence. On return to Armida, Callista ponders abandoning her position as Keeper of Arilinn to marry Andrew. For its romantic appeal, *The Spell Sword* appeared in French and Italian and two editions in German.

Sources

Bradley, Marion Zimmer. *The Spell Sword*. New York: DAW, 1974.
Kimmel, Leigh. "The Spell Sword," http://darkover.apiacoa.org/guide/books/sword/summary.en.html, 1999.
Mcintire, Elliot G. "Exploring Alternate Worlds," *Yearbook of the Association of Pacific Coast Geographers* 44:1 (1982): 93–108.
Muller, Al, and C.W. Sullivan. "Young Adult Literature: Science Fiction and Fantasy Series Books," *English Journal* 69:7 (October 1980): 71–74.
Watson, Ian. "*The Spell Sword*" by Marion Zimmer Bradley, *Foundation* (1 September 1978): 92.

Star of Danger

A YA introduction to the Darkover series, *Star of Danger* took a decade to write for its perusal of teen identity crises, family secrets, and interethnic relations. The popular story of the friendship between two sixteen-year-olds—Terran Larry Montray and Darkovan Kennard Alton—appears in French and in two German editions. Aboard the ship *Pantomime*, Larry arrives from Earth to the Darkover spaceport and learns about intercultural prejudices toward the "barbarian world" (Bradley, 1965, 9). Aided by skill at reading and writing the alien language, he shops for doughnuts in market stalls. At casual encounter with a Kyrri, one of the exotic beings in the rough part of Trade City, Larry collapses from the exotic being's electric force field.

While concealing Larry's Darkovan parent, Marion stresses the differences in the two cultures' manhood training, which requires sword skills in Darkover boys and first aid for Earth-borns like Larry. Larry's curiosity about human and non-human residents impels him from his Spaceport quarters to a blacksmith shop, one of many medieval details of Darkover life. The author introduces the concept of civil policing on the turf of a Trade City gang, where bully-boys attack Larry until two guards intervene and reduce ten against one to an even one-on-one fight, a principle of fairness that elevates planetary ethics.

The crux of the action, a friendship with Kennard, raises questions about Larry's ease in a strange place. He lends Kennard picture books on starships and photography. Ironically, Kennard is illiterate, yet familiar with the crossbow and gifted with *laran*. Against his father's command, Larry agrees to summer at the country estate of Armida to promote interplanetary relations with the ruling Altons. Larry is well versed in such technology as making rain by seeding clouds with silver diode, but he's disquieted by finding the body of the dying ranger Garin on the roadside and unfamiliar with treating the ranger with a powerful liquid and a blue jewel pressed to the forehead. Marion used the dramatic halt to the journey to introduce Larry to his own telepathy and that of Lord Valdir Alton. Valdir exonerated ESP by stating a diplomatic ideal: "Maybe if more Terrans and Darkovans could read each other's minds they'd understand one another better, and not be afraid of each other" (*Ibid.*, 11). The statement refers indirectly to the disparity in the two boys' forestry skills and experience with cautery and antibiotics, a pocket knife, fire-making, and orienteering.

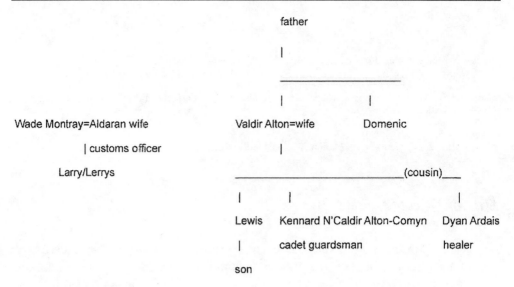

The narrative raises Kennard to the level of rescuer. On a trek through the mountains, the two boys fight wildfire. Kidnap and drugging by Cyrillon's raiders in the wintry backcountry leaves Larry helpless until Kennard frees him from the castle lock-up. Lost in the forest, they encounter first banshee birds, a trailman with a purulent wound, and Naradzinie the *chieri,* a clairvoyant humanoid who teleports them to the Montray home. At a peak of thematic significance, when the two boys intend to learn the history of Terra and Darkover, the story reminds the reader that "[a] civilization changes—or it dies" (*Ibid.,* 21), Marion's take on eras of insulation and ignorance.

Sources

Bradley, Marion Zimmer. *Star of Danger*. New York: Ace, 1965.
Breen, Walter. *The Darkover Concordance*. Houston, TX: Penny-Farthing Press, 1979.
_____. *The Gemini Problem: A Study in Darkover*. Baltimore: T-K Graphics, 1975.
Leith, Linda. "Marion Zimmer Bradley and Darkover," *Science Fiction Studies* 7 (1980): 28–35.

Stormqueen!

The second fantasy chronologically in an age of chaos, an early era of the Darkover series, Stormqueen! won a Locus sci-fi award and honorable mention for a Hugo, an annual recognition from the World Science Fiction Society. The novel, available in German and French, typifies the abuse of political dominance in struggles of the elite Aldarans two centuries after *Darkover Landfall* and two more before *Two to Conquer*. Begun like fairy tales that grace babies with special gifts, the epic opens at the Aldaran estate in the Hellers mountains in Lady Aliciane's birthing chamber, where, according to literary reviewer Dan Davidson for the *Whitehorse* (Yukon) *Daily Star*, "great families bred themselves like showdogs" (Davidson, 1981, 23).

Marion taps Gothic details for maximum suspense. On a stormy summer night, an "evil omen for the coming birth," fate bestows on the unborn infant Dorilys the hyper-magical power of laran, Marion's version of telepathy that provides heat, light, energy, and conveyance by elevator, glider, and aircar via the manipulation of matrix crystals (Bradley, 1978, 3). Bearers of the extrasensory prescience divine past and future, manipulate magnetic fields, or adapt lightning to their will, a threat equivalent to twentieth-century atomic power that introduces tragic results and losses to petty fiefdoms. Donal's widowed mother warns her ten-year-old to "use that gift only to save a life," an ironic comment coming from the woman who dies giving life to an infant already equipped with laran (*Ibid.*, 4).

```
                _____              _____              _____

                 |    Vardo   Rockraven  |                 |                          |
Clariza Leynier  |        |       |           |          Regis II      Dom Stephen Hastur
 |               |        |   Caryl          |            |                        |
 |  Deonara=Mikhail=Lady Aliciane   Lord Rakhal Aldaran   Felix    _____
 |        |      | of Rockraven   of Scathfell  |                    |              |
 |        |      | widowed harper               |                 Damon-Rafael   Allart=Cassilde
 |_____|_____|_____|       |                 of Elhalyn     Hastur  |Aillard-
                                                 |                 tormented monk and      |Hastur
 |        |         |            |        |       |                 heir to Thendara        son
three   stillborn  Donal Delleray=Dorilys=/=Darren
dead    sons       fosterling    Rockraven
```

For the backstory of Darkover, Marion groups patriarchal themes, from genetic diversity and parenting of sons to speciesism and the sources of bullying, enmity, and slaughter. The ruling class attempts to control *laran* with selective breeding, a failed system that produces unstable children who die young in both the Aldaran and Rockraven lineages. Written in 1978 during the Vietnam War about a feudal system, the narrative incorporates torture and dramatizes a generation gap in the midst of a reproductive revolution. To Lady Aliciane, the system of eugenics equals "[breeding] mankind like cattle for desired characteristics" (*Ibid.*, 5).

Dorilys's coming of age sets an example of oppositions—Age/Youth and, to a minor degree, Artificial/Natural and Rational/Intuitive. By age fourteen, she manipulates Darkover's electromagnetic field. Because youth has taught her nothing about self-restraint, Allart asks, "What are we to do with her?" (*Ibid.*, 98). Her foster brother Donal agrees that she must marry at an early age, a medieval suppression of women that removed them from a father's mastery to that of a husband. He hires Renata Leynier, an empath and monitor from Hali Tower, to control the effect of his sister/wife's tantrums on kingdom affairs. In deference to patrimony, the plot views the daughter's maturation and her threats to the vulnerable, Renata's main concern. On a broader plane, the application of psionics to clingfire leaves most Darkovans unshielded from possible annihilation, the author's allusion to the Cold War arms race, ballistic missiles, and napalm.

At the height of violence between dynasties that topples a tower, Marion views the all-out assault against Castle Aldaran from a medieval perspective, a style of tactical siege that J.R.R. Tolkien dramatizes in *The Lord of the Rings* in the face-off between Gondor and Sauron. The aura of belligerence contrasts Dom Stephen Hastur, a master of female breeders, with his son Allart, a tolerant *cristoforo* and reviled "sandal-wearer" whose scruples demand respect for females (*Ibid.*, 47). The most tragic figure, Dorilys bears both inheritance rights and a regrettable affliction that enables her to wreak havoc at will with the "brilliant white flare" that fells Darren for trying to rape her at their betrothal (*Ibid.*, 104). The plot contrasts the blitzkrieg death of Darren with the "healing-spell" that grips the castle (*Ibid.*, 254). Renata's magic intervention ferries Dorilys to the Overworld to view the disaster she has caused by smiting Donal. With the sobriety of a Greek chorus, the author surveys the death and interment of Dorilys at Hali to stress the subsequent millennia free of a wielder of instant doom.

Sources

Bradley, Marion Zimmer. *Stormqueen!* New York: DAW, 1978.
Davidson, Dan. "Paranoid Media Fantasye," *Whitehorse* (Yukon) *Daily Star* (11 December 1981): 23.
del Rey, Lester. "Review: *Stormqueen*," *Analog Science Fiction/Science Fact* 99:8 (August 1978): 173.
Leith, Linda. "Marion Zimmer Bradley and Darkover," *Science Fiction Studies* 7 (1980): 28–35.

Storytelling

Marion, like most fiction writers, valued oral narrative for its contributions to character and culture, a worthy trade-off in the confrontation of a Terran, a Darkovan, and Naradzinie the *chieri* in *Star of Danger* and in the catastrophe that strands Andrew Carr in *The Spell Sword*. In the opinion of Zambian essayist Carla Namwali Serpell, "Stories are one of our oldest technologies…. They give us a kind of perverse pleasure in reverse: not of seeing the worst come true, but of seeing the worst *without* it coming true" (Serpell, 2019, 15). Even adages carry the power of plot. In the introduction to *The Heritage of Hastur,* Regis parses the elements of "an old proverb: The mouse in the walls may look at a cat, but he is wise not to squeak about it" (Bradley, 1975, 4).

Marion applies a pro-narrative philosophy to the quest novel *Black Trillium,* the fairy tale *The Gratitude of Kings,* the ballad of sisterhood that Lythande sings in "Goblin Market," and the concepts she shares with the blind women of Jumathe in "Somebody Else's Magic." A parallel narrative, the tale of a raging dryad and the reports of alluring sea-maidens in "Sea Wrack" prove more sidebar than paradigm. At a tense moment in *The Forbidden Tower,* Callista's longer iambic harp song "What Sound Was That Upon the Moor" bears elements of Alfred Noyse's Gothic tragedy "The Highwayman." With similar control of suspense, Marion balanced visual with aural stimuli and rounded out the first two verses with the comforting solace, "Child, do not fear" (Bradley, 1977, 86). The admonition recurs in *The Shattered Chain* on the tense ride from Shainsa, when Kindra n'ha Mhari's mercenaries entertain twelve-year-old Jaelle n'ha Melora with stories and songs.

In a critique for the (New Brunswick) *Central New Jersey Home News,* reviewer Roland J. Green lauded Marion for "sheer skill in storytelling and wordbuilding, for wit, for strikingly intelligent development of the concept of telepathy, above all for continuous concern for people" (Green, 1982, D4). In "The Incompetent Magician," the magician-mercenary Lythande recalls an exemplum told to postulant Adepts about passing through stone walls. A failed Adept lost courage and ended his life "shrieking with pain" because his wavering confidence left him trapped, half in and half out, a terror that sci-fi author Octavia E. Butler reset in *Kindred* (Bradley, 2013, 26). For the wandering mage-minstrel, rumors about her sorcery and affairs with Myrtis the inn-keeper make for intriguing gossip, as did the split rule in the reigning family of Tschar-dain in "The Wandering Lute." Of the lute's provenance, Lythande urges the raconteur, "The night is young; long live the night. Tell on" (*Ibid.,* 89). At story's end, Lythande becomes the teller of how she obtained the lute, a swapping of roles that suggests that good listeners may become fascinating narrators.

RECOUNTING CULTURE

In the opening chapter of *The Forest House,* the elder teller declares the story of the House of Women a necessity: "That story must not be forgotten," a standard claim of folklorists worldwide (Bradley, 1993, 3). Expert Carol Patrice Christ, a feminist theo-logian and historian, warns that "if women's stories are not told, the depth of women's souls will not be known" (Christ, 1995, 1). A parallel cautionary tale by Celto-Roman boy Gaius Macellius's nurse warns him of forest dangers among the Celts of Britan-nia; his Silurian mother gave better instruction about the hospitality of Britons. At the Forest House, a rainy autumn turns the inmates to riddles, songs, and narrative of the mystic voyage of Bran, a mythic Irish quester to another realm. In the mode of Homer's *Odyssey,* Apollonius's *Argonautica,* and Virgil's *Aeneid,* Bran's daring exploration be-yond the known world comes at a price—never returning to Ireland or crumbling to dust on contact with native soil. The session concludes with "The King and the Three Hags." With a standard ploy, Dieda, the teller, opens the Samaine tale on better times, when people had greater access to the netherworld. One hearer compares the skillful telling to the recitals of Dieda's father, "one of the greatest bards" (Bradley, 1993, 161).

Embedded stories legitimize older-to-younger reclamation of past lore, as with Mother Lauria's story time for Cloris, Rafaella, Magda, and Janetta with "The Legend of Lady Bruna" in *Free Amazons of Darkover* and in Lady Rohana Ardais's singing of the origination poem "The Ballad of Hastur and Cassilda" in *The Shattered Chain.* For a more complex project, *The Firebrand,* the author introduces the elderly Kassandra's memories with a rebuke to the harper for perpetuating androcentric biases of the Trojan War in 1200 BCE. At the beginning of nuptials for Creusa and Aeneas, the appearance of Odysseus, the noted sea captain and brigand, promises engaging tales for the Trojan court. For a witty exchange in Andromache's discussion of childbirth with Kassandra, the new mother proposes overturning war stories and male-centered genealogies with "bards [making] ballads about the bravery of Hecuba, mother of Hector!" (Bradley, 1987, 185).

PARABLES AND ALLEGORIES

The author permeates plots with didactic dialogue in the form of stories. A par-able in *The Fall of Atlantis* speaks the love of fifteen-year-old Micail for his cousin, thirteen-year-old Tiriki. The wistful exemplum of a forest dweller awaiting the blos-soming of a passion flower illustrates to Tiriki her admirer Micail's willingness to await her maturity before initiating romance. With greater longing, former senator Hermes-Gabriel "Herm" Aldaran, a Darkover seer in *Traitor's Sun,* recalls particulars of the cautionary tale about an empire that precedes space travel. His relation of a nation that "had devoted itself to preparations for a war that never came" repeats a line from H.G. Wells's *The Research Magnificent* (Bradley, 1999, 12). Marion applies the lesson to the U.S. stockpiling of nuclear weapons, planes, submarines, satellites, and drones. She regrets that the nation endures dismemberment and bankruptcy and "collapsed into bits and pieces, by its own fear" (*Ibid.*). For the "complex political intrigue side-by-side with acute personal drama," *Library Journal* reviewer Jackie Cassada found the novel "both involving and intricate" (Cassada, 1999, 165).

Marion blended stock narrative with gynocentric reportage in *The Mists of Avalon*. At the start of Queen Igraine's "moon flux," she ponders the lot of the barren female, a motif of the story "Women Only," and wonders if Duke Gorlois of Cornwall may be at fault for their lack of a son (Bradley, 1983, 52). Her musings seize on the age-old anecdote about the old man's wife who lies with a shepherd to produce a long-awaited child, a ploy that influences Offred, the kept woman of Commander Fred, a sterile male in Margaret Atwood's dystopia classic *The Handmaid's Tale*. A surrealistic trance plunges Igraine into a cosmic survey of all time incorporating a string of legends and myths of Atlantis, Hy-Brasil, and the temple of the hunter Orion, a cult hero in Boeotia. Because of her fight with Gorlois and departure from London, harpers compose a ballad surmising that Igraine committed adultery. In a retelling, Morgause appears to substitute her sister for "the heroine of some old romantic tale" (*Ibid.*, 81). Viewing Marion as a "catalyst" for her reshaping of Arthurian stories with feminist telling, critic Marion Wynne-Davies declared the author's perspective "inevitable" (Wynne-Davies, 2016, 177). The radical restructuring "challenged the dominant male discourse of the legends" and made possible "more complex gendered reworkings" (*Ibid.*, 176–177).

Illustrative Story

The writer embeds subsequent yarns with mythic visions of the unfathomable—Lancelet's Welsh ballads of Queen Arianrhod ("Silver Wheel") and Blodeuwedd ("Flower-Faced"), the blossom woman, two mythic characters from the Mabinogion, an anthology of oral Celtic stories collected in Middle Welsh after 1100 CE. She gives to Taliesin the Merlin the tale linking Jesus, the "Nazarene prophet," with a school at Glass Town (Glastonbury) before fulfilling "the old Mystery of the Sacrificed God" (Bradley, 1983, 113). Merlin rounds out the story with the wonder tale of the staff that becomes a thorn tree and the erection of a chapel and monastery in Avalon, an otherworldly land removed from human access. The rendering inserts a brief Orphic myth about a Druidic bard who causes leaves to fall from tree limbs and ring stones to dance. The exemplum explains the dispensation to Orpheus to retrieve his wife Eurydice part way from the underworld. The motif repeats Genesis 19:26, the folk legend of Lot's wife, whom God transforms into a pillar of salt. Both settings emphasize the mortal punishment for disobedience of a divine command.

A myth from lunar lore exemplifies the use of Greek science stories to explain phenomena in nature. Avalon's postulants revere the moon, an icon of femininity and the female 28-day cycle. When the moon reaches "moon-dark," wisewomen explain that the Mother Goddess conceals her face while she consults with heavenly deities (*Ibid.*, 191). The meditation restores union with the Great Mother and rids priestesses of mundane thoughts. A more masculine coming-of-age tale explains why Achilles learned to spin and weave rather than go to war with the other Greeks. The claim that Archbishop Patricius (St. Patrick) drove serpents out of Ireland receives Morgaine's retooling as the symbolic expulsion of Druids, the "serpents of wisdom" (*Ibid.*, 769).

STORY AS BRITISH HISTORY

Marion inserts a story-within-a-story in a version of mythographer T.H. White's *The Sword in the Stone*. The legendary investiture of Arthur as heir to England's throne tumbles out with boyish enthusiasm for his first battle against Saxons. In league with his foster brother Cai/Caius, Arthur allows himself to be tricked into leaving the field to locate the sword of the former High King Uther Pendragon. Lying on a stone altar, the weapon seems useless to Arthur, who zealously plunges into warfare because of his advance from trainee to soldier. The commitment of foster father Ectorius and brother Cai astonishes the boy-king, but the author's second-hand retelling reduces a magic moment to a coming-of-age ritual.

At Arthur's eclipse as king in Camelot, Morgaine recalls Taliesin telling her the myth of Oedipus Rex, whose sin echoes that of the siring of Gwydion/Mordred at Beltane. Arthur's narration of the rape of Queen Boadicea's daughters by legionaries in 60 CE asserts to Gwenhwyfar the matriarchal basis of Celtic Britannia. Out of modesty, Lancelet mocks a song that circulates his "works and deeds … because the true tale is not exciting enough to tell by the fireside in winter" (*Ibid.*, 686). His self-effacing aside accounts for the value of oral lore, whether recited or sung, to entertain hearers while imparting the values and mystique of a nation.

At the "Great Magic" of Easter that prefaces the year-long Grail quest, Morgaine's transfiguration confuses viewers with its mystic light. Stories take shape from interpretations of the ray—an angel, a star, or the wine cup that served Christ at the Last Supper. Entries to Jesus's biography declare him the pupil of Druids and the foster son of Joseph of Arimathea, the planter of the Holy Thorn at Glastonbury. The sight of Nimue aiding Kevin Harper, a maimed musician, in packing his instrument recalls the original "Beauty and the Beast" legend, "La Belle et la Bête," a fairy tale completed in 1740 by Paris-born fiction writer Gabrielle-Suzanne Barbot de Villeneuve and rewritten as *Beauty* in 1978 by American fantasist Robin McKinley. The harper himself wishes he had the power of Orpheus, "that ancient bard who could play till the trees danced" (*Ibid.*, 785). The author turns the symbolism of the Fisher King into a parallel of the King Stag. Both represent the rise of majesty in a heroic monarch and the normal decline that accompanies age. Because Gwydion/Mordred's singing of the ballad startles Arthur, the harper turns to a rewriting of Isaiah 40:6–8 and the pervasive biblical image of withering grass, a metaphor of mortality.

See also The Shattered Chain, Part I: Lady Rohana Ardais.

Sources

Bradley, Marion Zimmer. *The Complete Lythande*. San Francisco: Marion Zimmer Bradley Literary Works Trust, 2013.
_____. *The Firebrand*. New York: Simon & Schuster, 1987.
_____. *The Forbidden Tower*. New York: DAW, 1977.
_____. *The Forest House*. New York: Michael Joseph, 1993.
_____. *The Heritage of Hastur*. New York: DAW, 1975.

_____. *The Mists of Avalon*. New York: Ballantine, 1983.
_____. *Traitor's Sun*. New York: DAW, 1999.
Cassada, Jackie. "Review: *Traitor's Sun*," *Library Journal* 124:1 (January 1999): 165.
Christ, Carol. *Diving Deep & Surfacing: Women Writers on Spiritual Quest*. New York: Beacon, 1995.
Green, Roland J. "'Hawkmistress' Continues Darkover Saga," (New Brunswick) *Central New Jersey Home News* (26 September 1982): D4.
Serpell, Namwali. "When Sci-Fi Comes True," *New York Times* (17 March 2019): 15.
Wynne-Davies, Marion. *Women and Arthurian Literature: Seizing the Sword*. London: Springer, 2016.

Survey Ship

Marion's warmly received young adult adventure novella *Survey Ship* anticipates futurist training to relieve overcrowding on Earth. The resulting space pilots for interstellar exploration travel the galaxy in search of habitable planets. From the age of five, 43 gifted cadets settle in Australia to focus on a twelve-year curriculum for the United Nations Expeditionary Planetary Survey covering agronomy, engineering, ESP, math and physics, navigation, meteorology, language, music, and surgery. On the day of the final cut from the original 100, students face a restless night pondering graduation to an elite corps aboard Survey Ship 103 representing "the United Nations—and Earth" (Bradley, 1980, 4). Later in the action, Hispanic psychologist Fontana summarizes intense training as brainwashing, a denigration questioning the loss of humanity from too much theory.

The narrative, which reviewer Dani Zweig typifies as "soft science fiction," identifies the cast by catchy in-house nicknames—Fly, Mei Mei, Huff, Zora, Jimson (Zweig). The crew members—South African physician David "Peake" Akami, Scots ship driver Ellen "Moira" Finlayson, James "Teague" McTeague, Ching, Fontana, and Ravi—dull the fear of failure with meditation, snappy humor, musical ensembles, ham sandwiches, flirting, a jacuzzi romp, and casual sex. Action reveals situational weaknesses, stressing Ching's isolation as the wonder child of technology. The introduction of variant family backgrounds, psychic powers, and heterosexual and homosexual pairing individualizes cadets, especially Ravi, a mystic philosopher from India's weaving caste; clairvoyant Moira; the homosexual Peake, who suffers angst at his separation from his lover Jimson; and Ching, the genetically engineered "human computer" and lonely oddball (*Ibid.*, 7).

In answer to the rhetorical question "How do you make a spaceman?," the author opens with a prologue musing on children, their physical and intellectual talents, and their introduction to lifetime careers as demanding as chess, ballet, trapeze, and space exploration (*Ibid.*, 1). In a perusal of teen foibles, she reveals the gawky, long-legged stage and resultant diffidence in immature youth. The team's physical gracelessness parallels emotional anomalies, particularly suspicion and paranoia about who is chosen and who passed over. Side issues of the validity of homosexuality in an all-male crew open discussions of the psychology of intimacy. In the final analysis of success or failure, Teague asserts a 50–50 chance: "Whatever way we go, we are equally likely, or unlikely, to find a good planet, or not to find one" (*Ibid.*, 49).

The theme of teamwork in lieu of adult supervision, the dominant concept in Orson Scott Card's *Ender's Game* series, glimpses the emergence of pragmatisms and leadership among teenagers. In a claustrophobic environment, the crew opts for Greenwich Mean Time vs. Universal Solar and enjoys body flips in a weightless cabin. Through trial and error, the team manages life support despite vehicle problems with a demagnetizer, a motif the novel shares with Marion's groundbreaking *Darkover Landfall*. The sudden din of collision with a meteor summons crew in training simultaneously with emergency alarms that test individual aptitude for quick solutions to deadly problems. Keith Roysdon, a book critic for the *Muncie* (Indiana) *Evening Press* admired the novella for its interplay of strong characters endowed with brilliance, compassion, and the standard youthful immaturity. The novel appeared in German and Portuguese.

See also Ambition.

Sources

Bradley, Marion Zimmer. *Survey Ship.* New York: Ace, 1980.
Roysdon, Keith. "Good Female Writers Abound in Science Fiction Category," *Muncie* (Indiana) *Evening Press* (14 November 1981): T8.
Zweig, Dani. "Review: Marion Zimmer Bradley," https://www.users.cs.york.ac.uk/susan/sf/dani/PS_017.htm.

The Sword of Aldones

A finalist for the 1963 Hugo award, *The Sword of Aldones* features Marion's favorite character, matrix mechanic Lew Alton, in a clash of powermongers fighting to recover the stolen matrix of the fire demon Sharra. The plot opens on a familiar motif, the reunion of an expatriate with the anti-technological milieu of Thendara, a spaceport on Cottman IV. Exposition simplifies the contrast between imperialistic wars on Terra and the one-on-one *code duello* of Darkover, where side arms—"power—or—propulsion—weapons—guns—disintegrators—or—blasters—atomic—isotopes…—or incendiaries" are contraband (Bradley, 1962, 8). In the estimation of critic Don D'Ammassa, the author gave "more emphasis on subtle shifts in alliances and the clash of cultures than in overt adventure" (D'Ammassa, 2013).

Almost immediately, Lew's involvement in a grudge match with Robert Kadarin introduces an unsettled antagonism, the energizer of Marion's plot.

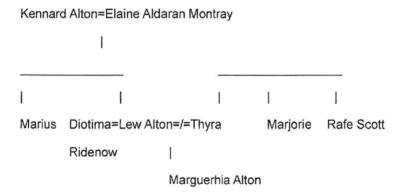

Kennard Alton=Elaine Aldaran Montray

Marius   Diotima=Lew Alton=/=Thyra   Marjorie   Rafe Scott
           Ridenow |
           Marguerhia Alton

In fast-paced action set in the late 21st century, Lew travels with the heirloom Sharra matrix, a precious "hunk of dull metal laced with little ribbons of shinier metal, and starred with a pattern of blue winking eyes" (*Ibid.*, 26). His daring transport of a lethal source of power precedes a roadway attack and theft by Karadin, who murdered Lew's brother Marius. The author tempers spurts of fury with the introduction of Lew to Marguerhia, his "unexpected daughter" conceived with Thyra during a drugged state (*Ibid.*, 62).

In one of Marion's most protracted struggles, Lew frees himself of the seductress Thyra and the fire demon. The restoration of Marguerhia and her appetite symbolize the resurgence of life and hope. In a melodramatic resolution, the story depicts the pull of family over power in Lew, who chooses to marry Dio and adopt Marguerhia. He exiles himself "the farther, the better" from the empire (*Ibid.*). In the author's advance to *Sharra's Exile,* the tangle of relationships and politics earned a rebuke from Keith Roysdon of the *Muncie* (Indiana) *Evening Press*: "It is just a bit too complex for me, and I couldn't tell the players even with a scorecard" (Roysdon, 1981, T8). Bill Williams, an editor on staff at the *Northwest Arkansas Times,* compared the novel to *The Planet Savers,* which he deemed "a fine study of life in a very alien community" (Williams, 1976, 10C).

Sources

Bradley, Marion Zimmer. *The Sword of Aldones.* New York: Ace, 1962.
D'Ammassa, Don. *Encyclopedia of Science Fiction.* New York: Facts on File, 2013.
Roysdon, Keith. "Good Female Writers Abound in Science Fiction Category," *Muncie (Indiana) Evening Press* (14 November 1981): T8.
Williams, Bill, ed. "Two Darkover Tales," *Northwest Arkansas Times* (5 December 1976): 10C.

Thendara House

A sequel to the rescue romance *The Shattered Chain* and the second in the three-part *The Saga of the Renunciates,* Marion's *Thendara House* follows the aims and misgivings of Terran linguist and spy Magdalen "Magda" Lorne and Darkovan travel coordinator Jaelle n'ha Melora, both of whom seek altered paths of self-expression. Critic Walter Breen typified the theme as "Man divided," an internal strife between origin and life story (Breen, 1975, n.p.). The narrative stresses isolation among individuals whom events alienate from their true personae, a difficulty for Magda while she surveys Darkovan customs at the collective known as the Guild House, an offshoot of the Sisterhood of the Sword. The same dilemmas afflict Jaelle during employment among Terrans at the Spaceport, which Marion describes in *The Bloody Sun* as "the clean, white, sterile world of the Terran Trade City" (Bradley, 2003, 12). The factory atmosphere exemplifies a techno-conspiracy by Planetary Investments Unlimited, the gargantuan eco-destroyer introduced in *The World Wreckers.*

Essential to each race's study of the other, the few who have "gone native" live among aliens and learn the slang, dress code, and behaviors, especially toward the opposite gender (Bradley, 1983, 71). Such incursions within boundaries intensify alienation, causing the motherless Jaelle n'ha Melora, the child of rape by the Dry Town brute Jalak of Shainsa, to think "I have never belonged anywhere except among my sisters in the Guild House" (*Ibid.*, 73). In extreme situations, she envisions the convent as a possible safety zone—a "walled building, windowless and blind to the street" (*Ibid.*,

18). The motif of the women's retreat supplied Marion with a Celtic learning and life development center that recurred a decade later in *The Forest House,* set around 80 CE during the Roman occupation of Britannia. Of the historical matriarchy, she stated in *The Forest House,* "Every culture without exception seems to have had shamanesses or healing sisterhoods ... even in the Middle Ages.... Women choosing to opt out of their society were allowed to go into convents" (Bradley, 1993, 13). She championed reformers Clare of Assisi and Teresa of Avila for revolutionizing the penitential atmosphere of abbeys that welcomed unattached females.

In Darkover, the mother house offers training in hand-to-hand combat as well as barn labor, gardening, sewing, cooking, management, medical care, midwifery, "farriery, metalworking and forging, veterinary medicine, dairying, cheesemaking, animal husbandry or bootmaking" (Bradley, 1983, 41). As a shelter for endangered females, the Guild House provides an all-female group shelter as well a source of mystical soul searching. Postulants profit from a boost to self-esteem, an issue for Keitha n'ha Casilda, the abused wife of Shann MacShann, and Byrna, who gives birth to a son with the aid of the monastic sisterhood, a counter force to chivalric brotherhood that the author continues in *Warrior Women.* Within the tight restrictions of the charterhouse, Magda feels alone and scorned for violating a rule of sword fighting by threatening to kill MacShann's henchman, who crouches in surrender pose. Marion describes Lauria as the mother superior and settler of infractions of house rule, but Rafaella n'ha Liriel carries significant authority among the women she bullies and taunts, including her own daughter Doria. The querulous classes and study sessions become unbearable to Magda, who exists under constant tension while concealing her ethnicity as a Terran.

Marion developed belonging into a controlling theme for both Magda and Jaelle, who suffer homesickness and self-doubt. For Magda, an official Guild House scolding for fighting a man after he dropped his sword derives from stern rules among Amazons about murder. Like Sophocles's tragic heroine Antigone, Magda must sort out her loyalties to self and country as well as to the Amazon sorority. For Jaelle, complicated social rules undermine her marriage to Peter "Piedro" Haldane, a Terran who treasures her less as an equal partner in wedlock more as a female possession and possible producer of a son. The concept of unbending strictures in each situation exasperates the protagonists, causing Jaelle to quarrel with Peter about balance in wedlock and Magda to recoil from the staunch warrior Camilla n'ha Kyria and Rafaella's harsh words about violating the *code duello.* The anxiety among Amazons and postulants illustrates that the formula for guiding a coterie of needy women has the potential to denigrate and vilify volunteers who retire to the sisterly hermitage for spiritual uplift and protection.

See also Sisterhood; *Thendara House;* Genealogy.

Sources

Bradley, Marion Zimmer. *The Bloody Sun.* New York: Ace, 1964.
_____. *The Forest House.* New York: Michael Joseph, 1993.
_____. *Thendara House.* New York: DAW, 1983.
_____. *A World Divided.* New York: DAW, 2003.
Breen, Walter. *The Gemini Problem: A Study in Darkover.* Baltimore: T-K Graphics, 1975.
Kaler, Anne K. "Bradley and the Beguines" in *Heroines of Popular Culture.* Bowling Green, OH: Bowling Green State University Popular Press, 1987.

Raddeker, Hélène Bowen. "Eco/Feminism and History in Fantasy Writing by Women," *Outskirts* 21 (November 2009).

Rogers, Michael. "Classic Returns," *Library Journal* 120:12 (1 July 1995): 128.

Thendara House Genealogy

A decade after *The Shattered Chain,* the tangled interrelations of Marion's Darkover series raise issues of kinship. In *Thendara House,* characters accept resultant responsibilities to orphaned and fostered children, particularly for Lord Lorill Hastur's cousin Melora Aillard. Implications of foster brother Kyril's incestuous rape of Jaelle n'ha Melora reveals violations of social and clan taboos. Notation in the family tree indicates sexual/marital ties:

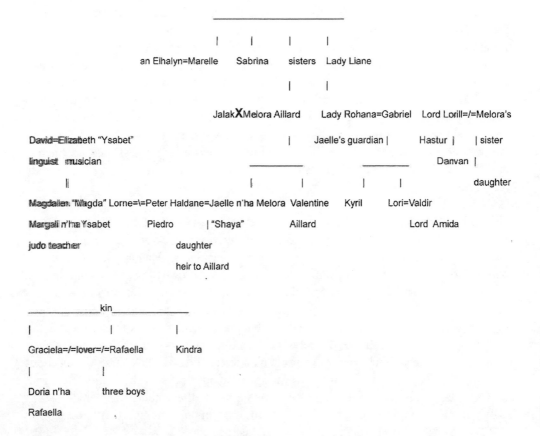

Literary analysts stress the author's interest in fostering, an issue in *The Firebrand, The Forest House,* and *The Mists of Avalon,* as well as her concern for pregnant women like Jaelle, who have no urge to mother their young. For both situations, the author highlights choice, the feminist byword, as the height of rational decisions governing birth children and voluntary parenting.

Sources

Bradley, Marion Zimmer. *Thendara House*. New York: DAW, 1983.
Breen, Walter. *The Darkover Concordance*. Houston, TX: Penny-Farthing Press, 1979.
_____. *The Gemini Problem: A Study in Darkover*. Baltimore: T-K Graphics, 1975.
Rogers, Michael. "Classic Returns," *Library Journal* 120:12 (1 July 1995): 128.

Thendara House Part One, Conflicting Oaths

The author spotlights elements of disparate cultures by having two women, a Terran and a Darkovan, swap places. A researcher of slang, idioms, and jokes at Thendara, Magdalen "Magda" Lorne, posing incognito, excels at a job she abandons, leaving it to fellow Free Amazon Jaelle n'ha Melora. Factory supervisor Cholayna Ares assigns Magda to liaise between the new Terran medical department and potential Darkovan trainees. On Jaelle's first day taking Magda's place in the Trade City factory, Marion satirizes the technology and practicality of synthetic meals, disposable tunics and cups that dissolve down the drain, and machines that assess Jaelle's blood and teeth. By observing Jaelle scripting her adventures on the expedition to Sain Scarpa, the reader acquires a summary of action from the prequel, *The Shattered Chain*.

To make a case against me-centered husbands, the author dredges up the sulky, ogerish tyrant Peter Haldane, a stereotypical feminist target found in two nonfiction accounts, Faith McNulty's *The Burning Bed* and Betty Mahmoody's *Not Without My Daughter*. Harsh commands from Peter attest that the loving suitor has turned into Jaelle's controlling mate. For gendered reasons, he also resents ex-wife Magda's promotion to head of the Terran Intelligence Department. His egotistic murmurings of "My flesh. My woman. My son, immortality … mine, mine, mine" echo the rumblings of the misogynist Duke locked into greed and self-adulation in Robert Browning's narrative poem "My Last Duchess" (Bradley, 1983, 56). In the case of both Peter and the Duke, possessiveness in husbands destroys hopes for a loving union.

A WOMAN'S WORLD

Overall, Marion finds misogyny among both cultures to the detriment of both male and female contentment and industrial advancement. Her text disdains female servitude to males of any status and defames verbal battery of consorts for failure to anticipate their husbands' wants and aims. She details androcentric demands on Jaelle for uxorious service to Peter's libido, hygiene, and wardrobe, including dressing him for an evening out. The tyrannic male's behaviors foreshadow a major conflict between women and the men whose faults lurk "at the very depths and foundation of the masculine self" (*Ibid.,* 57). Despite Marion's precise dramatization of macho surliness, she earned from Susanna J. Sturgis, a writer for the *Vineyard Gazette,* and other feminist critics absolution of the epithet "man-hater."

Marion's energetic prose intersperses individual women's stories and personalities among the Darkovan and Terran protagonists, who each study the other's ethnicity. By introducing Keitha n'ha Casilda, a badly mauled Darkovan, and male gossips in the spaceport cafeteria, the text resumes the author's crusade against abuse of girls and women by deed or gossip. The narrative revisits the issue of properly addressing a

Renunciate by avoiding patronyms and satirizes the choice of "girl" to diminish a woman's maturity and significance (*Ibid.*, 67). A major glitch in the company hierarchy places a know-nothing, Russell "Russ" Montray, in charge of intelligence work. Repeated screw-ups sharpen the author's derision of office politics and the rise of fools to supervisory positions. Even Russ's son, Wade "Monty" Montray, recognizes the lame choice of Russ as liaison between Terra and the Cottman IV culture, which Russ openly mocks and despises.

SYSTEMS OF GOVERNANCE

During question and answer sessions in which Jaelle prepares agent Alessandro "Aleki" Li for spying on Darkover, Marion risks boring readers with a tedious explanation of governmental structures—Cottman IV, Comyn, Hastur—and the rise of feudalism. Key to the discussion is *laran*, an inborn precognition and ability to read minds, psychic perceptions available only to the elite Darkovan. Pacing of the action eases apprehensions with humor at Jaelle's flight from the technological beauty parlor. The somber atmosphere returns to her terror of becoming her husband's "valet, comrade-in-arms, personal servant, breeding-anima," the beginning of a marital schism (*Ibid.*, 109). In a demonstration of the dangers of operating a safe haven for women and children, Marion depicts the reaction of males to monastic life in a convent, which smirky visitors equate with lesbianism. In a later scene, Camilla, a neutered Amazon, regrets "that is the true horror of all our stories, that some men, hearing them would think them almost funny" (*Ibid.*, 123).

Threats of capture and violence constantly stalk Marion's protagonists. The burly, angry Shann MacShann and his hired bruisers at the door of the Guild House demand possession of Keitha n'ha Casilda, a runaway victim of battery. The author excels at the standard caricature—the oversized, loudmouth mate who is certain a paltry wife can't suffice without him. By picturing armed Amazons in action, the sword fight at the front steps proves why men hate and suspect able-bodied women, who overcome tormentors and leave one dead. The scene, according to Irish critic Linda Leith, follows a pattern of "quick to anger and quick to relent," a scenario that morphs into legend in *The Forbidden Tower* (Leith, 1980, 34). In a show of honor and integrity, Camilla insists on compensating the men for their loss, Marion's representation of Amazon ethics.

Sources

Bradley, Marion Zimmer. *Thendara House.* New York: DAW, 1983.
Jaffrey, Sheldon. *Future and Fantastic Worlds.* Rockville, MD: Borgo, 2007.
Leith, Linda. "Marion Zimmer Bradley and Darkover," *Science Fiction Studies* 7 (1980): 28–35.
Tetreault, Mary Ann. "Review: *Thendara House,*" *Minerva* 3:3 (30 September 1985): 89.
Williams, Lynn F. "Everyone Belongs to Everyone Else: Marriage and the Family in Recent American Utopias 1965–1985," *Utopian Studies* 1 (1 January 1987): 123–136.

Thendara House Part Two: Sundering

Marion returns the sci-fi plot from Cottman IV to the universal quandaries of coming of age. In retrospect of love at first sight, Jaelle n'ha Melora recognizes her faulty rationale for falling in love as "a delayed adolescent in the grip of her first infatuation"

(Bradley, 1983, 135). Marion gentles the unbearable tone of the first stave with pity toward both Jaelle and her husband, Peter "Pedro" Haldane, for their marital incompatibility. A bit of praise for Magda's command of judo raises her spirits and gains respect from other novices. In the author's rhythmic pacing of emotion at the guild hall, Errol's permanent custody of his infant son leaves Byrna distraught and the sisterhood helpless to console her grief. The downward turn of atmosphere overwhelms Magda amid an elated dinner table celebration of Jaelle's visit.

Marion outlines the dilemma that precipitates Magda's nightmares and hysteria. Magda is a psychological anomaly—"too much Darkovan to be Terran, too much Darkovan ever to be happy in the Terran Zone," an incongruence without an obvious solution (*Ibid.*, 165). The situation reveals a weakness in the guild system, a regimentation that lacks empathy for the individual who doesn't fit the mold of the Free Amazon. In a critique, Welsh analyst Jo Walton blames "a Galactic Empire run by rigid 1950s bureaucrats" for the malaise that later grips Magda and Jaelle, both in different roles at the spaceport (Walton, 2010). Irish critic Linda Leith characterizes a more personalized struggle from the individuals' attempts to "reconcile the opposites in [themselves]" and to accept "their own often complex sexuality," a reference to Magda's bisexual leanings (Leith, 1980, 29, 30).

The lengthy discussion of gender issues by guild inmates enables Marion to align arguments pro and con against men and their bent for possessing women and pride in siring sons. The past sufferings of sisters emerge in harsh criticism, rage, loss, laughter, and the urge to kill. Magda's psi capabilities admit drifting thoughts into her head from other minds and reveal that any woman, regardless of her circumstances, can suffer estrangement. The return to the business of training sisters at a Terran factory resumes the motif of heightened character assessment. A rough evening of philosophical debate generates bad dreams and bloody night phantasms, which Magda links to the onset of menstruation.

The narrative deluges Jaelle with a welter of sensations, indicators of the Darkovan's ability to read minds. Among the messages, she recovers evidence of a Terran spy plane that crashed into a ravine in Armida outside the Trade Zone. During examination of the remains, Coordinator Russell "Russ" Montray demeans the intelligence and integrity of the local discoverers. He intends to conceal the purpose of fly-overs and the significance of the wreckage and flight recorder, which Darkovans value as scrap metal. In contrast, Lord Danvan Hastur, Jaelle's Darkovan kinsman, maintains nobility and a sense of courtesy and honor based on civility that Russ Montray lacks. In a display of arrogance, the coordinator snarls that he "didn't bow down to feudal lords from any damned pre-space culture" (Bradley, 1983, 210). The gibe contains the core conflict between techno-proud earthlings and the intuitive tribes of Darkover.

Marion dramatizes Magda's lesbian tendencies and Jaelle's long coming of age and her stubborn rejection of birth obligations to the Aillard dynasty. When the Amazons volunteer to fight a forest blaze on Alton land, Magda suffers burned feet. More painfully, she battles ambivalence toward women who love women, especially Camilla. The disorderly genealogy of Aillards links Jaelle and her unborn daughter to a grand heritage. Peter's reversion to macho attitudes arouses hysteria in Jaelle to the point she considers withdrawal from wedlock to the Guild House. The break in her loyalty to marriage and to spaceport employment accounts for Marion's use of "sundering" as a subtitle.

Sources

Bradley, Marion Zimmer. *Thendara House*. New York: DAW, 1983.
Breen, Walter. *The Gemini Problem: A Study in Darkover*. Baltimore: T-K Graphics, 1975.
Leith, Linda. "Marion Zimmer Bradley and Darkover," *Science Fiction Studies* 7 (1980): 28–35.
Walton, Jo. "'Where Did He Belong?': Marion Zimmer Bradley's *The Bloody Sun*," (3 March 2010): ttps://www.tor.com/2010/03/03/qwhere-did-he-belongq-marion-zimmer-bradleys-lemgthe-bloody-sunlemg/.

Thendara House Part Three: Outgrowth

In the novel's culmination, Marion continues to use the narrative as a means of scrutinizing social issues. At Midsummer, the Amazon midwives debate the ethics of letting a weak baby die or saving it, even though it is a poor specimen of its race and a questionable addition to the gene pool. At the boot shop in the market place, Magda debates with Wade "Monty" Montray the training of boys and girls under gendered expectations that boys like trucks and girls like dolls. Her acquiescence to seduction by Monty, then to bedding by Camilla forces Magda to assess evident bisexuality. A survey of effeminate men at the Midwinter dance reassures her that men can flirt with girls and also love their own gender.

Like the conventions of Western walkdowns on Main Street in the films *High Noon* and *The Outsider*, Marion turns a Midwinter ball into an explosive face-off between adversaries. The arrogant, bumfuzzled Russell Montray pulls rank on his employees and challenges the elegant Darkovan Dom Ann'dra Carr, whom characters suspect of being a renegade Terran named Andrew Carr. Escaping from the emotional melee to a street celebration, Amazons dance with local men and drink too much, two proofs that matriarchal women have normal weaknesses. In a drunken state, Peter tries to reunite with Magda, who again rejects him. The mix of confused loyalties with alcohol ends the holiday with individual regrets.

Marion compresses the final action into layers—galloping on horseback to rescue ambassador Alessandro "Aleki" Li from a dangerous snowstorm and the intrusive, yet reassuring mind reading that disconcerts Magda. In a cave, she grapples with mental torment, cold, and exposure to save Jaelle during a miscarriage. The rescue of both women by Andrew Carr and his associates restores harmony to a cast of distinctive personalities and raises hope that a more equitable, inclusive society is possible. Marion rids Jaelle of the curse of baby hating and offers another chance at motherhood, this time with Damon Ridenow. Unfortunately, in the grand finale, the author's admixture of self-discovery, mind reading, and women's and gay rights burdens the narrative with overwritten polemics, a frequent criticism of her fiction.

Sources

Bradley, Marion Zimmer. *Thendara House*. New York: DAW, 1983.
Raddeker, Helene Bowen. "Feminism and Spirituality in Fantastic Fiction: Contemporary Women Writers in Australia," *Women's Studies International Forum* 44 (1 May 2014): 154–163.
Tolmie, Jane. "Medievalism and the Fantasy Heroine," *Journal of Gender Studies* 15:2 (2006): 145–158.
Williams, Lynn F. "Everyone Belongs to Everyone Else: Marriage and the Family in Recent American Utopias 1965–1985," *Utopian Studies* 1 (1 January 1987): 123–136.
_____. "The Machine at Utopia's Center," *Utopian Studies* 3 (1 January 1991): 66–71.

Traitor's Sun

Marion orchestrated a turning point in Darkover politics with *Traitor's Sun,* her last published work before her death. Concluding the trilogy begun by *Exile's Song* and *The Shadow Matrix,* the novel, co-authored by Adrienne Martine-Barnes, extends a dominant motif of Terran imperialism and guile versus Darkoveran wielding of psi powers to suppress high-tech weapons that cost "trillions of credits … disbursed every year to create new technologies" (Bradley, 1999, 3). The action opens on diplomat Herm Aldaran's ominous dream of a time of "wariness and paranoia" and a major power shift following the disabling of ruler Regis Hastur from stroke after his handling of the fabled Sword of Aldones (*Ibid.,* 6).

Completing the novel in late 1998, nine months before her death, the author depicted a fictional era marked by constant surveillance, travel restrictions, and vast sums invested in a superfluous "fleet of dreadnaughts" (*Ibid.,* 3). The saga's details echo a period of real world plight over thermonuclear tests in India, wars in Kosovo and the Congo, embassy bombings in Kenya and Tanzania, a massacre of babies and adults in Algeria, Pakistan's underground missile tests, and Saddam Hussein's arming of Iraq. In the novel, enemies of Cottman IV use Regis's state funeral and its passage to holy ground at *rhu fead* as an opportunity to attack and overthrow the ruling Comyn via a murky combination of "military dominance and oppression" (Bradley, 1999, 2).

Some 35 years after the World Wreckers assaulted Darkover, the author pairs unusual methods of expressing opinion, for example, Kate Alderan's belief in the goddess Birga, deity of crafts. Kate asserts that "each person has a purpose, or more than one, and that we are obligated to discover what that is" (*Ibid.,* 75). Essential to security, telepathic messaging enables security guard Nico Hastur to warn his grandfather, former senator Lew Alton, of insurgents posing as a traveling troupe of puppeteers, a subtle satire of world tyranny. The stage show mirrors the cabal of Terrans, who hope to quell Darkoveran threats to reduce the planet to peonage.

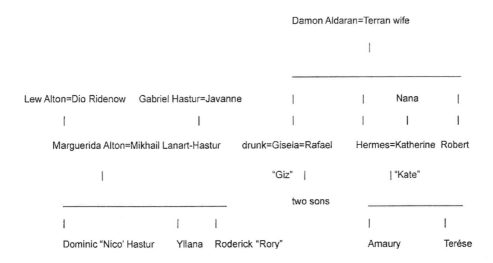

The stage play rids the coterie of menace by linking the propagandist Mathias with an innocent puppet van, a peripatetic entertainment for children that parks at old

Tanner's Field by the North Gate. Instead of the usual road show, however, the puppet play voices unseemly dialogue and rude denigration of Regis Hastur bordering on obscenity.

Cooperation between Nico and Senator Herm Aldaran plus intel from Captain Rafe Scott and advice from puppeteer Illona Rider disclose the conspiracy of station chief Lyle Belfontaine, a corrupt Terran climber, to turn the funeral cortege into a debacle. He "wanted to be the man who destroyed Cottman's Protected status and brought them into the Federation" (*Ibid.,* 40). He intends the assault to preface civil war and his rise to governor of the planet. The author extends the motif of cooperation in a band of Darkoveran opponents, who foil the Terran plot by destabilizing each attacker's confidence. In a show of mystic intervention, the story inserts a ghost—Regis returned from the Overworld to the planet to insist on his choice of Mikhail for the next ruler.

At the core of the culture war, Marion stresses the value of psychic energy, a peaceful means of guiding Darkover away from tyranny toward democracy and peace. Mikhail and his wife Marguerida unleash nonviolent matrix powers to shield the ruling family at Comyn Castle from assassination and to oust Terrans from their Darkover spaceport at Thendara. Even with laran intervention, the story erupts into gory face-to-face skirmishes on the Old North Road marked by "the twang of bowstrings and a flight of arrows," a medieval face-off (*Ibid.,* 208). By blurring recall of the events in Terran minds, Lew and daughter Marguerida rid Cottman IV of intrigues by the Terran federation. William Marden, reviewer for the *Orlando Sentinel,* framed the story with a single rhetorical question: "Can a small planet of technologically backward humans who have evolved strange mental powers stand against the might of a scientifically advanced empire intent on destroying its way of life?" (Marden, 1999, F9). Jeff Zaleski, a book critic for *Publishers Weekly,* offered a mixed review chastising Marion for "repetition and glacial pace," but praised characters for their "warm, humanistic values" (Zaleski, 1998, 61).

See also Ritual.

Sources

Bradley, Marion Zimmer. *Traitor's Sun.* New York: DAW, 1999.
Cushman, Carolyn. "Review: *Traitor's Sun,*" *Locus* 457 (February 1999).
D'Ammassa, Don. "Review: *Traitor's Sun,*" *Science Fiction Chronicle* 20:4 (February/March 1999): 43.
Marden, William. "Bradley Delves into Future of Planet Known as Darkover," *Orlando Sentinel* (28 March 1999): F9.
Zaleski, Jeff. "Review: *Traitor's Sun,*" *Publishers Weekly* 245:50 (14 December 1998): 61.

Treachery

Marion rated betrayal as a heinous sin and demonstrated her repugnance in a court scene in *The Forbidden Tower* in which Desiderio Leynier, guilty of "cold-blooded, fiendish murder" of his brother Domenic, tries to steal power from his brother-in-law Andrew Carr (Bradley, 1977, 184). In such theatrical situations, the author corroborated the ethics of Dante Alighieri of Florence, whose early Renaissance moral epic *Inferno* confined violators of trust, friendship, kinship, guests, and homeland to the ninth and last circle of hell. Marion incorporated deceit and conniving in her strongest fiction, especially the trickery of naive Darkovans by exploitive Terrans in *Thendara House,* of conspirator Lyle Belfontaine against the Comyn in *Traitor's Sun,* and of wives and concubines against atrocious males in *The Shattered Chain.* The author outlined examples in the creation of pseudo-enemy spaceships in "Peace in the Wilderness," for *In the Rift* when Kate Beacham bests the Fort Lauderdale wizard, and in *Gravelight,* a dynastic breach of faith between Ahanais Dellon and her great uncle Quentin Blackburn over possession of the magical Wellspring. The author underscored perfidy as the height of depravity, illustrated by gendered sins—the theft of Mary from her grandmother in "The Footsteps of Retribution," the suppression of Lord Aldaran's manhood in *The Ages of Chaos,* and the conception of an unwanted child in "Centaurus Changeling." In each example, harm radiates from the core crime to the guilty and the innocent.

To parody psychological treatment in the future, Marion's Dr. Rhoum in "The Crime Therapist" kills Frank Colby in order to rid Colby of the urge to murder his wife Helen. Too late, Frank realizes how easily Rhoum can remand a dangerous patient to the electric chair for instant execution. With a deft squiggle, Rhoum's stylus scratches "cured" in the treatment logbook (Bradley, 1954, 100). For the Lythande series, the thieving career of Roygan the Proud in "The Incompetent Magician" causes the roving mercenary to retrieve stolen goods. For punishment, she forces Roygan to wear a nose ring, a suggestion of the taming of a bull. Lythande humiliates him for double dealing with the rejoinder, "Wear this … in memory of your treachery, and that honest folk may know you and avoid you" (Bradley, 2013, 21).

Double-Dealers

In *The Fall of Atlantis,* faithlessness takes varied forms—the Arch-Administrator Talkannon rejects his lover and her daughter Karahama, Arvath abandons his lover Elis and her baby Lissa, and the Grey-Robes violate saffron-veiled women who serve their order like "chained flames" (Bradley, 1983, 192). The narrative anchors the Black-Robes to guile in the form of torture and by the blinding of Micon, an imprisoned Atlantean prince. On his deathbed, the scrying of his brother Reio-ta to learn Ahtarrath's whereabouts identifies the brother's allegiance to magician Riveda as an apostle. Using a neutral color to reveal a two-timer, Marion depicts Reio-ta as a gray shadow that threatens Micon's survival.

The author builds high drama from the reunion of the Atlantean brothers and concludes with compassion for Reio-ta, the apostate. At their parting, Micon offers partial forgiveness: "I love you still. I do not abandon you utterly" (*Ibid.,* 188). The scene imparts Marion's belief in humane treatment, even of sellouts. Unfortunately for the narrative, the confrontation founders under weighty melodrama arising from Riveda's control of Deoris, his lover and tool.

The role of false-heartedness and trickery in human events reaches a Homeric height in *The Firebrand* with the gradual disclosure of venality and inconstancy in the seaman Odysseus. On a *prima facie* evaluation, he appears jolly, frisky among females, and eager to tell tales of his voyages and distribute gifts. On return to Troy, he flirts with Kassandra and pats Polyxena's buttocks, yet makes a show of cleaning his language of man-talk lest he shock the womenfolk. Kassandra surmises that Odysseus maintains camaraderie "as long as it was to his advantage to do so" (Bradley, 1987, 251). Her astute evaluation of his character foreshadows Odysseus's role in the final assault on the Trojan gates, the preface to arson, pillage, rape, kidnap, and slaughter, notably, the baby prince Astyanax. Even at his worst, Kassandra "could not help thinking of the old pirate as a friend" (*Ibid.*, 534).

IMPERIAL ROME

At a father-son discussion in *The Forest House,* Marion reveals Prefect Macellius Severus's willingness to criticize the Roman Empire and Titus, its emperor, for the handling of rebellions and the recruitment of non–Romans into state legions. In a candid evaluation that could cause his dismissal or worse, the prefect characterizes the reigns of Caligula, Commodus, and Caracalla and the suicide of Nero in 68 CE as "Chaos…. The world upside down. The time of the four Emperors, or the Killer Queen again," a reference to the corrupt emperors and to the Iceni queen Boudicca, who rebelled against Roman legions in 60 CE (Bradley, 1993, 75). The summary places the first century of the Roman Empire in an unsteady state that arouses from old-timers nostalgia for the Roman Republic, which collapsed in 44 BC at the assassination of Julius Caesar.

In 93 CE, as paranoia increases in Domitian's inner circle, the emperor executes doubters of his legitimacy to rule. Macellius Severus reveals a plan to end the Flavian dynasty with "Imperial housecleaning," which his son Gaius Macellius Severus evaluates as "sedition on a grand scale" (*Ibid.*, 355). The plot parallels the heroic end of the Roman monarchy in 509 BCE with the assassination of King Lucius Tarquinius Superbus by Lucius Junius Brutus. To spare the gullible Gaius from a charge of treason and public execution, the aging father advises, "Try to live without ever coming to the attention of a prince," a restatement of "keep your head down" (*Ibid.*, 76). The wise counsel further corroborates the perilous state of individual freedoms in Rome.

THE PENDRAGON ASCENDANCE

For the basis of Arthuriana, in *The Mists of Avalon,* Marion spotlights dishonesty and broken pledges to Avalon as the downfall of King Arthur's Camelot. Beginning with the future high king's conception, she describes the enchantment and deceit that allow Uther Pendragon to transgress the Tintagel stronghold and impregnate Queen Igraine, wife of Duke Gorlois of Cornwall. The result, the birth of Arthur Pendragon, derives both from the spell of Taliesin the Merlin of Britannia and the human passion of Igraine for a mate less cruel, less despotic than Gorlois. Uther, crowned the high king in Londinium, swears vengeance on Gorlois, the "oathbreaker (and) betrayer" and "damnable traitor" for breaking his vows of fealty to the successor of Aurelius Ambrosius, a respected leader (Bradley, 1983, 102). Pakistani essayist and columnist Umer Mumtaz identifies deceit as the universal theme: "This story belongs to everyone. An archetypical good king, a wife that strays, friends that betray, fighting for God and Country, and love that turns to hate but never dies completely; all are part of a timeless concoction in which we can see ourselves and our leaders" (Mumtaz, 5).

Marion ventures into the theme of mercy killing during the long illness of Priscilla. The mother of Balin and surrogate mother of Balan, Viviane's son, Priscilla offers grace to her birth son and generous fostering to Balan. At her bedside, she welcomes Viviane's fatal potion, a single draught that ends protracted suffering from a wasting disease. The two brothers, emblematic of Druidic and Christian beliefs, squabble over the decision. Balin distorts shock and grief into anger toward the Lady of Avalon, whom he calls a "foul, murdering witch" and sorcerer of the "evil fiend-Goddess" (Bradley, 1983, 342). The maledictions on the Lady of the Lake and the Earth Mother foreshadow Balin's mad axe blow on Viviane's head, an example of retribution out of proportion to the crime.

The author epitomizes the height of treachery in Camelot lore as a symbolic act. King Arthur's abandonment of the Pendragon guidon at the Battle of Mount Badon in February 482 CE for a Christian banner "of the cross and the Holy Virgin" denotes forsaking Avalon, his grandmother and mother's realm (*Ibid.*, 414). Historically, the shift in loyalties characterizes a loss of the old ways—worship out of doors, venerating the earth and oak groves, making tools and weapons of flint rather than iron, burial in unconsecrated ground, and memorizing ritual rather than writing scripture. In place of belief in fairies and ancient herbal lore, Christians substitute orthodoxy bound by a fear of sin and temptation, which priests foist on Eve and the entire female gender.

Guile in the resolution of *The Mists of Avalon* reaches the extremes of James Goldman's play *The Lion in Winter*, a *tour de force* of cabals and rancor involving Henry II and Eleanor of Aquitaine in the choice of a king from three sons, Richard, Geoffrey, and John. Marion's concluding duplicities, according to critic Bridgette Da Silva, are "so embedded in the consciousness of Western society they could be deemed 'master narratives'—those well known stories that help us make sense of ourselves and our world" (Da Silva, 2007). Morgaine's request that Accolon steal Excalibur identifies her as a "kin-slayer" and precipitates Accolon's death in rebellion against her brother Arthur (*Ibid.*, 676).

Subsequent betrayals fragment Arthur's doomed realm. Foreshadowing ruin, salacious banners over the thrones demean the royal family of morality and dignity. Morgaine declares the new Merlin, Kevin Harper, a turncoat and blames herself for failing Avalon by abandoning a holy trust. Hatreds pile up—Arthur, Lancelet, Gwenhwyfar, and Uwaine. In the Great Hall, Nimue, an Arthurian temptress, bedazzles Kevin for profaning a hallowed oath. According to Sara Douglass's *The Betrayal of Arthur,* the final plot—the banishment of Lancelet and Gwenhwyfar for adultery and for the murder of Niniane—reveals the lengths to which Gwydion/Mordred will go to unseat his father from Camelot's throne. Lacking Arthur's depth of character and commitment to an ideal, Gwydion has nothing to offer the doubly royal Avalon-Pendragon dynasty.

See also Religion.

Sources

Bradley, Marion Zimmer. *The Complete Lythande.* San Francisco: Marion Zimmer Bradley Literary Works Trust, 2013.

_____. "The Crime Therapist," *Future Science Fiction* 5:3 (October 1954): 93–100.

_____. *The Fall of Atlantis.* Riverdale, NY: Baen Books, 1983.

_____. *The Firebrand.* New York: Simon & Schuster, 1987.

_____. *The Forbidden Tower.* New York: DAW, 1977.

_____. *The Mists of Avalon.* New York: Ballantine, 1983.

_____. *The Shattered Chain.* New York: DAW, 1976.

Da Silva, Bridgette. "Medieval Mindsets: Narrative Theory and *The Mists of Avalon*," *Strange Horizons* (1 October 2007).

Fuog, Karen E.C. "Imprisoned in the Phallic Oak: Marion Zimmer Bradley and Merlin's Seductress," *Quondam et Futurus* 1:1 (Spring, 1991): 73–88.

Mumtaz, Umer. "Love-Hate Relationship between King Arthur and Morgan le Fay," ttps://s3.amazonaws.com/academia.edu.documents/51543768/Arthurian_ Love_Hate_Paper.pdf?.

Two to Conquer

A dramatic contrast between premarital Celtic handfasting and a race toward mass destruction via psi weaponry, Marion's novel surveys the best and worst in human behavior. Because of the possibility of redemption and social refinement, the narrative thrived in English, French, and Dutch. Opening in the Hundred Kingdoms era two centuries after *Stormqueen!,* the plot introduces vast changes in Darkover politics, the military, and religion. Magic retrieves Paul Harrell/Paolo Harryl, an alien felon, from Earth and situates him in the milieu of his physical double, warmonger Bard di Asturien, a sci-fi version of the *doppelgänger* and the Roman *miles gloriosus* (arrogant soldier).

In a medieval atmosphere of feasting and joy, Bard's bride-to-be, his foster sister Carlina di Asturien, prepares for a year of engagement to a sadistic egotist, wizard, and serial rapist. The festive atmosphere derives from lighted torches, the bride-to-be's veiled gown, and servants bearing a "dole of food and wine and sweets" to a press of guests, foreign and local (Bradley, 1980, 173). To herself, she admits that she would rather join the followers of Avarra in altruistic service on the Island of Silence, a post–Arthurian version of Avalon that visitors approach by boat through fog-shrouded waters.

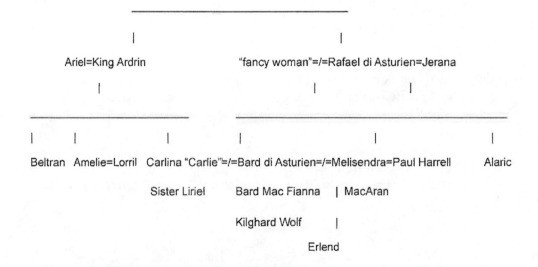

Marion accentuates crime and punishment in Bard's maiming of foster brother Geremy Hastur, rape of Melisendra, and murder of Carlina's brother Beltran. The killing results in Bard's seven-year exile to outlawry, a common ruling in medieval courts. Critic Jane Donawerth credits sadomasochism in *Two to Conquer* as a result of man's "quest for recognition" (Donawerth, 1997, 50). To succeed, the ambitious male objectifies the female victim as "only a thing to be used" (Bradley, 1980, 272). Donawerth cites

Bard di Asturien as a model thrill killer blessed with psi power that control the women he stalks. Burdened by inferiority and illegitimacy, he assaults the single mother Lilla, twelve-year-old Lisarda, and Melisendra MacAran, his foster sister. Donawerth adds, he "repeatedly rapes women, violating and attacking them to prove his own manly differ-entiation from them and to still his anxious fears of unworthiness" (Donawerth, 1997, 50). To still inner doubts, Bard baits the female victim with a taunt: "In your hearts you desire a man who will take you, and master you" (Bradley, 1980, 269).

Paul Harrell/Paolo Harryl, Bard's Earth-born double, internalizes the myth of manhood as power: He trivializes "looking for some fun" as "what women wanted and they loved it" (*Ibid.*, 207, 8). Melisendra corroborates the appeal of the macho seducer by admitting that "many women lie with a man under a glamour, and sometimes they do not even know it" (*Ibid.*, 268). From another perspective, Carlina, a devotee of the Mother Goddess, suffers two rapes by Bard and feels "mortal terror, and awful humilia-tion, as she lay with her clothes torn off, impaled, tearing pain, but worse…, the horror of knowing herself only a thing to be used" (*Ibid.*, 272). She fears pregnancy for placing "a horrid, hateful parasite" into "her clean body," a vilification that denies her the joy of normal motherhood (*Ibid.*, 166). During a period of civilizing neutrality and unifi-cation of 100 small realms and religious sisterhoods, the righting of persistent wrongs frees Bard from his cruel obsession with conquest.

Sources

Bradley, Marion Zimmer. *Two to Conquer.* New York: DAW, 1980.

Donawerth, Jane. *Frankenstein's Daughters: Women Writing Science Fiction.* New York: Syracuse University Press, 1997.

Huckfeldt, Cynthia Rose. "Avoiding 'Teapot Tempests': The Politics of Marion Zimmer Bradley's *Darkover.*" Laramie: University of Wyoming, 2008.

Renk, Thorsten. "Mapping Darkover," http://www.phy.duke.edu/~trenk/darkover/darkover_map.html#mental_map.

Violence

As unexpected as skirmishes resulting from the cabal plotted by Lyle Belfontaine against Darkover in *Traitor's Sun* and the blow against Jeff Kerwin's head during his stroll in Old Town in *The Bloody Sun,* Marion inserts vicious enmity in multiple epi-sodes of fiction. For song catcher Margaret Alton in *Exile's Song,* even the folk ballad "The Outlaw" bears its onus of bloodshed:

> How came this blood on your right hand?
> Brother, tell me, tell me.
> It is the blood of an old gray wolf,
> That lurked behind a tree.
> No wolf would prowl at this hour of the day,
> Brother, tell me, tell me.
> It is the blood of my own brothers twain
> Who sat at the drink with me [Bradley, 1996, 34].

The pattern continues in action stories in the suspension of the sorceress Mayra's remains for predators to peck in *Stormqueen!,* Sybil-Mhari's murder of a would-be seducer in "The Waterfall," Teresa's lashing of Count Angelo Fieresi, a vampire in

"Treason of the Blood," and the fistfight in *Star of Danger* between Larry Montray and a roughneck.

The author advocates a rule of law controlling weaponry and its use. In a fitful memory of loss in *The Heritage of Hastur*, she blames smugglers for importing contraband weapons from Earth that cause Rafael Hastur to be "blown to bits" at age thirty-five (Bradley, 1975, 2). For Allira, a quavering virgin in *Winds of Darkover*, a childhood amulet offers no shield against her ravisher Brynat, an amoral brigand. In *Two to Conquer*, the author stresses the virulence of Brad di Asturien, a bloodthirsty mercenary who attacks Geremy Hastur with a poisoned dagger that permanently cripples him. Brad exonerates himself as a professional: "I am a soldier; I know very little of other kinds of courage," a rationale that fails to explain his bloodlust (Bradley, 1980, 11).

The author's first story, "Outpost," published in *Spacewarp* in 1948, introduced hot tempers and lethal threats against democratic votes. Because the minority of twenty-six residents rejects the thirty votes to scuttle a spaceship, the protagonist faces death threats. Marion remarks, "The fools, can't [Conner] realize we can't risk any crazed and homesick person giving away our hiding place?" (Bradley, 1949, 143). The sentiment echoes the rationale of Spanish conquistador Hernan Cortes, who burned his ships upon reaching Veracruz, Mexico, in February 1519 as a demonstration of commitment to New World exploration. The same logic results in the sabotage of a mangled starship in *Darkover Landfall*, which gives survivors no vote in the possibility of escaping Cottman IV.

Some cataclysmic scenes rely on natural forces, as with Mike's one-on-one battle with an eagle in *Falcons of Narabedla* and his "thrust blindly upward with the knife, ripped, slashing, hearing the bird's scream of pain" (Bradley, 1954, 2). Because of a less dramatic altercation in *Darkover Landfall*, geologist Gabriel "Gabe" MacAran slaps mathematician Camilla Del Rey to stop her hysterics over a banshee-like scream in the night. In "The Stars Are Waiting," messenger Julian Flanders reprises an era of natural cataclysms that preceded worldwide savagery, the kind of subversion and radiation burns that Pharigs allegedly inflicted on humankind during the "Three Days War" in Marion's story "Peace in the Wilderness" (Bradley, 1956, 58). The creation of the imaginary Pharig allows authorities to blame aliens for wrongdoing and "[destroy] the superficial glamor around crime and violence" (Bradley, 1956, 77). The author enlarges on animosities by depicting squabbles over an elected council, a nonviolent verbal motif that invests much of the Darkover series.

VIOLENCE AS ENTERTAINMENT

Marion rebukes humankind for its tendency to enjoy mayhem. Among Terrans in *The Shattered Chain* who regard dueling as "the most popular indoor sport," Free Amazon leather traders brave a clutch of foul-mouthed men in Dry Town and threaten to emasculate brawlers with their daggers (Bradley, 1976, 103). A court knife fight at dinner in "A Sword Called Chaos" depicts drunken bandits mauling each other over women until Narthen, their chief, commands "Find another wench or take turns with this one" (Bradley, 1982, 96). In the bandit raid in "To Keep the Oath," the fearful onset pits Scarface and his killers and arsonists against "menfolk [who] drove 'em off with pitchforks," a vicious attack similar in barbarity and crude self-defense to the Lawrence,

Kansas, massacre led by William's Quantrill's guerrillas on August 21, 1863 (Bradley, 1985). After the Amazon leader Kindra n'ha Mhari calls for rope, Jaella n'ha Melora creates womanly humor by binding a wounded bandit in clothesline, domestic equipment common to women's lives.

The ripping apart of a horse by a banshee in *The Shattered Chain* produced a Gothic clash elaborated with "the beak plunging into the pack animal's soft underbelly and rearing up, dripping gore" (Bradley, 1976, 185). The scene applauds Magdalen "Magda" Lorne's swift knife hand in *mano a mano* rampage for the sake of self-preservation. For gendered psychology, the author probes more thoroughly the roots of masculine warfare and men's uncivil treatment of animals, women, children, and each other. She identifies reprehensible patterns of human behavior, for example, the children's shoving game of king of the hill in *Thendara House,* the "living pain" of Micon's tortured hands in *The Fall of Atlantis,* and mention in *The Catch Trap* of the bombing of Hiroshima on August 6, 1945 (Bradley, 1983, 35).

Medieval Mayhem

In Thieves Quarter, a dark alley in "Somebody Else's Magic," the skewering, beheading, and dismembering of brigands is not unusual, nor the sword thrust of the Lord of Sathorn in "The Children of Cats" that kills his adulterous wife nor the torture of Lythande's confidante in "The Walker Behind." A plot twist pictures Lythande, a woman disguised as a mage-mercenary, armed with a mystic knife "fashioned for supernatural menaces, to kill ghosts and anything else from specters to werewolves" and capable of ending her own life if she should choose suicide (Bradley, 2013, 116). To save her secret identity in "The Incompetent Magician," she stabs Roygan the Proud in the mouth before he can reveal her gender, then stabs him "through his heart, in the merciful release from agony" (*Ibid.,* 29). Regretful that secrecy requires slaughter, the itinerant bard celebrates "a small victory for the cause of Law" (*Ibid.,* 30).

Marion tempers havoc in *The Forest House* to tides of drama. Arch-Druid Bendeigid Vran's slap on Eilan's mouth and the threat to drown her hardly compare with the onslaught of Hibernian raiders under Red Rian and the torching of Eilan's home. As vengeance builds between Romans and Celts, they forge an alliance and advance on Hibernians at the shore, where stinking latrines attest to their barbarity. The battle scene peers through Cynric's slashing sword and spear in rapid defeat of the enemy, the blinding of the only surviving Gael, and Cynric's queasiness at the smell of burning flesh. In contrast to the howling Celts, Romans conduct warfare mechanically, the result of a lifetime of training in the killing arts. Still leery of Romans, Cynric admits a fact of war: "You could see now there might be something to be learned from them," a prediction Marion clarifies in the detailed strife at the Battle of Mons Graupius in 83 CE (Bradley, 1993, 128).

International Bloodshed

To illustrate contrast in Roman and Celtic demeanor, the author reprises Domitian's anti–Christian colosseum games in the mid–80s, when Gaius Macellius learns of the Emperor Nero's excessive backlash against believers following the Great Fire of

Rome in 64 CE. The pairing of lion with giraffe and panther with wild boar prepares Gaius for ghastly gladiatorial events. In a trance, Eilan speaks for the mother goddess a weariness of combat: "Is there ever justice in the wars of men?" (*Ibid.*, 296). Gaius later muses on the Emperor Augustus's "Pax Romana" (Roman Peace), an ironic concept of pacification through domination and exploitation (*Ibid.*, 304). The era of peace anticipates a similar "pax" in *The Mists of Avalon* under the rule of King Arthur and his Knights of the Round Table and a collapse of rule into anarchy.

In the best of action scenes, Marion applied hand-to-hand combat into high drama, as with the invisible catmen who cut Reidel's throat and rip out Bethiah's eyes in *The Spell Sword* and the unidentified corpse hacked apart and stripped of his face in *Castle Terror*. An early novel, *The Door Through Space*, turns war on the catmen into a slashing, snarling melee that concludes with a snapping spine, disemboweling, and bestial mewling, ending with a fatal slash to the throat with a skean, a two-edged bronze Celtic dagger. In the aftermath, humans discover a dead combatant: "His throat had been torn completely out" (Bradley, 1961, 43). For *Tiger Burning Bright*, psychological dread extends the threat to Merina of "Emperor Balthasar and his Imperial Army ... the largest conquering army this world had ever seen" (Bradley, 1995, 3). With an allusion in *Witchlight* to the Massachusetts setting of the Lizzie Borden axe murders in 1892, the author turns the destruction on small animals at Fall River into "some ghoulish offering" (Bradley, 1997, 46).

The gendered threat in *The Firebrand* from hostile Kentaurs forces Penthesilea and the Amazons to gallop toward female sanctuary in the east. Star recalls the kidnapping stratagems of their lustful enemies, who break women's legs to keep them from fleeing. In counterpoint to Troy's army maneuvers and praise for warriors, Marion treats Odysseus, "that Master of Sneaks," as an avuncular pacifist who appears to prefer roving and flirting to fighting (Bradley, 1987, 539). Akhilles, at age seventeen "crazy for the kill," glorifies battles and insists on "man's talk," which rejects negotiation and reduces all women to idiots (*Ibid.*, 388, 281). Kassandra observed that such hot-headed heroes "do not live long enough to learn better.... Perhaps the world is better without such men" (*Ibid.*, 283).

Marion's rewriting of the Trojan War gradually builds on savagery. During the winter when the Akhaians raid Troy, they seize goats and olives from food stores and burn coastal houses and flammable buildings made from logs and timber. Farther up the slope, stone materials prevent fire. A flanking raid around Troy to Mount Ida enables Agamemnon's forces to seize Priam's herds. As the fighting progresses, the Akhaians move on to rifle grain stores and treasure. The author mentions fire arrows that burn victims alive and a rape victim who goes mad and hurls herself from a wall. Even Kassandra fantasizes about bedding with Akhilles and slitting his throat while he sleeps, a re-enactment of the biblical heroism of Jael, who freed Israel from the marauder Sisera in Judges 5:24–26.

Gods and Carnage

Volume Three of *The Firebrand* escalates discussion of the purpose and place of conflicting deities in human warfare. Andromache posits that the gods enjoy watching fights to the death, a ghoulish voyeurism enhanced by the slaughter of sacrificial horses to Poseidon. Marion builds dramatic tension from Homer's depiction of Akhilles dragging Hector's lifeless remains around the city and the return of a mangled body, a grisly detail missing from Homer's *Iliad*. An extreme of retribution, the violation of a war code between gentlemen occurs in sight of Troy's royal women, including Hector's wife, sister, and mother.

Perpetuating the motif of massacre for the joy of butchery, Marion's *The Mists of Avalon* surveys English history in the late fifty century CE during the Celtic struggle to drive Saxon raiders from their shores and rid the land of dragons, a task that obsesses Pellinore, Gwenhwyfar's maternal uncle. Galahad/Lancelet, an atheistic warrior, grows up amid man talk about strife, courage, and kill or be killed and gentles a dangerous horse to display to Leodegranz skill with pike and sword. In answer to what faith he professes, he touches his sword hilt and declares, "I have no faith in any God but this," thus ruling out Druidism and Christianity (Bradley, 1983, 146). His beliefs equate a soldier's skill with manhood. Both Galahad/Lancelet and Arthur study Greek and Roman texts on battlefield strategy; Caius attains combat experience before his foster brother Arthur, who frets he is "young and unblooded" to join the war against Saxon raiders (*Ibid.*, 163). To ensure alliance with Pict tribes, Arthur learns to stalk deer and shoot elf bolts, the stone or flint arrowheads favored by fairy folk.

In the estimation of critics Paul and Dominique Battles, Marion's novel "gives prominent place to the Theban motifs of incest and kin-slaying," the source of mortality for Viviane, Gwydion/Galahad, and Arthur and of Lot's commentary on the curse of the kinslayer (Battles & Battles, 2017). Part of the deer ritual calls for Morgaine to "give birth to her Dark Son who will bring the King Stag down," a motif acclaiming the promising offspring for supplanting his sire through patricide (Bradley, 1983, 177). While reflecting on human thoughts, Morgaine sees copulation with the noble male as "a barbarian mummery," represented by red berries tied around her lower torso to enhance mystic regeneration (*Ibid.*). Freudian symbols inundate the seduction scene with phallic shapes (horns, antlers, chalk penis, flint knife, torch) and vaginal/uterine quintessence (cave, blood, moon, belly, womb). The narrative alleviates both shock and anguish in Morgaine and Arthur by her motherly cradling.

The explosive third book of *The Mists of Avalon* piles bodies in view, the result of retribution and gratuitous slaughter. Balin's unforeseen axe murder of the aged Lady of the Lake precipitates a retaliatory strike. Meleagrant's accosting and rape of Gwenhwyfar requires another recompense for Arthur's dishonored queen. Even Gawaine's music encapsulates a grim, grisly Saxon scenario from Beowulf. Lancelet explains, "Most Saxon tales are so. War and bloodshed and heroes with killing in battle and not much else in their thick noddles" (*Ibid.*, 531). Ironically, Marion concludes the episode with Lancelet's longing for action in the field against Pellinore's horse-headed dragon, which burns victims and dissolves their flesh with its slime. On reflection of past glories over fifteen years, Uriens reduces them to "murder and ravage and blood and the slaughter of the innocent," a refutation of the glory and honor associated with the Arthuriad (*Ibid.*, 575).

Marion slows the pace of the declining action to intensify Morgaine's ambition to rescue Avalon from the closed-mindedness of Archbishop Patricius (St. Patrick) and Christianity. Standing over the prostrate form of her brother Arthur, she ponders killing him with Excalibur or slitting his throat with a dagger. The decision to let him live elevates Morgaine's humanity while increasing her ambivalence toward obeying the Great Mother. She tallies two losses in the previous three days—stepson Avalloch and her aborted baby—and decides, "There has been too much death" (*Ibid.*, 749).

See also Feud; Rape; Retribution; Treachery.

Sources

Battles, Paul, and Dominique Battles. "From Thebes to Camelot: Incest, Civil War, and Kin-Slaying in the Fall of Arthur's Kingdom," *Arthuriana* 27:2 (2017): 3–28.
Bradley, Marion Zimmer. *The Complete Lythande.* San Francisco: Marion Zimmer Bradley Literary Works Trust, 2013.
_____. *The Door Through Space.* New York: Ace, 1961.
_____. *Exile's Song.* New York: DAW, 1996.
_____. "Falcons of Narabedla," *Dimensions* 14–15 (May 1954).
_____. *The Fall of Atlantis.* Riverdale, NY: Baen Books, 1983.
_____. *The Forest House.* New York: Michael Joseph, 1993.
_____. *Free Amazons of Darkover.* New York: DAW, 1985.
_____. *Greyhaven.* New York: DAW, 1983.
_____. *The Heritage of Hastur.* New York: DAW, 1975.
_____. *The Mists of Avalon.* New York: Ballantine, 1983.
_____. "Outpost," *Amazing Stories* 23:12 (December 1949): 143–144.
_____. "Peace in the Wilderness," *Fantastic Universe* 5:6 (July 1956): 55–79.
_____. *The Shattered Chain.* New York: DAW, 1976.
_____. "The Stars Are Waiting," *Saturn* 1:5 (March 1958): 84–94.
_____. *Sword of Chaos.* New York: DAW, 1982.
_____. *Tiger Burning Bright.* New York: William Morrow, 1995.
_____. *Two to Conquer.* New York: DAW, 1980.
_____. *Witchlight.* New York: Tor, 1997.

Warrior Woman

A *tour de force* rendering of barbaric abuse and bondage of a silenced female, *Warrior Woman* delves into hopelessness relieved by preparation of a manacled slave for sexual bondage. The narrative details protagonist Zadieyek/Amber's brain-numbing pain, nightmares, nakedness, hunger, and thirst on a desert trek in iron shackles to Jemmok. Suffering gives place to disembodied care from "skilled fingers kneading my muscles and ointments to soothe the hurts of days in the saddle," a preface to lesbian longings for womanly tending (Bradley, 1985, 6). Upon arrival at a gladiatorial school, she attempts to differentiate inchoate yells and rejects a future as an obscure comfort girl "spreading my legs for these brutes" (*Ibid.*, 8). In a perverse form of ambition, she chooses a cycle of fighting against "Old Bloody's hand stern on my shoulder," the gladiatorial image of death (*Ibid.*, 31).

Contributing drama and raising issues of women's rights and sexuality, Zadieyek's "white fire" (amnesia) arouses thoughts of past human normality she can only imagine, a problem she shares with the hospital patient in *The Brass Dragon* (*Ibid.*, 1). The punishments that await disobedience—torture, burning, gang rape and her "body flung on the swill-pile for the pigs to devour"—force her to adapt to a grim milieu that "is all unreal, everything is unreal, as I am unreal" (*Ibid.*, 15). Amid "death-stink and blood," her transformation into a dread fighter elicits curled lips and sneering retorts equivalent to the posturing of males and the bribes and sweetmeats from a possible patron (*Ibid.*, 24). From the trainer Hassim, she learns the savvy ways of the survivor; from Beizun, a slave, who chooses arena fighting to the copper mines, Zadieyek accepts the generosity of a friend and eventual soul mate.

Veering into a masculine subgenre, Marion's YA pro-woman fiction reveals strength in multiple female roles—as patron, fighter, survivor, servant, advocate, healer, and midwife. Inklings of courage like those displayed by Xena and Wonder Woman replace past experiences expunged from Zadieyek's brain and empower her to become more than bondwoman, harlot, or entertainment for a savage crowd. Although disjointed because of Zadieyek's affliction, the narrative salutes female agency by depicting takeover of a city by women gladiators. In *Women of Ice and Fire,* editor Anne Gjelsvik stresses that the enslaved gladiator "represents the *possibilities* of a feminist insistence on women's visibility in the (pre-feminist) mythical past" (Gjelsvik, 2016, 181).

Bradley fans embraces *Warrior Woman* for deviating from set sci-fi patterns and clichés. Book critic Jan W. Whiteley praises the author's ingenuity: "A risky narrative device in a novel of this length, the first person gives great emotional depth to this tale … modelled on conscious or unconscious perceptions of ancient Earth" (Whiteley, 1987, 74). By saving until last the identification of the heroine as an alien wounded in a spaceship crash, empowering her flight, and enabling an escape, the author reprises themes and events in *Darkover Landfall* and anticipates Penthesilea and her band of Amazons in *The Firebrand* and Morgaine, the trailblazer of *The Mists of Avalon.*

See also Dreams; Rape.

Sources

Bradley, Marion Zimmer. *Warrior Woman.* New York: DAW, 1985.
Gjelsvik, Anne, and Rikke Schubart, eds. *Women of Ice and Fire: Gender, Game of Thrones and Multiple Media Engagements.* New York: Bloomsbury, 2013.
Whiteley, Jan W. "Warrior Woman: The Adventures of Zadieyk of Gyre," *Minerva* 1 (1987): 74.

Wicca

In an era that saw the redemption of witches from centuries of feminized evil and the pan-tolerance of Wicca, Marion promoted feminist Neo-Pagan spirituality of covens, initiations, and occult mysteries as a survival of primal Dark Ages theology. She identified what analyst Janice C. Crosby called "the desire for the Goddess as a continuing human need" and applied a vigorous theology to the Divine Mother, eight annual Celtic festivals, and an egalitarian ministry of both male and female clergy in veneration of nature (Crosby, 2000, 43). In *The New Generation Witches,* Hannah E. Johnson and Peg Aloi named self-liberation as a motivation for "adults who had been raised with other traditions. Many Catholics found their way to Witchcraft, perhaps drawn to a form of ritual that contained the church's drama, but not its dogma" (Johnston & Aloi, 2017, 4).

The author's canon allocates a normality to Wiccan folk traditions through informational references—yule logs, holy wells, amulets, baby naming, phases of the moon, love feasts, croning rituals, agrarian blessings, and flowered garlands, joyous specifics in *The Mists of Avalon.* For the story "Bride Price," Rohana muses on the meaning of "handfasting," an archaic Celtic term for "betrothal," the ceremonial "true binding" that opens *Two to Conquer* (Bradley, 1980, 10). Beltran, the bride's brother, respects the ceremony that makes Bard "Carlina's lawful husband and she cannot take another while you live" (*Ibid.*). The Wiccan practice continues to glorify committed love before couples take the permanent step of wedlock. In reference to the ancient rituals and beliefs, Robert Ellwood, a former religion expert at the University of Southern California, defined Wicca's esoteric context as "significant truth about reality—truth unknown to most people either because it has been deliberately concealed or because it is by its very nature unknowable without special training or initiation" (Elwood, 1988, 712).

WICCAN HERITAGE

Marion's landmark novel differentiates opinions about the endurance of the roots of Wicca. At Camelot, High King Arthur Pendragon encourages Beltane rites for farmers, but declares that more urbane citizens have no need of pagan ritual and feasting that bolster the agrarian lifestyle. Conversely, Kevin Harper, the new Merlin, explains the deathlessness of the Great Mother: "Avalon will always be there for all men to find if they can seek the way thither" (Bradley, 1983, 470). According to J. Gordon Melton, author of *The Encyclopedia of Religious Phenomena,* practitioners accept that the "true secrets of their craft are revealed not in the texts but in the practice," the cultural remnant that "Morgaine of the Fairies" promotes among the aboriginal Welsh (Melton, 2008, 132).

In an overview of late twentieth-century revivals of paganism, Graham Harvey, a professor at Great Britain's Open University, lauds the "shift away from Protestant Christian stress on correct belief towards a more indigenous stress on action and performance" (Harvey, 2004, 326). Arthurian critic Nicole Evelina reported in *The Once and Future Queen* that Marion's bestselling novel "complemented a growing neo-paganism that was emerging in the latter twentieth century" (Evelina, 2017, 152). The revival of prehistoric woman lore contributed to "the general awareness of female potential and equality ... in keeping with the trends of the times" (*Ibid.*). Evelina declared Dianic Wicca, a theology based on the Roman nature goddess Diana, and the wise-woman ideal in the early 1980s an "alternative to the oppression of Christianity," which had previously curbed female emancipation (*Ibid.*, 153).

THE LIBERATED WICCAN

The author's promotion of woman-based religion takes shape in a series of fictional scenarios, such as the inscription of a pentagram at a cursed barn in "The Wuzzles" and the numerology of a thirteenth sacred oak within a circle of twelve oaks in *The Forest House*, a representation of womanly energy in an odd number. In the 1989 essay "The Household Altar," the author cited practical means of keeping a shrine and supplying it with earth, air, wind, and fire from inexpensive items, e.g., an earthenware dish to hold rock salt. She featured a naming ceremony in *The Firebrand,* croning in *The Forest House,* handfasting between Dorilys and Darren in *Stormqueen!* and *Two to Conquer* and between Alastair and Floria in *The Heirs of Hammerfell,* and a Year's End sacrament in *The Forbidden Tower.* For Kate, hero of *In the Rift,* the nature-based religion sanctions her defiance of wizardry, a threat from the alternate realm of Glenraven.

Don Riggs, an expert on Celtic worship, noted the dynamics of the conquering religion over deities of the past, which include "demonization of the previous ... manifestations of the Goddess into sirens, harpies, and gorgons—to be slain or outwitted by patriarchal heroes—in the Greek tradition" (Riggs, 1998, 15). In a ruse to silence purveyors of witchery and monster lore, Marion employs wit in "A Feminist Creation Myth," which she dated Wiccan style "Lughnasadh 1975," a reference to the harvest festival honoring first fruits each August 1. By parodying Genesis 1 with a snippy tone, she devised womanly fiction that dramatizes the perennial angst of the female artisan—the mother interrupted at her work by a demanding daughter. Marion concludes, "And so God held Her hand, which is why this world is still in such an unGodly mess" (Bradley, 2009, 282). A whimsical thrust at anti-woman disparagement of Wicca and its practitioners, the author links the protagonist with creativity and motherhood rather than hexes and evil. She states the goal of womanly advancement in *City of Sorcery*: "In the fullness of time, everyone who comes to this world shall become everything that he or she can be or do or accomplish. Perfection is for the individuals, one at a time.... The end of every quest is to become what you are" (Bradley, 1984, 353, 371).

SPIRITED REVERENCE

Marion asserts joy in Wicca, especially the dance around the maypole in *The Forest House* after a night of bonfires fed with nine holy woods. In the shadows, the narrative celebrates unfettered lovemaking between couples who "seemed one being" (Bradley, 1993, 129). Eilan enjoys the purity of spring water and anticipates Beltane or May Day, one of the four annual Gaelic festivals, for its vigor and optimism. Midsummer brings athletic games and selection of a year-king. A reference to Samaine/Samhain, the final harvest festival on October 31, suggests a more plentiful time than May Day or Midsummer for its accounting of fruits and grain. The allusion to the tying of ribbons on hazel branches validates the sanctity of the tree and the god Mercury, disseminator of healing, wisdom, and dowsing for water.

Wiccans gravitate toward the equality of the male/female aspect of the divine. At a crucial point in Eilan's training, she ponders men's fear of the hag, an energized crone or woman past menopause who "knows all the secrets of birth and death" (Bradley, 1993, 126). Eilan's mentor Caillean exults that menopause brings renewed spirituality and strengthening of "the ties of power" (*Ibid.*, 314). In the Lythande episode "The Malice of the Demon," the roving protagonist champions older women for the "beauty which comes of age and wisdom" (Bradley, 2013, 130). The author hints that eras of witch burnings and hangings derived less from female behaviors than men's terror of the autonomous wisewoman freed of biological shackles.

Sources

Bradley, Marion Zimmer. *City of Sorcery*. New York: DAW, 1984.
_____. *The Complete Lythande*. San Francisco: Marion Zimmer Bradley Literary Works Trust, 2013.
_____. *The Forest House*. New York: Michael Joseph, 1993.
_____. *Green Egg Omelette*. New York: Career Press, 2009.
_____. *The Mists of Avalon*. New York: Ballantine, 1983.
_____. *The Other Side of the Mirror*. New York: DAW, 1987.
_____. *Two to Conquer*. New York: DAW, 1980.
Crosby, Janice C. *Cauldron of Changes: Feminist Spirituality in Fantastic Fiction*. Jefferson, NC: McFarland, 2000.

Ellwood, Robert. "Occult Movements in America" in *The Encyclopedia of the American Religious Experience.* New York: Scribner, 1988, 711.

Evelina, Nicole. *The Once & Future Queen: Guinevere in Arthurian Legend.* Maryland Heights, MO: Lawson Gartner, 2017.

Fry, Carrol L. "The Goddess Ascending: Feminist Neo-Pagan Witchcraft in Marion Zimmer Bradley's Novels," *Journal of Popular Culture* 27:1 (1993): 67–80.

Harvey, Graham, "Initiations," in *The Paganism Reader.* New York: Routledge, 2004.

Johnston, Hannah E., and Peg Aloi, eds. *The New Generation Witches.* New York: Routledge, 2017

Melton, J. Gordon. *The Encyclopedia of Religious Phenomena.* Canton, MI: Invisible Ink, 2008.

"Review: *In the Rift*," *Kirkus* (1 April 1998).

Riggs, Don. "The Survival of the Goddess in Marie de France and Marion Zimmer Bradley," *Journal of the Fantastic in the Arts* 9:1 (1998): 15–23.

Spivack, Charlotte. *Merlin's Daughters: Contemporary Women Writers of Fantasy.* Westport, CT: Greenwood, 1987.

_____. *Popular Arthurian Traditions.* Bowling Green, OH: Bowling Green State University Popular Press, 1992.

The Winds of Darkover

A terse view of punitive blindness, taboo breaking, and rape available in French and German translations, *The Winds of Darkover* exemplifies the use of psi powers to control mind and body of a male and a female. Daniel "Dan" Firth Barron, a disgruntled dispatcher at the Thendara Spaceport, makes a difficult choice by exiting his post at the flight tower after five years because of visions of a castle. His inattention to air traffic control over Cottman IV nearly crashes a spaceship. On a new assignment to instruct Darkovans in glass grinding for binocular lenses and telescopes, Dan aids Armida estate in setting up a sentry system to alert residents of fire and raiders. He follows Larry "Lerrys" Montray into the Hellers Mountains, a jagged, impassable terrain that epitomizes ancient notions of assault and seizure by men devoid of mercy. When raider Brynat Scarface of Dry Town assails the Storn estate, he captures Allira Storn for his bride, but stops short of taking the castle.

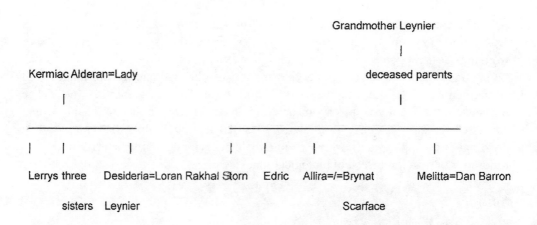

As a balance to muscle power, the author inserts a wistful ballad of Cassilda's love played by the gentle Allira on water harp. Her airy lyrics set the stage for Brynat's lust and abuse.

The author uses Gothic detail and psi powers as dynamic sources of energy in the Darkover series. Through telepathy, Loran Storn, blind and imprisoned, summons his sister Melitta and Dan to Carthon, an ancient planetary ruin. For strength, Melitta prays to a mythic divinity, Sharra, a pagan light goddess, who recurs in *Sharra's Exile* and *The Heritage of Hastur*. The deity appears also to Dan as an exotic female: "Sharra! Sharra, flame-haired, flame-crowned, golden-chained—Sharra! Child of Fire!" (*Ibid.,* 61). To evade a pollen-laden Ghost Wind, Dan and Lerrys at first shelter at a mountain fire station, but Dan hurries on to Carthon. Melitta recognizes Loran's ability to control Dan's thinking, a key issue in earthling adaptation to extraterrestrial life.

Marion enhances urgency with "the thundering nightmare noise of klaxons, the all-quarters alarm of sirens and whoopers and bells, the wreck lights blazing everywhere" and a possible space catastrophe halted by "seat-of-the-pants navigation" (Bradley, 1970, 3). At Aldaran, Dan and Melitta encounter Keeper Desideria Leynier and Kermiac Aldaran, who offers no aid. Summoning the dynamism of an amulet, Desideria directs matrix potency from Sharra. Aided by the unified energies of Forge Folk of the hill caverns, adherents of Sharra, Desideria blasts Brynat and his brigands. Free of his ties to Earth, Dan allies with Melitta, a self-reliant female partner, in the remaking of Darkover.

The messy resolution of Brynat's violation of a tender girl reflects medieval thinking about ownership of females. Like the unmapped Hellers declivities, the bandit chief's sexual intimidation reveals an uncurbed bent toward human exploitation, especially of nubile and vulnerable girls. By the law of the jungle, Allira becomes the war prize and "lady wife" of a despoiler (*Ibid.,* 14). In a twist of Christian philosophy, like the characters of *A Sword Called Chaos,* Allira and Brynat undergo a shotgun union, a travesty of priestly altar vows between bride and groom and "a fine subject for sagas and tales" (*Ibid.*). The survey of anti-woman crime established the novel as a fount of female science fiction. For Marion's presentation of sexual arousal, Alyssa Rosenberg, reviewer for the *Washington Post,* declared the work "beautiful and evocative in ways that much contemporary pop culture could learn from" (Rosenberg, 2014).

See also rape.

Sources

Bradley, Marion Zimmer. *The Winds of Darkover*. New York: Ace, 1970.
Huckfeldt, Cynthia Rose. "Avoiding 'Teapot Tempests': The Politics of Marion Zimmer Bradley's *Darkover*." Laramie: University of Wyoming, 2008.
Rosenberg, Alyssa. "Re-reading Feminist Author Marion Zimmer Bradley in the Wake of Sexual Assault Allegations," *Washington Post* (27 June 2014).

Womanhood

The majority of females of Marion's canon embody the primeval concerns of their gender—home, children, food, healing, and fiber work. In retrospect of giving birth to two scorned daughters, Kindra n'ha Mhari, leader of the mercenary band in *The Shattered Chain,* recalls thinking "A woman's lot in our world was wholly accursed," her response toward shaming, isolation, and violence against the lone female (Bradley, 1978, 73). In stating Lady Aliciane's choices for surviving in widowhood, the author of *Stormqueen!* cites "drudge or sewing-woman, or at best minstrel in a stranger's household" and possible "wife to a tinker or ragpicker ... blacksmith or charcoal-burner," all objectionable futures for the survivor (*Ibid.,* 10, 11). In *Traitor's Sun,* Hermes "Herm" Aldaran echoes the importance of sewing to artistic women, who "satisfy themselves with vast amounts of unnecessary needlework" (Bradley, 1999, 81). Narrow-minded Terrans scorn spinning, looming, and stitchery as "a pointless way of passing time for women who had no useful work to do," a sentiment shared by Romy, the repressed fifteen-year-old raptor-tender in *Hawkmistress!* (Bradley, 1976, 239). The generalization demeans children's and adult clothing, towels, tapestries, floor and window coverings, bed linens, bandages, footwear, and ritual costumes that female fiber workers provided for the home and community.

Marion's commentaries on autonomy memorialize the milestones that follow a girl's coming of age. Wedlock precedes a bride's delight in "The Wuzzles" in "her own house and her own kitchen" after the marriage of Frennet (Bradley, 2013, 145). In "The Wandering Lute," Prince Tashgen typifies such housebound women as "bored with la-dylike accomplishments" and open to assignations with a lecher like him (Bradley, 2013, 92). In *Thendara House,* lack of the five determiners of feminine domesticity abases linguist Magdalen "Magda" Lorne for her inability to cook, grow herbs, weave, dye, sew, or embroider, causing her to admit she belonged nowhere. An assignment to vegetable prep, waiting at table, clearing, and dishwashing reduces her status to near-servant. In *The City of Sorcery,* she enters house confinement for a year to refine homemaking skills.

Magda's rescuer and mentor, Camilla n'ha Kyria, the neutered woman, makes her own break from obstacles to a full life by seeking the Grey Sisterhood. Anne K. Kaler explains "that suffering and denial of the self, the purgative step of mysticism, alone leads to the illuminative step" of joining a sorority (Kaler, 1987, 83). Magda's advance in womanhood involves venturing into the unknown to find "the real me, the truest me" (Bradley, 1983, 17). One of the Grey Sisters acknowledges Magda's accomplishment in committing to a contemplative cloister: "Few of thy sisters have had such trials. How shall the fruit grow unless the blossoms are pruned from the tree?," a restatement of the philosophy of Hildegard of Bingen, a twelfth-century German abbess and feminist visionary (Bradley, 1984, 346).

The Womanly Tradition

At significant moments, Marion reconnects female characters to inklings of the Great Mother. In *The Mists of Avalon,* the author acknowledges the sweet fragrance and contentment of the still-room, the drying shed and preparation lab for kitchen recipes, pot herbs, salves, poultices, and bakery overseen by Alienor, the fourth wife of Leode-granz. Psychologist Adam Anczyk summarizes, "It is the women who are the keepers of the ancient pagan mysticism, and it is because of their effort that the mystical tradition is not lost and forgotten in the times of cultural change" (Anczyk, 2015, 10). At a tense point in the action, Marion extols Gwenhwyfar and other court women for huddling at Caerleon and stitching a royal banner while Arthur and the Round Table army face off against the Saxons. Critic James Noble blames the queen for deceit in posing as the good wife—"justifying her personal insecurity as a woman by imposing upon her husband and his subjects the very value system that has made her so desperately fearful and unhappy" (Noble, 1997, 148).

Unlike Arthur's Queen, Igraine, the future mother of the High King Arthur Pendragon, feels trapped inside Tintagel castle during a blustery winter while her husband, Duke Gorlois of Cornwall, wages war beyond Cornwall. Of the misery and boredom of waiting, she complains, "It was a woman's fate to sit at home, in castle or cot" (Bradley, 1983, 90). She uses the snug retreat as a time to weave, teach her child to spin fleece into thread, and tell stories she learned in Avalon, a verbal preservation of the old ways similar in scope to women's narratives in Anita Diamant's *The Red Tent*. On Igraine's first assignation with Uther, she realizes that marital coitus with Duke Gorlois of Cornwall had always been "something done to her" which she could observe with detachment (*Ibid.*, 102). In contrast, her daughter Morgaine, a fully realized woman, "believes that a woman's body is her own to give to whomever she wishes," a precept devoid of the Christian hierarchy of husbands and fathers above all females (Farwell, 1996, 99).

While men absorb themselves in land, money, dynasty, control, and violence, in *The Forest House,* High Priestess Eilan debates the future of orphaned girls victimized by political intrigue. With some pride, she declares, "I have a reputation for sheltering motherless children," an addition to Marion's ongoing salute to foster mothers (Bradley, 1993, 336). Celtic initiates learn the importance of spreading lavender (*Lavandula stoechas*) among clean sheets, a female touch that introduces aromatherapy into their hermitage. In addition to lightening despair with wispy purple stalks, the dispensing of mugwort (*Artemis vulgaris*) eases sore muscles, anxiety, and menstrual cramps. Chervil (*Anthriscus cerefolium*) and feverfew (*Tanacetum parthenium*), which resemble each other, both dispel indigestion and stomach ache. Wild thyme (*Thymus vulgaris*), a minty evergreen that heightens aromas in incense, cleanses wounds, and promotes sleep; stitchwort (*Stellaria media*) treats skin, skeletal, and lung disease. Bell-shaped foxglove (*Digitalis purpurea*) bears a two-pronged vigor to stimulate the heart and kidneys. The healer Latis warns, "That which is most powerful for good is also powerful for evil," an alert to novices that women must practice discernment in dosage (Bradley, 1993, 122). Because of the opportunity to use herbs for evil, females evolved a reputation for witchery, hexing, and poisoning, the historic reputation of Lucrezia Borgia and Livia Drusilla, wife of the emperor Augustus.

LABOR AND SACRIFICE

In age-old retrospects on female biology, obligations, impotence, and agency, Marion focused on matriarchal self-determination, the controlling theme of *The Ruins of Isis,* "Somebody Else's Magic," and *The Winds of Darkover*. Her liberation of Amazons in *The Shattered Chain* opens the way for females to be "mercenary soldiers … trackers, hunters, horsebreakers, blacksmiths, midwives, dairy-women, confectioners, bakers, ballad-singers and cheese-sellers … any honest trade," incorporating strength and daring with creativity (Bradley, 1976, 120). In *The Forbidden Tower,* the *leronis* Leonie Hastur forgives Ellemir "Elli" Lanart for floury hands and apron: "Don't apologize for being a conscientious housekeeper," an essential role in civilized society (Bradley, 1977, 11). To Floria Elhalyn, a potential daughter-in-law in *The Heirs of Hammerfell,* Erminie

Leynier reminds her of the value of independence to a satisfying life: "It would be a pity if you left your work because of a man's selfishness" (Bradley, 1989, 84).

Beyond concern for the dominated female, the author respected the hardships of poverty, referring in *The Mists of Avalon* to the female peasant as "beast of burden and brood mare in season" and the fears of mothers that parturition destroyed their beauty (Bradley, 1983, 21). The author's nod to Igraine for causing Duke Gorlois of Cornwall to blush acknowledges a wifely facility with seductive language. Countering Igraine's depth of character and intelligence, the narrative poses the duke and the other warlords, who dismiss their womenfolk for shopping at the London marketplace while a self-important male council determines how to select the next king of Britannia. Ironically, Igraine already knows the outcome from the prescience of her sister Viviane, the Lady of the Lake, who assures Igraine that she will give birth to Britain's greatest king.

WOMAN TALK

Marion breaks a taboo on women's motifs by referring to Rohana's menstrual cycle before her wedding to Gabriel Ardais in "Bride Price," Morgaine's heavy dark menstrual flow in *The Mists of Avalon*, and Hillary's cramping, weakness, contractions, and convulsions in "The Keeper's Price." In *Rediscovery*, Lorill, Heir to Hastur, summarizes the "influence of moons" with euphemisms: "Everyone knows how sensitive women are to the moons—and how dramatic their influence can be" (Bradley, 1993, 12). Author interest in female biology broadens in *The Forest House*, to menstrual cramps, the cause of Eilan's discomfort. In the opening paragraphs of "The Lesson of the Inn," the narrative summarized the agony of dysmenorrhea, an inescapable monthly pain caused by uterine contractions. Protagonist Hilary Castamir, a postulant Keeper, turns to prayer to inquire, "What am I doing wrong that I cannot keep the channels pure and untainted as befits a virgin?" (Bradley, 1982, 182). A brief encounter at a roadway inn revives Hilary's courage, leaving her assured "I can do anything" (*Ibid.*, 195).

The link between menstruation and action recurs in *The Mists of Avalon* while Morgaine cuts and sews a scabbard from doeskin and velvet, emblematic of moist vaginal depths from a female mammal. The image takes on personal sacrifice after the priestess smears blood on the three-day project from a deliberate cut on her arm. Under cycles of the moon, Marion dramatizes the act: "It was Arthur who had shed the blood of her virginity" (Bradley, 1983, 198). She must guard his royal blood by casting a protective spell on the sheath wrought from sacrifice: "blood of her maidenhood, strength of the King Stag who had died and shed his blood" (*Ibid.*). Ironically, Morgaine realizes that ritual coitus and conception have halted her "moon-dark bleeding" (*Ibid.*, 210). In book two, the scabbard and sword return to prominence where they hang over the royal bed of Arthur and Gwenhwyfar. The pairing of sheath with weapon anticipates what Raymond Thompson, author of *The Return from Avalon*, describes as universal suffering: "The heroism that wins victories on the battlefield is replaced by the grief of those who must count the cost" (Thompson, 1985, 135).

The themes of female ordeals and bravery dominate Marion's most urgent reprises of affliction—sexual assault in *The Fall of Atlantis* and *Warrior Woman* and the bondage of royal women and the murder of their offspring during the Trojan War in *The Firebrand*. For "The Walker Behind," liberation of Frennet, an enslaved comfort girl in the Hag and Swine, results in jubilation: "I'm me own mistress now, sir. And I ain't for sale" (Bradley, 2013, 127). She continues developing confidence in "The Wuzzles," in which she "would like makin' me own choice" (*Ibid.*, 141). Fictional scenarios contrast the imposition of celibacy on virgin Keepers in *The Forbidden Tower* and the competent research of parapsychologist Truth Jourdemayne of *Ghostlight* and *Witchlight* in the Light series.

Marion's canon returns repeatedly to strength and encouragement from the Great Mother, a protective deity. In the introduction to *The Saga of the Renunciates,* the author states "The Oath of the Free Amazons," a pledge of the resolute female. Chief among promises in the credo, the Guild of Free Amazons refuses to surrender naming or conception rights and promises to ward off male aggression and offers of money or help from men. The oath guarantees "allegiance only to my oath-mother," the Goddess whom the sisterhood exalts (Bradley, 2002, ii).

FEMALES AND FORCE

Marion alternates motifs of arranged nuptials such as Allira's vile wedlock with the highwayman Brynat in *The Winds of Darkover* by advocating a woman-with-woman union, a source of joy in "The Legend of Lady Bruna." The narrative of *Two to Conquer* substantiates Lady Bruna's proposal to Margali with warnings of father-arranged nuptials "forced on her for political reasons" or "issues of clan and inheritance" (Bradley, 1985, 104). In "The Secret of the Blue Star," Marion depicts lesbian intimacy as the subject of a rumor that Lythande, a frequent overnight guest at Aphrodisia House, "called up female demons from the Grey Wastes, to couple in lechery" (Bradley, 2013, 2). For a Renaissance-style wedlock based on stereotypical man-with-woman romance, *The Fall of Atlantis* centers on a satisfying relationship between the Atlantean Micon and Domaris, an acolyte in Ancient Land. The author enumerates wifely qualities—"beautiful, modest, conventional, and submissive … compliant, affectionate, even tender" (Bradley, 1983, 318–319). Yet, these traits mean nothing when love is absent from the marriage, a defining trope in the story of Rohana's wedding in "Bride Price," in which the marriage is "for the pleasure of [her] kin" (Bradley, 1987, 81).

Marion introduced sci-fi character alternatives in 1953 with the birth of a synthandroid infant in the story "Women Only" and Dr. Helen Murray's shielding of her fetus in an alien environment in "The Wind People." Out of jealousy for her sister Domaris's attention, Deoris, the rebel of *The Fall of Atlantis,* renounces motherhood, the biological duty that binds Domaris to her lover Micon and their unborn son Micail. On a separate plane, the novel depicts the *saji,* a sisterhood of pariahs, the comfort girls of the Grey Temple who join priests in carnal depravity like lab rats in psychic experiments. At the sound of the outcast Semalis wailing in labor, Domaris breaks Caratra rules and delivers the baby of the female untouchable. She justifies intervening midwifery as an act of mercy: "At such a time all women are one," even sexual reprobates (*Ibid.*, 304). The self-justification reverences the work of the midwife as a service more binding than the laws and depravities of men.

THE WOMAN'S FATE

In volume one of *The Firebrand*, Marion summarizes female destiny as "the realms of women—the darkness of birth and death," paired fates that often claim mother and/ or newborn (Bradley, 1987, 77). She later muses, "How deeply the woman is in subjugation to her body" to bring another life into being (*Ibid.*). Of the central achievement in adult women, Helen claims greater love for her toddler son Bynomos than for her lover Paris or her husband Menelaus. Sister-in-law Andromache reverences the mother-child bond: "No woman could bring herself to leave a child she had borne," a belief that Elis repeats in *The Fall of Atlantis* (*Ibid.*, 299). Marion implies an inborn gift for mothering in the priestess Kassandra, who rides home from Colchis with Honey, a newborn foundling. The two scenes accentuate the pervasive nature of compassion in women.

The Firebrand acknowledges female ancestry in the care of twelve-year-old Kassandra among her mother's tribe of horse-folk, a communal fostering repeated in *The Forest House* among the sons of priestesses of Mona raped by Roman invaders. As symbols of heritage, Kassandra claims men's weapons—a sword, scabbard, and spear from Hecuba's girlhood, when the queen rode with her sister Penthesilea and the Amazons. Star and Kassandra debate the extremes of female devotion—a hypothetical intimacy with a man versus chaste service to the Earth Goddess. The arguments continue to a moot finish between Queen Imandra and her sassy daughter Andromache, who advocates girlish frippery over her mother's warlike pose.

Through the words of the Amazon queen Penthesilea, Marion emphasizes the limited choices the "house-bred" women of antiquity have over their lives: "Why should women live as slaves to men?" (*Ibid.*, 514, 313). For daily activity, Trojan women remain sequestered indoors to spin, weave, and embroider or venture out to fill water jars at the cistern. To set Queen Hecuba apart from the other Trojan women, the novel pictures "the great loom," an emblem of domestic industry that contrasts the massive double-headed ax, an icon of the macho heritage of slaughter that ends Priam's rule at Troy (*Ibid.*, 299).

Of the issue of polygyny, Creusa, the betrothed of Aeneas, prefers monogamy, but yields to a marriage system skewed to male preferences. After the birth of Astyanax, Priam's first grandson, Andromache mocks Hector's pride in siring the boy. In comparison to Hector's delight in a son, she equates labor and delivery with battle and wonders "how brave my dear Hector would have been in *this* battle!" (*Ibid.*, 188). The drollery speaks a common boast among women who believe birthing pains beyond male tolerance and snicker at the thought of Paris giving birth.

RITUALIZED WOMANHOOD

In volume two of *The Firebrand*, standard categories—girl, barren women, virgin, mother, crone—separate female worshippers at the spring planting ritual. The gendered ritual takes on reproductive significance: Priam's wielding of the wood plow illustrates the male role in fertilizing the furrow, a vaginal symbol. Female miming of the sprinkling of milk from bare breasts on the field precedes the sowing of seeds. Aeneas identifies the ritual as something "done for decency and custom," a conservative explanation of ancient seasonal protocols (*Ibid.*, 263).

While studying the reactions of Helen to the initial Akhaian raid on Troy, Kassandra realizes that she admires the Spartan queen's logic and obduracy amid a city of gossips and backbiters. Both Hecuba and Kassandra display affection toward Helen, especially in the birthing chamber. With a cool assessment of the demands of a court harper, Helen agrees that "[n]o working girl wants to be burdened with carrying and birthing" (*Ibid.,* 271). After the safe arrival of Bynomos, Kassandra acknowledges the boy Amazon style, as Helen's son rather than the child of Paris. Imandra, queen of Colchis, expands on women's rights by deriding the arrogant Akhaian concepts of kings and their dynasties. Volume three widens the divide between genders with Priam's self-satisfying question "Why can a woman never be reasonable," which suggests Henry Higgins's rhetorical question-song in *My Fair Lady,* "Why Can't a Woman Be More Like a Man?" (*Ibid.,* 493). Marion derides the king for his use of "reasonable" as a synonym and template for "male."

See also Details; Mother Goddess; Reproduction; *The Shattered Chain.*

Sources

Anczyk, Adam. "Druids and Druidesses: Gender Issues in Druidry," *Pantheon* 10: 1(2015): 3–15.

Bradley, Marion Zimmer. *City of Sorcery.* New York: DAW, 1984.

_____. *The Complete Lythande.* San Francisco: Marion Zimmer Bradley Literary Works Trust, 2013.

_____. *The Fall of Atlantis.* Riverdale, NY: Baen Books, 1983.

_____. *The Firebrand.* New York: Simon & Schuster, 1987.

_____. *The Forbidden Tower.* New York: DAW, 1977.

_____. *The Forest House.* New York: Michael Joseph, 1993.

_____. *Free Amazons of Darkover.* New York: DAW, 1985.

_____. *The Heirs of Hammerfell.* New York: DAW, 1989.

_____. *The Mists of Avalon.* New York: Ballantine, 1983.

_____. *The Other Side of the Mirror.* New York: DAW, 1987.

_____. *Rediscovery.* New York: DAW, 1993.

_____. *The Saga of the Renunciates.* New York: DAW, 2002.

_____. *The Shattered Chain.* New York: DAW, 1976.

_____. *Stormqueen!* New York: DAW, 1978.

_____. *Thendara House.* New York: DAW, 1983.

_____. *Traitor's Sun.* New York: DAW, 1999.

Farwell, Marilyn R. *Heterosexual Plots and Lesbian Narratives.* New York: New York University Press, 1996.

Kaler, Anne K. "Bradley and the Beguines" in *Heroines of Popular Culture.* Bowling Green, OH: Bowling Green State University Popular Press, 1987.

Noble, James. "*The Mists of Avalon*: A Confused Assault on Patriarchy" in *The Middle Ages After the Middle Ages in the English-Speaking World.* Cambridge, UK: Brewer, 1997.

Thompson, Raymond. *The Return from Avalon: A Study of the Arthurian Legend in Modern Fiction.* Westport, CT: Greenwood, 1985.

Glossary

aberration abnormality ("The Crime Therapist," 100)

adept a master of a particular skill. ("The Incompetent Magician," 137)

adiutrix Latin for "rescue." (*The Forest House*, 61)

aedile Latin for "magistrate." (*The Forest House*, 276)

agape Christian lovefeast. (*The Forest House*, 364)

agoraphobic fearful of open spaces. (*Darkover Landfall*, 40)

Aldebaran the brightest star in the Taurus constellation. ("The Crime Therapist," 97)

aleph the first letter of the Semitic alphabet. ("Elbow Room," 331)

allez-y French for "Let's go." (*The Catch Trap*, 83)

Alpha Centaurus the nearest star system to the sun. (*Thendara House*, 9)

alpha rhythms normal brain waves during consciousness. (*The Spell Sword*, 60)

amnesiac a patient who is unable to remember. (*Falcons of Narabedla*, 20)

anachronistic belonging to the wrong time period. ("The Crime Therapist," 100)

analogue a comparable object or being. (*City of Sorcery*, 54)

Andiamo, ragazzi Italian for "Let's go, kids." (*The Catch Trap*, 170)

android a robot resembling a human. ("The Crime Therapist," 95)

angelus the church bells rung daily at 6:00 a.m., noon, and 6:00 p.m. (*The Mists of Avalon*, 729)

anis an herb with a licorice taste. (*Falcons of Narabedla*, 10)

anoxia a lack of oxygen. (*Darkover Landfall*, 22)

anthropomorphism in human shape. (*Ghostlight*, 298)

anticlimax a letdown or disappointment. (*The Bloody Sun*, 31)

anti-matter a substance with negative gravity. (*Darkover Landfall*, 10)

aphasia an inability to speak. ("The Stars Are Waiting," 87)

apostasy retreat from religious fealty and beliefs. (*The Fall of Atlantis*, 40)

apotheosis a maximum point of development. (*Heartlight*, 16)

archon Greek for "magistrate." ("Centaurus Changeling," 86)

armistice a signed agreement ending a war. (*Falcons of Narabedla*, 7)

arras tapestry or heavy cloth hanging. ("Treason of the Blood," 215)

atavistic anachronistic or extinct. ("Hero's Moon," 272)

aura the energy field or atmosphere surrounding a living creature. ("The Secret of the Blue Star," 12)

auspices predictions based on animal sacrifice. (*Warrior Woman*, 40)

autarchy government by a single despot or dictator. (*The Sword of Aldones*, 1)

avanti Italian for "Go on." (*The Catch Trap*, 151)

avatar in Hinduism, the appearance a deity takes on earth. (*The Fall of Atlantis*, 272)

Aventine the southernmost of Rome's seven hills and the home of laboring-class people and immigrants. (*The Forest House*, 307)

azimuth the horizon. (*Darkover Landfall*, 15)

babbo Italian for "Daddy." (*The Catch Trap*, 523)

bacaudae Latin for "free-roving peasant rebels." (*The Forest House*, 391)

banewolf a demonic hellhound. (*The House Between the Worlds*, 39)

bannock a Scots flatbread. (*The Mists of Avalon*, 238)

banshee a female fairy who shrieks, howls, and mourns. (*The Dark Intruder*, 6)

barm the foam atop beer as it ferments. (*The Mists of Avalon*, 440)

barragana Spanish for "concubine." (*Sword of Chaos*, 86)

barrow a raised tomb of earth and stone. (*The Forest House*, 47)

basalt volcanic rock. (*Gravelight*, 9)

basque tight bodice or jacket. (*Bluebeard's Daughter*, 10)

basso profundo Italian for "deep bass." (*Exile's Song*, 124)

bating struggling. (*Hawkmistress!*, 12)

beglamoured smitten, enchanted. (*The Mists of Avalon*, 685)

Bellissima Italian for "most beautiful." (*The Forest House*, 383)

Bilitis a Greek writer of erotica. (*Checklist: A Complete, Cumulative Checklist of Lesbian, Variant and Homosexual Fiction*, ii)

bilocation being in two places at the same time. (*The House Between the Worlds*, 48)

biofeedback the training of the mind through electronic monitoring to control pain, blood pressure, or other physical anomalies. (*The House Between the Worlds*, 75)

birthchair a chair that supports a parturient woman with handholds and backboard to provide leverage during contractions. (*The Firebrand*, 334)

Bishop of Rome the Roman Catholic Pope. (*The Mists of Avalon*, 262)

bladder wrack a brown algae (*Fucus vesiculosus*) of the Atlantic and Baltic oceans. ("Sea Wrack," 79)

bloodleaf an herb (*Iresine herbstii*) that heals wounds and strengthens brain and nerves. ("Somebody Else's Magic," 40)

bodhran an Irish frame drum. ("The Wandering Lute," 88)

bolt paleolithic stone or flint dart or arrow. (*The Mists of Avalon*, 85)

Bona Dea a women's deity in ancient Rome whose rituals excluded men. (*The Forest House*, 151)

boon a good deed or favor. ("The Secret of the Blue Star," 5)

breechclouts diapers. (*The Mists of Avalon*, 221)

breeks breeches. (*The Mists of Avalon*, 455)

Brigantia the festival of St. Brigid, held on February 1. (*The Forest House*, 251)

Brigid the Irish deity of fertility, healing, and invention. (*The Mists of Avalon*, 875)

brimstone sulfur. ("Fool's Fire," 173)

Buon' giorno, Nonnina, come sta? Italian for "Good day, Granny, how are you?" (*The CatchTrap*, 61)

Buon' notte Italian for "Good night." (*The Catch Trap*, 214)

byre-woman dairy maid. (*The Forest House*, 29)

cadenza an ornamental phrase decorating a melody. (*Survey Ship*, 5)

cairn a landmark of mounded stones. (*The Mists of Avalon*, 505)

camelopard giraffe. ("Here There Be Dragons," 180)

Candlemas a Catholic festival on February 2, the date of Jesus's presentation at the temple in Jerusalem. (*The Mists of Avalon*, 236)

carboy jug. (*Darkover Landfall*, 89)

cari figli, cari fanciulli … tutti, tutti Italian for "dear sons, dear children, all, all." (*The Catch Trap*, 265)

cariole one person vehicle. ("Centaurus Changeling," 85)

castellan castle governor. (*The Mists of Avalon*, 363)

catatonic a stuporous state of immobility. (*Falcons of Narabedla*, 7)

catharsis relief from strong emotion. ("The Crime Therapist," 98)

ceilidh house party. ("The Bardic Revel," 78)

centering calming the mind and controlling emotions to enhance relaxation and alertness. (*Witchlight*, 56)

Cepheid variables cosmic pulsations for determining distances. (*Darkover Landfall*, 42)

Cerberus the three-headed dog in Greek myth that guards the entrance to the Underworld. ("Elbow Room," 339)

chantry an altar dedicated to prayers or masses for the dead. (*The Fall of Atlantis*, 37)

charge nurse managing nurse. ("Women Only," 36)

che il Dio ha fatto due Italian for "Whom God has made two." (*The Catch Trap*, 130)

chela the Hindu term for an apostle. (*The Fall of Atlantis*, 21)

chilblains patches of skin reddened and blistered by cold. (*The Mists of Avalon*, 93)

Child Francis James Child, a collector of English and Scots ballads published in 1898. (*Exile's Song*, 36)

chimera a female monster with a snake tail, goat body, and lion's mouth that breathes fire. (*The Gratitude of Kings*, 34)

chitarrone a long-necked Renaissance lute. ("Bitch," 107)

chronometer clock. ("The Climbing Wave," 1)

circadian set around a 24-hour day. (*Thendara House*, 44)

circumambulation walking in a circle. ("The Malice of the Demon," 54)

citadel the fortified center of a town. (*Black Trillium*, 7)

clabber cheese yogurt. (*The Mists of Avalon*, 307)

clairaudience an auditory perception of something beyond normal hearing. (*Traitor's Sun*, 14)

clavier a keyboard instrument invented in the late 1600s. ("The Wandering Lute," 94)

clingfire an incendiary siege weapon reminiscent of napalm. (*Stormqueen!*, 285)

code duello the rules governing an armed clash. (*The Door Through Space*, 10)

codex an ancient book, the forerunner of printed manuscripts. (*The Fall of Atlantis*, 75)

coemptio a Roman marriage arrangement symbolized by a bride price. (*The Forest House*, 267)

cognomen Latin for "nickname" or a military additive identifying a foreign victory, e.g., Germanicus, Africanus, Britannicus. (*The Forest House*, 152)

cohort one-tenth of a Roman legion, approximately 500–600 men. (*Lady of Avalon*, viii)

collective unconscious ancestral actions and memories that reside in the unconscious mind. (*The House Between the Worlds*, 105)

comfit a nut, seed, or dried fruit coated in candy. (*The Mists of Avalon*, 495)

conjure summon by sorcery. (*The Shadow Matrix*, 1)

conjure-man witch doctor. (*Gravelight*, 3)

conscript fathers Latin term for Roman senators. (*The Forest House*, 310)

consensus majority opinion. (*Rediscovery*, 68)

conservatory greenhouse. (*The Heirs of Hammerfell*, 5)

contraband illegal or banned goods. (*Star of Danger*, 2)

Cornovii an Iron Age tribe in England's West Midlands. (*The Forest House*, 46)

corona borealis a semicircle of stars known as the north crown. (*Endless Voyage*, 5)

crevasse a great abyss. (*The Spell Sword*, 2)

croft an enclosed home. ("The Incompetent Magician," 22)

crop a throat pouch in birds that stores food and begins digestion. (*Hawkmistress!*, 3)

Cuchulain an Irish mythic hero from Ulster in the first century CE. (*The Mists of Avalon*, 189)

cullion wretch; knave. (*The Mists of Avalon*, 65)

Curia Latin for "assembly." (*The Forest House*, 71)

curragh an Irish boat made from animal hides stretched over a wood frame. (*The Forbidden Tower*, 41)

cuyones gonads. (*The Shattered Chain*, 15)

cyclopean massive. (*Heartlight*, 80)

Cyclopeans a primordial race of one-eyed giants related to the Titans. (*The Firebrand*, 289)

dalmatica an ornate shirt or tunic. (*The Forest House*, 362)

Dammerung German for "twilight." (*The Planet Savers*, 14)

darkleaf oregano (*Origanum vulgare*). ("Somebody Else's Magic," 40)

daub and wattle grids of woven twigs and sticks covered in clay or mud to keep out harsh weather. (*The Mists of Avalon*, 30)

deadfall a trap made from a heavy weight balanced on a stick. (*The Forest House*, 9)

deja vu French for "seen before." (*The Brass Dragon*, 30)

denarius the basis of the Roman money system. (*The Forest House*, 392)

Deneb a supergiant star in the top of the Northern Cross constellation. ("Outpost," 143)

denouement French for "conclusion." (*Souvenir of Monique*, 179)

di catenas Spanish for "in chains" placed on married women. (*The Forbidden Tower*, 179)

discarnate body-less. ("Measureless to Man," 81)

distaff a spindle rotated to wind flax or wool for thread. (*The Firebrand*, 24, 236)

dom a lord or monk's title, taken from the Latin *dominus* (lord). ("The Shadow," 175)

Dominus et Deus Latin for "Lord and God," the designation that the Emperor Augustus chose for himself after his deification on January 16, 27 BCE. (*The Forest House*, 309)

domna a female title of respect, taken from the Latin *domina* (lady). ("The Word of a Hastur," 195)

Dôn a mythic matriarch of Welsh clans. (*The Forest House*, 65)

doppelgänger a twin or apparition of a living person. ("The Secret of the Blue Star," 4)

dorje a two-ended symbol in Tibetan Buddhism. (*The Fall of Atlantis*, 92)

draughts checkers. (*The Mists of Avalon*, 670)

dreamroot an herb (*Silene undulata*) causing vivid dreams. ("Somebody Else's Magic," 40)

drop spindle a rotating disk dangled from yarn for spinning fleece into thread. (*The Mists of Avalon*, 5)

dropsy swelling in tissues from water retention. (*The Forest House*, 213)

dryad a forest nymph or tree spirit. ("The Wind People," 198)

Dyaus the Hindu god of thunder, lightning, wind, and rain. (*The Fall of Atlantis*, 272)

dymaxion a maximum application of technology and resources with minimal effort and material. (*Darkover Landfall*, 7)

Eagles icon of the Roman military standard, the *aquila* (eagle). (*The Forest House*, 164)

Ebbene, Signor Mario Italian for "Well, Mr. Mario." (*The Catch Trap*, 197)

ecosystem a network of interrelated living things. (*Darkover Landfall*, 12)

ectoplasm a sticky substance that a seer exudes to call up a spirit. ("Footsteps of Retribution," 139)

effloresce blossom and proliferate. (*To Save a World*, i)

eglantine sweetbriar or wild rose. (*The Forest House*, 376)

Ego te absolvo Latin for "I forgive you." ("Elbow Room," 336)

eldritch unearthly; weird. (*The Mists of Avalon*, 167)

elemental a power of nature. (*The Gratitude of Kings*, 5)

elf bolts triangular flint points commonly found in Scotland. (*The Mists of Avalon*, 314)

ell an archaic measure equaling 45 inches. (*The Mists of Avalon*, 622)

entropy a decline toward disorder. ("Firetrap," 75)

epigraph a brief, cryptic wording of wisdom. (*A Darkover Retrospective*, introduction)

eques member of the Roman senatorial class. (*The Forest House*, 265)

esoteric concerning secret knowledge; the occult. (*The Fall of Atlantis*, 158)

euphoria a buoyant sense of wellness and joy. (*Rediscovery*, 173)

evensong evening prayer service. (*The Mists of Avalon*, 354)

exemplum a narrative illustrating a moral. (*The Ruins of Isis*)

ex officio Latin for "out of office." (*Traitor's Sun*, 78)

exorcism the banishing of an evil spirit. ("The Household Altar," 166)

eyas newborn hawk. (*Hawkmistress!*, 4)

factor a purchaser of goods for an estate. (*The Shattered Chain*, 252)

fairing a gift from a market or fair. (*The Mists of Avalon*, 6)

fard a facial colorant. ("Somebody Else's Magic," 61)

farriery a specialty in trimming hooves and fitting shoes on them. (*Thendara House*, 42)

fells barren moors. (*The Mists of Avalon*, 235)

fetch a double or shadow, a precursor of death. ("The Secret of the Blue Star," 4)

fibulae garment pins. (*The Forest House*, 18)

filleting narrow binding or banding of hair. (*The Fall of Atlantis*, 77)

fifth columnist traitor or supporter of the enemy. ("Peace in the Wilderness," 66)

firth an inlet or estuary. (*The Forest House*, 231)

fission the splitting of a substance into multiple parts. (*The Planet Savers*, 11).

flamma red veil at a Roman wedding. (*The Forest House*, 270)

Floralia a Roman spring fertility holiday celebrated on April 28. (*The Forest House*, 176)

flotsam wreckage or cargo floating in the sea or outer space. (*Rediscovery*, 6)

footpad a robber of pedestrians. ("The Walker Behind," 116)

forsworn committed perjury; lied. (*The Mists of Avalon*, 56)

fräulein German for "girls." (*The Catch Trap*, 381)

fretwork open spaces in ornamental design. (*The Fall of Atlantis*, 32)

Frisian person from northwestern Germany or Holland. (*Lady of Avalon*, ix)

fuller's earth absorbent clay. (*Darkover Landfall*, 136)

fustian a rough weave of linen with cotton. (*The Mists of Avalon*, 825)

gainsay contradict; deny. (*The Firebrand*, 446)

galactic arm a segment of a spiral of stars. (*Darkover Landfall*, 16)

gauntlet a falconer's padded glove. (*Hawkmistress!*, 4)

geas Irish for "obligation or spell." ("North to Northwander," 183)

genius Latin for "guardian spirit." (*The Forest House*, 384)

Gesù e Maria! Che Italian for "Jesus and Mary! What." (*The Catch Trap*, 440)

ghast a terror. ("The Wandering Lute," 97)

Giants' Dance Stonehenge. (*The Forest House*, 171)

glamour enchantment. (*The Gratitude of Kings*, 40)

glyph a pictographic symbol. ("Bird of Prey," 119)

Gnostic mystics who believe that an evil force created the world. ("Thoughts on Avalon," 2)

gorgon a mythic female monster whose gaze turned humans to stone. (*The Firebrand*, 36)

grand-dame grandmother. ("The Footsteps of Retribution," 133)

Gra'mère French for "Grandmother." (*Souvenir of Monique*, 174)

graz' tanto Italian for "Thanks a lot." (*The Catch Trap*, 307)

Great Wain Ursa Major or the Big Dipper. (*The Forest House*, 123)

greaves shin guards. (*Warrior Woman*, 35)

handfasting a Celtic commitment pledge before marriage. (*Two to Conquer*, 173)

hardtack a flat, hard biscuit made of a slurry of flour and flavorings and slow-baked to preserve it for a long shelf life. (*The Spell Sword*, 16)

haruspex the official who inspected a sacrificial animal at a Roman wedding. (*The Forest House*, 266)

haw a red berry of the hawthorn bush. (*The Mists of Avalon*, 155)

hearth-witch domestic sorcerer. ("To Kill the Undead," 162)

hedge-witch herbalist. ("Chalice of Tears," 34)

henge a circular monument made of timbers and stone. (*Lady of Avalon*, 46)

Hibernia Latin for "Ireland." (*The Forest House*, 83)

hierophant a guide or interpreters of religious mysteries. (*Gravelight*, 337)

Hittites a Middle Eastern people who occupied Anatolia and Syria from 1700 to 1200 BCE. (*The Firebrand*, 88)

holt a thicket or grove. ("Sea Wrack," 82)

Hound and Jackal an Egyptian board game dating to Thebes in 2100 BCE. (*The Firebrand*, 130)

hoy Dutch for "stop." ("The Incompetent Magician," 29)

hubris overweening pride. (*The Mists of Avalon*, 479)

humanoid resembling humans in shape, action, or character. (*The Planet Savers*, 5)

Hyades a star cluster in the Taurus constellation. (*The Door Through Space*, 7)

hyperadrenal overactive production of human steroids. (*The Bloody Sun*, 32)

hyperspace a method of traveling faster than light. ("Jackie Sees a Star," 98)

hypocaust under-floor furnace. (*The Forest House*, 354)

Iceni Iron Age tribe of eastern Britannia. (*Lady of Avalon*, x)

ides mid-month. (*The Forest House*, 302)

integument hide or covering. (*The Survivors*, 16)

iron maiden a cabinet filled with spikes that pierce the victim shut on the inside. ("Treason of the Blood," 216)

isotope the altered form of an element. ("Peace in the Wilderness," 76)

jack leather drinking vessel sealed with tar. (*The Firebrand*, 54)

jackdaw crow. ("The Walker Behind," 127)

jesses leather straps on a bird leg to which owners fasten leashes. (*Hawkmistress!*, 3)

Jochanan Greek for "John the Baptist." (*The Forest House*, 371)

joiner carpenter. (*The Forest House*, 44)

karmic concerning action that decides human destiny. (*The Fall of Atlantis*, 92)

keep the part of a palace that secures the royal family. (*The Firebrand*, 232)

ken know. ("The Secret of the Blue Star," 5)

Kerberos the three-headed hound of the Greek

underworld who guarded the gate. (*The Firebrand*, 45)

kirtle an overskirt, jumper, or loose gown. (*The Mists of Avalon*, 105)

kite a predatory raptor similar in size to a hawk. (*The Mists of Avalon*, 188)

knucklebones gaming dice made of bone, ivory, or metal. (*The Firebrand*, 18)

kylix Greek for a two-handled stemmed drinking bowl used at all-male drinking parties. (*The Inheritor*, 8)

kyrie eleison, criste [*sic*] *eleison* Greek for "Lord, have mercy; Christ have mercy." (*The Forest House*, 369)

lacunae gaps. (*Darkover Landfall*, 146)

lanai deck, porch. (*Exile's Song*, 28)

leechcraft medical treatment. (*The Mists of Avalon*, 327)

legatus juridicus Latin for "law officer." (*The Forest House*, 68)

lennavan a Celtic girl's name. (*The Mists of Avalon*, 239)

levin-bolt lightning. ("The Children of Cats," 229)

lexicon vocabulary. (*Exile's Song*, 20)

liana vine. (*The Planet Savers*, 59–60)

light-year the distance light can travel in one year. (*Rediscovery*, 4)

lingua franca the unofficial patois spoken between people of differing language groups. (*The Shattered Chain*, 99)

liturgy the language of ritual. (*Lady of Avalon*, 49)

locus/loci Latin for "place/places." (*Witchlight*, 42)

lordling a petty authority. ("Goblin Market," 188)

lughnasad the Gaelic harvest festival each August 1. ("A Feminist Creation Myth," 282)

lustration purification. ("The Household Altar," 165)

madonna Old French for "my lady." ("Treason of the Blood," 217)

Madre Santissima Italian for "Most Holy Mother." (*The Catch Trap*, 77)

maenad in Greek mythology, one of the raving women who followed Dionysus on his earthly travels. ("The Day of the Butterflies," 245)

mage an alchemist or magician learned in the natural elements. (*The Gratitude of Kings*, 34)

Magnificat the "Canticle of Mary," a Christian hymn. (*The Mists of Avalon*, 357)

magus a learned person; a philosopher. (*Ghostlight*, 23)

Malthusian theories principles of planet control based on the rapid growth of population and the decline of means of subsistence. (*Thendara House*, 17)

M-AM drive a theoretical rocket propulsion derived from dense antimatter. (*Darkover Landfall*, 118)

Mataguchi blade Japanese sword used in World War II. (*The Survivors*, 1)

matrix crystal a mineral constituted of pieces of crystal held together by other igneous rock. (*The Shadow Matrix*, title)

maw jaws. ("The Incompetent Magician," 27)

melanin dark skin pigment. ("Centaurus Changeling," 65)

messire Old French for "my lord." ("Treason of the Blood," 217)

mews stables. (*Hawkmistress!*, 3)

midden trash dump. (*Hawkmistress!*, 2)

mnemonic a pattern of letters or concepts that serves as a memory aid. ("Elbow Room," 340)

mo chridhe Celtic for "my heart." (*The Forest House*, 348)

moonblood menstruation. (*The Forest House*, 126)

moon flux menstruation. (*The Mists of Avalon*, 52)

mother-right the matrilineal ownership of land and realms. (*The Firebrand*, 192)

mummery playacting. (*The Mists of Avalon*, 746)

murrain plague. (*Black Trillium*, 3)

mutagenic capable of altering DNA. (*Thendara House*, 27)

mutch Scotswoman's linen or muslin cap. ("The Wandering Lute," 100)

Myrmidons rough warriors from Thessaly in northeastern Greece. (*The Firebrand*, 294)

nadir low point. (*The Fall of Atlantis*, 20)

narcosynthesis administration of sodium amytal and pentothal to cause patients to recall the past. ("The Stars Are Waiting," 89)

Nazarene Jesus. (*The Forest House*, 22)

nebula cloud; haze. (*The Colors of Space*, 14)

necropolis graveyard. ("Bitch," 113)

Neo-Gandhism passive resistance. ("The Stars Are Waiting," 91)

Neo-Luddites a society that shuns technology. (*Rediscovery*, 59)

nimbus a glowing cloud, aura, or halo. (*Gravelight*, 10)

noblesse oblige French for "nobles owe" assistance to the underclass. (*Darkover Landfall*, 30)

nock to load an arrow onto a bowstring. (*The Firebrand*, 101)

noncausal not related to stimulus and response. (*The Spell Sword*, 26)

nonna Italian for "grandmother." (*The Catch Trap*, 78)

noonday office noontime prayer. (*The Mists of Avalon*, 212)

nosegay a small bunch of fragrant flowers. (*The Heirs of Hammerfell*, 46)

novice an apprentice nun before the taking of final vows. ("The Heart of the Hill," 2)

Nunc Dimittis Latin for "Now you send forth," the opening phrase of an evening prayer. (*The Mists of Avalon*, 201)

O dulcis…. / O pie…. / O Jesu, Fili Mariae / Miserere Mei, Domine Latin for "O sweet; O worthy; O Jesus, son of Mary, Pity me, Lord," text from Mozart's hymn "Ave Verum Corpus." (*Survey Ship*, 127)

ogham an alphabet used in prehistoric Britannia. (*Ghostlight*, 56)

omphalos the metaphoric navel of the earth, the hub of all life. ("The Heart of the Hill," 6)

optio Latin for "sergeant, second in command." (*The Forest House*, 103)

orichalcum a mythic metal from Atlantis. (*The Mists of Avalon*, 57)

padrón/padrone Spanish/Italian for "master." (*The CatchTrap*, 5)

palfrey a smooth-gaited, lightweight horse suitable for a female rider or courier. (*The Mists of Avalon*, 300)

Palladium a sacred wood statue of Athene that Aeneas carries from Troy. (*The Firebrand*, 23)

pandemic a disease that engulfs residents of an entire planet. (*The Planet Savers*, 6).

Pan pipes a line of flutes of different lengths connected into a single musical instrument. ("The Day of the Butterflies," 245)

paps breasts. ("The Secret of the Blue Star," 10)

parapsychologist an expert on paranormal events. ("Jackie Sees a Star," 100)

pastille an aromatic wafer or pellet. ("Bird of Prey," 108)

patrician nobleman; aristocrat. (*The Forest House*, 323)

Pax Romana the Emperor Augustus's concept of international peace across the Roman Empire, which lasted 200 years. (*The Forest House*, 305)

pectoral an ornamental breastplate. (*The Fall of Atlantis*, 292)

pentagram a five-pointed star. ("The Wuzzles," 144)

Pentecost the Christian holiday marking the descent of the Holy Spirit on Jesus's apostles. (*The Mists of Avalon*, 413)

pentothal a psychotherapy to relax a subject and elicit concealed information. (*City of Sorcery*, 15)

peristyle a central court in a Roman house edged by columns. (*The Forest House*, **per nome di Dio** Italian for "In God's name." (*The Catch Trap*, 80)

persona non grata Latin for "unacceptable person or interloper." (*The Bloody Sun*, 51)

phantom pain suffering from amputation. (*Sharra's Exile*, 6)

picara a self-confident, autonomous heroine, such as Lythande.

piccino Italian for "little one." (*The Catch Trap*, 319)

Pict a tribesman from northeastern Caledonia during the Dark Ages. (*The Mists of Avalon*, 8)

pidgin an everyday lingo. (*Exile's Song*, 12)

pietas Latin for "duty and obedience." (*The Forest House*, 308)

pigeon-cote pigeon house. (*Hawkmistress!*, 11)

pillion a lady's pillow for sitting behind a rider on a saddle. (*The Mists of Avalon*, 68)

piton ice pick to aid mountain climbing. (*Rediscovery*, 8)

poltergeist a rambunctious ghost or specter. (*Witchlight*, 5)

polymath an intellect skilled in multiple disciplines. (*Survey Ship*, 2)

posset a hot restorative drink made with spiced wine and milk. (*The Mists of Avalon*, 329)

postural hypotension the dizziness resulting from a sudden drop in blood pressure. (*Exile's Song*, 7)

precognitive of future sight or visions. (*The House Between the Worlds*, 3)

Prefect Castrorum chief officer of a Roman camp. (*The Forest House*, 68)

preordained previously determined. (*Heritage and Exile*, 22)

priapic relating to an engorged penis or male sexuality. (*The Inheritor*, 172)

priedieu a kneeling bench for private prayers, devotions, or meditation. ("Treason of the Blood," 215)

procalamin a synthetic protein nutrient. (*Sword of Aldones*, 7)

procurator a provincial agent of Roman law and taxation. (*The Forest House*, 207)

prop plane an airplane moved by propellers. (*Hunters of the Red Moon*, 2)

proto-simian the forerunner of apes. (*The Survivors*, 18)

psychedelic mind-altering; hallucinogenic. (*The House Between the Worlds*, 1)

psychism an example of mental or intuitive alertness. (*The Inheritor*, 228)

psychodynamics the mental forces or energy that motivate emotion and behavior. (*The Planet Savers*, 11)

psychokinetic causing motion without applying force. (*The Planet Savers*, 9)

psychosomatic bodily disease or pain caused or worsened by stress or mental illness. (*The House Between the Worlds*, 47)

punt a flat-bottomed boat. (*Lady of Avalon*, 32)

quaestor a Roman investigator or judge. (*The Forest House*, 397)

quartern one-fourth. ("Somebody Else's Magic," 40)

Quel cretin French for "What an idiot." (*Souvenir of Monique*, 181)

Que pasó? O Dio, mi duele—duele tanto Spanish for "What's happening? Oh God, it hurt—it hurt so much." (*Darkover Landfall*, 46)

querido Spanish for "dear." (*Darkover Landfall*, 98)

quick alive. (*The Mists of Avalon*, 221)

ragazzo Italian for "kid." (*The Catch Trap*, 332)

reaver pillager. (*The Mist of Avalon*, 560)

retarius [*sic*] the Roman retiarius (net-fighter) used fishing trident and net to fight an armed pursuer in the Coliseum. (*The Forest House*, 307)

rheum runny nose. (*The Forest House*, 134)

rick haystack. (*The Heirs of Hammerfell*, 6)

Rigel the brightest star in the Orion constellation. (*Seven from the Stars*, 8)

roc a predatory bird in Arabian folklore. ("Here There Be Dragons," 180)

roll underworld slang for a sudden attack and theft of belongings. (*The Bloody Sun*, 31)

Roman wall Hadrian's Wall, begun in northern Britannia in 122 CE to protect the central and southern regions from Pict attack. (*The Mists of Avalon*, 482)

rune a mystic letter that confers protection. ("The Walker Behind," 126)

Sacré, quelle nuit de diable! French for, "God, what a devilish night!" (*Souvenir of Monique*, 5)

Sakti Sidhana the Hindu concept of devotion to the Divine Mother. (*The Fall of Atlantis*, 257)

salto mortale Italian for "the mortal leap." (*The Catch Trap*, 214)

salve Latin for "good morning." (*The Forest House*, 71)

Samurai medieval Japanese warrior. (*The Survivors*, 1)

sapience wisdom. (*Hunters of the Red Moon*, 10)

Sargent a portrait painter. (*Bluebeard's Daughter*, 6)

scrying a supernatural means of observing the past, present, and future. (*Lady of the Trillium*, 2)

scull to row with oars. ("Sea Wrack," 78)

Scythian bow a bow shaped with an upward curve at each end. (*The Firebrand*, 96)

serge a lustrous twill fabric used for suits and coats. ("The Day of the Butterflies," 242)

Serpent Mother a faience statue of a snake-wielding deity or priestess discovered in Knossos and dating to 1700 BCE. (*The Firebrand*, 154)

serried zigzagged. ("Measureless to Man," 79)

sestercius [*sic*] Rome devalued the sestertius to small change. (*The Forest House*, 332)

shriven absolved of sin. (*The Mists of Avalon*, 484)

sigil a magic sign, seal, or symbol. (*The Fall of Atlantis*, 140)

simples herbal cures. (*The Mists of Avalon*, 6)

sipwell a source of water in damp sand that

collects drinkable moisture in a pad of leaves and grass. (*Warrior Woman*, 2)

siren singer of an alluring song. (*Star of Danger*, 4)

Sirius the brightest star in Earth's night sky. ("Death Between the Stars," 129)

sistrum an Egyptian rattle, a percussion instrument consisting of metal rods on a frame. ("The Wandering Lute," 88)

skean a double-edged bronze Celtic dagger. ("Bird of Prey," 100)

soeur French for "sister." (*Souvenir of Monique*, 162)

solar private chamber. (*The Gratitude of Kings*, 40)

sooth truth. (*The Mists of Avalon*, 44)

Southern Cross a constellation visible only to Earth's Southern Hemisphere. (*Survey Ship*, 2)

spatha long sword. (*The Forest House*, 241)

spell-candler a creator of verbal charms. ("To Kill the Undead," 162)

spell-singer magician who uses notes and ritual lyrics to cast enchantment. (*Falcons of Narabedla*, 512)

spell-wright wizard wordsmith. ("To Kill the Undead," 162)

sphincter a circular closure similar to the muscles surrounding the human anus. ("Death Between the Stars," 74)

spinnaker a sail that balloons toward the prow. (*Hunters of the Red Moon*, 1)

spinosa martis a Latin plant name for a spiny Martian shrub. (*The Dark Intruder*, 9)

strappado a suspension device that lifts a torture victim by the hands behind the back until the shoulders dislocate. ("Treason of the Blood," 216)

strophe/antistrophe opening line and reply. (*The Fall of Atlantis*, 337)

subliminal subconscious. (*Darkover Landfall*, 146)

subsidiary auxiliary, secondary. (*The Planet Savers*, 18).

supernova an exploding star. ("Jackie Sees a Star," 100)

surcoat overcoat. (*The Mists of Avalon*, 487)

sventura Italian for "ill luck, misfortune." (*The Catch Trap*, 38)

symbiotic sharing powers that benefit all parties. (*Sharra's Exile*, 4)

Syrtis Major a dark spot on Mars. ("Year of the Big Thaw," 116)

tabularium Rome's record office and treasury. (*The Forest House*, 211)

taints heir to a Celtic chief. (*The Mists of Avalon*, 644)

talisman amulet or good luck charm. (*The Bloody Sun*, 17)

tambour a small hand drum. ("The Wandering Lute," 88)

tapster bartender, who directs ale from the barrel through the tap. ("The Secret of the Blue Star," 3)

tarlatan loosely woven cheese cloth. (*Souvenir of Monique*, 7)

Tay-Sachs a crippling genetics disorder of brain and spine. (*Survey Ship*, 8)

telempath a reader of emotions. (*Seven from the Stars*, 10)

telepathic capable of reading the thoughts of others; clairvoyant. (*The Heritage of Hastur*, 32)

Théâtre Étoile French for "Star Theatre." (*Souvenir of Monique*, 6)

Theta Centaurus a star in the Centaurus constellation. ("The Crime Therapist," 94)

threnody lament. ("The Wild One," 203)

tile meats cold cuts. ("The Secret of the Blue Star," 4)

tisane an herbal tea or medicinal infusion. (*Black Trillium*, 10)

Titus the emperor of Rome from 79 to 81 CE. (*The Forest House*, 7)

toga picta embroidered Roman uniform for male citizens. (*The Forest House*, 311)

tor a bare spire of rock. (*Lady of Avalon*, 15)

Transfiguration a church festival on August 6 venerating Jesus's return to his apostles in glory. (*The Mists of Avalon*, 543)

trews trousers or tights. (*The Forest House*, 11)

triangulate divide space into triangles for the purpose of determining location and mass. (*Darkover Landfall*, 42)

vambraces forearm guards. (*Warrior Woman*, 36)

vanguard leading riders. (*Hawkmistress!*, 67)

vassal a subordinate or underling. (*The Mists of Avalon*, 63)

vector any organism that infects a host with a pathogen; a carrier. (*The Planet Savers*, 4)

Vega the brightest star in the Lyra constellation. (*The Colors of Space*, 8)

Vestal a celibate woman who tends Rome's sacred hearth of Vesta. (*The Forest House*, 144)

vizier prime minister. (*The Gratitude of Kings*, 25)

VTOL vertical takeoff and land. (*Thendara House*, 208)

wain dray cart. (*Lady of Avalon*, 78)

warp-drive a fictional speed faster than the speed of light. (*The Colors of Space*, 7)

wattle and daub twigs and mud woven into panels and covered in mud mixed with animal dung. (*The Mists of Avalon*, 280)

wencher womanizer or lecher. (*The Mists of Avalon*, 295)

wenching profligate sexual conquest of women. (*Two to Conquer*, 3)

were-dragon a human who can shapeshift into a winged dragon. ("The Wandering Lute," 87)

wicker-withes willow twigs. (*The Mists of Avalon*, 403)

will-o'-the-wisp phosphorescent marsh gas. ("Well Met By Moonlight," 32)

winding sheet burial shroud. (*Lady of Avalon*, 25)

wing-struts shock absorbing braces on a plane's wing. (*Stormqueen!*, 27)

witchfire a ritual display of a sorcerer's power. ("The Footsteps of Retribution," 133)

woad a blue dye extracted from a yellow wildflower, the *Satis tinctoria*. (*The Mists of Avalon*, 99)

xenobotanist an expert in alien plants. (*Darkover Landfall*, 19)

xenologist expert at the study of alien or extraterrestrial culture and biology. (*The Forbidden Circle*, 28)

xenophobia suspicion and distrust of foreigners. (*Thendara House*, 183)

xenopsychology the study of the thinking process in foreign people. (*Rediscovery*, 60).

zygote tissue formed by the union of sperm with ovum. (*Exile's Song*, 86)

Appendix A:
A Guide to Places

Marion situates fiction in identifiable locales, both ancient and modern, such as Colchis, the realm of Queen Imandra in *The Firebrand*; *Survey Ship* in Australia; and *The Inheritor*, a ghost tale set in San Francisco in sight of the Bay Bridge. For *Witch Hill*, she acknowledges using place names created by H.P. Lovecraft.

Akhaia a northwestern region of the Peloponnesus southwest of Athens and home to the Akhaians.

Anglia a kingdom in southeastern England adjacent to Kent *q.v.*

Aquae Sulis a temple and bath complex built by Romans in the 60s CE that evolved into the English city of Bath.

Argos a city on the northeastern shore of the Peloponnesus and home of the Argives.

Atlantis Plato's fabled lost civilization on an island possibly west of Gibraltar.

Basque country a wedge on the Atlantic coast between Spain and France, the home of a unique people and language.

Bithynia a coastal area on the Black Sea in Asia Minor northeast of Anatolia.

Caerleon a Romano-Celtic administrative center in southern Wales.

Caledonia the Roman name for Scotland.

Camlann site of Arthur's last battle in 537 CE in western Cumbria.

Cappadocia a Turkish region from Mount Taurus to the Black Sea after 332 BCE.

Celidon Wood the location south of the Clyde and Tweed rivers in Scotland where Arthur fought his seventh battle after 465 CE.

Colchis a city in Thracian territory south of the Black Sea.

Colonia Agrippensis the Roman camp that became Cologne, Germany.

Crete an island south-southeast of Greece that featured the Minoan civilization, begun in 2700 BCE.

Dacia a land west of the Black Sea in modern-day Romania.

Delos a sacred Greek isle in the Cyclades, the birthplace of twin deities, Apollo and Artemis.

Deva the origin of Chester, England, established by Romans north of Wales in 79 CE.

Eboracum the fortified capital of northern Britannia, the foundation of York, dating to the 70s CE.

Elam a coastal region west of the Tigris and Euphrates settled in 4000 BCE.

Etruria west central Italy north of Rome, settled by northerners in the 800s BCE.

Galilee a mountainous region of northern Israel ruled by Naphtali around 1200 BCE.

Glastonbury a town in Somerset in southeastern Britannia built in 300 BCE, the supposed burial site of King Arthur and Queen Guinevere.

Glastonbury Tor a hill overlooking Glastonbury terraced by a spiral path known as the Processional Way. *See Also* Ynis Witrin.

Glevum the origin of Gloucester, a city established by Romans in south central England in 97 CE.

Gobi an Asian desert lying between Mongolia and the Himalayas.

Hibernia the name for Ireland during the Roman invasion of Britannia on August 22, 55 BCE.

Hy-Brasil a mythical island west of Ireland that is invisible from land.

Hyperborea a region of Thrace north of Anatolia.

Isle of Apples a designation for Glastonbury Tor or Avalon, reputedly named in 440 CE by St. Benignus.

Judea an upland of Palestine encompassing the Dead Sea from 720 BCE.

Kallistos an island also called Thera or Santorini, destroyed by an earthquake in 1500 BCE.

Karnak a temple complex built by Senusret I outside Luxor, Egypt, after 1970 BCE.

Kent a settled shire in southeastern England allied with the Jutes in the late 400s CE.

Knossos a city on Crete that dates to a neolithic settlement from 7000 to 1100 BCE.

Labyrinth a subterranean maze designed by Daedalus to contain the monstrous Minotaur under the Knossos palace on Crete.

Lenacum a Roman encampment near the Great Wall separating England from Scotland.

Less Britain the early medieval name for Brittany, a jut of land in northwestern France.

Libya a North African coastal country settled in 8000 BCE.

Londinium the Roman forerunner of London, established on the Thames River in 43 CE.

Lothian the lowlands of southeastern Scotland, settled around 420 CE.

Lyonesse a region adjacent to Cornwall in Arthurian literature.

Magdala an ancient town west of the Sea of Galilee, home of Mary Magdalene.

Media an ancient Iranian land dating to 800 BCE after the decline of Assyria.

Mendip Hills limestone hills south of Bristol and Bath, England.

Mesopotamia a fertile region in the Tigris and Euphrates valley from 10,000 BCE.

Minoans a civilization on Crete that flourished from 3500 to 1100 BCE and declined before the Trojan War.

Mona Anglesey, a holy island northwest of Wales.

Mons Graupius a battleground in northern Scotland in 83 CE between Scots tribes and the Roman general Agricola's forces.

Montmartre a hill in Paris known for artists displaying their works outside the Basilica of the Sacré-Coeur.

Moridunum a Roman sea fort built in 75 CE in southern Wales.

Mount Badon Arthur's Celtic army overcame the Anglo-Saxons at the Battle of Mount Badon near Bath or Swindon in February 482 CE.

Mount Ida, a mountain southeast of the Troad in Anatolia where King Priam proposed sending Prince Paris to be reared by a shepherd.

Mull a Scots island in the Inner Hebrides first inhabited in 6000 BCE.

Mykene a stronghold in the northeastern Peloponnesus and home of the Argives from 1350 BCE.

Mytilene the capital of Lesbos, an island off northwestern Anatolia.

New Hebrides a South Pacific island cluster renamed Vanuatu.

Orkneys an archipelago north of Scotland first settled around 6820 BCE.

Pamphylia a coastal region of south central Turkey settled in 1200 BCE.

Parthia a northeastern part of Iran south of the Caspian Sea ruled by Cyrus the Great from 559 to 530 BCE.

Phoenicia a trading center on the eastern Mediterranean shore south of Anatolia from 2500 to 539 BCE.

Phrygia a west central region of Turkey from 1200 BCE.

Pinnata Castra a Roman camp on the northern shore of Moray, Scotland, from the 80s CE.

Provençal related to Provence in southeastern France on the Mediterranean shore.

Rhenus Latin name of the Rhine River.

Salisbury a cathedral city in south central England near the neolithic monument of Stonehenge.

Scamander a river flowing by Mount Ida where the battles of the Akhaians and Trojans took place in 1200 BCE.

Scythia a central Asian region northeast of the Black Sea.

Segontium a Roman fort in northern Wales at Carnarvon.

Skye a Scots island in the Inner Hebrides first inhabited around 7000 BCE.

Summer Country the dry lake bed at Ynis Within, q.v.

Tara a hill in east central Ireland where kings ruled from the 600s-1169 CE.

Tarentum a Roman city on the southeastern tip of Italy.

Tartarus a great chasm in the underworld.

Thera an ancient city on the island of Santorini north of Crete.

Thessaly a region in northeastern Greece.

Thrace an area of southeastern Europe adjacent to northeastern Greece.

Tintagel a jut of land into the Atlantic ocean in southwestern Britannia, the supposed birthplace of King Arthur.

Tyre a Lebanese city founded in 2750 BCE that marketed Tyrian purple, a dye extracted from murex sea snails.

Ultima Thule a Latin designation for lands farthest north of Britannia, including Iceland and Greenland.

Venta Silurum a Roman market town built in southern Wales in 75 CE.

Ynis Witrin the Welsh name of Glastonbury Tor, *q.v.*

Ys a mythical Breton city that sank into the ocean.

Zakynthos an island retreat off the west coast of the Peloponnesus.

Appendix B:
A Guide to Writing, Art
and Research Topics

1. Discuss the effectiveness of the following rhetorical and linguistic devices:

- *rhyme* Though stars like weeds be thickly sown, no world of stars can match your own. (*The Bloody Sun*)
- *anachronism* half-pint, not quart (*The Forest House*)
- *conjecture* No benefits could ultimately come from a paralyzed parliament. (*Traitor's Sun*)
- *litotes* It is troublesome to be a woman. (*The Shattered Chain*)
- *cacophony* the rock-cliff as a gust of wind struck. (*The Spell Sword*)
- *hyperbole* If the projectile didn't ricochet and kill half the people in the room it would undoubtedly puncture the wall, vent the room to space, and kill *everyone* in the room. ("The Dance at the Gym")
- *rationalizing* Men do such things now and again, and women are expected to accept them. (*Two to Conquer*)
- *fallacy* They say you can never hear the one that has your name on it. (*City of Sorcery*)
- *pidgin* Heart—kind of you … I keep in grateful wishing. (*Death Between the Stars*)
- *headline* PIGTAIL KILLER TRAPPED BY PSYCHIC. (*The Inheritor*)
- *citation* Sufficient to the day is the evil thereof. (*Darkover Landfall*)
- *cliché* double-jointed fingers. (*Survey Ship*)
- *iambic tetrameter-trimeter* As one who on a lonesome road/Doth walk in fear and dread.. ("The Walker Behind")
- *caesura* Oh, Lew! There was … such music! (*The Shadow Matrix*)
- *alarum* Who grudges his blood to a blade had better earn his living behind the plow. (*Thendara House*)
- *logo* MZB Limited. (*The Best of Marion Zimmer Bradley Fantasy Magazine*, i)
- *solecism* not never no more. (*The Mists of Avalon*)
- *cynicism* Slaying dragons for your fair lady. (*The Spell Sword*)
- *synecdoche* this nest of evil birds—feather, wing, and egg (*The Fall of Atlantis*)

- *repetition* something stirring, nagging at his mind, something wrong. Something rotten. (*The Forbidden Circle*)
- *allusion* Xanadu. Not the Xanadu of Coleridge's poem. (*The Dark Intruder*)
- *archaism* Come, thou elemental prince. (*Gravelight*)
- *cognate* There is no parting a fool and his folly. (*The Forest House*)
- *neologism* They were sworded. (*Falcons of Narabedla*)
- *etymology* the personalities had forked so sharply apart and separated, Jason from Jay. (*The Planet Savers*)
- *aphorism* In seeking to avert fate, men often bring it closer. (*The Firebrand*)
- *sibilance* source of so much psychic disturbance. (*Gravelight*)
- *periodic sentence* The thing most important to the beauty of a married woman is her husband's love. (*The Gratitude of Kings*)
- *embedded narrative* Mother Lauria opened the book, and began to read … ("The Legend of Lady Bruna")
- *enigma* They had hidden the prey inside the hunter's door, hidden the leaf inside the forest. (*The Bloody Sun*)
- *masculine rhyme* And as the leaves within the forest fall,/Your memories will not remain at all. ("The Secret of the Blue Star")
- *simile* Like a row of dominoes … we'd gone down. (*Witch Hill*)
- *command* Wherever your soul is hiding, I call it forth! (*The Inheritor*)
- *pathetic fallacy* smoke of burned housesteads darkened the weeping sky. (*The Forest House*)
- *rhetorical question* A return to the past or a new beginning? (*The Catch Trap*)
- *adage* only men laugh, only men dance, only men weep. (*Sharra's Exile*)
- *truism* A tree is a tree, you might think. (*Exile's Song*)
- *dialect* it's a tarnal funny yarn. ("Year of the Big Thaw")
- *tone* playing Achilles-sulking-in-his-tent. ("Hero's Moon")
- *assonance* Hail to thee, thou new moon. (*The Forest House*)
- *Gothicism* the hotmetal stink of blood clogged the air. (*In the Rift*)
- *parallelism* So it was, so it is, so shall it be. ("The Wandering Lute")
- *fragment* Come robbery, rape, arson, blood feud, or the strange doings of wizards. ("Somebody Else's Magic")
- *sequel* The Shadow Matrix, World Wreckers, Heritage of Hastur, Exile's Song
- *acronym* the remnants of the wartime OSS. (*Heartlight*)
- *execration* Sweet Evanda, you're half frozen. (*Zandru's Forge*)
- *threnody* Alas for the land that none could save—/The knowledge lost that gods once gave. (*The Forest House*)
- *couplet* and to the shores Cassilda came/and called him by a mortal name. ("The Ballad of Hastur and Cassilda")
- *consonance* the dread fetch of the death-doomed. (*The Mists of Avalon*)
- *alliteration* I might have felt a fellow father's feeling. (*The Firebrand*)
- *personification* apple trees in gnarled files marching down to the river. (*Witchlight*)
- *malediction* May his bones rot unburied on the shores of the Styx! (*The Firebrand*)
- *prayer* All the Gods grant it. (*Stormqueen!*)

- *synesthesia* I am soaring with wings of light. (*The Forest House*)
- *nuance* combat troops sent to keep order. (*Traitor's Sun*)
- *inversion* this illusion—for illusion it must be. (*The Forbidden Circle*)
- *metaphor* The tight knot in his chest dissolved. (*The Catch Trap*)
- *allusion* Maybe Chicken Little was right. (*Witchlight*)
- *internal rhyme* I am bending to thee my knee. (*The Forest House*)
- *prophecy* Our fates spin their web. (*The Fall of Atlantis*)
- *advisory* Never underrate the power of intellectual curiosity. (*The Fall of Atlantis*)

2. Account for the significance of two secondary characters and the impact on plot and theme, especially these:

- psychiatrist Randall Forth in *The Planet Savers*
- Elizabeth and David in *Rediscovery*
- Romy's grandfather in *Hawkmistress!*
- Cyrillon in *Star of Danger*
- oddlings in *Black Trillium*
- Lady Deonara in *Stormqueen!*
- Sarmato or Elaria in *The Firebrand*
- Nonna Santelli in *The Catch Trap*
- Jimson in *Survey Ship*
- Alnath the salamander in *The Gratitude of Kings*
- Dr. Judith "Judy" Love in *Darkover Landfall*
- Valentine in *The Shattered Chain*
- Isis Cinderella in *The Ruins of Isis*
- Mother Lauria in *Thendara House*
- Balin and Balan or Raven in *The Mists of Avalon*
- Esteban in *The Forbidden Tower*.

How do these characters influence significant action? emotions? memories? dialogue? Which secondary cast member would you omit? What role would you create for yourself as a secondary character in the Lysande or Darkover series?

3. Contrast the settings and sources of drama, satire, or humor in two of these fictional situations:

feeding a verrin hawk	trading horses with Kentaurs
jousting at Pentecost	turning into a female dog
locating cat-men in the forest	treating clingfire burns
being teleported	graduating from space flight school
showing Jackie a distant star	selling a skirt to Lythande
saying mass for crash victims	destroying boots during a forest fire
charting Cottman IV	freed from bondage to catmen.

Which scenes provide visual effects for film or stage? Which suit oral storytelling, radio, mural, puppetry, anime, or pantomime?

4. Characterize the importance of setting to these scenes:

the birth of Rohana's baby	Khryses's attempt to seduce Kassandra
finding the dying grail bearer	visiting Atlantis

Leonie's location of a crash	grieving for the pony Dancer
avoiding Trailmen	attending mass with Bishop Patricius
Gaius Macellius's wedding	studying language and behaviors in a foreign town
conferring knighthood	learning ritual from a mentor.

5. Compose an annotated map featuring these landmarks in Marion's stories and novels:

Salisbury	Thera	Mona	Caerleon
Green Planet	Tara	Isle of Apples	Celidon Wood
Segontium	Hibernia	Londinium	Orkney
Ynis Witrin	Akhaia	Moridunum	Crete
Lothian	Kent	Mount Ida	Glastonbury Tor
Colchis	Less Britain	Troy	Hadrian's Wall.

List possible locations of Atlantis and cite archeological attempts to find its ruins.

6. Account for the significance of three of the following terms to the action of Marion's works:

oracle	coemptio	doppelgänger	skean
humanoid	scabbard	were-dragon	scry
posset	Nazarene	peristyle	matrix
liturgy	humanoid	knucklebones	exorcism
harper	esoteric	anthropomorphism	jesses
light-years	ecosystem	pentothal	*catenas.*

7. Locate three examples of destinations for visits and journeys as symbols of ambition, escape, loyalty, worship, and patriotism, particularly these:

House of the Maidens	Sparta	Round Table
mythic mountain city	Trade City	holy well
Tintagel	Darkover	Caratra's Temple
Beltane fire	circus tour	Colchis
Hag and Swine	Charmides	Hammerfell's castle
Imandra's throne	Cornwall	Mons Graupius
Old Gandrin	Roygan's lair	Shrine of Laritha
Grey Temple	Imperial Rome	St. Valentine's monastery
gates of Troy	Stonehenge	Terra
King Tashgen's court	tree nests	spaceport.

8. Debate the wisdom of two of the following choices and explain the characters' motivation:

making a mass grave on Darkover	marrying Julia Licinia
treating hurt hawks	riding with Penthesilea's band
interbreeding with humanoids	buying men's work boots
seducing Oberon	abandoning the Pendragon banner
loving Kevin Harper	summoning lightning storms
giving up the Sight	accepting hospitality at Castle Chariot
jousting against Lancelet	traveling on pilgrimage with Manuela
teaching judo	lancing and cauterizing an infected wound
becoming a tower Keeper	closing Darkover to outsiders.

9. Discuss the role of history in two of Marion's scenarios. Include background facts about these:

Saxon invasions of Britannia	Bishop Patricius's denunciation of Druids
the building of Stonehenge	Rome's seizure of southern Wales

adoration of the Virgin Mary	the loss of Penthesilea during the Trojan War
Rome's four bad emperors	the first flight out of Earth's atmosphere
Agamemnon's fleet	Boudicca's revolt against Rome.

10. Discuss the pervasive motif of women's accomplishments in three of Marion's works, especially these:

"Here There Be Dragons"	*Tiger Burning Bright*	"Elbow Room"
Warrior Woman	"Sea Wrack"	*The Gratitude of Kings*
"Well Met by Moonlight"	*Hawkmistress!*	"The Wind People"
"The Engine"	"The Waterfall"	*Heartlight*
The Planet Savers	*The Bloody Sun*	*Exile's Song*
"The Legend of Lady Bruna"	*Survey Ship*	"Fool's Fire."

Explain why the author values collaboration as well as self-liberation or self-rescue, the fate of questers in *City of Sorcery*.

11. Survey the rewards and recriminations of advanced age or declining health in two of Marion's characters. Consider the actions of these:

Taliesin the Merlin	Pellinore	Eilan	Viviane
Macellius Severus	Priam	Priscilla	Kevin Harper
Queen Imandra	Igraine	Khryses	Mother Lauria
Talkannon	Camilla	Uther	Gabriel
Duke Gascard	Domaris	Alexis	Esteban
Old Ones	Ashara	Gavin	Ivor Davidson

How do elderly or sickly characters make themselves indispensable?

12. Summarize two of the following quandaries as themes in Marion's stories and novels:

unbridled jealousy	intimidation by an enchanter
harassment of lone women	forced motherhood
bi-species offspring	disagreements between siblings or fosterlings
self-absorbed parents	feuding authority figures
illegitimate birth	loss of magical powers
Amazon training	epidemic illness
unrequited love	identity crisis.

13. Contrast two romantic relationships from Marion's writings. Choose from these examples:

Ravi/Moira	Magdalen "Magda" Lorne/Camilla n'ha Kyria
Dr. Judy Love/an alien	Kassandra/Aeneas
Morgaine/Arthur	Domaris/Reio-ta of Ahtarrath
Paris/Oenone	Cara/Ryn Kenner
Arvath/Elis	Rohana/Gabriel Ardais
Gaius Macellius/Eilan	Lythande/Frennet
Mario/Tommy	Akhilles/Khryses's daughter
Elizabeth/David Lorne	Andrew Carr/Ellemir
Jason Allison/Kyra	Danilo Syrtis/Regis Hastur.

What attracts one person to another? Why are some romances unwise or dangerous?

14. Describe how Marion presents two social issues in stories or novels, such as these:

Akhilles's bloodlust	epidemic Trailman fever
Gabriel's alcoholism	Roman exploitation of Celtic miners

Honey's abandonment	Leodegranz's patriarchal marriage arrangement
alienation from a brother	Gwenhwyfar's religious fanaticism
Kevin's disability	Kassandra's pregnancy with Agamemnon's child
Klytemnestra's adultery	extermination of Celtic folk culture
permanent paralysis	the rigid gender system in Isis Cinderella.

15. Arrange a literature seminar to introduce students to Arthurian lore in Marion's *The Mists of Avalon, Sir Gawain and the Green Knight,* Wolfram von Eschenbach's *Parzival,* and the Merlin Trilogy of Mary Stewart: *The Crystal Cave, The Hollow Hills,* and *The Last Enchantment.* Conclude discussion of historical fiction with proposals for cover art, a collection of lore or balladry, oral interpretation, genealogies, chronologies, maps, costume or banquet sketches, or illustrations.

16. Give the meaning and propose reasons for three of Marion's story or novel titles:

"The Year of the Big Thaw"	"Treason of the Blood"	*The Spell Sword*
"The Wild One"	*Gravelight*	"Measureless in Man"
The Firebrand	*Rediscovery*	"Blood Will Tell"
"Everything But Freedom"	"Witch Hill"	*Star of Danger*
The Heritage of Hastur	*The Winds of Darkover*	"Oathbreakers."

Suggest new titles for *In the Rift,* "The Wind People," *Two to Conquer, The Bloody Sun, The Inheritor, The Shadow Matrix, Traitor's Sun,* and "The Day of the Butterflies."

17. What does Marion's application of dreams, travel, music, food, dance, recitation, bawdy humor, and song as antidotes to despair have in common with forms of escapism in one of these works:

Madeline Miller's *Circe*	Kurt Vonnegut's *Slaughterhouse-Five*
Marjane Satrapi's *Persepolis*	Voltaire's *Candide*
Orson Scott Card's *Ender's Game*	Ursula LeGuin's *A Wizard of Earthsea*
Jamaica Kincaid's *Annie John*	Leslie Marmon Silko's "Lullaby"
Ruth Downie's *Medicus*	Toni Morrison's *The Bluest Eye*
Ray Bradbury's *Fahrenheit 451*	Isabel Allende's *The House of the Spirits*
Diane Gabaldon's *Outlander*	Sherman Alexie's *The Absolutely True Diary*
Robert Jordan's Wheel of Time	of a Part-Time Indian.

Which of Marion's protagonists embrace storytelling as a refuge and outlet for confusion, pain, and rage? How do ordered events in narrative or song restore mental and spiritual harmony?

18. Summarize the wisdom of Goddess worship in *The Fall of Atlantis, City of Sorcery, The Ruins of Isis, Sharra's Exile, The Forest House,* and *The Mists of Avalon.* What do postulants learn from living in cloisters, singing liturgy, scrying in calm water, celebrating harvest festivals and processions, drinking from a holy well, and cultivating magic and telepathy? Why do Christian zealots consider followers of the old ways heathen or satanic?

19. Characterize the motivation and purpose of daring in Darkover novels and the Lythande series.

- Why do Kennard and Larry fight a forest fire?
- Why does Lythande choose so isolated a life?
- How does Andrew rescue Callista from catmen?

- How do tower Keepers enrich themselves?
- What does Lady Rohana contribute to the rescue of Lady Melora?
- How do Rafaella and Magda track Alexis into the mountains?
- How does Camilla n'ha Kyria mentor Magdalen "Magda" Lorne?
- What does Jason/Jay Allison risk by formulating a serum?

20. Analyze the effects of sibling rivalry on two of these pairs from Marion's novels and stories:

Cai/Arthur	Menelaus/Agamemnon	Deoris/Domaris
Igraine/Viviane	Hector/Paris	Micon/Reio-ta of Ahtarrath
Gawaine/Gareth	Hecuba/Penthesilea	Gwenhwyfar/Meleagrant
Balan/Balin	Morgause/Viviane	Conn/Alastair
Leonie/Lorill	Dezi/Callista	sisters in "Goblin Market."

21. Summarize the significance of three of these details in Marion's novels and stories:

gesture of surrender	Pentecost	sacred snake
red dragon banner	church bells	flying salamanders
embroider scabbard	Earth's gravity	haunted house
gifts from Odysseus	Scotti	Tarot
chervine pack animals	elf bolts	disguise
St. Valentine monastery	Picts	judo
deadfall	mercy killing	*laran*
facial scar	light-year	travel by litter
double-bladed ax	psychodynamics	fire goddess.

22. Propose the choice of Marion's *The Mists of Avalon* as a community read. Suggest an annotated ballad or character web, taped readings, improvised dialogue, addition of a secondary character or characters or an exotic beast, and new and untried weaponry such as clingfire or matrix. Make a dramatic timeline to express periods of exhilaration or change in the lives of King Arthur's family and court, Taliesin the Merlin, Kevin Harper, the Lady of the Lake, and Grail seekers.

23. Compare aloud the turmoil of political, religious, and socio-economic change in *The Fall of Atlantis* and the stories in Mike Ashley's *Lost Mars: Stories from the Golden Age of the Red Planet*. Include adaptations to women's rights, Goddess worship, and postulant training. How do torture and treachery threaten lives? Why does gendered status endanger progress?

24. Account for two different types of confrontations in Marion's writing. Choose from these:

- romance and student rivalry in *Survey Ship*
- setting up a vendors' booth among hostile men
- releasing Preciosa in *Hawkmistress!*
- protecting Cholayna from altitude sickness
- executing a patient in an electric chair
- belittling of illegitimate and biracial children
- Gwydion/Mordred's regret at his destiny
- refusing entry to Shann MacShann and his mercenaries

- Priam's war council with Odysseus and Akhilles
- Gaius Severus's refusal of Eilan for a daughter-in-law
- formulating a serum against Trailman fever
- Deoris's charge against Riveda for practicing black magic
- delegating experts to repair a spaceship and its computer
- Meleagrant's insistence on a seat at the Round Table
- Lythande's threats against an old enemy Adept.

25. Contrast types of resistance in several of Marion's works. Include the following models:

- against oppression in *Two to Conquer*
- against enchantment in "Bitch"
- against a kidnapper in *The Shattered Chain*
- against ocean perils in "Sea Wrack"
- against falsehood in "The Word of a Hastur"
- against tradition in *The Forbidden Tower*
- against ecstatic worship in *The Fall of Atlantis*
- against grief in "The Wild One" or *City of Sorcery*
- against optimism in *Darkover Landfall*
- against evil in *Castle Terror*
- against distrust in "Chalice of Tears"
- against shapeshifting in "The Gratitude of Kings"
- against rules in "Hero's Moon" or *Hawkmistress!*
- against trickery in "Footsteps of Retribution"
- against males in *The Ruins of Isis*
- against a plague in *The Planet Savers*
- against a sexual predator in *The Mists of Avalon*
- against a brutal mining camp in *The Forest House*.

26. Compare the maturation and aging of decisive women in *The Forest House, Rediscovery, The Forbidden Tower, City of Sorcery,* or *The Mists of Avalon* with the last days of an English professor suffering from ovarian cancer in Margaret Edson's one-act play *Wit.* Explain how the paired works fulfill the definition of *reifungsroman.*

27. List types of creativity in such works as *Survey Ship,* "The Wind People," *The Catch Trap, Glenraven, Exile's Song,* and "Well Met by Moonlight." How do protagonists achieve great satisfaction from effort? from the supernatural? from romance? from solitude? from collaboration? from recognition?

28. Summarize Marion's views on marginalization in *City of Sorcery,* "To Keep the Oath," "To Kill the Undead," "Measureless to Man," and "Women Only." How does speciesism vary from ageism or racism?

29. Outline sources of pride in Marion's "The Climbing Wave," "Somebody Else's Magic," "Hero's Moon," *Rediscovery,* or *Sharra's Exile.* How do training, hard labor, community, unity, altruism, and strength produce contentment?

30. Account for humor in difficult times in the Lythande series as compared to Jacqueline Carey's *Miranda and Caliban,* Gore Vidal's *Visit to a Small Planet,* Diane Gabaldon's *Outlander,* or Karel Capek's play *R.U.R.* Compare situational satire among the customers in pubs and inns. How does Marion illustrate ignorance among country folk? Why does Lythande stay in the background, eat in privacy, and shave her eyebrows in private?

31. Compare institutionalized behavior for girls and women in Marion's *The Mists of Avalon, The Forbidden Tower, Hawkmistress!,* "Bride Price," or *Lady of Avalon* with similar expectations in one of these works:

Ursula LeGuin's "Sur"	Kathryn Forbes's *Mama's Bank Account*
Ruth Downie's *Medicus*	Sigrid Undset's *Kristin Lavransdottir*
Mary Chase's *Harvey*	Edward White's *The Unwilling Vestal*
Oscar Hammerstein's *The King and I*	Jessamyn West's *The Friendly Persuasion*
Harper Lee's *To Kill a Mockingbird*	Adrienne Rich's "Diving into the Wreck"
Anne McCaffrey's *Dragonsong*	Jeanne Houston's *Farewell to Manzanar*
Diane Gabaldon's *Outlander*	William M. Thackeray's *Vanity Fair*

32. Account for forcible isolation and for positive images of solitude in four of these characters:

Beccolo	Elaine	Caillean	Dom Gabriel Ardais
Hammerfell	Titania	Kennard Alton	tower Keepers
Huw	Renunciates	Kamellin	Theradin
Lori	Robin	*Chieri*	Macellius Severus
Cynric	lion tamer	Arvath	Robin Murray.

How do rituals at Forest House, Gandrin, and the House of Maidens ease alienation? Why do Terrans long to reunite with Earth's people?

33. Select contrasting scenes from Marion's stories and novels and describe their pictorial qualities, for example:

- locating a distant glimmer and protecting the village in "Fool's Fire"
- reuniting Micail and with his cousin Tiriki in *The Fall of Atlantis*
- arriving at Sanctuary and greeting Myrtis in "The Secret of the Blue Star"
- rejoining Penthesilea and watching Akhilles dishonor Hector's corpse in *The Firebrand*
- Ferrika's midwifery and Damon Ridenow's fear for Ellemir in *The Forbidden Tower*
- discussing music with Riella and regretting her death in "Sea Wrack"
- enchantment and racing dogs in "Bitch"
- viewing the face of the Goddess in *City of Sorcery*
- discovering the purpose of a pilgrimage and changing an opinion in "Chalice of Tears"
- Kindra's fear of blood and her dedication to healing in "To Keep the Oath"
- giving birth during a lightning storm in *Stormqueen!*
- shaping candles and Alnath's birthing of children in *The Gratitude of Kings.*
- Morgause's lust for young men and Priscilla's fostering of Balin in *The Mists of Avalon.*

34. Discuss the sources of affection or antipathy or both between one of these pairs:

Alart Hastur/serfs	Jalak/Jaelle n'ha Melora	Rafe MacAran/Camilla del Rey
Deoris/Demaris	Arthur/Cai	Gwenhwyfar/Archbishop Patricius
Eilan/Caillean	Agamemnon/Akhilles	Countess Teresa/Angelo Fieresi
Myrtis/Lythande	Black-robes/Eilantha	Javanne Hastur/Lew Alton
Red Rian/Cynric	Gorlois/Uther	Lady Rohana/Gabriel Ardais
Jaelle/Magda	Jay/Jason Allison	Lythande/Roygan the Proud

In which relationships have emotions stabilized? What outside forces alter affection?

35. Contrast flaws and strengths in two of these secondary characters from Marion's stories and novels:

Gareth	Accolon	Julia Licinia	Riveda
Oenone	Harry Leicester	Talkannon	Pellinore
Ysaye Barnett	Ryn Kenner	Fiora	Broca
Leonie Hastur	Lot of Orkney	Emperor Nero	Carlina di Asturien
Narthen	Leodegranz	Leonie	Byrna
Ysabet	Uwaine	Marco Zabal	Russ Montray
Ferrika	Agathon	Beltran	Lyle Belfontaine

Which characters recognize their own weaknesses? talents? inescapable memories? needs for control, rest or medical treatment, and camaraderie?

36. Write an extended definition of *conflict* using as an example the atmosphere of two of these examples:

- use of the Sword of Aldones
- toy making in "Bird of Prey"
- self-identification in *The Bloody Sun*
- investigating arson and slaughter by Scotti in *The Forest House*
- relationships among Keepers in *The Forbidden Tower*
- love between Oberon and Titania in "Well Met by Moonlight"
- celebration during Beltane bonfires in *The Forest House*
- discussion at Kassandra's meeting with Cheiron in *The Firebrand*
- Morgaine's wedding to King Uriens in *The Mists of Avalon*
- Akhaian ritual before Patroklos's funeral in *The Firebrand*
- Tommy's "coming out" in *The Catch Trap*
- priestesses at the stone circle at Glastonbury Tor in *The Mists of Avalon*
- anxiety after Max's levitation in "Phoenix"
- psychotropic drug experiments in *The House Between the Worlds*.

Incorporate changes in characters from triumphs or failures, for example, Eilan's hesitance to make love with a Roman prefect's son in *The Forest House* and the kidnap of Khryses's daughter in *The Firebrand*.

37. List types of comfort in these scenes. Explain why the characters are in need of treatment or solace:

- locating a plane crash on Cottman IV
- bandaging the shoulder wound on a deadfall victim
- treating the High King's illness with a posset

- escaping a hostile town on the road to Northwander
- eluding prowl cars in "Peace in the Wilderness"
- drinking from a holy well
- escaping a bad marriage in *Hawkmistress!*
- locating the Grail in "Chalice of Tears"
- measuring Darkover's mass
- watching a new colony digging a garden
- spoken words from a mute priestess
- sharing the bed of a sister-in-law
- enjoying visions in "The Day of the Butterflies"
- an alien spy in *The Colors of Space*
- ending a mother's pain with herbal poison.

38. Compose letters to characters offering support for their troubles and advice in difficult situations, especially these:

- boys born after mass rape on the holy island of Mona
- Gwenhwyfar during bouts of agoraphobia
- a Darkover spaceman's orphan
- a paraplegic lord and former soldier
- a visitor finding Rome to be a different place than imagined
- Rohana before her wedding to Gabriel in "Bride Price"
- the troubled patient in *The Brass Dragon*
- Andrew Carr's longing for the perfect woman in *The Spell Sword*
- Rafe MacAran after the death of his sister in *Darkover Landfall*
- acrobats learning flying techniques for the circus.

39. Cite occasions for computation in Marion's works. Name the particulars of each situation, such as these:

- 24 leagues of forest destroyed in *Rediscovery*
- a census of species in "Death Between the Stars"
- staff music to accompany Gaelic songs at New Hebrides
- the travel speed of Gwenhwyfar's retinue on the way to her wedding
- the demographics of disease in *To Save a World*
- the value of copper rings and bars in medieval Britannia
- a primitive way for Marco Zabal to chart a heart rate
- the range of *kireseth* pollen over open land
- gale damage in *The Winds of Darkover*
- principles of physics introduced in "The Climbing Wave"
- the number of pupils a school can enroll in *Survey Ship* and the percentage that graduate
- the size of an unknown planet and its period of rotation in *Darkover Landfall*
- the number of diners at a Pentecostal feast in *The Mists of Avalon*
- the territory covered by a raptor's flight in *Hawkmistress!*
- accounting for war costs in *Traitor's Sun*.

Compare the level of mathematical and scientific skills demanded in other sci-fi novels, especially Michael Crichton's *Airframe* or *The Andromeda Strain,* Marge Piercy's *He, She and It,* Orson Scott Card's *Ender's Game,* Daniel Keyes's *Flowers for Algernon,* Arthur C. Clarke's *2001,* Octavia Butler's *Kindred,* Robert Heinlein's *Strangers in a Strange Land,* Madeleine L'Engle's *A Wrinkle in Time,* or Ray Bradbury's *I Sing the Body Electric.*

Bibliography

Primary Sources

Black Trillium. New York: Doubleday, 1990. (co-authors Julian May and Andre Norton)

The Bloody Sun. New York: Ace, 1964.

The Brass Dragon. New York: Ace, 1969.

Can Ellen Be Saved? New York: Grosset & Dunlap, 1975.

Castle Terror. New York: Lancer, 1965.

The Catch Trap. New York: Random House, 1979.

Checklist: A Complete, Cumulative Checklist of Lesbian, Variant and Homosexual Fiction. Alexandria, VA: Library of Alexandria, 1980.

City of Sorcery. New York: DAW, 1984.

The Colors of Space. New York: Perennial Press, 1963.

Costume and Clothing as a Cultural Index on Darkover. Berkeley, CA: Thendara House, 1977.

Dark Satanic. New York: Berkeley Medallion, 1972.

The Door Through Space. New York: Ace, 1961.

Drums of Darkness. New York: Ballantine, 1976.

Endless Universe. New York: Ace, 1975.

The Endless Voyage. New York: Ace, 1975.

Exile's Song. New York: DAW, 1996. (co-author Adrienne Martine Barnes)

The Fall of Atlantis. Riverdale, NY: Baen Books, 1983.

The Fall of Neskaya. New York: New York: Ace, 2001.

The Firebrand. New York: Simon & Schuster, 1987.

The Forbidden Tower. New York: DAW, 1977.

The Forest House. New York: Michael Joseph, 1993.

The Forests of Avalon. New York: Penguin, 1998.

Ghostlight. New York: Tor, 2002. (co-author Rosemary Edghill)

Glenraven. New York: Baen, 1996. (co-author Holly Lisle)

The Gratitude of Kings. New York: Wildside, 1997.

Gravelight. New York: Tor, 1997. (co-author Rosemary Edghill)

Hawkmistress! New York: DAW, 1982.

Heartlight. New York: Tor, 1998. (co-author Rosemary Edghill)

The Heirs of Hammerfell. New York: DAW, 1989.

The Heritage of Hastur. New York: DAW, 1975.

The House Between the Worlds. New York: Doubleday, 1980.

Hunters of the Red Moon. New York: DAW, 1973. (co-author, Paul Edwin Zimmer)

I Am a Lesbian. Derby, CT: Monarch, 1962. (pseudonym Lee Chapman)

In the Rift. Wake Forest, NC: Baen, 1998. (co-author Holly Lisle)

The Inheritor. New York: Tor, 1984.

Knives of Desire. San Diego, CA: Corinth, 1966. (pseudonym Morgan Ives)

Lady of Avalon. New York: Viking, 1997. (co-author Diana L. Paxson)

Lady of the Trillium. New York: Bantam Spectra, 1995. (co-author Elisabeth Waters)

Lythande. New York: DAW, 1986.

Men, Halflings, and Hero Worship. Baltimore: T-K Graphics, 1973.

The Mists of Avalon. New York: Ballantine, 1983.

My Sister, My Love. New York: Monarch, 1963. (pseudonym Miriam Gardner)

The Necessity for Beauty. Baltimore: T-K Graphics, 1974.

Night's Daughter. New York: Del Rey, 1985.

No Adam for Eve. San Diego, CA: Corinth, 1966. (pseudonym John Dexter)

Rediscovery. New York: DAW, 1993. (co-authors Mercedes Lackey and Elisabeth Waters)

The Ruins of Isis. New York: Starblaze, 1978.

Seven from the Stars. New York: Ace, 1962.

The Shadow Matrix. New York: DAW, 1997. (co-author Adrienne Martine-Barnes)

Sharra's Exile. New York: DAW, 1981.

The Shattered Chain. New York: DAW, 1976.

Souvenir of Monique. New York: Ace, 1967.

Spare Her Heaven. New York: Monarch, 1963. (pseudonym Morgan Ives)

The Spell Sword. New York: DAW, 1974. (co-author Paul Edwin Zimmer)

Star of Danger. New York: Ace, 1965.

Stormqueen! New York: DAW, 1978.

The Strange Women. New York: Monarch, 1962. (pseudonym Miriam Gardner)

Survey Ship. New York: Ace, 1980.

The Survivors. New York: DAW, 1979. (co-author Paul Edwin Bradley)

The Sword of Aldones. New York: Ace, 1962.

Thendara House. New York: DAW, 1983.

Tiger Burning Bright. New York: William Morrow, 1995. (co-authors Mercedes Lackey and Andre Norton)

Traitor's Sun. New York: DAW, 1999. (co-author Adrienne Martine-Barnes)

Twilight Lovers. Derby, CT: Monarch 1964. (pseudonym Miriam Gardner)

Two to Conquer. New York: DAW, 1980.

Warrior Woman. New York: DAW, 1985.

Web of Darkness. New York: Starblaze, 1983.

Web of Light. New York: Starblaze, 1983.

The Winds of Darkover. New York: Ace, 1970.

Witch Hill. New York: Tor, 1972. (pseudonym Valerie Graves)

Witchlight. New York: Tor, 1997. (co-author Rosemary Edghill)

The World Wreckers. New York: Ace, 1971.

Zandru's Forge. New York: DAW, 2001.

Anthologies

The Age of Chaos. New York: DAW, 2002. (*Stormqueen!* and *Hawkmistress!*)

The Best of Marion Zimmer Bradley. Chicago: Academy Chicago, 1985. (*The Planet Savers, the Colors of Space, the Door Through Space, Year of the Big Thaw*)

The Best of Marion Zimmer Bradley's Fantasy Magazine. New York: Aspect, 1994. ("Introduction," "About Dorothy J. Heydt and 'Moonrise,'" "About Jennifer Roberson and 'Final Exam,'" "About L.A. Taylor and 'Counterexample,'" "About Mary C. Aldridge and 'The Adrinka Cloth,'" "About Pat Cirone and 'To Father a Sohn,'" "About Susan Urbanek Linville and 'Born in the Seventh Year,'" "About Peter L. Manly and 'Dragon Three Two Niner,'" "About Lynne Armstrong-Jones and 'The Case of Kestra,'" "About Lawrence Watt-Evans and 'The Palace of Al-Tir Al-Abtan,'" "About Mercedes Lackey and 'Nightside,'" "About Jacqueline Lichtenberg and 'Aventura,'" "About Jo Clayton and 'Change,'" "About Phyllis Ann Karr and 'The Truth About the Lady of the Lake,'" "About Diana L. Paxson and 'The Dancer of Chimaera,'" "About Elisabeth Waters and 'The Lesser Twin,'" "About Kit Wesler and 'The Bane of the Red Queen,'" "About Deborah Millitello and 'The Reluctant Vampire,'" "About Tanya Huff and 'Be It Ever So Humble'")

The Best of Marion Zimmer Bradley's Fantasy Magazine, Vol. II. New York: Aspect, 1995.

The Bloody Sun. New York: Ace, 1964. ("To Keep the Oath")

A Century of Science Fiction. New York: Dell, 1963. ("The Wind People")

Children of Hastur. New York: Doubleday, 1982. (*The Heritage of Hastur, Sharra's Exile*)

The Complete Lythande. San Francisco, CA: Marion Zimmer Bradley Literary Works Trust, 2013. ("The Secret of the Blue Star," "The Incompetent Magician," "Somebody Else's Magic," "Sea Wrack," "The Wandering Lute," "Bitch," "The Walker Behind," "The Malice of the Demon," "The Footsteps of Retribution," "The Wuzzles," "The Virgin and the Volcano," "Chalice of Tears," "To Kill the Undead," "To Drive the Cold Winter Away," "Fool's Fire," "Here There Be Dragons," "North to Northwander," "Goblin Market," "The Gratitude of Kings," "The Children of Cats")

The Dark Intruder. New York: Ace, 1964. ("The Dark Intruder," "Jackie Sees a Star," "Exiles of Tomorrow," "Death Between the Stars," "The Crime Therapist," "The Stars Are Waiting," "Black and White")

Darkover Grand Council VII Program Book. Wilmington, DE: Friends of Darkover, 1984. ("Oathbreakers")

Darkover Landfall. New York: DAW, 1972. (*No Tradition I Can Withstand, the Ghost Wind's Gale*)

A Darkover Retrospective. New York: Ace, 1980. (*The Planet Savers,* "The Waterfall," *The Sword of Aldones*)

Domains of Darkover. New York: DAW, 1990. ("Introduction and Contrariwise," "Firetrap")

Excalibur. New York: Aspect, 1995. ("Here There Be Dragons")

Experiment Perilous. New York: Algol, 1976. ("Experiment Perilous: The Art and Science of Anguish in Science Fiction")

The Forbidden Circle. New York: DAW, 2002. (*The Spell Sword, the Forbidden Tower*)

Four Moons of Darkover. New York: DAW, 1988. ("Introduction," "A Man of Impulse," "House Rules")

Free Amazons of Darkover. New York: DAW, 1985. ("About Amazons," "The Legend of Lady Bruna," "Knives")

The Future Is Female! New York: Penguin, 2018. ("Another Rib")

Grails: Quests, Visitations and Other Occurrences. Atlanta, GA: Unnameable, 1992, 43–52. ("Chalice of Tears")

Grails: Quests of the Dawn. New York: Penguin, 1994. ("Chalice of Tears")

Green Egg Omelette. New York: Career Press, 2009. ("The Household Altar," "A Feminist Creation Myth")

Greyhaven. New York: DAW, 1983. ("The Bardic Revel," "From Various and Sundry Bardic Revels," "The Incompetent Magician")

Jamie and Other Stories. Chicago: Academy Chicago, 1993. ("Introduction," "Women Only,"

"Centaurus Changeling," "The Climbing Wave," "Exiles of Tomorrow," "Death Between the Stars," "Bird of Prey," "The Wind People," "The Wild One," "Treason of the Blood," "The Jewel of Arwen," "The Day of the Butterflies," "Hero's Moon," "The Engine," "The Secret of the Blue Star," "To Keep the Oath," "Blood Will Tell," "Elbow Room," "Jamie")

The Keeper's Price. New York: DAW, 1980. ("A Word from the Creator of Darkover," "The Keeper's Price," "The Hawk-Master's Son," "Blood Will Tell")

Legends of Hastur and Cassilda. Berkeley, CA: Thendara House, 1979. (*The Legend of Lady Bruna*)

Leroni of Darkover. New York: DAW, 1991. ("Introduction")

Marion Zimmer Bradley Super Pack. New York: Simon & Schuster, 2015. (*Falcons of Narabedla,* "Death Between the Stars," "The Dark Intruder," *The Door Through Space,* "Black and White," "Treason of the Blood," "Jackie Sees a Star," *The Planet Savers,* "The Stars Are Waiting," *Exiles of Tomorrow, the Colors of Space,* "The Crime Therapist," "Year of the Big Thaw," "The Wild One," "The Wind People")

Marion Zimmer Bradley's Darkover. New York: DAW, 1993. ("Introduction," "To Keep the Oath," "Free Amazons," "House Rules," "Knives," "Firetrap," "The Keeper's Price," "The Lesson of the Inn," "Hilary," "Hilary's Homecoming," "Hilary's Wedding," "Everything but Freedom," "Oathbreaker," "The Hawk-Master's Son," "Man of Impulse," "The Shadow," "Bonds of Sisterhood," "Amazon Fragment," "Rohana," "Dyan Ardais")

Moonsinger's Friends. New York: Bluejay, 1985. ("Sea Wrack")

Music of Darkover. San Francisco, CA; Marion Zimmer Bradley Literary Works Trust. ("Introduction," "The Ballad of Hastur & Cassilda," "The Outlaw")

The Other Side of the Mirror. New York: DAW, 1987. ("Introduction," "Bride Price," *Everything but Freedom,* "Oathbreaker")

Out of Avalon. New York: Penguin, 2001. ("The Heart of the Hill")

The Planet Savers. New York: Ace, 1976. (*The Planet Savers,* "The Waterfall")

Red Sun of Darkover. New York: DAW, 1987. ("Introduction," "The Ballad of Hastur and Cassilda," "The Shadow")

Renunciates of Darkover. New York: DAW, 1991. ("Introduction," "Amazon Fragment")

The Saga of the Renunciates. New York: Daw, 2002. (*The Shattered Chain, Thendara House, City of Sorcery*)

Snows of Darkover. New York: DAW, 1994. ("Introduction," "The Word of a Hastur")

Songs from Rivendell. privately printed, 1960. ("The Rivendell Suite")

Space Opera. New York: DAW, 1996. ("To Drive the Cold Winter Away")

Spells of Wonder. New York: DAW, 1989. ("Introduction")

Summer Butterflies. Los Angeles, CA: Gafia Press, 1955. ("Summer Butterflies," "Song to Patrice")

Sword and Sorceress: An Anthology of Heroic Fantasy. New York: DAW, 1984.

Sword and Sorceress IV: An Anthology of Heroic Fantasy. New York: DAW, 1987.

Sword and Sorceress XI: An Anthology of Heroic Fantasy. New York: DAW, 1994.

Sword of Chaos. New York: DAW, 1982. ("Introduction," "A Sword Called Chaos," "The Lesson of the Inn")

Tales by Moonlight II. New York: Tor, 1989. ("The Haunted Street")

Tales of the Free Amazons. Berkeley, CA: Thendara House, 1980. ("Thendara House")

Thieves' World. New York: Ace, 1979. ("The Secret of the Blue Star")

To Save a World. New York: DAW, 2004. (*The World Wreckers, the Planet Savers,* "The Waterfall")

Towers of Darkover. New York: DAW, 1993. ("Introduction," "Ten Minutes or So")

The White Knight Cookbook. Berkeley, CA: Thendara House, 1981. (Recipes)

A World Divided. New York: DAW, 2003. (*The Bloody Sun, Star of Danger, the Winds of Darkover*)

Media Fiction

"Adventure in Charin," *Ghuvna* (August 1952): 26–35.

"Amazon Excerpt," *Darkover Newsletter* 9–10 (January 1978): 7–16, 41.

"Amazon Fragment," *Darkover Newsletter* 9–10 (January 1978): 42.

"Announcement: Off with the Old and on with the New," *Marion Zimmer Bradley's Fantasy Magazine* 11:3 (Winter 1991).

"Another Rib," *Fantasy and Science Fiction* 24:6 (June 1963): 111–126. (co-author Juanita Coulson)

"The Bardic Revel," *East Bay Review* 11:19 (1977): 77–79.

"Bird of Prey," *Venture* 1:3 (May 1957): 92–120.

"Bitch," *Fantasy & Science Fiction* 72:2 (February 1987): 104–110.

"Black and White," *Amazing Stories* 36:11 (November 1962): 76–85.

"Blood Money," *Uncensored Confessions* 3:10 (February 1962): 7–8, 10–11, 63–69.

"Blood Will Tell," *The Keeper's Price.* New York: DAW, 1980.

"The Blue Strangers," *Teen Trends*. Canada, n.d.

"Bonds of Sisterhood," *Free Amazons of Darkover*. New York: DAW, 1985.

"Cassandra Marceau-Leynier," *Astra's Tower Leaflet* 1 (August 1952): 7–10.

"Centaurus Changeling," *Fantasy and Science Fiction* 6:4 (April 1954): 85–123.

"Child of Fire," *Astra's Tower* 4 (May 1950): 1.

"The Children of Cats," *The Complete Lythande*. San Francisco, CA: Marion Zimmer Bradley Literary Works Trust, 2013.

"The Chimes in the Cathedral," *Astra's Tower* 1:2 (December 1947): 7.

"The Climbing Wave," *Fantasy and Science Fiction* 8:2 (February 1955): 3–55.

"Collector's Item," *Satellite* 2:5 (June 1958): 118–127.

"Conquering Hero," *Fantastic Science Fiction Stories* 8:10 (October 1959): 47–76.

"Cover-Up Girl," *True Romance* 75:4 (December 1962): 32–35, 78–79, 81.

"Crime Story," *Day*Star* (May 1961): 11–14.

"The Crime Therapist," *Future Science Fiction* 5:3 (October 1954): 93–100.

"Cross Currents," *Obsc'zine* 4 (November 1980): 72–73.

"The Dance at the Gym," *San Francisco Chronicle* (17 September 1987): B3, B7.

"The Day of the Butterflies," *DAW Science Fiction Reader* (July 1976): 183–194.

"Death Between the Stars," *Fantastic Universe* 5:2 (March 1956): 70–83.

"Dio Ridenow of Serre," *Astra's Tower Leaflet* 1 (August 1952): 4–7.

"Doom of the Thrice-Cursed," *Ghor, Kin-Slayer* (August 1997): 152–162.

"A Dozen of Everything," *Day*Star* (May 1955): 5–7.

"Elbow Room," *Stellar #5* 1 (May 1980): 124–144.

"The Engine," *Viva* 4:6 (March 1977): 63, 108–110.

"Everything but Freedom," *Darkover Newsletter* 9–10 (January 1978): 20.

"Exiles of Tomorrow," *Fantastic Universe* 3:2 (March 1955): 117–122.

"Falcons of Narabedla," *Dimensions* 14–15 (May 1954): continued.

"Falcons of Narabedla," *Other Worlds* (May 1957).

"A Feminist Creation Myth," *GE* 8:72 (Lughnasad 1975).

"The Final Bet," *Marion Zimmer Bradley's Fantasy Magazine* (Summer 1988): 30–31.

"Firetrap," *Domains of Darkover*. New York: DAW, 1990. (co-author Elisabeth Waters)

"Fool's Fire," *Marion Zimmer Bradley's Fantasy Magazine* 26:7 (January 1995): 60–62.

"Footsteps," *Marion Zimmer Bradley's Fantasy Magazine* 11 (January 1991): 32–36.

"A Genuine Old Master," *Galileo* 5 (October 1977): 24–29.

"Giant Step," *Mattachine Review* 7:4 (April 1961): 8–26.

"Goblin Market," *Marion Zimmer Bradley's Fantasy Magazine* 44:11 (July 1999): 23–25.

"Green Thumb," *Amazing Stories* 52:1 (November 1978): 71–72.

"The Hawkmaster's Son," *The Keeper's Price*. New York: DAW, 1980.

"Hello Daddy, This Is Margaret," *Marion Zimmer Bradley's Fantasy Magazine* (July 1990): 28.

"Here There Be Dragons," *Excalibur* (1995): 183–192.

"Hero's Moon," *The Magazine of Fantasy and Science Fiction* 51:4 (October 1976): 79–89.

"The House on the Borderland," *The Ladder* 4:8 (May 1960): 5–6.

"House Rules," *Free Amazons of Darkover*. New York: DAW, 1985.

"The Immovable Object," *The Other Side of Paradise* 2 (1977): 34.

"In the Steps of the Master," *Sixth Sense* 2 (January 1973): 1–155.

"The Inevitable Secret," *Altitudes* (1947).

"Jackie Sees a Star," *Fantastic Universe* 2:2 (September 1954): 97–101.

"The Jewel of Arwen," *I Palantir* 2 (August 1961): 1–39.

"The Keeper's Price," *Starstone* (January 1978): 48–57. (co-author Elisabeth Waters)

"Keyhole," *Vortex Science Fiction* 1:2 (1953): 123–132.

"The Lesson of the Inn," *Starstone* 2 (June 1978): 68–76.

"The Malice of the Demon," *Magazine of Fantasy & Science Fiction* 75:3 (September 1988): 53–55.

"Mama, Don't Let Him Have My Babies!" *True Experience* 69:2 (July 1961): 28–32, 46, 48.

"Marga of the Darriells," *Astra's Tower Leaflet* 1 (August 1952): 2–4.

"Measureless to Man," *Amazing Stories* 36:12 (December 1962): 74–107.

"A Meeting in the Hyades," *Anduril* (December 1962): 14–29.

"Moonfire," *Two "Lost" Tales* (April 2011): 18–32.

"Naughty Venusienne," *Caper* 1:3 (December 1956): 16–17, 21.

"North to Northwander," *Marion Zimmer Bradley's Fantasy Magazine* 36:9 (July 1997): 20–23.

"The Once and Future Merlin," *TV Guide* (April 1998).

"Orcs and Elfstones," *Day*Star* 15 (August 1961): 18–22.

"Outpost," *Amazing Stories* 23:12 (December 1949): 143–144.

"The Parting of Arwen," *I, Palantir* 5 (August 1964): 1–10.

"Peace in the Wilderness," *Fantastic Universe* 5:6 (July 1956): 55–79.

"Phoenix," *Amazing Stories* 37:2 (February 1963): 88–98. (co-author Ted White)

"The Place in the Marshes," *Astra's Tower* 1:2 (December 1947): 11.

"The Planet Savers," *Amazing Stories* (November 1958): 81–148.

"The Pledged Word," *The Merlin Chronicles* (1995): 130–136.

"The Priestess," *Astra's Tower* 1:2 (December 1947): 11.

"Saga of Carcosa," *Astra's Tower* 1 (July 1947): 5–6. (pseudonym Astra of the Spheres)

"Sea Wrack," *The Magazine of Fantasy and Science Fiction* 69:4 (October 1985): 82–102.

"The Seeker of Arrath," *MEZRAB* 4 (Spring 1951): 13–16.

"Seven from the Stars," *Amazing Science Fiction Stories* 34:3 (March 1960): 48–148.

"Somebody Else's Magic," *The Magazine of Fantasy & Science Fiction* 67:4 (October 1984): 101–134.

"The Stars Are Waiting," *Saturn* 1:5 (March 1958): 84–94.

"A Sword Called Chaos," *Sword of Chaos*. New York: DAW, 1982.

"To Err Is Inhuman," *Science Fiction Stories* 10:4 (September 1959): 30–44.

"To Keep the Oath," *Free Amazons of Darkover*. New York: DAW, 1985.

"To Kill the Undead," *Marion Zimmer Bradley's Fantasy Magazine* 23:6 (April 1994): 42–45.

"Toe Heaven," *Marion Zimmer Bradley's Fantasy Magazine* 9:1 (October 1996): 32–33.

"Treason of the Blood," *WEB Terror Stories* (August 1962): n.p.

"Veteran," *Astra's Tower* 1:3 (July 1949): 1–2.

"The Vigil," *Astra's Tower* 1:5 (December 1950): 4.

"The Walker Behind," *The Magazine of Fantasy & Science Fiction* 73:1 (July 1987): 101–115.

"The Wandering Lute," *The Magazine of Fantasy & Science Fiction* 70:2 (February 1986): 88–108. (novella)

"The Waterfall," *The Planet Savers*. New York: Ace, 1976.

"Well Met by Moonlight," *Marion Zimmer Bradley's Fantasy Magazine* 11:1 (October 1998): 32–33.

"Who Am I, Where I Am, and Where I Came From," *Triskelion* 1 (1977).

"The Wild One," *A Book of Weird Tales* 1:1 (January 1960): 104–116.

"The Wind People," *If* 9:2 (February 1959): 14–27.

"Women Only," *Vortex Science Fiction* 1:2 (1953): 36–40.

"The Word of a Hastur," *Snows of Darkover*. New York: DAW, 1994.

"World After Destruction," *Gorgon* 5 (November 1947).

"The Wuzzles," *Marion Zimmer Bradley's Fantasy Magazine* 14:4 (October 1991): 24–28.

"Year of the Big Thaw," *Fantastic Universe* 1:6 (May 1954): 110–116.

Verse

"Amazon Fosterlings' Rhyme," *Starstone* (June 1978): 33.

"The Ballad of Hastur and Cassilda," *Red Sun of Darkover*. New York: DAW, 1987, 21–27.

"A Carol for Patrick," *Allerlei* 25 (February 1965): 16.

"Chieri Lament," *Starstone* 2 (June 1978): 25.

"Cover," *Thrilling Wonder Stories* (October/November 1951).

"Dawns at the Window," *Ugly Bird* 1 (Summer 1956): 6–7.

"Fannish Executioner's Song," *Yandro* 10:2 (February 1962): 9.

"The Femfan's Lament," *Anything Box* 1 (1958): 2.

"Fragilities," *Allerlei* (February 1962): 6.

"The Haunted Street," *Nekromantikon* 2 (1950).

"In Search of Arkham," *Allerlei* (February 1972): 1.

"Introvert," *Anything Box* 1 (1958): 10.

"Katwen," *Allerlei* (February 1972): 18.

"Leaf," *Day*Star* 8 (May 1959): 3.

"The Long Hot Summer: Three Moods," *FAPA* (August 1959): 1.

The Maenads. Portland, OR: Garvin & Levin, 1978.

"Maidenhood," *Star*Line* (November/December 1980): 17–18.

"Nova," *Nekromantikon* 5 (1951): n.p. (pseudonym Astra)

"Oh-Oh, Another Po,'" *Startling Stories* 21:3 (July 1950). (pseudonym Astro)

"The Outlaw" in *The Heritage of Hastur*. New York: DAW, 1975, 273–275.

"A Parting Gift," *Starstone* 3 (December 1978): 28–32. (pseudonym Elfrida Rivers)

"The Place in the Marshes," *Astra's Tower* 2 (December 1947): 11.

"The Priestess," *Astra's Tower* 2 (December 1947): 11.

"Reflections on the Fugghead," *Yandro* 10:10 (October 1962): 18–19.

"The Sabre Jets," *FAPA Nonesuch* (Summer 1952): 8.

"Sapphic Song," *Day*Star* (August 1956): 9.

"Shangri La," *Allerleib* (February 1972): 6.

"The Sorceress," *Gorgon* 2:3 (March 1949): 33. (pseudonym Marion Astra Zimmer)

"Spaceman's Song," *Nekromantikon* 1:4 (1950–1951).

"Spinning Song," *Beyond the Fields We Know* (January 1978): 47–48.

"The Sterner Season," *Day*Star* 2 (May 1955): 2.

"Symphonic Suite," *Day*Star* 1 (November 1954): 5–9.

"Three Moods," *Day*Star* (May 1961): 10.

"To Evelyn from Mars," *MEZRAB* 3 (Winter 1951): 3.

"Tomboy," *Day*Star* 2 (May 1955): 7.

"Two Christmas Cards, Out of Season," *Day*Star* 8 (May 1959): 3.

"Veteran," *Astra's Tower* 3 (July 1949): 1.

"The Vigil," *Astra's Tower* 1:5 (December 1950): 4.

"Women ... at War," *Astra's Tower* 1:5 (December 1950): 3.

"World After Destruction," *Gorgon* 1:5 (November 1947): 37–46.

"Year's Beginning," *Day*Star* 13 (February 1961): 1.

Essays

"...and Strange-Sounding Names," *Amra* 2:10 (1960).

"About the Birthgrave, by Tanith Lee," *Fantasiae* 3:11–12 (November-December 1975): 1, 3–4.

"Alas All Maturity," *Vagabond* 2 (Summer 1955).

"Appreciation of Donald A. Wollheim," *Locus* 359 (December 1990).

"Appreciation of Randall Garrett." *Locus* 325 (January 1988).

"The Art of Speaking Forsoothly," *Marion Zimmer Bradley's Fantasy Magazine* (Fall 1992).

"Astra—Logically Speaking," *Astra's Tower* 1:2 (December 1947): 2.

"Astra's Tower," *Astra's Tower* 1 (July 1947): 3.

"At Science Fiction Conventions, Fans Can Sometimes Be a Second Family," *Science Fiction Age* 1:2 (January 1993): 22–23.

"The Attraction of Fantasy," *Marion Zimmer Bradley's Fantasy* 9 (July 1990): 35–36.

"The (Bastard) Children of Hastur," *Nyctalops* 6:1 (February 1972).

"Behind the Borderline," *Ladder* 5:1 (October 1960): 6–11. (pseudonym Miriam Gardner)

"Block That Title," *Allerlei* 25 (February 1965): 16. (co-author Walter Breen; pseudonym Marion Breen)

"Breather," *Astra's Tower* 3 (March 1959): 14–16.

"The Chief Value of Science Fiction" *The Double-Bill Symposium* (1969): 25–26.

"Child-Mother," *Day*Star* 3 (August 1955): 6.

"Children's Fantasy," *Fantasiae* 4:8 (August 1976): 5.

"C.L. Moore: An Appreciation," *Locus* 326 (March 1988): 69.

"Clunkers," *Fantasiae* 3:2 (February 1977): 8–9.

"Clutch of Vampires," *Niekas* 45 (July 1998): 33, 43.

"Convenient Earthquake," *Marion Zimmer Bradley's Fantasy* 18:5 (January 1993): 28.

"Darkovans Have Dirty Minds, Too!" *Darkovan Language Review* 1 (Spring 1978): 55.

"Darkover," Audio Records, 1980.

"Dear Editor: Stop Right There," *Writer's Digest* 68:9 (September 1988): 31.

"Death, Taxes, and the Writer," *Marion Zimmer Bradley's Fantasy Magazine* (October 1998).

"The Devil Made Me Do It," *Writer* 101:4 (April 1988): 16–17.

"Dialogue," *Marion Zimmer Bradley's Fantasy* 23:6 (April 1994): 32.

"Discovery," *Marion Zimmer Bradley's Fantasy Magazine* 16:4 (Spring/Summer 1992).

"Do You Know the Way to Miskatonic!," *Marion Zimmer Bradley's Fantasy Magazine* (October 1993): 30.

"Dungaree Doll: Inquiring Into a Modern Phenomenon," *Day*Star* (August 1956): 2–4.

"Editorially Speaking," *Legends of Hastur and Cassilda* (1979): 21.

"An Evolution of Consciousness: Twenty-Five Years of Writing About Women in Science Fiction," *Science Fiction Review* 6:3 (August 1977): 34–45.

"The Evolution of Women's Fantasy," *Sword and Sorceress III* (July 1986): 7–10.

"Excellence or Elitism?" *Marion Zimmer Bradley's Fantasy Magazine* 4:3 (Winter 1992).

"Fandom: Its Value to the Professional," *Inside Outer Space,* ed. Sharon Jarvis. New York: Ungar, 1985.

"Fantasy Vs. Disney," *Marion Zimmer Bradley's Fantasy Magazine* 3:3 (Winter 1991).

"Feminine Equivalents of Greek Love in Modern Fiction," *International Journal of Greek Love* 1:1 (1965): 48–58.

"The Fine Art of Collecting Rejection Slips," *Marion Zimmer Bradley's Fantasy Magazine* (October 1990): 47–48.

"Foreword," *Harper's Encyclopedia of Mystical and Paranormal Experience.* San Francisco, CA: Harper, 1991.

"Foreword," *In Search of the Woman Warrior.* Rockport, MA: Element Books, 1998, vii-x.

"God Hears Short Prayers Just as Well as Long Ones," *Marion Zimmer Bradley's Fantasy Magazine* (July 1990): 55–56.

"Grabbing the Reader," *Marion Zimmer Bradley's Fantasy Magazine* (January 1994): 32.

"Grammar I Learned in Fifth Grade," *Marion Zimmer Bradley's Fantasy Magazine* (October 1998).

"Grandchildren of the Lens," *Astra's Tower* 3 (July 1949): 4.

"Happy Endings," *Marion Zimmer Bradley's Fantasy Magazine* 5:3 (April 1993): 32.

"The Heroic Image of Women: Woman as Wizard and Warrior," *Sword and Sorceress I* (May 1984): 9–16.

"Holes in My Yard," *Darkover Newsletter* 58 (September 1992): 1.

"I'm Not in This Business for My Health," *Marion Zimmer Bradley's Fantasy Magazine* 5:2 (January 1993): 1–3.

"An Interview with Diana Paxson," *Marion Zimmer Bradley's Fantasy Magazine* (Autumn 1990).

"Introduction," *Encyclopedia of the Strange, Mysti-*

cal, & Unexplained. New York: Gramercy, 1991, ix.

"Introduction," *Leroni of Darkover.* New York: DAW, 1991: 1–3.

"Introduction: And Contrariwise," *Domains of Darkover* (March 1990): 9–12.

"The Last Word," *MEZRAB* (First Quarter, 1952).

"Lovecraftian Sonnetry," *Astra's Tower* 2 (December 1947): 10. (co-author Robert Carson)

"The Major Question," *Marion Zimmer Bradley's Fantasy Magazine* (April 1990): 53–56.

"Men, Halflings, and Hero Worship," *Astra's Tower* 5 (May 1961): 1–52.

"More Rejection," *Marion Zimmer Bradley's Fantasy Magazine* (January 1990): 57.

"My Life on Darkover," *Fantasiae* 2:11 (November 1974): 1, 5, 12; 2:12 (December 1974): 1, 5–6, 14.

"My Trip Through Science Fiction," *Algol* 15:1 (Winter 1977/1978): 10.

"My Very Own Slush Pile," *Marion Zimmer Bradley's Fantasy Magazine* 6:4 (July 1994): 38.

"A New Magazine," *Marion Zimmer Bradley's Fantasy Magazine* 1:1 (Summer 1988): 4.

"The Nine Basic Science Fiction Plots," *Marion Zimmer Bradley's Fantasy Magazine* 7:3 (January 1989): 49–50.

"Notes on Chronology," *The Spell Sword.* New York: DAW, 1974.

"Nova," *Nekromantikon* (June 1951): 56. (pseudonym Astara Zimmer Bradley)

"Now, Marion," *Starstone* (December 1978): 84–91.

"Ode on Imitations of an Immortal," *Astra's Tower* 1:2 (December 1947): 6.

"Of Cabbages and Kings," *Astra's Tower* 1:4 (May 1950): 4.

"On Night's Daughter and Mozart's *The Magic Flute*," *Night's Daughter* (1985): 247.

"The One Reason for Rejection," *Marion Zimmer Bradley's Fantasy Magazine* 6:4 (October 1994): 50.

"The Perfect Cover Letter," *Marion Zimmer Bradley's Fantasy Magazine* 14:4 (October 1991): 29–30.

"Programming the Centipede," *Marion Zimmer Bradley's Fantasy Magazine* (Autumn 1988): 55–56.

"Rejection, Continued," *Marion Zimmer Bradley's Fantasy Magazine* 2:2 (September 1989): 56.

"Rejection, Rejection ... Acceptance!," *Marion Zimmer Bradley's Fantasy Magazine* 2:1 (June 1989): 53–54.

"The Sense of Wonder," *Sword and Sorceress X* (June 1993): 7–10.

"Sex and Bad Language," *Marion Zimmer Bradley's Fantasy Magazine* 5:4 (April 1999): 46.

"Spaceman's Song," *Nekromantikon* (November 1950): 34.

"Speaking of Hacks," *Astra's Tower* 1:4 (May 1950): 3.

"Stencil Gazings," *Astra's Tower* 3 (July 1949): 1. (pseudonym Astra)

"A Subject I Wish Had Never Come Up," *Marion Zimmer Bradley's Fantasy Magazine* 1:2 (Autumn 1988): 54.

"Suspension of Disbelief," *Marion Zimmer Bradley's Fantasy Magazine* (July 1993): 34.

"Ten Minutes or So," *Towers of Darkover.* New York: DAW, 1993.

"Thoughts on Avalon," http://mzbworks.com/thoughts.htm, 1986.

"Tools of the Trade," *Marion Zimmer Bradley's Fantasy Magazine* 5:1 (October 1992): 34.

"Translations from the Editorial," *The Alien Critic* 6 (1973).

"Trialogue," *Marion Zimmer Bradley's Fantasy Magazine* 1:1 (Summer 1988): 45–49. (co-authors Walter Breen and Fritz Leiber)

"Twice the Work and Half the Money," *Marion Zimmer Bradley's Fantasy Magazine* 4:4 (April 1992): 24.

"Two Worlds of Fantasy," *Haunted* 1:3 (June 1968): 82–85.

"Variations on an Old Theme," *Astra's Tower* 1:3 (July 1949): 5–6.

"A View from the Other Side of the Desk," *Marion Zimmer Bradley's Fantasy Magazine* 4:1 (March 1989): 51–52.

"The Voice of the Myth-Maker," *Anduril* 3 (November 1972): 7–13.

"What I Reject and Why," *Marion Zimmer Bradley's Fantasy Magazine* 4:3 (January 1992): 32.

"What Is a Short Story," *Marion Zimmer Bradley's Fantasy Magazine* 8:2 (January 1996): 44.

"What Makes a Fanzine Crud?," *Vega* 12 (1953).

"What's My Name in Darkovan?," *Darkovan Language Review* 1 (April 1978): 50–54.

"What's Your Story About, Anyway?," *Marion Zimmer Bradley's Fantasy Magazine* 10:2 (January 1998): 57.

"When I Ignore My Own Guidelines," *Marion Zimmer Bradley's Fantasy Magazine* 4:1 (July 1991): 41.

"Why Did My Story Get Rejected," *Marion Zimmer Bradley's Fantasy Magazine* 9:2 (January 1997): 46–48.

"The Writer's Toolbox," *Marion Zimmer Bradley's Fantasy Magazine* 26:7 (January 1995): 50.

Secondary Sources

Arbur, Rosemarie. *Leigh Brackett, Marion Zimmer Bradley, Anne McCaffrey: A Primary and Secondary Bibliography.* Boston, MA: G.K. Hall, 1982.

_____. *Marion Zimmer Bradley.* Mercer Island, WA: Starmont, 1985.

Archibald, Elizabeth, and Ad Putter, eds. *The Cambridge Companion to the Arthurian Leg-*

end. Cambridge, UK: Cambridge University Press, 2009.

Ashley, Mike, ed. *The Merlin Chronicles.* New York: Carroll & Graf, 1995.

Auerbach, Nina. *Woman and the Demon: The Life of a Victorian Myth.* Cambridge: Harvard University Press, 1982.

Baert, Barbara. *A Heritage of Holy Wood: The Legend of the True Cross in Text and Image.* Leiden, Holland: Brill, 2004.

Barefield, Laura. *Gender and History in Medieval English Romance and Chronicle.* New York: Peter Lang, 2003.

Barr, Marleen S., ed. *Future Females: A Critical Anthology.* Bowling Green, OH: Popular Press, 1981.

Bernard, Miriam, Pat Chambers and Gillian Granville, eds. *Women Ageing: Changing Identities, Challenging Myths.* London: Routledge, 2000.

Breen, Walter. *The Darkover Concordance.* Houston, TX: Penny-Farthing Press, 1979.

_____. *The Gemini Problem: A Study in Darkover.* Baltimore: T-K Graphics, 1975.

Broderick, Damien. *Psience Fiction: The Paranormal in Science Fiction Literature.* Jefferson, NC: McFarland, 2018.

Browne, Ray B., ed. *Rituals and Ceremonies in Popular Culture.* Bowling Green, OH: Bowling Green University Popular Press, 1980.

Brownmiller, Susan. *Against Our Will: Men, Women and Rape.* New York: Simon & Schuster, 1975.

Busby, Keith, ed. *The Arthurian Yearbook III.* New York: Garland, 1992.

Campbell, Lori M. *A Quest of Her Own: Essays on the Female Hero in Modern Fantasy.* Jefferson, NC: McFarland, 2014.

Chivers, Sally. *From Old Woman to Older Women: Contemporary Culture and Women's Narratives.* Columbus: Ohio State University Press, 2003.

Christ, Carol. *Diving Deep & Surfacing: Women Writers on Spiritual Quest.* New York: Beacon, 1995.

Crosby, Janice C. *Cauldron of Changes: Feminist Spirituality in Fantastic Fiction.* Jefferson, NC: McFarland, 2000.

D'Ammassa, Don. *Encyclopedia of Fantasy and Horror.* New York: Facts on File, 2006.

_____. *Encyclopedia of Science Fiction.* New York: Facts on File, 2013.

Davin, Eric Leif. *Partners in Wonder.* Lanham, MD: Lexington Books, 2006.

Davis-Secord, Jonathan. *Joinings: Compound Words in Old English Literature.* Toronto: University of Toronto Press, 2016.

Dixon, Joy. *Divine Feminine: Theosophy and Feminism in England.* Baltimore, MD: John's Hopkins University Press, 2001.

Donaworth, Jane. *Frankenstein's Daughters:* *Women Writing Science Fiction.* New York: Syracuse University Press, 1997.

DuPont, Denise, ed. *Women of Vision.* New York: St. Martin's, 1988.

Elliott, Andrew B.R. *Handbook of Arthurian Romance: King Arthur's Court in Medieval European Literature.* Berlin, Ger.: De Gruyter, 2017.

Evans, Richard, ed. *Prophets and Profits: Ancient Divination and Its Reception.* New York: Routledge, 2017.

Evelina, Nicole. *The Once & Future Queen: Guinevere in Arthurian Legend.* Maryland Heights, MO: Lawson Gartner, 2017.

Evola, Julius. *The Mystery of the Grail: Initiation and Magic in the Quest for the Spirit.* New York: Simon & Schuster, 2018.

Farwell, Marilyn R. *Heterosexual Plots and Lesbian Narratives.* New York: New York University Press, 1996.

Fenster, Thelma S., and Norris J. Lacy. *Arthurian Women: A Casebook.* New York: Routledge, 2015.

Fiedler, Leslie. *Love and Death in the American Novel.* New York: Stein & Day, 1960.

Filmer-Davies, Kath. *Fantasy, Fiction and Welsh Myth: Tales of Belonging.* New York: St. Martin, 1996.

Frye, Northrop. *Anatomy of Criticism.* Princeton, NJ: Princeton University Press, 2000.

Gilbert, Sandra M., and Susan Gubar. *The Madwoman in the Attic.* London: Yale University Press, 1979.

Gilliam, Richard, Martin H. Greenberg, and Edward E. Cramer, eds. *Grails: Quests of the Dawn.* New York: Penguin, 1994.

Gimbutas, Marija. *The Language of the Goddess.* San Francisco, CA: HarperCollins, 1989.

Gjelsvik, Anne, and Rikke Schubart, eds. *Women of Ice and Fire: Gender, Game of Thrones and Multiple Media Engagements.* New York: Bloomsbury, 2013.

Gordon-Wise, Barbara Ann. *The Reclamation of a Queen: Guinevere in Modern Fantasy.* New York: Praeger, 1991.

Harty, Kevin J., ed. *Cinema Arthuriana.* Jefferson, NC: McFarland, 2002.

Hebert, Jill M. *Morgan Le Fay, Shapeshifter.* New York: Palgrave Macmillan, 2013.

Herald, Diana Tixier. *Fluent in Fantasy.* Englewood, CO: Libraries Unlimited, 1999.

_____. *Genreflecting.* Englewood, CO: Libraries Unlimited, 2005.

Higham, N.J. *King Arthur: Myth-Making and History.* London: Routledge, 2002.

Hildebrand, Kristina. *The Female Reader at the Round Table: Religion and Women in Three Contemporary Arthurian Texts.* Uppsala, Sweden: University of Uppsala Press, 2001.

Howey, Ann F. *Rewriting the Women of Camelot.* Westport, CT: Greenwood, 2001.

_____, and Stephen R. Reimer. *A Bibliography of Modern Arthuriana (1500–2000).* Cambridge, UK: D.S. Brewer. 2006.

Huckfeldt, Cynthia Rose. *Avoiding "Teapot Tempests": The Politics of Marion Zimmer Bradley's Darkover.* Laramie: University of Wyoming, 2008.

Hutton, Ronald. *The Triumph of the Moon: A History of Modern Pagan Witchcraft.* New York: Oxford University Press, 1999.

_____. *Witches, Druids and King Arthur.* London: Hambledon and London, 2003.

Jaffrey, Sheldon. *Future and Fantastic Worlds.* Rockville, MD: Borgo, 2007.

James, Edward. "Marion Zimmer Bradley" in *St. James Guide to Fantasy Writers.* New York: St. James Press, 1996.

Johnston, Hannah E., and Peg Aloi, eds. *The New Generation Witches.* New York: Routledge, 2017.

Kaler, Anne. *The Picara: From Hera to Fantasy Heroine.* Bowling Green, OH: Bowling Green State University Popular Press, 1991.

Keller, Rosemary Skinner, Rosemary Radford Ruether, and Marie Cantion, eds. *Encyclopedia of Women and Religion in North American.* Vol. 1. Bloomington: Indiana University Press, 2006.

Koelling, Holly, ed. *Best Books for Young Adults.* Chicago: American Library Association, 2006.

Larbalestier, Justine. *The Battle of the Sexes in Science Fiction.* Middletown, CT: Wesleyan University Press, 2002.

Lefanu, Sarah. *In the Chinks of the World Machine: Feminism and Science Fiction.* London: Women's Press, 1988.

Lennard, John. *Of Sex and Faerie.* Penrith, CA: Humanities-Ebooks, 2010.

Little, Judith A., ed. *Feminist Philosophy and Science Fiction: Utopias and Dystopias.* Amherst, NY: Prometheus, 2007.

Lykke, Nina, and Rosi Braidotti, eds. *Between Monsters, Goddesses and Cyborgs: Feminist Confrontations with Science, Medicine and Cyberspace.* London: Zed Books, 1996.

Mahoney, Dhira B., ed. *The Grail: A Casebook.* New York: Routledge, 2000.

Malinowski, Sharon, ed. *Gay & Lesbian Literature.* Detroit, MI: St. James, 1994.

Melton, J. Gordon. *The Encyclopedia of Religious Phenomena.* Canton, MI: Invisible Ink, 2008.

Mendlesohn, Farah. *Rhetorics of Fantasy.* Middletown, CT: Wesleyan University Press, 2008.

Mink, JoAnna Stephens, and Janet Doubler Ward. *The Significance of Sibling Relationships in Literature.* Bowling Green, OH: Bowling Green State University Popular Press, 1993.

Morgane, Judith S. *The Spirituality of Avalon: The Religion of the Great Goddess in Marion Zimmer Bradley's Avalon Cycle.* Munich, Ger.: AVM, 2010.

Nelson, Hilde Lindemann. *Damaged Identities: Narrative Repair.* Ithaca, NY: Cornell University Press, 2001.

Orenstein, Gloria Feman. *The Reflowering of the Goddess (Athene).* Oxford, UK: Pergamon, 1990.

Ortiz, Luis. *The Science Fiction Fanzine Reader: Focal Points: 1930 –1960.* New York: Nonstop Press, 2019

Pagès, Meriem, and Karolyn Kinane. *The Middle Ages on Television: Critical Essays.* Jefferson, NC: McFarland, 2015.

Paxson, Diana L. *Costume and Clothing as a Cultural Index on Darkover.* San Francisco, CA: Friends of Darkover, 1981.

Pearson, Joanna, ed. *Belief Beyond Boundaries: Wicca, Celtic Spirituality and the New Age.* Burlington, VT: Ashgate, 2002.

Rabinovitch, Shelley. *The Encyclopedia of Modern Witchcraft and Neo-Paganism.* New York: Citadel, 2002.

Riddle, John M. *Eve's Herbs.* Cambridge: Harvard University Press, 1999.

Roberson, Jennifer, ed. *Return to Avalon: A Celebration of Marion Zimmer Bradley.* New York: DAW, 1996.

Roberts, Adam. *Silk and Potatoes: Contemporary Arthurian Fantasy.* Amsterdam, Holland: Rodopi, 1998.

Sadovsky, Sonja. *The Priestess & the Pen: Marion Zimmer Bradley, Dion Fortune & Diana Paxson's Influence on Modern Paganism.* Woodbury, MN: Llewellyn Worldwide, 2014.

Sampson, Fay. *Return to Avalon.* New York: DAW, 1996.

Shichtman, Martin B., and James P. Carley, eds. *Culture and the King: The Social Implication of the Arthurian Legend.* Albany: SUNY Press, 1992.

Spivack, Charlotte. *Merlin's Daughters: Contemporary Women Writers of Fantasy.* Westport, CT: Greenwood, 1987.

_____. *Popular Arthurian Traditions.* Bowling Green, OH: Bowling Green State University Popular Press, 1992.

_____, and Roberta Lynn Staples. *The Company of Camelot: Arthurian Characters in Romance and Fantasy.* London: Greenwood, 1994.

Staicar, Tom, ed. *The Feminine Eye: Science Fiction and the Women Who Write It.* New York: Ungar, 1982.

Starhawk. *The Spiral Dance: A Rebirth of the Ancient Religion of the Great Goddess.* San Francisco, CA: Harper & Row, 1979.

Tanner, William E., ed. *The Arthurian Myth of Quest and Magic.* Dallas, TX: Caxton's Modern Arts Press, 1993.

Thompson, Diane P. *The Trojan War: Literature*

and *Legends from the Bronze Age to the Present.* Jefferson, NC: McFarland, 2013.

Thompson, Raymond. *The Return from Avalon: A Study of the Arthurian Legend in Modern Fiction.* Westport, CT: Greenwood, 1985.

Weedman, Jane B., ed. *Women Worldwalkers: New Dimensions of Science Fiction and Fantasy.* Lubbock: Texas Tech Press, 1985.

Wheeler, Bonnie, and Fiona Tolhurst, eds. *On Arthurian Women.* Dallas, TX: Scriptorium, 2001.

Wheeler, Rebecca S., ed. *The Working of Language: From Prescriptions to Perspectives.* Westport, CT: Greenwood, 1999.

Wise, Sandra. *The Darkover Dilemma: Problems of the Darkover Series.* Baltimore: T-K Graphics, 1976.

Wynne-Davies, Marion. *Women and Arthurian Literature: Seizing the Sword.* London: Springer, 2016.

Periodicals, Texts, and Journals

Adrian, Jack. "Obituary: Marion Zimmer Bradley," *Independent* (30 September 1999).

Ahern, Stephen. "Listening to Guinevere: Female Agency and the Politics of Chivalry in Tennyson's Idylls," *Studies in Philology* 101:1 (2004): 88–112.

Anczyk, Adam. "Druids and Druidesses: Gender Issues in Druidry," *Pantheon* 10:1 (2015): 3–15.

_____. "The Image of Druids in Contemporary Paganism: Constructing the Myth," *Walking the Old Ways: Studies in Contemporary European Paganism* (2012): 99–118.

Barr, Marleen. "Food for Postmodern Thought" in *Feminism, Utopia, and Narrative.* Knoxville: University of Tennessee Press, 1990, 21–33.

Battles, Paul, and Dominique Battles, "From Thebes to Camelot: Incest, Civil War, and Kin-Slaying in the Fall of Arthur's Kingdom," *Arthuriana* 27:2 (2017): 3–28.

Benko, Debra A. "Morgan Le Fay and King Arthur in Malory's *Works* and Marion Zimmer Bradley's *The Mists of Avalon*" in *The Significance of Sibling Relationships in Literature.* Bowling Green, OH: Popular Press, 1992, 23–31.

Bianco, Robert. "'Mists' Features Strong Women, Acting," *USA Today* (13 July 2001).

Bowman, Marion I. "Ancient Avalon, New Jerusalem, Heart Chakra of Planet Earth," *Numen* 52:2 (1 January 2005): 157–190.

_____. "Learning from Experience: The Value of Analysing Avalon," *Religion* 39:2 (2009): 161–168.

Brennan, Patricia. "King Arthur's Tale—With a Twist," *Washington Post* (15 July 2001).

Calhoun, John. "Parting the Mists," *Entertainment Design* 35:7 (July 2001): 5.

Cassada, Jackie. "Review: *Traitor's Sun,*" *Library Journal* 124:1 (January 1999): 165.

Chism, Christine. "Romance," *The Cambridge Companion to Medieval English Literature.* Cambridge, UK: Cambridge University Press, 2009, 57–69.

Coker, Catherine. "The *Contraband* Incident: The Strange Case of Marion Zimmer Bradley," *Transformative Works and Cultures* 6 (2011): 1–6.

Cortiel, Jeanne. "Risk and Feminist Utopia: Radicalizing the Future," *American Journal of Economics and Sociology* 77:5 (November 2018): 1353–1376.

Craig, Paul. "Bradley's Science Fiction World a Huge Success," (Santa Rosa, CA) *Press Democrat* (15 May 1989): B5.

Crater, Theresa. "The Resurrection of Morgan Le Fey: Fallen Woman to Triple Goddess," *Femspec* 3:1 (December 2001): 12–22.

Cushman, Carolyn. "Review: *Traitor's Sun,*" *Locus* 457 (February 1999).

Da Silva, Bridgette. "Medieval Mindsets: Narrative Theory and *The Mists of Avalon,*" *Strange Horizons* (1 October 2007).

D'Ammassa, Don. "Review: *Traitor's Sun,*" *Science Fiction Chronicle* 20:4 (February/March 1999): 43.

_____. "Review: *A World Divided,*" *Science Fiction Chronicle* (1 February 2004): 34.

D'Aries, Dawn. "Books We Can't Quit: *The Mists of Avalon,* by Marion Zimmer Bradley," *Pank Magazine* (3 June 2014).

Davidson, Dan. "Clear Choices Unmade," *Whitehorse* (Yukon) *Daily Star* (5 November 1982): 24.

_____. "Paranoid Media Fantasye," *Whitehorse* (Yukon) *Daily Star* (11 December 1981): 23.

del Rey, Lester. "Review: *The Forbidden Tower,*" *Analog Science Fiction/Science Fact* 97:11 (November 1977): 170–171.

_____. "Review: *Stormqueen,*" *Analog Science Fiction/Science Fact* 99:8 (August 1978): 173.

Dell, Helen. "'Yearning for the Sweet Beckoning Sound': Musical Longings and the Unsayable in Medievalist Fantasy Fiction." *postmedieval* 2:2 (2011): 171–185.

De Weever, Jacqueline. "Morgan and the Problem of Incest" in *Cinema Arthuriana: Twenty Essays.* Jefferson, NC: McFarland, 2002, 54–63.

Donawerth, Jane. "Galactic Suburbia: Recovering Women's Science Fiction," *Tulsa Studies in Women's Literature* 28:1 (Spring 2009): 179–180.

_____. "Teaching Science Fiction by Women," *English Journal* 79:3 (1 March 1990): 39.

Ellwood, Robert. "Occult Movements in America" in *The Encyclopedia of the American Religious Experience.* New York: Scribner's, 1988, 711.

Engelking, Tama Lea. "Renée Vivien and the

Ladies of the Lake," *Nineteenth-Century French Studies* 30:3–4 (2002): 363–380.

Epstein, Warren. "So You Want to Be a Science Fiction Writer, Kid?," *Tampa Tribune- Times* (14 June 1987): C5.

Ertell, Dee. "Busy Season at McCullough," *Bennington* (Vermont) *Banner* (22 December 1989): 4.

Fayad, Mona. "Aliens, Androgynes, and Anthropology," *Mosaic* 30:3 (September 1997): 59–73.

Felperin, Leslie. "The Magic Sword Quest for Camelot," *Sight and Sound* 8:8 (August 1998): 50–51.

Fox, Cheryl. "Review: *The Forest House*," *Park Record* (Park City, UT) (4 August 1994): B8.

Frederick, Sally R. "Review: *The Firebrand*," *English Journal* 78:1 (January 1989): 85.

Friedman, Mickey. "A Trend to Science Fantasy Books," *San Francisco Examiner* (16 November 1981): E4.

Fries, Maureen. "Trends in the Modern Arthurian Novel" in *King Arthur Through the Ages*. New York: Garland, 1990.

Fry, Carrol L. "The Goddess Ascending: Feminist Neo-Pagan Witchcraft in Marion Zimmer Bradley's Novels," *Journal of Popular Culture* 27:1 (1993): 67–80.

_____. "What God Doth the Wizard Pray To," *Extrapolation* 31:4 (1990): 333–346.

Fuog, Karen E.C. "Imprisoned in the Phallic Oak: Marion Zimmer Bradley and Merlin's Seductress," *Quondam Et Futurus* 1:1 (Spring, 1991): 73–88.

Gale, Mary Ellen. "Rape as the Ultimate Exercise of Man's Domination of Women," *New York Times* (12 October 1975).

Gidlow, Christopher. "Top 10 Clues to the Real King Arthur," (London) *Independent* (12 July 2010).

Godwin, Parke. "The Road to Camelot: A Conversation with Marion Zimmer Bradley," *Science Fiction & Fantasy Review* (April 1984): 6–9.

Goodman, Tim. "Women Take Over Camelot," *San Francisco Chronicle* (13 July 2001).

Gordon, Joan. "Review: Playing the Field," *Science Fiction Studies* 36:1 (March 2009): 161–163.

Green, Roland J. "'Hawkmistress' Continues Darkover Saga," (New Brunswick) *Central New Jersey Home News* (26 September 1982): D4.

Griffith, Nicola, and Kelley Eskridge. "War Machine, Time Machine" in *Queer Universes: Sexualities in Science Fiction*. Liverpool, England: Liverpool University Press, 2008.

Gubar, Susan. "C.L. Moore and the Conventions of Women's Science Fiction," *Science Fiction Studies* 7:1 (March 1980): 16–27.

Gulley, Alison. "Marion Zimmer Bradley" in *Arthurian Writers: A Biographical Encyclopedia*. Westport, CT: Greenwood, 2007.

Hagen, Michael. "Fantasy Writers to Visit," (Wilmington, DE) *News-Journal* (21 November 1986): D4.

Harvey, Graham, "Initiations," in *The Paganism Reader*. New York: Routledge, 2004.

Haught, Leah. "A Moment in the Field: Voices from Arthurian Legend by Margaret Lloyd," *Arthuriana* 17:4 (2007): 125–126.

Hernandez, Nelson. "Greek Students Savor 'The Iliad' and the Oddity," *Washington Post* (7 September 2003).

Hildebrand, Kristina. "The Other Cornwall Girl: Morgause in Twentieth-Century English Literature," *Journal of the International Arthurian Society* 6:1 (2018): 25–45.

Hollinger, Veronica. "Feminist Science Fiction: Breaking Up the Subject," *Extrapolation* 31:3 (October 1990): 229–239.

Howey, Ann F. "Belief and Acting on It Go Hand-in-Hand," *Edmonton Journal* (3 January 1991): F7.

Hughes, Melinda. "Dark Sisters and Light Sisters: Sister Doubling and the Search for Sisterhood in *The Mists of Avalon* and *The White Raven*," *Mythlore* 19 (1993): 24–28.

Hutton, Ronald. "King Arthur," *History Today* 60:4 (April 2010): 54–55.

Jones, Libby Falk. "Gilman, Bradley, Piercy, and the Evolving Rhetoric of Feminist Utopias" in *Feminism, Utopia, and Narrative*. Knoxville: University of Tennessee Press, 1990, 116–129.

Jordison, Sam. "Can Homer's Iliad Speak Across the Centuries?," *The Guardian* (9 February 2016).

Judge, Virginia. "*Firebrand* Tells Woman's Views of the Legend of Trojan War," (Rock Hill, SC) *Herald* (16 January 1988).

Kaler, Anne K. "Bradley and the Beguines: Marion Zimmer Bradley's Debt to the Beguinal Societies" in *Heroines of Popular Culture*. Bowling Green, OH: Popular Press, 1987.

Kaveney, Roz. "Review: *The House Between the Worlds*," *Foundation* (1 October 1980): 89.

_____. "Science Fiction in the 1970s." *Foundation* (1 June 1981): 5.

Keinhorst, Annette. "Emancipatory Projection: An Introduction to Women's Critical Utopias," *Women's Studies* 14:2 (1987): 91–99.

Kelso, Sylvia. "The Matter of Melusine: A Question of Possession," *Literature in North Queensland* 19:2 (2016): 134–144.

Killheffer, Robert K.J. "Fantasy Charts New Realms," *Publishers Weekly* 244:24 (16 June 1997): 34–40.

Kirchhoff, H.J. "An Old Story 'The Firebrand,'" (Toronto) *Globe and Mail* (26 December 1987).

Łaszkiewicz, Weronika. "Religious Conflicts and Their Impact on King Arthur's Reign in Marion Zimmer Bradley's *The Mists of Avalon*," *Acta Neophilologica* 19 (2017): 133–143.

Le Guin, Ursula. "Sur," *New Yorker* (1 February 1982): 38.

Lefkowitz, Mary. "What the Amazons Taught Her," *New York Times* (29 November 1987): A27.

Leith, Linda. "Marion Zimmer Bradley and Darkover," *Science Fiction Studies* 7 (1980): 28–35.

_____. "Tales of Earth: Terraforming in Recent Women's SF," *Foundation* 29 (1 April 2000): 34.

Lifshitz, Felice. "Destructive Dominae: Women and Vengeance in Medievalist Films," *Studies in Medievalism* 21 (2012): 161–190.

Livingstone, Josephine. "Old English," *New York Times Magazine* (6 January 2019): 24–25.

Madrigal, Alix. "A Female Vision of the Arthurian Legend," *San Francisco Examiner* (27 February 1983): 3.

Marden, William. "Bradley Delves Into Future of Planet Known as Darkover," *Orlando Sentinel* (28 March 1999): F9.

_____. "The Darkover Series Out of Exile; Swords; Angels," (Fort Lauderdale, FL) *Sun Sentinel* (15 September 1996): F10.

_____. "Otherworldly Entries in Fantasy Fiction Genre," *Orlando Sentinel* (8 August 1993): D11.

Margoulick, Mary. "Frustrating Female Heroism," *Journal of Popular Culture* 39:5 (2006): 729–754.

"Marion Zimmer Bradley, 69, Writer of Darkover Fantasies," *New York Times* (29 September 1999).

Maryles, Daisy. "Rising from the Mists," *Publishers Weekly* (30 July 2001): 18.

McCash, Vicki. "A Feminist Reworking of Mythology," (Broward, FL) *Sun Sentinel* (17 April 1988).

McClain, Lee Tobin. "Gender Anxiety in Arthurian Romance," *Extrapolation* 38 (Fall 2000).

McDaniel, Maude. "Review: *The Mists of Avalon*," *Washington Post* (28 January 1983).

McIntire, Elliot G. "Exploring Alternate Worlds," *Yearbook of the Association of Pacific Coast Geographers* 44:1 (1982): 93–108.

McIntyre Vonda N. "Review: *Darkover Landfall*," *The Witch and the Chameleon* 2 (November 1974): 19–24.

Mendlesohn, Farah. "Women in SF: Six American SF Writers Between 1960 and 1985," *Foundation* (October 1991): 53.

Miller, Steve. "The Arthurian Legend: Returned to Epic Status," *Baltimore Sun* (30 January 1983): D4.

Mink, Eric. "'Avalon' Gradually Improves Its Caliber," *New York Daily News* (13 July 2001): 120.

Monk, Patricia. "Frankenstein's Daughters: The Problems of the Feminine Image in Science Fiction," *Mosaic* 13:3–4 (1 April 1980): 15.

_____. "The Future Imperfect of Conjugation: Images of Marriage in Science Fiction," *Mosaic* 17:2 (1 April 1984): 207–222.

Muller, Al, and C.W. Sullivan. "Young Adult Literature: Science Fiction and Fantasy Series Books," *English Journal* 69:7 (October 1980): 71–74.

Murphy, Laura. "Marion Zimmer Bradley," *Dictionary of Literary Biography* vol. 8, Detroit, MI: Gale, 1981, 77–80.

Mutter, John. "Review: *Lythande*," *Publishers Weekly* 229:26 (27 June 1986): 82.

Nastali, Dan. "Arthur Without Fantasy: Dark Age Britain in Recent Historical Fiction," *Arthuriana* 1 (April 1999): 5–22.

_____. "Arthurian Pop: The Tradition in Twentieth-Century Popular Music," *King Arthur in Popular Culture* (2002): 138–167.

Nesselrath, Heinz-Günther. "Where the Lord of the Sea Grants Passage to Sailors Through the Deep-Blue Mere No More," *Greece & Rome* 52:2 (Oct 2005): 153–171.

Nichols, Nichelle. "Influences of 'Star Trek' on Her Writing," *Amani* 15/16 (1976).

Noble, James. "Guinevere, the Superwoman of Contemporary Arthurian Fiction," *Florilegium* 23:2 (2006): 197–210.

_____. "*The Mists of Avalon*: A Confused Assault on Patriarchy" in *The Middle Ages After the Middle Ages in the English-Speaking World*. Cambridge, UK: Brewer, 1997.

O'Hare, Kate. "The Once and Future Women of 'The Mists of Avalon,'" *Reporter-Times* (Martinsville, IN) (14 July 2001).

Oliver, Myrna. "Marion Bradley; Writer of Fantasy Novels," *Los Angeles Times* (30 September 1999): A24.

Orenstein, Gloria. "Letter to Christine Downing," *Women's Studies Quarterly* 21:1–2 (1993): 42–47.

Panchyle, Dave. "Review: *The Shadow Matrix*," (Regina, Saskatchewan) *Leader-Post* (21 February 1998): D2.

Paxson, Diana L. "Marion Zimmer Bradley and *The Mists of Avalon*," *Arthuriana* 9:1 (Spring 1999): 110–126.

_____. "The Priestess of Avalon," *Sagewoman* 48 (Winter 1999–2000): 31–34.

Prater, Lenise. "Monstrous Fantasies: Reinforcing Rape Culture in Fiona McIntosh's Fantasy Novels," *Hecate* 39:1/2 (2013): 148–167, 218.

Quilligan, Maureen. "Arthur's Sister's Story," *New York Times* (30 January 1983): 11.

Raddeker, Hélène Bowen. "Eco/Feminism and History in Fantasy Writing by Women," *Outskirts* 21 (November 2009).

_____. "Feminism and Spirituality in Fantastic Fiction: Contemporary Women Writers in Australia," *Women's Studies International Forum* 44 (1 May 2014): 154–163.

Ramstedt, Martin. "Metaphor or Invocation? the Convergence Between Modern Paganism and Fantasy Fiction," *Journal of Ritual Studies* 1:1/5 (2007): 1–15.

"Review: *The Catch Trap*," *Kirkus* (1 April 1979).

"Review: *The Firebrand*," *Publishers Weekly* (1 October 1989).

"Review: *The Forest House*," *Kirkus* (1 April 1994).

"Review: *The Forest House*," *Publishers Weekly* (1 April 1994).

"Review: *The Heirs of Hammerfell*," *Publishers Weekly* (29 November 1989).

"Review: *In the Rift*," *Kirkus* (1 April 1998).

"Review: *Lythande*," *Publishers Weekly* (27 June 1986): 82.

"Review: *The Mistress of Avalon*," *Los Angeles Times* (30 September 1999): A24. "Review: *The Mistress of Avalon*," *New York Times* (29 September 1999): A25.

"Review: *The Mistress of Avalon*," *Washington Post* (3 October 1999): C6.

"Review: *The Mists of Avalon*," *Fort Lauderdale News* (10 April 1983): 10G.

"Review: *The Mists of Avalon*," *Kirkus* (1 January 1982).

"Review: *The Mists of Avalon*," *San Francisco Examiner* (27 February 1983).

"Review: *The Mists of Avalon*," *Science Fiction Review* (Summer 1983).

"Review: *The Mists of Avalon*," *Washington Post* (28 January 1983).

"Review: *Rediscovery*," *Kirkus* (14 April 1993).

"Review: *Rediscovery*," *Publishers Weekly* (29 March 1993).

"Review: *Thendara House*," *School Library Journal* 30 (1 January 1984): 91.

"Review: *Traitor's Sun*," *Kirkus* (December 1998)

"Review: *Traitor's Sun*," *Kirkus* (December 1998)

Riggs, Don. "The Survival of the Goddess in Marie De France and Marion Zimmer Bradley," *Journal of the Fantastic in the Arts* 9:1 (1998): 15–23.

Ringel, Faye J. "Genetic Experimentation: Mad Scientists and the Beast," *Journal of the Fantastic in the Arts* 2:1 (1989): 64–75.

Robeson, Lisa. "Pawns, Predators, and Parasites: Teaching the Roles of Women in Arthurian Literature Courses," *Medieval Feminist Forum* 25:1 (1998).

Rogers, Michael. "Classic Returns," *Library Journal* 120:12 (1 July 1995): 128.

Rosen, Jeremy. "An Insatiable Market for Minor Characters," *New Literary History* 46:1 (Winter 2015): 143–163, 188.

Rosenberg, Alyssa. "Re-reading Feminist Author Marion Zimmer Bradley in the Wake of Sexual Assault Allegations," *Washington Post* (27 June 2014).

_____. "The Rules of Fictional Worlds," *The Atlantic* (24 September 2010).

Roysdon, Keith. "Good Female Writers Abound in Science Fiction Category," *Muncie* (Indiana) *Evening Press* (14 November 1981): T8.

Rubenstein, Roberta. "Feminism, Eros, and the Coming of Age," *Frontiers: A Journal of Women's Studies* 22:2 (2001): 1–19.

Salmon, Catherine, and Don Symons. "Slash Fiction and Human Mating Psychology," *Journal of Sex Research* 41:1 (February 2004): 94–100.

Schneider, Wolf. "My World," *Southwest Art* 35:6 (November 2005): 106–107.

Schwartz, Susan. "Women and Science Fiction," *New York Times* (2 May 1982).

Schweitzer, Darrell. "Bradley's Arthurian Novel Is Hardly the Stuff of Legend," *Philadelphia Enquirer* (6 March 1983): 6.

_____. "Interview," *Science Fiction Review* 7 (February 1992).

_____. "Review: *The Mist of Avalon*," *Philadelphia Inquirer* (6 March 1983): 6.

Serpell, Namwali. "When Sci-Fi Comes True," *New York Times* (17 March 2019): 15.

Sharpe, Victoria. "The Goddess Restored," *Journal of the Fantastic in the Arts* 9:1 (1998): 36–45.

Shaw, Jan. "Feminism and the Fantasy Tradition: *The Mists of Avalon*" in *A Companion to Arthurian Literature*. Oxford, UK: Blackwell, 2009, 463–478.

_____. "Troublesome Teleri," *Sidney Studies in English* 35 (2009): 73–95.

Shimmel, Lawrence. "Review: *The Mistress of Avalon*," *Lambda Book Report* (December 1999): 30.

Shuey, Andrea Lee. "Review: *The Firebrand*," *Library Journal* (15 October 1987).

Shwartz, Susan. "Marion Zimmer Bradley" in *St. James Guide to Science Fiction Writers*. New York: St. James Press, 1996.

_____. "Marion Zimmer Bradley's Ethic of Freedom" in *The Feminine Eye: Science Fiction and the Women Who Write It*. New York: Ungar, 1982, 73–88.

_____. "Women and Science Fiction," *New York Times* (2 May 1982): A11.

Smith, Jeanette C. "Marion Zimmer Bradley," *Gay & Lesbian Literature*. Detroit, MI: Gale, 1994.

_____ "The Role of Women in Contemporary Arthurian Fantasy," *Extrapolation* 35:2 (1994): 130–144.

Smol, Anna. "Oh … Oh … Frodo!: Readings of Male Intimacy in *The Lord of the Rings*," *Modern Fiction Studies* 50:4 (Winter 2004): 949–979.

Steffens, Daneet. "Review: *The Forest House*," *Entertainment Weekly* (20 May 1994).

Steinberg, Sybil S. "Review: *Heartlight*," *Publishers Weekly* 245:35 (31 August 1998): 53.

_____. "Review: *Gravelight*," *Publishers Weekly* 244:35 (25 August 1997): 50–51.

_____. "Review: *Lady of Avalon*," *Publishers Weekly* 244:20 (19 May 1997): 71.

_____. "Review: *Witchlight*," *Publishers Weekly* 243:34 (19 August 1996): 56.

Sullivan, C.W. "Folklore and Fantastic Literature," *Western Folklore* 60:4 (Fall 2001): 279–296.

Tetreault, Mary Ann. "Review: *Thendara House*," *Minerva* 3:3 (30 September 1985): 89.

Thompson, Raymond H. "Darkness Over Camelot: Enemies of the Arthurian Dream" in *New Directions in Arthurian Studies*. Cambridge, England: D.S. Brewer, 2002.

_____. "The First and Last Love: Morgan Le Fay and Arthur," *The Arthurian Revival*. New York: Routledge, 1992, 230–247.

_____. "Humor and Irony in Modern Arthurian Fantasy: Thomas Berger's Arthur Rex," *Kansas Quarterly* 16:3 (1984): 45–49.

Tobin, Lee Ann. "Contemporary Medievalism as a Teaching Tool," *Studies in Medieval and Renaissance* 1:2 (1990): 13–19.

_____. "Why Change the Arthur Story? Marion Zimmer Bradley's *The Mists of Avalon*," *Extrapolation* 34:2 (1993): 147–157.

Tolmie, Jane. "Medievalism and the Fantasy Heroine," *Journal of Gender Studies* 15:2 (2006): 145–158.

Tucker, Ken. "Mists of Avalon," *Entertainment Weekly* (13 July 2001).

Tutor, Laura. "Back to Avalon," *Anniston* (Alabama) *Star* (15 July 2001): 4B.

Unger, Rhoda K. "Science Fictive Visions: A Feminist Psychologist's View," *Feminism & Psychology* 19:1 (1 February 2009): 113–117.

Vaughn, Sue Fisher. "The Female Hero in Science Fiction and Fantasy: 'Carrier-Bag' to 'No-Road,'" *Journal of the Fantastic in the Arts* 4:4 (1 January 1991): 83–96.

Viars, Karen, and Cait Coker. "Constructing Lothiriel: Rewriting and Rescuing the Women of Middle-Earth from the Margins," *Mythlore* 33:2 (Spring/Summer 2015): 35–48.

Vincelette, Bob. "Bradley Lectures on Morgan LeFey," *Trinity Tripod* 86:11 (24 January 1989): 1.

Volk-Birke, Sabine. "The Cyclical Way of the Priestess," *Anglia* 108:3/4 (1990): 409–428.

Watson, Chris. "Today Meets Yesterday," *Santa Cruz Sentinel* (5 January 1992): D2.

Watson, Ian. "*The Spell Sword*" by Marion Zimmer Bradley," *Foundation* (1 September 1978): 92.

Wege, Beverly S. "Review: *The Black Trillium*," *Alternative Index* (Westmoreland, KS) (27 December 1990): 7.

Wehrmann, Jürgen. "Jane Eyre in Outer Space: Victorian Motifs in Post-Feminist Science Fiction" in *A Breath of Fresh Eyre*. Amsterdam, Holland: Brill Rodopi, 2007, 149–165.

Whiteley, Jan W. "Warrior Woman: The Adventures of Zadieyk of Gyre," *Minerva* 1 (1987): 74.

Wicks, Pat. "Novel Focuses on Telepathic Woman," *San Bernardino Sun* (6 October 1996): E10.

Wiebe, Sheldon. "Dance of Knives Sharp First Novel," *Calgary Herald* (16 June 2001): ES11.

Wilder, Cherry. "Review: *The Forbidden Tower*," *Foundation* (1 January 1979): 105.

Williams, Bill, ed. "Mostly About Books," *Northwest Arkansas Times* (11 january 1976): 10D.

_____. "Two Darkover Tales," *Northwest Arkansas Times* (5 December 1976): 10C.

Williams, Lynn F. "Everyone Belongs to Everyone Else: Marriage and the Family in Recent American Utopias 1965–1985," *Utopian Studies* 1 (1 January 1987): 123–136.

_____. "The Machine at Utopia's Center," *Utopian Studies* 3 (1 January 1991): 66–71.

Winick, Mimi. "Modernist Feminist Witchcraft," *Modernism/Modernity* 22:3 (September 2015): 565–592.

Zaerr, Linda Marie. "Women and Arthurian Literature," *Rocky Mountain Review* 51:1 (1997): 109–112.

Zaleski, Jeff. "Review: *Traitor's Sun*," *Publishers Weekly* 245:50 (14 December 1998): 61.

Electronic

Angeli, Anna. "Rape and Male Identity in Arthurian Romance, Chrétien De Troyes to Marion Zimmer Bradley," digitalrepository.unm.edu, 2010.

Busch, Jenna. "Rediscovering Marion Zimmer Bradley's Sword and Sorceress Anthologies," *SYFYWire* (6 November 2018), https://www.syfy.com/syfywire/rediscovering-marion-zimmer-bradleys-sword-and-sorceress-anthologies.

Clark, Mary Higgins. "Review: *The Planet Savers*," https://webcache.googleusercontent.com/search?q=cache:KqTaaNfTkFoJ:https://www.tisec.org.uk/6d188f/the-planet-savers.pdf+&cd=18&hl=en&ct=clnk&gl=us.

Engler, L.S. "Worlds Unknown," https://webcache.googleusercontent.com/search?q=cache:EfR7taZnFJsJ:https://lsengler.com/2015/02/18/review-the-planet-savers-and-the-waterfall-by-marion-zimmer-bradley/+&cd=4&hl=en&ct=clnk&gl=us

"Excalibur," http://www.britannia.com/history/arthur/excalibur.html.

"From Couch to Moon," couchtomoon.wordpress.com/2016/06/15/heritage-of-hastur-1975-by-marion-zimmer-bradley/

Jernigan, Jessica. "The Book That Made Me a Feminist Was Written by an Abuser," https://electricliterature.com/the-book-that-made-me-a-feminist-was-written-by-an-abuser-4c6891f548cf, 2017.

Kimmel, Leigh. "The Saga of the Renunciates," http://billionlightyearbookshelf.com/reviews/sagaoftherenunciates.shtml, 2015.

_____. "The Spell Sword," http://darkover.apiacoa.org/guide/books/sword/summary.en.html, 1999.

Lewis, Jone Johnson. "Who Was Andromache?,"

https://www.thoughtco.com/what-is-andro mache-3529220.

Long, Steven S. "Defining Fantasy," http://static1.1. sqspcdn.com/static/f/1150388/15767768/1325081308097/Defining+Fantasy.pdf?token=B pTlEYX04ph3gRydeNhAzN%2BO9qI%3D.

MacDonald, Margo. "Review: *The Gratitude of Kings,*" https://www.sfsite.com/04a/grat30.htm, 1998.

Miller, Kate Spitz. "Review: *The Firebrand,*" https://katespitzmiller.com/2017/03/27/book-review-the-firebrand-by-marion-zimmer-bradley/.

"Morgan Le Fay: How Arthurian Legend Turned a Powerful Woman from Healer to Villain," https://www.ancient-origins.net/history/morgan-le-fay-0011428.

Mumtaz, Umer. "Love-Hate Relationship Between King Arthur and Morgan Le Fay," ttps://s3.amazonaws.com/academia.edu.documents/51543768/Arthurian_Love_Hate_Paper.pdf?

Nelson-Deutsch, Hannah. "Nine Books That Have Subtle Feminist Sneak Attacks Lurking in Their Pages," https://www.bustle.com/articles/63025-9-books-that-have-subtle-feminist-sneak-attacks-lurking-in-their-pages (6 March 2015).

Palojärvi, Maija Päivikki. "Morgaine the Maiden, Morgaine the Mother, Morgaine the Death-crone: Female Ageing in Marion Zimmer Bradley's *The Mists of Avalon,*" Humanities thesis, University of Eastern Finland (1 November 2013): http://epublications.uef.fi/pub/urn_nbn_fi_uef-20131005/urn_nbn_fi_uef-20131005.pdf.

Renk, Thorsten. "Mapping Darkover," http://www.phy.duke.edu/~trenk/darkover/darkover_map.html#mental_map.

"Review: *The Mists of Avalon,*" *The Heretic Loremaster,* http://themidhavens.net/heretic_loremaster/2009/05/the-mists-of-avalon-reviewed/, 2009.

Ross, Deborah J. "Proofreading *The Catch Trap,*" http://deborahjross.blogspot.com/2014/04/proofreading-catch-trap.html, April 9, 2014.

"Santelli Family Tree," https://www.mzbworks.com/santelli.htm.

Sturgis, Susanna J. "What's a P.C. Feminist Like You Doing in a Fantasy Like This?" http://www.susannajsturgis.com/article.php?id=34.

Tichelaar, Tyler. "Children of Arthur," https://childrenofarthur.wordpress.com/tag/t-h-white/.

Trowbridge, Serena: "Review: *The Fall of Atlantis,*" http://trashotron.com/agony/reviews/2003/bradley-fall_of_atlantis.htm.

Vain, Madison. "The Mists of Avalon," *Entertainment* (25 July 2014), https://ew.com/article/2014/07/25/mists-of-avalon-marion-zimmer-bradley/.

Walton, Jo. "A Heroine's Journey: Marion Zimmer Bradley's *Hawkmistress,*" www.tor.com/2010/03/05/a-heroines-journey-marion-zimmer-bradleys-lemghawkmistresslemg/

_____. "'Where Did He Belong?': Marion Zimmer Bradley's *The Bloody Sun,*" (3 March 2010): ttps://www.tor.com/2010/03/03/qwhere-did-he-belongq-marion-zimmer-bradleys-lemgthe-bloody-sunlemg/

Zanghi, Deborah L. "An Exploration of Alternate Realities: Women's Contemporary Speculative Fiction," master's thesis, digital commons.brockport.edu, 1997.

Zweig, Dani. "Review: Marion Zimmer Bradley," https://www-users.cs.york.ac.uk/susan/sf/dani/PS_017.htm.

Index

Numbers in **bold** indicate main entries

293